GW00776350

News and rumour in Jacobean England

MANCHESTER
1824

Manchester University Press

Politics, culture and society in early modern Britain

General editors

DR ALEXANDRA GAJDA
PROFESSOR ANTHONY MILTON
PROFESSOR PETER LAKE
DR JASON PEACEY

This important series publishes monographs that take a fresh and challenging look at the interactions between politics, culture and society in Britain between 1500 and the mid-eighteenth century. It counteracts the fragmentation of current historiography through encouraging a variety of approaches which attempt to redefine the political, social and cultural worlds, and to explore their interconnection in a flexible and creative fashion. All the volumes in the series question and transcend traditional interdisciplinary boundaries, such as those between political history and literary studies, social history and divinity, urban history and anthropology. They thus contribute to a broader understanding of crucial developments in early modern Britain.

Recently published in the series

Chaplains in early modern England: Patronage, literature and religion
HUGH ADLINGTON, TOM LOCKWOOD AND GILLIAN WRIGHT *(eds)*

The Cooke sisters: Education, piety and patronage in early modern England
GEMMA ALLEN

Black Bartholomew's Day   DAVID J. APPLEBY

Insular Christianity   ROBERT ARMSTRONG AND TADHG Ó HANNRACHAIN *(eds)*

Reading and politics in early modern England   GEOFF BAKER

'No historie so meete'   JAN BROADWAY

Republican learning   JUSTIN CHAMPION

This England   PATRICK COLLINSON

Sir Robert Filmer (1588–1653) and the patriotic monarch   CESARE CUTTICA

Brave community   JOHN GURNEY

'Black Tom'   ANDREW HOPPER

Impostures in early modern England: Represenations and perceptions of frauduent identities   TOBIAS B. HUG

The politics of the public sphere in early modern England
PETER LAKE AND STEVEN PINCUS *(eds)*

Henry Neville and English republican culture   GABY MAHLBERG

Royalists and Royalism during the Interregnum
JASON MCELLIGOTT AND DAVID L. SMITH

Laudian and Royalist polemic in Stuart England   ANTHONY MILTON

Full details of the series are available at www.manchesteruniversitypress.com.

News and rumour in Jacobean England

Information, court politics and diplomacy, 1618–25

DAVID COAST

Manchester
University Press
Manchester and New York

distributed exclusively in the USA by Palgrave Macmillan

Published by Manchester University Press
Oxford Road, Manchester M13 9NR, UK
and Room 400, 175 Fifth Avenue, New York, NY 10010, USA
www.manchesteruniversitypress.co.uk

Distributed exclusively in the USA by
Palgrave Macmillan, 175 Fifth Avenue, New York, NY 10010, USA

Distributed exclusively in Canada by
UBC Press, University of British Columbia, 2029 West Mall,
Vancouver, BC, Canada V6T 1Z2

British Library Cataloguing-in-Publication Data
A catalogue record for this book is available from the British Library

Library of Congress Cataloging-in-Publication Data applied for

ISBN 978 0 7190 8948 0 *hardback*

First published 2014

The publisher has no responsibility for the persistence or accuracy of URLs for external or any third-party internet websites referred to in this book, and does not guarantee that any content on such websites is, or will remain, accurate or appropriate.

Typeset in Scala with Pastonchi display by
by Koinonia, Manchester

Printed in Great Britain by
TJ International Ltd, Padstow

Contents

Acknowledgements

I have accumulated more debts in writing this book than I will ever be able to remember, let alone repay. This book was made possible with the generous support of the Arts and Humanities Research Council, the Huntington Library and the Leverhulme Trust. My thanks are due to the kind and patient staff at the British Library and the National Archives, as well as at the other university libraries and local archives where I have spent a fair chunk of my time for the past few years.

The History Department at the University of Sheffield was a wonderful place to do my PhD, and I would like to thank George Newberry, Matt Phillpott, Sarah Rawlins, Jack Rhoden, Gary Rivett, Robin Scaife and Daniel Turner for conversation, games of Risk and cups of tea. James Shaw and Mark Greengrass, as secondary supervisors, provided some very useful perspectives and suggestions. I would particularly like to thank Peter Lake and Michael Braddick, the examiners of my PhD thesis, who both made invaluable criticisms and suggestions.

I would also like to thank all the staff in the History department (and beyond) at Durham University, where (among others), Alex Barber, John Clay, David Gehring, Natalie Mears, Nicole Reinhardt, Stephen Taylor, Philip Williamson and Andy Wood have welcomed me and created a fantastic research culture. I'd particularly like to thank Alex Barber for getting in touch with me and inviting me to apply for a fellowship, as well as Stephen Taylor and Philip Williamson, who helped me to thrash out the proposal, using up a lot of red ink in the process.

I am grateful to the editors and staff at the *Journal of Early Modern History* for their kind permission to use some of the material that appeared as 'Misinformation and disinformation in late Jacobean court politics', *Journal of Early Modern History* 16 (2012).

I would also like to thank the series editors and staff at Manchester University Press for their kind help. I would particularly like to thank the reviewers of my proposal and typescript, including Alastair Bellany, Thomas Cogswell and Richard Cust, for taking the time to make such useful comments and suggestions.

I am deeply indebted to Alex Barber, David Cressy, Janet Dickinson, Alex Gajda, Mark Greengrass, Chris Kyle, Steve May, J. Sears McGee, Natalie Mears, George Newberry, Stephen Taylor, Lizzy Williamson and Neil Younger, among others, for discussing ideas, providing references or allowing me to read unpublished drafts of their own work. Four people deserve special thanks. Simon Healy and Michael Questier read early drafts of my thesis when they had many better things to be doing. They have both been extremely kind, helpful and generous, and gossiping with them about Jacobean politics has been fun and hugely enlightening. Thomas Cogswell gave me some extremely useful advice about the structure and scope of this book, and although I'm not sure the end product matches his ambitions for it, I am very grateful for his generous help. Noah Millstone was kind enough to give a draft of the book a very

Acknowledgements

thorough critical reading, and I'd like to thank him for all his help. As with all of those who have been generous enough to read drafts and provide feedback, any errors or inadequacies that remain in this book are entirely my own.

It was my good fortune to have Anthony Milton as my PhD supervisor. Ever since I emailed him to ask if there might be a way for me to return to historical research, he has been unfailingly helpful, encouraging, generous and funny. His acute comments and observations have improved this study tremendously, and it could never have been written without his help and support. The debt I owe him is greater than I could possibly acknowledge.

Finally, I owe my greatest debt to Georgina Lyons for her love, help and forbearance.

Editorial conventions

Contractions and abbreviations have been expanded throughout for ease of reading. Square brackets denote editorial additions, usually to expand words that have been abbreviated without a mark of contraction, or where words are cut off by the binding of a volume. On occasion, square brackets are also used to provide translations or other additional information not provided in the manuscript, as in 'Sir Dudley [Carleton]'. Original spelling is retained throughout, although thorns have been modified in line with modern orthography.

Contemporaries writing to and from the continent used a mixture of old style and new style dates. Writers sometimes state the convention that has been followed, or give both old and new style dates. Where writers have given some indication of the convention followed, I have reproduced it here. The year is taken to begin on 1 January.

Abbreviations

Add.	British Library additional manuscripts
APC	*Acts of the Privy Council*
Bod. Ms.	Bodleian Library Manuscripts
CSPD	Mary Anne Everett Green (ed.), *Calendar of State Papers, Domestic Series, of the reign of James I, 1603 – 25* (4 vols, 1857–9)
CSPV	Allen B. Hinds (ed.), *Calendar of state papers and manuscripts relating to English affairs existing in the archives and collections of Venice and in other libraries of Northern Italy,* vols 14–18, 1615–25 (London, 1908–12)
Downshire	Sonia P. Anderson, A. B. Hinds, Gerain Dyfnallt Owen, E. K. Purnell (eds) *Report on the manuscripts of the Most Honourable the Marquess of Downshire, formerly preserved at Easthampstead Park, Berkshire,* vols II–VI (London, 1936–95)
Eg.	British Library Egerton manuscripts
EL	Huntington Library Ellesmere manuscripts
Harl.	British Library Harleian manuscripts
HMC	Historical Manuscripts Commission
Larkin	James F. Larkin, and Paul L. Hughes (eds), *Stuart Royal Proclamations Volume I: Royal Proclamations of King James I 1603–1625* (Oxford, 1973)
Lee	Maurice Lee (ed.), *Dudley Carleton to John Chamberlain, 1603–1624: Jacobean Letters* (New Brunswick (NJ), 1972)
McClure	N. E. McClure, *The Letters of John Chamberlain* (2 vols, Philadelphia, 1939)
NLW	National Library of Wales
PRO	Public Record Office
SP	National Archives, state papers
Stowe	British Library Stowe manuscripts

Introduction

In the early seventeenth century, news was often compared to a fountain. 'You that know all things from the Fountaynes', as John Castle told his friend, the diplomat William Trumbull, 'can tell me how far I err that take things by durtie channells'.[1] When a well-informed courtier, Sir George Goring, visited Sir Dudley Carleton, ambassador at The Hague, Carleton's friend John Chamberlain employed similar imagery to contrast their access to accurate information. Thanks to Goring's visit, Carleton would be sufficiently informed of all the news from court, 'for he brings yt from the well head, whereas we are driven to draw our intelligence from by-channels which many times alter both colour and tast'.[2] News, like water, might be free flowing, and potentially accessible to all, but there was a significant difference between those who were forced to draw it second-hand from stagnant by-channels and those who were privileged enough to drink from the source itself. The stream of news could be diverted or stopped altogether by those who controlled it, but the image also implied reciprocity, since water eventually returned to the fountainhead before being recirculated. News could provide refreshment and sustenance, but it was not a pristine resource, and a common source of information, like a common source of water, could become polluted with use.[3]

King James I had the best access to news – indeed he was the source of much of it. James sat at the centre of a network of diplomats and advisers, and a large proportion of the news and speculation that circulated around the country concerned his intentions, motives and decisions. As such, he was in a unique position to conceal or manipulate the news. At the same time, he found it difficult to prevent leaks, and was surrounded by courtiers and foreign ambassadors who constantly struggled to shape his perceptions. James presided over a court in which rivals for office and patronage used political rumours to boost their own chances of success or to damage their opponents. This was the world inhabited by court insiders like John Castle and John Beaulieu, who used their relatively minor positions in the Jacobean bureaucracy to keep friends like the diplomat William Trumbull abreast of events at home. Courtiers like John Holles or the Earl of Kellie also corresponded with their friends and relatives.

Slightly further from the centre were the men like John Chamberlain or Simonds D'Ewes, who met in the nave of St Paul's Cathedral, at the Exchange or in private houses to share and discuss news with courtiers, diplomats, merchants and Members of Parliament (MPs). The membership of this circle overlapped considerably with the court. Men like John Chamberlain had contacts at the centre but also exchanged news with English diplomats abroad. John Pory, a former courier of diplomatic letters, was one of a growing number of news gatherers who provided a subscription newsletter service for clients outside of London.

The recipients of these letters were members of a much wider circle; provincial observers like Viscount Scudamore in Herefordshire or Joseph Mead in Cambridge, who eagerly consumed news from the centre or passed it on to others like Sir Martin Stuteville. They were also fed information from the centre by friends pursuing legal cases, by MPs returning to their constituencies, or by a regular flow of printed, written and oral news spread by itinerant merchants and other travellers. Distance militated against accuracy, and inhabitants of this circle were sometimes forced to drink from the 'durtie channells' of rumour and speculation. Observers like John Rous and Walter Yonge recorded this uncertain stream of information in their diaries.

News and public politics has been one of the most fertile areas of research in early Stuart history in recent decades. This was not always the case. In the 1970s, some revisionist historians downplayed the potential for news to generate political conflict, arguing that much of it was gossipy and frivolous. While pamphlets and newsletters circulated widely, as John Morrill wrote, most of them 'treated great affairs of state in a surprisingly trivial manner', leaving the reader 'knowing a good deal that was distasteful and unpleasant about the Court, but knowing and understanding less about the real constitutional issues'.[4] As a result, the provincial gentry were 'surprisingly ill-informed' about important political matters.[5] Morrill's argument about news circulation was part of a wider revisionist project which stressed the insularity of county communities and their interest in local, rather than national, matters.

Much of what has been written about early Stuart news culture since has in one way or another reacted against this account, and has instead stressed the wide social and geographical circulation of news and the important political consequences of its circulation. Printed news, in particular, has received a great deal of attention.[6] F. J. Levy highlighted the range of ways in which news could circulate in the country, arguing that the provincial gentry had a much greater degree of access to information than revisionist historians had realised.[7] Historians who have studied the impact of news have tended to stress its role in creating political conflict. Levy argued that the spread of news down the social scale helped to undermine the mystery of kingship by making foreign policy a matter of public debate, and Alastair Bellany has demonstrated how scurrilous poetry helped to 'create, express and sustain a set of political perceptions that diverged markedly from the perceptions held by the king'.[8] Richard Cust argued that news tended to polarise political opinion in the decades preceding the English Civil War, while Thomas Cogswell argued that access to news was 'essential ... if contemporaries and their parliamentary representatives aspired

to a political role higher than that of rubber-stamps', and that accurate information was 'the key to all "opposition" to royal policies'.[9] More recently, David
Randall has highlighted royal concerns that the free circulation of news represented an inherent threat to the crown because it encouraged subjects to offer
unsolicited advice.[10]

This work has increasingly transcended the boundaries of the debate on the
causes of the English Civil War, and can be said to represent an independent
research agenda for the political history of early modern Britain. The founda-
tions of this broader approach were laid by the German sociologist Jürgen
Habermas, who argued that a 'public sphere' in which individuals rationally
debated political and economic matters emerged for the first time in late
seventeenth-century England.[11] By applying Habermas's framework to earlier
periods, often altering it in the process, historians have greatly enriched our
understanding of the nature and extent of popular political consciousness and
how and why it changed over time.[12]

The 1620s were a particularly important period in the development of a
'public sphere' in England. As Peter Lake and Steven Pincus wrote, it was
during this time that 'the heady mixture of international confessional conflict,
domestic religious dispute, royal marriage, war and the rise to power of a
classic evil counselor combined to create a sustained pitch of public political
discourse equal to that achieved in the 1590s'.[13] While much of the early part
of James's reign in England was relatively politically quiescent, the outbreak
of the Thirty Years' War in Europe in 1618, together with James's unpopular
attempts to negotiate a marriage between his son, Prince Charles, and the
Spanish Princess, Donna Maria, plunged the Kingdom into a period of political conflict and uncertainty. The King's subjects were increasingly knowl-
edgeable about state business, and increasingly willing to discuss and criticise
his policies. This was a period during which James's kingship, and particularly
his ability to shape the opinions of his subjects and potential foreign allies,
was put to the test.

This study investigates how political information was manipulated,
concealed and distorted during this tumultuous period. It analyses the ways in
which news was managed at the centre by James, his diplomats and councillors. It examines James's attempts to restrict access to information and the
opportunities this created for the King to present a misleading impression
of political events and his own intentions. Finally, it explores how contemporaries interpreted these attempts to shape their perceptions, and how the false
rumours that emerged as news circulated from the centre to the periphery
were analysed and used as political weapons.

An investigation of the politics of news and rumour during the period has
the potential to enrich and extend our understanding of a wide range of issues
and debates to do with royal counsel, the formation and realisation of foreign

policy, censorship and secrecy, image-making and propaganda, the spreading and exploitation of political rumours and the relationship between elite and popular politics. This study aims to advance new arguments about these matters, which reach across the politics and political culture of the reign and which can be fruitfully applied well beyond it.

The first chapter examines the circulation of information at the centre of government. While Elizabeth I's councillors had a considerable influence over the Queen's policies, James's ministers and diplomats have traditionally been seen as playing a much more subordinate role.[14] By controlling the flow of information to and from the King, however, secretaries and ambassadors could shape the King's perceptions, and this chapter will examine whether this allowed them to play a greater part in the formation and realisation of policy than historians have previously recognised. On occasion, they altered or delayed James's instructions and messages, or withheld them altogether, but the King may have tacitly approved of this apparently disobedient behaviour, which allowed him to change his mind or disavow policies while giving different audiences a variety of impressions about his true intentions. On some occasions, and particularly after 1623, this administrative buffer between the King and the implementation of his policies was used in order to encourage the King to adopt certain policies, and in particular to steer him towards war with Spain. James was never simply a dupe, however, and this chapter considers the King's suspicions about the information he was sent and their consequences. An examination of the diplomatic machinery of Jacobean government adds an important new dimension to our understanding of decision-making and the extent to which the King retained full control over foreign policy until his death in 1625.

While Chapter 1 examines the manipulation of information at the centre, Chapter 2 considers how political news was concealed or manipulated as it spread around the kingdom as a whole. Much of the existing historiography on this topic has focused on censorship, on the ways in which printed and verbal expressions of opinion were punished or suppressed.[15] This chapter attempts to shift the focus of this debate on to secrecy, examining how James tried to prevent information about his policies from reaching the public in the first place. It investigates the leaking of diplomatic news by bureaucrats and ministers as well as the King's attempts to withhold information from his increasingly news-hungry subjects, and his reasons for doing so. It will consider whether accusations that James ignored his own councillors, which were made by contemporaries and which have sometimes been repeated in modern historiography, were really justified. In part, this chapter will examine the consequences, both intended and unintended, of the King's secretive behaviour and the way it was interpreted by his subjects, casting new light on existing debates about the regulation of speech.

Historians who have examined 'public relations' during this period have tended to focus on formal ceremonies and other forms of image-making and propaganda that were intended to shape views about the regime and its policies as a whole.[16] Elizabeth I's skills in this area are often contrasted with those of the early Stuarts.[17] James's secretive and ambiguous style of rule meant that observers of court and international politics watched his every outward word and gesture for hints as to his intentions and the future course of politics. Knowing that observers read the political auguries in his outward speech and behaviour, James orchestrated public 'performances' – informal pronouncements and gestures which were calculated to mislead domestic and foreign audiences about his intentions and motivations. These hints and gestures, which contemporaries often called 'outward shows', were often intended to appease the frustration that many of James's subjects felt about the direction of his foreign policy or to elicit concessions from the foreign powers he was negotiating with. By shifting the focus away from formal propaganda, an examination of James's 'outward shewes' offers a fresh perspective on the nature of royal engagement with the 'public sphere'. This chapter will ask how convincing his performances were, what effect they had on the bonds of trust between the King, his subjects and his potential foreign allies, and how this might affect our understanding of James's kingcraft.

Historians have drawn attention to the sceptical and analytical way in which political news was interpreted in the sixteenth and seventeenth centuries. A renewed interest in Roman historians, particularly Tacitus, stimulated a suspicious reading of political news which sought to uncover the truth behind the outward appearance of political events.[18] A series of writers from Machiavelli to Justus Lipsius and Francis Bacon sought to examine and justify various forms of royal simulation and dissimulation.[19] Many contemporaries, as Perez Zagorin argued, 'viewed the world they lived in as filled with duplicity'.[20] While historians have analysed the broad historical causes for the growth of this sceptical, analytical approach to the news and the ways in which it was manifested in political literature, this chapter allows us to consider the specific political circumstances in which it may have been particularly useful. An analytical attitude towards the news was often entirely sensible during the reign of monarchs such as James who habitually concealed his intentions and created misleading impressions about the likely course of future events. Nevertheless, this monograph will question whether a sceptical reading of the news was always justified, or whether individuals sometimes searched for hidden truths and motivations that simply were not there.

Political rumours proliferated in the dramatic and uncertain political circumstances of the early 1620s. An absence of definite information encouraged speculation about the King's intentions and about the momentous events occurring on the continent. Rumours were represented in literature from

Virgil to Shakespeare as harbingers of popular sedition.[21] False reports could play a crucial role in generating the mutual suspicions and conspiracy theories which were the breeding ground for popular uprisings and civil war, and naturally monarchs attempted to suppress them. Historians who have relied on the court records of individuals prosecuted for spreading false rumours have tended to overlook evidence of popular scepticism, and have underestimated the involvement of elites in spreading and exploiting misinformation, effectively repeating early modern stereotypes about the susceptibility of the uneducated multitude to false news. An analysis of the formation, scrutiny and political uses of rumours during the period will deepen and complicate our understanding of the interaction between elite and popular politics and news culture.

Rumour is a difficult concept to pin down.[22] It does not cover a clearly delineated area of meaning, but shares permeable borders with several closely related concepts. The first of these is 'news'. A 'rumour' is defined in the *Oxford English Dictionary* as 'a statement or report circulating in a community, of the truth of which there is no clear evidence'.[23] Almost all reports could be so defined during this period, and indeed it could be argued that all news was 'rumour'. The marginal annotations of news diarists, who wrote 'proved true' or 'false' after reports, confirms that reports only attained the status of fact after they had been reinforced by further information. The sociologist Tamotsu Shibutani has argued that rumours only become news when a stable consensus about their truth is reached. One might ask whether a unanimous consensus about the veracity of a report ever develops, because there will always be those who believe in the truth of a rumour long after others have ceased to believe it. For our purposes, however, 'rumours' were news reports that individuals were unsure of at the time of writing. Almost all of the rumours used here were designated as such by contemporaries, who referred to them as 'rumours' 'bruits', 'fables' and so on, or who communicated doubts about their truth in other ways, even if these specific words were not used. Attention will also be paid to reports which contemporaries believed but which historians now know to have been false, and those which they disbelieved but which were actually true.

Chapter 3 investigates how the process of oral transmission transformed speculation that events *might* happen into apparently conclusive reports that they *had* happened. The illness of a ruler created reports that he or she had died, and political crisis was misreported as rebellion. An analysis of these rumours allows us to understand how observers simplified and explained political events as well as the psychological functions they fulfilled. In contrast to much of the existing work on this topic, which has focused on rumours spread by ordinary people, this chapter also considers the ways in which elites engaged with false reports. Despite their denunciations of 'vulgar' rumours, elites were often willing to seize upon and exploit false reports that circulated more widely in order to damage their political enemies or influence the perceptions of the King. Rumours may not have simply been a plebeian mode of discourse, but may have been a form of interaction between elite and popular politics.

False reports about appointments and demotions at court were an important facet of elite rumour-mongering. Chapter 4 will investigate the spreading of these and similar rumours about promotions and demotions and their role in making or breaking careers. In doing so, it will attempt to shed light on the ways in which perceptions were manipulated in the particularly uncertain political culture of the late Jacobean court. It will examine the part these rumours played in shaping royal decisions about appointments, also questioning whether they were spread deliberately, as observers tended to assume, or whether the use of rumours as political weapons was exaggerated. Finally, like Chapter 1, it will ask what opportunities such rumours created for individuals beneath the most powerful patronage brokers to influence James's decisions.

The danger of the thematic approach taken by the first four chapters is that individual examples of the manipulation of information or the spreading of rumours can become divorced from their original context. The last two chapters, which are extended narrative case studies, are intended to address this problem. They examine how these phenomena operated and interacted with each other in particular political circumstances.

The first of these case studies examines ways in which diplomatic information was suppressed and manipulated in 1623. Between February and October, Prince Charles and the royal favourite, the Duke of Buckingham, travelled to Madrid in an attempt to conclude negotiations for a Spanish marriage alliance. This was a period when the success of James's most treasured policy relied on his ability to shape perceptions and when the conciliar government described in earlier chapters almost entirely broke down. Historians have tended to focus on the course of the Prince's negotiations in Madrid, but this chapter shifts attention to James and the battle over perceptions of the match at home. It considers his extraordinary efforts to keep details of the negotiations secret from his own councillors, and his reasons for doing so, as well as the opportunities this near-monopoly over information created to present a misleading impression of events in Madrid. The sceptical and often cynical reaction of many of James's subjects to his behaviour show how the secrecy and 'outward shows' discussed earlier could backfire in ways which could potentially undermine royal authority.

The final chapter addresses the intersection between court rumours and foreign policy. It focuses on a series of reports that circulated about the Duke of Buckingham during his illness in the summer of 1624. The first set of rumours, that Buckingham planned to shut the King away in one of his hunting lodges and take the direction of affairs in to his own hands, were enthusiastically taken up by various Spanish ambassadors, who wished to create conflict between the favourite and James in order to derail Buckingham's anti-Spanish foreign policy. When the Duke later fell ill, it was rumoured that he had been poisoned, had died or had become mentally unstable, and when a guard was put on his door to prevent the access of suitors who were hindering his recovery, it was rumoured that James had imprisoned him. This chapter considers what effect these rumours had on Buckingham's political standing and the foreign policy he was trying to promote. It also examines contemporary beliefs that disgruntled Catholics were responsible for inventing and spreading these rumours, and why this sort of attribution was so plausible and appealing. In doing so, it aims to understand how the confessional divide shaped the way in which news was assessed.

Although this study is primarily concerned with James's later years, comparisons and contrasts will also be drawn with the reigns of Elizabeth I and Charles I. It will attempt to understand what was distinctive about James's style of rule, thus contributing to ongoing debates about the strengths and weaknesses of his reign and the extent to which Charles's accession to the throne represented a decisive break.

The collections of correspondence on which the core of this study is based have tended to be used simply as reference material for political and diplomatic history. While these letters are indeed excellent sources for understanding who said and did what to whom, this study also uses them to understand the role that perceptions played in Jacobean politics. It is therefore as much concerned with 'what really happened' during the later years of James's reign as with what people *thought* was the case. It examines how individuals attempted to shape these views and what their political consequences were. While the primary focus of the monograph is on the management of information within the Jacobean government, attempts will also be made to analyse the wider reception of this behaviour, and the ways in which information was distorted as it spread beyond the court. In studying these phenomena, I hope to understand the role of news and rumour as sources of influence and even power during the later years of James I's reign.

NOTES

1 John Castle to William Trumbull, 12 September 1619, Add. 72275, fol. 72r.

2 John Chamberlain to Dudley Carleton, 6 December 1623, McClure vol. II, p. 528.

3 It is surely no coincidence that patronage and moral reform were also supposed to start at the King's elbow and flow outwards. See Linda Levy Peck, *Court Patronage and Corruption in Early Stuart England* (Cambridge, MA, 1990), pp. 1–2. See also Alastair Bellany,

The Politics of Court Scandal in Early Modern England: News Culture and the Overbury Affair, 1603–1660 (Cambridge, 2002), pp. 1–3.

4 John Morrill, *The Revolt of the Provinces: Conservatives and Radicals in the English Civil War, 1630–1650* (London, 1976), pp. 22–3. It is of course debateable whether news media have ever achieved or even aspired to achieve such aims.

5 *Ibid.*, p. 22.

6 Michael Frearson, 'The distribution and readership of London corantos in the 1620s', in Robin Myers and Michael Harris (eds), *Serials and their Readers: 1620–1914* (Winchester, 1993), pp. 1–25; Joad Raymond, *The Invention of the Newspaper: English Newsbooks 1641–1649* (Oxford, 1996); Jason Peacey, 'Print and public politics in seventeenth-century England' *History Compass* 5:1 (2007), pp. 85–111.

7 F. J. Levy, 'How information spread amongst the gentry, 1550–1640', *Journal of British Studies* 21:2 (1982), pp. 11–34. For the circulation of news in the provinces, see also Anthony Fletcher, 'National and local awareness in the county communities', in Howard Tomlinson (ed.), *Before the English Civil War: Essays on Stuart Politics and Government* (London, 1983), pp. 151–74; Anthony Fletcher, *The Outbreak of the English Civil War* (London, 1981), pp. 25–7. For the circulation of news in London, see Ian Archer, 'Popular politics in the sixteenth and early seventeenth centuries', in Paul Griffiths and Mark Jenner (eds), *Londinopolis: Essays in the Cultural and Social History of Early Modern London* (Manchester, 2000), pp. 26–46; Dagmar Freist, *Governed by Opinion: Politics, Religion and the Dynamics of Communication in Stuart London, 1637–1645* (London, 1997).

8 F. J. Levy, 'The decorum of news', in Joad Raymond (ed.), *News, Newspapers, and Society in Early Modern Britain* (London, 1999), p. 17; Alastair Bellany, 'Rayling rymes and vaunting verse: Libellous politics in early Stuart England, 1603–1628', in Kevin Sharpe and Peter Lake (eds), *Culture and Politics in Early Stuart England* (London, 1994), p. 117.

9 Richard Cust, 'News and politics in early seventeenth century England', *Past and Present* 112 (1986), pp. 60–90; Thomas Cogswell, *The Blessed Revolution: English Politics and the Coming of War, 1621–1624* (Cambridge, 1989), pp. 23–4; Thomas Cogswell, 'England and the Spanish match', in Richard Cust and Ann Hughes (eds), *Conflict in Early Stuart England: Studies in Religion and Politics 1603–1642* (Harlow, 1989), p. 128. See also Ian Atherton, 'The itch grown a disease: Manuscript transmission of news in the seventeenth century', in Joad Raymond (ed.), *News, Newspapers and Society in Early Modern Britain*, pp. 36–65.

10 David Randall, *Credibility in Elizabethan and Early Stuart Military News* (London, 2008), pp. 35, 43–5.

11 Jürgen Habermas, *The Structural Transformation of the Public Sphere: An Inquiry into a Category of Bourgeois Society* (Boston (MA), 1989); Craig Calhoun (ed.), *Habermas and the Public Sphere* (Cambridge (MA), 1992).

12 See in particular Peter Lake and Steven Pincus (eds), *The Politics of the Public Sphere in Early Modern England* (Manchester, 2007).

13 Peter Lake and Steven Pincus, 'Rethinking the public sphere in early Modern England', pp. 1–30 in Lake and Pincus (eds), *Public Sphere*, p. 9. While many of the more dramatic conflicts over these matters did not occur until after James's death, they were all present in the early 1620s.

14 For Elizabeth's relationship with her councillors, see in particular Christopher Haigh, *Elizabeth I* (London, 1988), ch. 4; Patrick Collinson, 'The monarchical republic of Queen

Elizabeth I' in Patrick Collinson (ed.), *Elizabethan Essays* (London, 1994), pp. 41–2. It has been argued that the Duke of Buckingham subverted the Privy Council's authority during the 1620s. See Kevin Sharpe, 'Crown, parliament and locality: Government and communication in early Stuart England', *The English Historical Review* 101:399 (1986), p. 337; 'The rhetoric of counsel in early modern England', in Dale Hoak (ed.), *Tudor Political Culture* (Cambridge, 1995), p. 306. The Secretaryship of State under James has been viewed as a 'routine clerkship'. See F. M. Evans, *The Principal Secretary of State: A Survey of the Office from 1558 to 1680* (Manchester, 1923), p. 61. For the traditional view of the poverty and relative irrelevance of Jacobean diplomats, see Maurice Lee, 'The Jacobean diplomatic service', *The American Historical Review* 72:4 (1967), pp. 1264–82.

15 Cyndia Clegg, *Press Censorship in Jacobean England* (Cambridge, 2001); Sheila Lambert, 'State control of the press in theory and practice: the role of the Stationers' Company before 1640', in Robin Myers and Michael Harris (eds), *Censorship & the Control of Print in England and France 1600–1910* (Winchester, 1992), pp. 1–29; Anthony Milton, 'Licensing, censorship, and religious orthodoxy in early Stuart England', *The Historical Journal* 41:3 (1998), pp. 625–51. For the regulation of speech, see David Cressy, *Dangerous Talk: Scandalous, Seditious, and Treasonable Speech in Pre-Modern England* (Oxford, 2010); Adam Fox, 'Rumour, news and popular opinion in Elizabethan and early Stuart England', *The Historical Journal* 40:3 (1997), pp. 597–620. For the suppression of criticism of the Spanish match in sermons and other forms in the early 1620s, see Cogswell, *Blessed Revolution*, pp. 20–34.

16 See in particular Kevin Sharpe, *Image Wars: Promoting Kings and Commonwealths in England, 1603–1660* (London, 2010); for the Duke of Buckingham's engagement with 'popularity', see in particular Thomas Cogswell, 'The people's love: The Duke of Buckingham and popularity', in Thomas Cogswell, Richard Cust and Peter Lake (eds), *Politics, Religion and Popularity* (Cambridge, 2002), pp. 211–34.

17 For Elizabeth's skill at public relations, see Haigh, *Elizabeth I*, ch. 8; Malcolm Smuts, 'Public ceremony and royal charisma: The English royal entry in London, 1485–1642', in A. L. Beier, David Cannadine and James Rosenheim (eds), *The First Modern Society: Essays in English History in Honour of Lawrence Stone* (Cambridge, 1989), pp. 65–93; David Cressy, *Bonfires and Bells: National Memory and the Protestant Calendar in Elizabethan and Stuart England* (London, 1989), pp. 50–66, 120. For contrasts with James, see Tim Harris, 'Venerating the honesty of a tinker: The King's friends and the battle for the allegiance of the common people in Restoration England' in Tim Harris (ed.) *The Politics of the Excluded, c. 1500–1850* (Basingstoke, 2001), pp. 198–200.

18 Malcolm Smuts, 'Court-centred politics and the uses of Roman historians, c. 1590–1630' in Sharpe and Lake (eds), *Culture and Politics*, pp. 21–43; J. H. M. Salmon, 'Seneca and Tacitus in Jacobean England', in Linda Levy Peck (ed.), *The Mental World of the Jacobean Court* (Cambridge, 1991), pp. 169–88.

19 Nicolo Machiavelli, *Il Principe* (1532), ch. 18. For the English reception of Machiavelli, see Felix Raab, *The English Face of Machiavelli: A Changing Interpretation* (London, 1965); Jan Waszink (ed.), *Politica: Six Books of Politics or Political Instruction* (Assen, 2004), pp. 507–19; Francis Bacon, 'Of simulation and dissimulation' in James Spedding (ed.), *The Works of Francis Bacon* vol. XII (London, 1857–74), pp. 95–8. It is perhaps a testament to the interest in political lying during this period that writers made these quite fine distinctions between simulation – pretending not to be what one was, and dissimulation – pretending to be what one was not.

20 Perez Zagorin, *Ways of Lying: Dissimulation, Persecution, and Conformity in Early Modern*

Europe (London, 1990), p. 255.

21 See Virgil's *Aeneid*, book IV; Chaucer, *The House of Fame;* Shakespeare, *Henry IV Part II* (I.i.); Francis Bacon, 'Of fame' in Spedding (ed.), *The Works of Francis Bacon*, pp. 283–4. For a detailed investigation of the representation of rumour in ancient and early modern literature, see Philip Hardie, *Rumour and Renown* (Cambridge, 2012).

22 For the difficulty in defining rumours, see Jean-Nöel Kapferer, *Rumors: Uses, Interpretations and Images* (New Brunswick, 1990), ch. 1.

23 See 'rumour, n.'. OED Online. March 2012. Oxford University Press. 30 July 2012. www.oed.com/view/Entry/168836?rskey=7CkM53&result=1&isAdvanced=false#eid (accessed 29 July 2012).

Chapter 1

◆

Controlling the flow of
diplomatic information

INTRODUCTION

Historians have provided valuable insights into the ways in which the flow of information to and from the monarch was managed during the reign of Elizabeth I.[1] Secretaries Cecil and Walsingham both tried to influence Elizabeth's decisions through the selection, presentation and suppression of information, and Robert Beale even wrote a treatise about how Secretaries of State should manage the Queen.[2] It was common practice to chat with Elizabeth in order to distract her while she signed official papers, and to quickly dispatch important documents before the Queen had a chance to change her mind, as she often did. Elizabeth's secretaries even attempted to guide her foreign policy by directing English ambassadors abroad to doctor their official dispatches to encourage the Queen to take a particular course of action.[3] These practices were part of wider attempts by Elizabeth's advisers to gang up on her and pressurise her into adopting the policies they wished to advance.

Elizabeth was not simply manipulated by her councillors, however. She regularly asserted her independence by ignoring her councillors' advice, by changing her mind about policies that she had reluctantly agreed to, and by sabotaging military expeditions by starving them of funds. Very often, of course, the Queen and council worked in harmony, and on occasion, she may even have secretly connived at her servant's apparently disobedient behaviour. When privy councillors dispatched the execution warrant for Mary, Queen of Scots without the Queen's approval in 1587, Elizabeth was publicly outraged. Suspicions remain, however, that she secretly approved of their actions and merely wished to avoid the blame for Mary's death.[4]

While Elizabeth's councillors have been well studied, rather less attention has been paid to the relationship between James and his councillors. Historians have instead focused on the battle for control over foreign policy at the very top of Jacobean government, between James, Charles and Buckingham. It was once thought that the King was sidelined during his later years by his increasingly assertive son and favourite.[5] More recent scholarship has argued that James remained firmly in charge of foreign policy until his death, and he successfully resisted Charles and Buckingham's attempts to steer him towards war with Spain from late 1623 onwards.[6] The role of the Spanish match, the proposed marriage between Prince Charles and the Spanish Infanta, in generating conflict between King and Parliament has received particular attention.[7] Those who have studied foreign policy as a subject in its own right have tended to concentrate on the minutiae of diplomatic interactions during James's attempts to bring an end to the Thirty Years' War, which broke out on the continent in 1618.[8]

While attention has focused on the struggle between James, Charles and Buckingham for control of foreign policy, the King's councillors, Secretaries of State and diplomats have generally been seen as playing a fairly minor role in decision-making. The contrast between James and Elizabeth seems clear, and in part it was a product of their different circumstances and styles of rule. Where Elizabeth struggled against contemporary assumptions about the weakness of female rule, James came to the throne as an experienced King with a secure succession, and faced no such doubts about his ability or right to make decisions. His councillors appear to have played a much more subordinate role, and his habit of fostering divisions between them meant that they were unable to combine against him.

This chapter examines the formation and realisation of foreign policy during the later years of James's reign. While the historiography has tended to limit itself to the decision-making role of James, Charles and Buckingham, this chapter takes a broader approach by examining the activities of his other servants and ministers. It investigates how the fountain of news was fed from abroad as well as how information was managed at the centre. As we shall see, Secretaries of State and diplomats could influence policy by feeding James selective or misleading information, or by altering, delaying or ignoring his instructions. Ministers and servants often expressed scepticism that the King was the author of the orders they received, and suspected that intermediaries were issuing instructions on James's authority but without his knowledge.

For the most part, the relationship between James and his ministers appears to have been rather less antagonistic than it had often been under Elizabeth. Indeed, for much of the time, the apparently disobedient behaviour of James's subordinates was carried out with his tacit consent and was part of the normal running of government. The conciliar and diplomatic bureaucracy acted as a kind of buffer between the King's initial impulses and the implementation of his final decisions. James's ministers sometimes queried, delayed or palmed his messages and orders, giving him the opportunity to reconsider rash decisions. The softening of James's instructions allowed him to rebuke neighbouring powers or make verbal threats against them in front of courtiers and foreign ambassadors, while a much more moderate and conciliatory message was in fact delivered abroad. At the same time, James gave his secretaries and diplomats a degree of latitude and independence, creating uncertainty about whether they were acting on his orders or had used their own initiative. This preserved his freedom of manoeuvre, allowing him to take credit for successful policies and disown those that went wrong, even if he had ordered them himself. The apparently unwarranted behaviour of James's secretaries and diplomats often worked in James's favour, but they sometimes crossed the boundary between 'excusable disobedience' and actively thwarting or manipulating the King, for instance by feeding him information designed to encourage him into adopting particular policies. On occasion, James's servants took it upon themselves to act according to their interpretation of the interests of the King or the kingdom, even if this was different from what James had actually ordered them to do. This chapter will seek to understand how effective these attempts to shape James's perceptions were, and how the King's suspicious and sceptical attitude as well as the bureaucratic structure of Jacobean government might have limited the degree to which he could be manipulated. Before examining these issues, however, it is worth surveying the complicated and almost intractable foreign policy problems James faced during the later years of his reign. The dramatic events of the later 1610s and 1620s deepened the ideological rift between supporters and opponents of a Spanish marriage alliance, creating incentives for individuals from both sides to shape the information James received in the hope of influencing policy.

JACOBEAN FOREIGN POLICY

James I's abhorrence of war was the most consistent element of his foreign policy. His first major foreign policy decision after succeeding to the English throne was to end the long Elizabethan war with Spain, and this set the pattern for the rest of his reign. James's Dutch allies were left to continue the war on their own for another five years before they signed a twelve-year truce with Spain in 1609.

The divisions between and within European powers meant that the continent was a powder keg for much of James's reign, and the King sought to prevent the religious war that repeatedly threatened to break out. The confessional rift was deepened by the creation in 1608 of a Union of Protestant princes within the Holy Roman Empire, itself a reaction to attempts to re-establish Catholicism in Donauwörth and to restore Church lands appropriated by Protestant princes.[9] In response, Catholic princes led by Maximilian of Bavaria formed the Catholic League the next year. A crisis over disputed claims to the territories of Cleves and Jülich in 1609 threatened to ignite a wider conflict when Henri IV of France threatened to make war on Spain in support of one of the claimants, but his assassination in 1610 put an end to these plans.[10] France would do little to check Spain during the minority of Henri's son, Louis XIII. James's response was to join the Protestant Union in 1612 and to marry his daughter Elizabeth to its leading member, Frederick V of the Palatinate, the next year.[11] At the same time, James pursued various potential marriage alliances for his son, Prince Charles. A match with the Infanta Maria Anna of Spain emerged as the preferred choice, and James hoped that an alliance with Spain would help to heal the confessional rift in Europe while also providing a large dowry to help pay off his debts.[12] The match was unpopular with James's subjects, many of whom were rabidly anti-Catholic.[13] The King repeatedly tried to strengthen his hand in negotiations with Spain by hinting that he might wage war against them. He dispatched Sir John Digby to Madrid in 1617 to begin serious negotiations for the match, but at the same time he allowed Sir Walter Raleigh to sail to Guiana, where he attacked Spanish settlements.[14]

The major crisis for Jacobean foreign policy came in 1618, when the Protestant nobility of Bohemia revolted against their Catholic King, Archduke Ferdinand, who was cousin and heir to the ageing Holy Roman Emperor, Mathias.[15] The rebels were successful at first, laying siege to Vienna in June 1619. They were forced to retreat, but their ally, the Transylvanian Prince Bethlen Gabor, renewed the siege the next year. In August 1619, the Bohemian rebels offered the vacant throne to James's son-in-law, Frederick. Bohemia, like Frederick's ancestral lands in the Palatinate, was an electorate, meaning that its ruler held one of seven votes used to elect the Holy Roman Emperor. By adding a second electoral title to the one he already possessed, Frederick threatened to upset the balance of power between Protestant and Catholic Electors and wrest control of the Imperial throne from the Austrian Habsburgs. While James strongly advised his son-in-law against accepting the crown, the Archbishop of Canterbury, George Abbot, hinted that the King would support him in the end. James's advice arrived too late. Frederick was crowned in Prague in November 1619.

Frederick's acceptance of the Bohemian crown threatened to drag James into the confessional war he had tried to prevent. The King came under pressure to give financial and military support for his son-in-law, but preferred to mediate the dispute, sending James Hay, Viscount Doncaster, to negotiate a peaceful settlement.[16] In the meantime, Ferdinand had forged an alliance with Maximilian, the Duke of Bavaria, who promised to use the army of the Catholic League against Frederick in return for his electoral title. Frederick's ancestral lands were also under threat. While the Upper Palatinate bordered Bavaria, the Lower Palatinate straddled the Rhine. With the deadline for the resumption of war with the Dutch Republic approaching, Philip III of Spain was keen to secure the route which would allow him to provide his army in the Spanish Netherlands with money and reinforcements. By attacking the Lower Palatinate, he could also relieve the pressure on his Austrian cousin, Ferdinand. Rumours began to circulate that Ambrosio Spinola, who commanded forces in one of Spain's client states, the Spanish Netherlands, was preparing to invade Frederick's lands. The Elector's representative in England, Christopher Dohna, managed to raise charitable funds for an English force led by Sir Horace Vere to defend the Palatinate, but James refused to support this cause directly. Nevertheless, the King did dispatch a small fleet led by Sir Robert Mansell. This force was tasked with suppressing North African pirates but it also served to remind Spain of England's ability to inflict damage at sea. Nevertheless, Frederick's ancestral lands in the Palatinate, as well as his new kingdom of Bohemia were threatened by Spanish and Imperial forces, and James, who was deeply in debt, was reluctant to provide any assistance.

Spinola's successful invasion of the Lower Palatinate in August and September 1620 was a disaster for Frederick, but the real blow came in November, when his Bohemian forces were crushed at the Battle of White Mountain, just outside of Prague. Frederick was forced to flee with Elizabeth and his children to the safety of the Dutch Republic, having been declared an outlaw by Ferdinand. While the rest of Bohemia was reconquered, a six month truce was arranged in April 1621 in the Palatinate between Spinola's army and the English force led by Vere. James sent Sir Edward Villiers to convince Frederick to renounce his claim to the Bohemian throne, but the Elector stubbornly refused to comply with his father-in-law's wishes, as he was to do many times in the following years.[17]

Faced with these disasters, James decided to call a Parliament, which met in January 1621.[18] The King hoped it would strengthen his negotiating position by voting him the funds which would allow him credibly to threaten military intervention. Since Spinola's army had fought in the name of the Emperor rather than Philip III, James did not necessarily have to fight Spain to restore the Palatinate. Now that the Spanish supply routes to Flanders had been secured, Philip had no particular interest in the continuation of the war in Germany, and James hoped that he could be persuaded to exert pressure on his ally, Ferdinand, to come to terms. Spain would be much more willing to complete the marriage alliance and provide diplomatic support for the restitution of the Palatinate if they could be convinced that the alternative was war with England. James hoped that parliamentary sabre-rattling and a grant of taxation would elicit the desired response.

James's political position between Spain and Parliament meant that he could pursue a favourite strategy – bargaining with both sides in order to get the best deal. This policy had been recommended by James's own diplomats. In 1617, Digby advised James to call a Parliament because it would strengthen his negotiating position over the Spanish marriage. If the Spanish dowry was James's only way of solving his financial problems, Philip would demand toleration for English Catholics, but Parliament might vote a generous supply just to prevent the match from taking place.[19] The Venetian ambassador also suspected that James wished to threaten Parliament with the completion of the match in order to blackmail it into giving him money.[20] Some were cynical enough to believe that James was fully aware that he was being deceived by the Spanish ambassadors about their willingness to conclude the match, but continued with the negotiations because it provided him with a bargaining chip against Parliament.[21]

The most obvious manifestation of James's policy of bluff and brinksmanship was his dissemination of the Commons' aggressive declaration of 1621. In it, MPs promised that 'if Religion and Right may not be restored by Treaty and peaceable Means ... we would be ready to adventure the Lives and Estates of all that belong unto us' to restore Frederick to his hereditary lands.[22] At the same time, John Digby was sent to the Archdukes and the Emperor, but when he returned in late October it was clear that neither Frederick nor Ferdinand were willing to compromise. When Parliament reassembled, members petitioned James to go to war with Spain if Philip would not intercede to restore the Elector, also urging the King to end the Spanish match.[23] James angrily dissolved Parliament when this disagreement over policy escalated into a constitutional dispute about MPs' freedom of speech. Two subsidies had been voted during the first session as a free gift, but the dissolution deprived James of a third, which had been voted but not enacted. Without parliamentary support, James's bargaining position was considerably weakened.

The King continued to work towards a negotiated settlement, sending Sir Richard Weston and Sir Edward Conway to take part in a peace conference in Brussels that lasted from April to September 1622. The problem with these negotiations was that monarchs such as James who sought peace were unable to control combative princes like Frederick, who in turn were unable to control their own mercenary generals. Fighting in the Empire tended to continue regardless of negotiations for a truce. James continued to make belligerent gestures, mustering 6,000–10,000 men in St James's fields in April 1622 for the benefit of the Emperor's ambassador, who also witnessed a tilt afterwards in which Charles, who was beginning to play a more prominent role in affairs, was shown off as a vigorous and martial prince.[24]

The string of military disasters for Frederick's side continued. In October 1621, Maximilian occupied the Upper Palatinate. In the following year, Frederick travelled in person to the Lower Palatinate to lead his forces, but was unable to prevent the armies of the Emperor and the Catholic League from defeating his allies at Wimpfen and Hochst. Frederick's mercenary general, Mansfeld, gained some small compensation for these defeats by pushing through Spanish forces at Fleurus in the Spanish Netherlands. War between Spain and the Dutch Republic had resumed, and Mansfeld helped to end Spinola's siege of the Dutch town of Berghen-op-Zoom. Nevertheless, Imperial forces were left to storm Heidelberg, Frederick's capital, where they massacred the English garrison. Early in 1623 the Imperial Diet of Regensburg formally transferred Frederick's electoral title to Maximilian. Frederick had lost virtually everything.

These events led many to believe that James would once again call a Parliament, but he continued to hope that the match between Charles and the Infanta would encourage Spain to put pressure on the Emperor to restore the Palatinate and end the war. The slow pace of negotiations led many to suspect that the Spanish did not want to conclude them, but were merely stringing James along to prevent him joining with the Dutch in a war against them. In February 1623, Charles and Buckingham made a dramatic incognito trip to Madrid. There were many reasons for this journey, but perhaps the most important was that they hoped to force the pace of negotiations and find out once and for all whether Philip IV, who succeeded his father in 1621, was negotiating in good faith. After further talks, the match seemed on the point of conclusion, but more delays and the raising of new demands soured relations. Charles realised that even if the match went ahead, Spain would not intervene to restore the Palatinate, and he returned with Buckingham in October intent on war with the Habsburgs.

In the months after their return from Spain, Charles and Buckingham forged a fragile alliance with anti-Spanish elements at court. They pressured the King to break off negotiations with Spain and to call a Parliament which would vote the funds necessary for war.[25] At the same time, they began diplomatic preparations for a grand anti-Habsburg alliance. James resisted pressure to declare war on Spain, hoping once again that a belligerent Parliament would encourage new Spanish offers. Parliament duly voted three subsidies, much less than the amount James insisted would be necessary for a war, but enough to make a start. MPs were suspicious that James would merely use the money to pay off his debts, so parliamentary commissioners were appointed to supervise their spending. Negotiations began for a marriage between Charles and the French Princess, Henrietta Maria, which was intended to secure a military alliance. James continued to seek the restoration of Frederick's lands and titles while resisting pressure to go to war with Spain. An English expeditionary force led by Mansfeld was intended to march for the Palatinate through France, but Louis XIII had little interest in restoring Frederick's lands, and when his Protestant subjects began an uprising against him, he refused to allow English forces to land in French ports. James had forbidden his troops from relieving the Spanish siege of Breda, so they were left to rot aboard ship in Dutch ports without achieving anything. To the end, James resisted war with Spain and never entirely gave up hope of coming to an understanding with Philip. The Count of Gondomar, the Spanish ambassador, was on his way to England when James died in March 1625.

SECRETARIES OF STATE: GLOSSING AND SUPPRESSING NEWS

These dramatic events deepened divisions at court and in the diplomatic service between those who supported a Spanish marriage alliance and those who wanted James to break with Spain and provide military support for Frederick. Like all court factions, these two groups were loose and shifting alliances, often organised as much around individuals as policies, and the division between the two was greater at some points than others. Historians have drawn particular attention to the conflict between James on the one hand, and Charles and Buckingham on the other, following the return of the Prince and the favourite from Spain in 1623. We will now consider what role other ministers and diplomats could play in the formation and realisation of policy, beginning with Secretaries of State, who held responsibility for handling diplomatic correspondence. While they exerted only a limited control over the flow of information, their position nevertheless provided them with opportunities to shape James's perceptions of foreign affairs and to influence the way in which his wishes were put into action.

James's Secretaries of State have traditionally been seen as playing a fairly minor role. Garrett Mattingly argued that the secretaryship degenerated into a 'routine clerkship' after 1612, and James's 'second rate' secretaries have been viewed as poor successors to the likes of Sir Francis Walsingham and Sir Robert Cecil.[26] A secretaryship of state was a particularly ill-defined office. The secretaries handled the King's correspondence and set the agenda for meetings of the Privy Council, as well as sitting in Parliament, but their practical powers could vary enormously. The office was also precarious under James, and a secretary's authority was often open to question.[27] As Robert Cecil wrote, while the powers of other ministers were defined by patent or oath, secretaries had no other warrant for their activities but the word of the King.[28] If their actions displeased James, or if he wanted to get rid of them, they could not claim, as other ministers did, that they had simply acted within the terms of their commission, and they were always vulnerable to accusations that they had overstepped the bounds of their authority. The insecure and ill-defined nature of a Secretary of State's authority allowed James to disavow their actions, if necessary, even if they had merely done as the King asked. Sir Robert Naunton was suspended from the secretaryship for making enquiries about a French match, even though James had directed him to do so.[29]

Other ministers played a similar role in taking the blame for decisions which might create discontent among courtiers or foreign princes. The Lord

Keeper did so by scrutinising the warrants for offices, pensions or pardons that were sent to him to be sealed. James was able to grant suitors their wishes, and thus display his largesse, while his Lord Keeper was blamed when their requests were finally diminished or denied. Lord Keepers could also take the blame for more important matters. In 1623, when James was offering concessions to English Catholics in the hope of completing the Spanish match, Lord Keeper Williams offered to accept the responsibility if James decided to renege on his promises and reinforce the recusancy laws when the Infanta was safely in England.[30] Shortly before Charles and Buckingham returned to England, James promised pardons for English Catholics but was reluctant to produce them, fearing an anti-Catholic backlash. With James's blessing, Williams created artificial bureaucratic delays in preparing the documents, and once again offered to accept full responsibility for doing so.[31] James did not always simply betray ministers by allowing them to take the fall for actions that he had privately approved – on occasion, they willingly offered to shield James from blame.

Although Secretaries of State were never very secure in their office, their control over the flow of letters to and from James could give them real power. Control over correspondence provided them with diplomatic information which was the basis for their office and gave them an excuse for close personal attendance on the King. It also gave them greater influence as interpreters of diplomatic information, both in selecting and summarising news in order to steer the King's perceptions, and in interpreting his wishes and communicating them to his representatives abroad.

Control over dispatches allowed secretaries to encourage diplomats to emphasise news that might provoke James to adopt particular policies. Those who advocated English military intervention to restore James's son-in-law Frederick to his ancestral lands and titles sometimes sought to shape James's perceptions about the situation on the continent. In 1619, for instance, Naunton secretly wrote to Sir Dudley Carleton and encouraged him to stress how enthusiastically the Dutch were assisting Frederick. The Secretary evidently hoped to convince James that if he decided to help his son-in-law, the Dutch would be committed and dependable allies.[32]

Conway behaved similarly when Charles and Buckingham attempted to steer James towards a breach with Spain following the breakdown of the Spanish match negotiations in 1623–24. Conway, who was a reliable ally of Buckingham, seized upon slights against James which might damage the King's relationship with Spain or even create a *casus belli*. Spain's client state, the Spanish Netherlands, which was ruled by the Archduchess Isabella, was a potential source of friction. In April 1624 Conway expressed his satisfaction at William Trumbull's attempt to seek the restitution of two English ships which had recently been taken by Dunkirk pirates, and asked to be informed of the result of his efforts, 'for iudgement wilbe thereby made, of the affection to continue in good corre-spondencie with his Maiestie'.[33] Trumbull was instructed to request an exten-sion to the sequestration of Frankenthal, a town in the Palatinate which the Archduchess had occupied on James's behalf in 1623. Conway urged Trumbull to demand a reply, 'soe as especially, if the Infanta shall giue you any negative Answere', he wrote, 'which may be laid hold off as a breach on her part; send the Answere hither with all speede'.[34] A few months later, Trumbull was told that Conway was 'very inclinable' to repay the Archduchess's government 'in their owne coyne' for recent attacks on English shipping and the mistreatment of James's subjects, and encouraged Trumbull to feed the Secretary informa-tion on this subject.[35] Trumbull thereupon wrote a letter to the Privy Council, stirring up anger against the outrages committed against English merchants, and leaving them resolved to inform James about the situation and to 'presse extraordinarily' for the augmentation of the fleet that he was setting out to transport Count Mansfeld and his forces across the channel.[36]

There is reason to believe that Conway also withheld information he did not want James to receive when summarising diplomatic dispatches for the King. A letter from Trumbull in December 1624 reported that ministers in the Spanish Netherlands were interested in negotiating a peaceful restitu-tion of the Palatinate.[37] A summary of Trumbull's letter does not mention this information.[38] Conway may not have wanted James to be distracted by further offers of negotiation while Charles and Buckingham were pushing for war, and while Mansfeld's expeditionary force was on its way to the continent, and he may well have omitted these peace offers on purpose.

Conway's behaviour appears to have been part of a larger attempt to control the flow of information to James during his final years. Buckingham intimi-dated and silenced diplomats whose actions might undermine his war policy. When Walter Aston sent a dispatch to England to prepare the ground for the embassy of Gondomar in early 1625, Buckingham reproached the English ambassador, saying that his behaviour was 'much wondered att here by all'. Gondomar, Buckingham said, 'was the instrument to abuse my master the prince and the state and if now by your meanes the kinge should be fetched on againe vpon a new tretie the blame would light vpon you'.[39] A few months later, when the French match was being negotiated, Charles appears to have coached messengers on how to gloss bad news from Paris so as to avoid provoking an angry reaction from James that might damage the negotiations.[40] James Hay, Earl of Carlisle fed the English commissioners for the marriage treaty with encouraging information so that they could 'drawe arguments to quicken his Maiesties affection to this match'.[41] Although James remained the final arbiter over foreign policy, there is a sense that the machinery of diplomatic news, if not decision-making, was being hijacked by Charles and Buckingham during his last years.

An episode in which Sir George Calvert 'palmed' diplomatic letters in 1623 shows how secretaries were able to influence the tone of dispatches, prevent them from being sent and even obstruct the implementation of the King's orders. The affair began in 1622, when two Dunkirk privateering ships, which had been pursued by the Dutch, took refuge in Scottish ports, one at Leith and the other at Aberdeen. They were both blockaded by Dutch ships, which would attack them as soon as they attempted to leave.[42] James demanded that the Dutch allow the Dunkirk ships to return to the Spanish Netherlands unmolested, but the Dutch denied his request. The King then gave Carleton instructions ordering him to protest the inadequate Dutch response, and to threaten to attack the Dutch ships if they continued their blockade.[43]

For much of the reign, one of the Secretaries of State stayed at Whitehall, while the other usually accompanied the King as he travelled between his favourite hunting lodges. On this occasion, James was not in London, and his instructions were initially given to Conway, who was attending him. Conway then passed the instructions on to Calvert at Whitehall, who was supposed to send a courier to deliver them to Carleton in the Dutch Republic.

In early May, Carleton received word from his nephew that the King was angry with him for failing to communicate his displeasure about the blockade to the Dutch.[44] Carleton had apparently ignored his instructions, and so the King had resolved to send two of his own ships to break the Dutch blockade before waiting for either Carleton or the Dutch to respond. Conway said that if James's feelings had been communicated in good time, conflict could have been avoided.[45] James was further angered when Dutch ships destroyed one of the Dunkirkers as it tried to break the blockade at Leith. With Charles and Buckingham in Spain, and marriage negotiations entering their most crucial phase, James wished to demonstrate the value of an English alliance, and he promised the Spanish ambassador that he would seek redress for the loss of the ship.[46] Conway suspected that James's instructions had been held up on their way to The Hague by Calvert, and wanted to know if Carleton had received them.[47]

As a later investigation established, Carleton had taken it upon himself to soften James's threats. Carleton was sympathetic to the Dutch position. If the Dunkirk ships were allowed to escape, they would simply go on to attack Dutch shipping, and if James continued to protect them, he would effectively turn his ports into operating bases for pirates.[48] Although Carleton had been commanded to request that the Dutch lift the blockade and to threaten the use of force if they did not, he decided to reserve the threat for a private meeting with Prince Maurice, only asking the States General to withdraw their ships.[49] Carleton claimed that the Prince would be able to inform James how the States would be likely to react to his threat, thereby giving James the opportunity to change his mind if it seemed likely to backfire and provoke an angry response.[50]

What the investigation into this episode did not discover was that Calvert had also played a part in undermining James's orders. The Secretary had delayed sending the King's demands to the Dutch, finding them 'so bitter that he is lofte to send them withowt some sweetening'.[51] Calvert was reputed to favour the Spanish match and might have been expected to encourage conflict with the Dutch, yet his 'palming' of the letter was intended to maintain good relations with the Republic. His attempts to moderate James's threats indicates that he was far from being a lackey of Spain.

Calvert's apparent subversion of James's wishes did not stop there. He promised Carleton that he was keeping an eye on the English ships that were being prepared to break the Dutch blockade, and would not allow them to leave before James had a chance to change his mind. He would send the instructions to Carleton only when 'he could not deferre so unpleasing a message any longer'.[52] Crucially, he went on to attribute the intemperate tone of the communications with the Dutch to Conway rather than James.[53] The implication was that it was Conway, not James, who was leading the push for decisive action, giving the King's instructions to Carleton, which bore 'M*aster* Secretary Conways military style' a more belligerent and implacable spin than the King would have intended. Carleton's nephew, who clearly shared Calvert's suspicions, decided to speak with the Marquis of Hamilton, who had been present when James dictated his instructions to Conway and who would be able to confirm independently what had taken place.[54] Unease over the potential misrepresentation of James's views forced Carleton to request that in future the King should sign all instructions sent to him on matters of such importance. Conway, however, insisted that this was not possible, and that when the King commanded him to write, he did so without further ceremony.[55] Relations with Conway appear to have been at a low point, and Carleton's nephew may well have been alluding to the Secretary when he wrote that someone close to James had lately done Carleton 'ill offices' by saying that his loyalties lay with Frederick, Elizabeth and the Dutch rather than with the King.[56]

Conway's behaviour was all the more surprising because he was so closely identified with the anti-Spanish party at court. He had lived and served for many years in the Dutch Republic and had a Dutch wife. His secretaryship was even rumoured to have been bought for him with Dutch money, and this perhaps explains his uncharacteristic behaviour during this episode.[57] Any belligerent gestures Conway could make against the Dutch would tend to contradict rumours that he was secretly in their pay, showing that his true loyalties lay with James. For different reasons, then, Conway, Calvert and Carleton all tried to influence the tone and delivery of James's letter, while Calvert had delayed James's order for the dispatch of English ships.

A compromise was eventually worked out with the Dutch by which James's ships would escort the Dunkirkers home, a solution which was reported to have greatly contented the Spanish.[58] The matter of Carleton's disobedience was finally cleared up when Calvert and other Privy Councillors explained his actions to the King:

> they and he joined together, and on Thursday last all of them at their comming to the king did remonstrate to his Maiesty that your endeauours in this busines were not understood aright the k[ing] at the same instant shewed him self uery well pacified; and your lordships white mule [Conway], who causelesly hath caused all this distemper, was not a little ashamed.[59]

Dudley Carleton's nephew assured him that Calvert had done him 'no meane seruice' by clearing his name.[60] His friend John Chamberlain, who had also heard about the episode, thought that Conway would now be 'more tractable', but if he continued with his 'jades tricks', Carleton had 'an antidot against all venome' in the shape of Calvert, 'for *saepe premente Deo fert Deus alter opem* [often when we are oppressed by one God, another comes to our help]'.[61] It was not until September 1623 that Conway's goodwill towards Carleton seemed assured, but Carleton's nephew thought his behaviour had only changed because the Secretary's attempt to undermine him had been exposed.[62] The matter appears to have rested there until Buckingham and Charles, newly committed to an anti-Spanish war which Calvert opposed, began to search for ammunition against the Secretary in 1624.[63]

While James had the final say in foreign affairs, this episode indicates that Secretaries of State held a potentially powerful position. As we have seen, secretaries could put a more aggressive or moderate spin on the King's words, and could delay his instructions in order to prevent him from following through on rash and intemperate sentiments. James's anger, as Conway noted, 'passeth as suddainely as it riseth', and by delaying actions that he might later regret, secretaries could function as an important safety mechanism within the machinery of foreign policy.[64]

Importantly, there are reasons to suppose that James actually welcomed the fact that his secretaries delayed his instructions. Calvert appears to have openly admitted his reasons for withholding Carleton's orders, even to Conway, and it is noticeable that James did not appear to punish him for it, but was reportedly 'uery well pacified' by Calvert's and the Privy Council's explanation.[65] This process allowed the King to let off steam by striking belligerent poses, perhaps intended to impress the Spanish ambassadors, without suffering the consequences of committing himself to a particular position in the fixed and less deniable form of an official letter. As we have seen, Elizabeth's secretaries were adept at dispatching orders which the Queen had only reluctantly agreed to before she had a chance to reconsider. When secretaries and diplomats delayed or simply ignored James's more intemperate instructions, they gave him a welcome chance to change his mind, an opportunity which Elizabeth's secretaries frequently denied her. Both the King and his secretaries were happy to uphold the outward dignity of kingship while tacitly acknowledging that royal instructions would be modified.

Conrad Russell praised James's political inertia. While Charles's determination and activity tended to create opposition, James was more often content to leave things as they were, and to avoid clearly defined policies.[66] This case study suggests that on occasion, James could actually be rather belligerent and interventionist, at least in show, while the delays and obstructions came from his ministers. This sort of 'excusable disobedience' may have been more common than historians have previously realised. In 1624, the Venetian ambassador reported that after a similar provocation, James had instructed Buckingham to arrest all Dutch ships in English ports, but that the Duke had not put these orders into action.[67]

Secretaries were not the only ministers who queried or delayed James's decisions. The Lord Keeper, as we have seen, scrutinised documents which he was asked to seal, raising objections about warrants and pardons and allowing James to reconsider hastily made decisions. Lord Keeper Williams, for instance, regularly challenged and edited the grants, patents and proclamations he was sent, informing Buckingham if they were likely to be unpopular or would drain the King's limited resources.[68] He occasionally queried whether James was even aware of orders made in his name, or whether other ministers had simply claimed his authority to pass petitions and warrants.[69] Such internal discussions ensured that the consequences of decisions were fully thought through before they were enacted, and that policies reflected James's wishes rather than those of his other ministers.

The Scottish Privy Council also disobeyed James's orders, for instance when they quietly refused to enforce the Five Articles of Perth. The articles were alterations to Scottish Church worship intended to bring the Kirk closer to conformity with the Church of England. The articles were hugely controversial, particularly the fifth, which required worshippers to receive communion on their knees from a minister. James relentlessly pushed for those who refused to conform to the articles to be punished, but his councillors in Scotland felt they understood Scottish politics better than their distant King. They refused to follow his orders, which they feared would provoke further confrontation and discontent.[70] This sort of behaviour was all the more remarkable in the case of Calvert's 'palming' of letters in 1623. Not just far-flung representatives, but even those at the heart of government felt they could act according to James's best interests, even if these weren't the same as what he had told them to do.

James was not simply duped and manipulated by his secretaries. He had good reason to be suspicious of those who managed his paperwork ever since Lord Balmerino slipped a letter to the Pope, hinting that the King might convert to Catholicism, into a pile of letters for him to sign in 1599, and there were other examples of similar behaviour to draw on from France and Spain.[71] This distrust may have been one of the reasons why James temporarily decided to act as his own secretary after the death of Cecil in 1612. There was a high rate of turnover among James's secretaries during his later years, and the inherent instability of their position may well have given them cause to refrain from risking blatant attempts at manipulation.

Safeguards were also built into the institutional framework of Jacobean government. James's practice of balancing competing secretaries who were associated with opposing factions prevented any single group or individual from forming a monopoly over the control of dispatches and instructions. Particularly helpful in this respect was the convention that while one secretary was in attendance on James, the other stayed at Whitehall. This meant that directions went through the hands of both secretaries before they were dispatched. By having his secretaries arranged in series rather than in parallel, James ensured that his directions would receive additional scrutiny which minimised the potential for any one secretary to exercise an improper degree of control. It should also be remembered that James had many other ways of receiving and sending information about foreign affairs, not least through foreign ambassadors residing at his court, and he often made use of unofficial envoys who could circumvent the normal diplomatic machinery.[72] Finally, as we have seen, at times James may have even tacitly approved of this diplomatic filtering mechanism. It allowed him to reconsider rash or unwise decisions, made his more undiplomatic statements more palatable to a foreign audience, and also allowed him to convey an impression of anger to one audience while sending a more moderate message to another.

DIPLOMATS: SELECTING THE NEWS

Historians have tended to characterise James's diplomats as ineffective and isolated, servants of a master who tended to ignore or undermine them.[73] Nevertheless, diplomats, like Secretaries of State, were engaged in the struggle over the direction of foreign policy. There are few if any cases in which diplomats overtly and independently attempted to use their dispatches to steer James's policies. Indeed they were constantly on their guard against accusations that they provided biased or ideologically slanted information. Instead, their superiors at home, and even their foreign hosts, tended to direct them to provide or highlight news designed to create conflict with Spain, particularly after 1623 when Charles and Buckingham attempted to lead the King towards war. The newsletter collections of William Trumbull and Sir Dudley Carleton are particularly useful in exploring these phenomena, not merely because they left some of the richest records of any Jacobean diplomats, but also because their positions in the Dutch Republic and the Spanish Netherlands meant that they straddled the European confessional divide.

While the most important Jacobean ambassadors might exert some influence over affairs by conducting important negotiations, most did not. Although the King's representatives in Spain and France were given some responsibility, many of James's other diplomats were tasked with conveying messages and settling minor disputes, but they had little influence over the most important affairs. While foreign nations, particularly Spain, often delegated authority to diplomats sent abroad, James preferred to negotiate at home.[74] Carleton was often frustrated that important diplomatic business, such as the sale of the cautionary towns, was removed from his jurisdiction and dealt with by the King and his ministers.[75] When major problems needed to be resolved, James tended to send extraordinary ambassadors rather than leaving things in the hands of his resident diplomats, although greater powers were sometimes given to those who were based far from home.[76]

If James rarely gave his diplomats as much responsibility as they might have liked, he also gave them little in the way of direction or guidance, and they often complained that the King gave them insufficient instructions. There is some justice to claims that James neglected paperwork and would rather go hunting than attend to official business. In this case, however, his *laissez faire* approach was the result of deliberate calculation rather than laziness. His instinct was to keep his distance from the actions of his servants, allowing him to claim credit if they succeeded and to disown them if they failed. As the Venetian ambassador explained, 'his nature is such that in his heart great strokes sometimes please him when they turn out well, but he has no inclination to devise or handle them, and if they turn out badly he wishes to be free from every imputation of having fomented or advised them'.[77] When Edward Herbert departed for France in 1621 he was told that he would not need instructions because James trusted his judgement. Herbert replied that this vote of confidence had merely given him 'greater power and latitude to err', but James once again refused to give him instructions.[78] As we have seen, the lack of a formal commission meant that secretaries had little to fall back on if their actions displeased the King. By failing to give his diplomats clear written instructions, James similarly deprived them of the ability to claim that they had merely followed orders if things went wrong and he found it necessary to use them as scapegoats. John Castle, a minor official and newsletter writer, was not the only one to observe that diplomats were 'subject to be charged and to suffer publikely for doeing that to which he was warranted privately by good commission'.[79]

While Jacobean diplomats had relatively little say over major decisions, the lesser negotiations they conducted still provided opportunities to influence foreign policy. James occasionally exerted or released pressure over relatively minor points of contention with his neighbours depending on the progress of other, more important negotiations. A large debt owed to James by towns in the

Spanish Netherlands functioned as just such an issue.[80] Anti-Spanish councillors who wished to create conflict could raise the matter of the debt and even use it to help to justify war against Spain. The Archdukes's agent in England, Van Male, warned his superiors at an early stage that the same councillors who wanted James to make a declaration in favour of Frederick were also encouraging him to demand the repayment of the loan.[81] In March 1620, as part of a process apparently orchestrated by Secretary Naunton, Trumbull requested that a letter 'of some resentment' should be sent to the Archduke, complaining about the delays and excuses the provincial estates were making about repaying the loan. Trumbull was reminded that when similar 'vndue and vnfitting' answers had been given in the past, Elizabeth I had been driven to 'take the course of Iustice by way of Arrests and Reprizalls, which was none of the least causes of producing those many fold acts of hostility which fell out betwixt her and the King of Spain and those countries'.[82]

In November, however, Trumbull was told that James thought it better to set the matter aside because England and Spain were 'betweene frends and enemies'.[83] In 1621, when the Archduke's support in mediating peace in the Palatinate was being sought, Trumbull was once again instructed not to press the issue because it might give the Archduke cause for offence.[84] A further attempt to raise the matter of the loan was made in October 1622, when Trumbull suggested that the debt might be comprehended in the Spanish marriage treaty.[85] When Charles was on the brink of war with Spain in the summer of 1625, Trumbull was once again instructed to reignite the dispute by demanding the repayment of the debt and indicating that no further excuses would be accepted, and he presented a remonstrance just before he was revoked in October 1625.[86] Trumbull appears to have been caught between the anti-Spanish faction at court and James himself. While the former encouraged him to raise contentious issues with the Archdukes, James was inclined to suppress anything which might create conflict, although the King realised that such matters could provide him with diplomatic leverage and allow him to elicit concessions from Spain.

Corona Regia, a libellous pamphlet printed against James in 1615, provided a similar diplomatic lever. James wanted the Archdukes to punish the authors and publishers of the pamphlet, but his pursuit was not a fixed issue of principle so much as a diplomatic tool that could be used or set aside as circumstances dictated.[87] If James wished to avoid conflict with the Archdukes and Spain because this served the interest of securing a Spanish bride and restoring the Palatinate by negotiation, the issue of *Corona Regia* could be overlooked. Depending on the diplomatic context, as Trumbull wrote, James could either press the issue of the pamphlet or bury it in a 'graue of oblivion' until a more suitable time.[88] Ultimately, the Spanish match was a far more important matter, and it was this that dictated whether Trumbull should pursue those responsible or not.[89]

From late 1623, Charles and Buckingham began to use these relatively minor issues to create friction with Spain. The dispute over *Corona Regia* could be used to exert pressure and extract concessions, to legitimise reprisals, or even as a *casus belli*. From as early as 1617 the Venetian ambassador hoped that James could use the failure of a recent mission to resolve the dispute as an excuse to dismiss the Spanish and Archducal ambassadors and break off friendly relations.[90] While Trumbull sporadically pursued the matter over the course of his time in Brussels, the major breakthrough had to wait for Charles and Buckingham's conversion to an anti-Habsburg foreign policy. It is probably no coincidence that a big push to identify and punish the publishers of *Corona Regia* came in 1623, just as the Prince was on his way back from Madrid.[91] By 1624, Trumbull's efforts to track down the publisher led Castle to hope that James would use the issue as a pretext to break with Spain.[92] Prior to 1623, then, James directed Trumbull to raise or quash matters depending on the progress of negotiations for the Spanish match, although supporters of Frederick, such as Naunton, may have occasionally played an independent role. After Charles and Buckingham's trip to Spain, however, an important shift in power took place, and Trumbull was repeatedly encouraged by Conway to create friction with Spain.

On occasion, English diplomats were asked by foreign powers to relay information about plots against James in order to shape his perceptions. The assassination of Henri IV of France in 1610 had panicked James into cracking down on Catholics at home while shoring up the Protestant Cause abroad.[93] Those who informed James of Catholic plots against him in the later 1610s and 20s, when the King was moving towards a Spanish alliance, hoped to provoke a similar reaction. Trumbull and Carleton sometimes warned James of assassination plots against him, and there is a strong sense that they encouraged him to believe those which might create distrust of Catholics and the Habsburg powers while downplaying those that were designed to alienate him from Frederick and the Dutch.

In 1615 Trumbull had come to England to warn James about an assassination plot being hatched by English Catholics, but the man who had provided the information turned out to be a charlatan.[94] Another attempt was made in 1620 to convince the King of an assassination plot, set to coincide with a Spanish invasion from Flanders. Although James did not believe in the plot, the Venetian ambassador saw it as an indication that the anti-Spanish faction had not lost hope of 'changing the aspect of affairs' by creating suspicions about Spanish intentions just as Spinola was invading the Palatinate.[95] Even if a plot itself were not believed, it might nevertheless help to raise suspicions about the aims and trustworthiness both of English Catholics and Spain.

Spain and the English Catholics were not the only parties implicated in plots against James. The unpopularity of the King's pacific foreign policy also raised the spectre of Dutch and puritan plotting. In 1622, Trumbull passed on 'malitious and infernall' news of a supposed plot, emanating from the Dutch Republic, in which Frederick would go in disguise into England, and would be on hand to assume the throne once James, Charles and Gondomar had been murdered.[96] Carleton realised that the plot was 'an artifice to bring his Ma*i*esty in jealosie of his best frende', the Dutch Republic, and Trumbull was no doubt relieved to hear that James did not take it seriously.[97]

There was no guarantee that rumours of assassination plots would be believed, and those who spread them could not control the ways in which they were subsequently interpreted. A supposed plot against Charles's life involving his sister Elizabeth, for instance, was interpreted by some as the mere 'deuise of some papists to make the Prince iealous of his sister'.[98] The Privy Council dismissed the whole episode as 'an idle matter', and it is an open question whether such an absurd and transparent attempt to sow distrust between Charles and Elizabeth was really hatched by 'papists' or by those who wished to make Catholics look mendacious and desperate.[99] James often treated reports of Catholic plotting with scorn, and Thomas Edmondes for one wished that he would take them more seriously.[100] Such reports could also have the opposite effect to that which their originators intended. The Venetian ambassador, Valaresso, believed that James's fear of Catholic plots against his life were a major reason for his attachment to a policy of peace with Spain.[101] At the very least, the multiplicity of interpretations that could be put upon these 'plots' and their potential to backfire must have severely limited their reliability and usefulness as weapons in the battle over royal perceptions.

Even if James did not believe these plots, however, they at least had the potential to convince him that there was no smoke without fire and to provide a context within which less dramatic suspicions might seem more plausible. The idea that the United Provinces were plotting to assassinate James and replace him with Frederick, for instance, would tend to vivify and sustain more moderate fears, such as that the Dutch were exerting inappropriate influence through friendly privy councillors and pushing him to support his son-in-law's wars.

Foreign rulers also sometimes tried to steer James's policies in a particular direction by supplying him with letters that they had supposedly intercepted, and English diplomats were often used as conduits for these. An episode that took place in July 1620, when Spinola was preparing to invade the Palatinate, helps us to understand the politics surrounding the provision of such intercepted letters. James was sceptical that Spinola would attack Frederick's ancestral lands, but Prince Maurice of Orange and three deputies of the States General supplied Carleton with a packet of intercepted letters that seemed to prove that he would.[102] The packet included Spinola's commission from the Emperor, together with a number of other enciphered letters written by the chief ministers of the Emperor and the King of Spain.[103] Since no man in the Dutch Republic could be found with the requisite skill to decipher them, however, Maurice asked Carleton to send them to England to see if better luck might be had there. When Carleton considered 'the good terms of amity, in which his majesty doth hitherto stand' with the Habsburg princes, he declined to send the letters himself, although he did send the commission. Carleton clearly did not wish to be seen as a tool of Dutch interests or to be blamed for any deterioration in Anglo-Spanish relations.

The recent treatment of Carleton's own letters by the Spanish side, however, gave him the justification for further action. An English courier had recently drowned while crossing the channel, and when his body washed up near Ostend, a letter he was carrying from Carleton to his superiors at home had been discovered. Despite being marked 'for his majesty's special service', this letter had been taken to Brussels.[104] Emboldened by this precedent, Carleton advised Maurice to send the enciphered Spanish letters to his own ambassador in England, Noel Caron. In London, Secretary Naunton directed Caron to the best person to decipher them.[105] By sending the letters to the Dutch ambassador rather than directly to Naunton, Carleton was ensuring that neither James nor his servants could be blamed for intercepting and deciphering them, even though the effect would be the same, since Caron would be sure to disclose their contents to the King. Since Caron had made copies of the letters and had taken charge of the deciphering, Naunton was able to politely return the originals to the Archduke via Trumbull, assuring him that neither he nor Carleton had made any attempt to decode them – which was strictly true.[106] News soon spread that Caron had received the letters, and with typical exaggeration and simplification, it was rumoured that these deciphered letters had been written from the King of Spain to Spinola, and that they ordered the general to massacre the inhabitants of Heidelberg before the English forces under Vere could arrive.[107]

The Archdukes's agent in England, Van Male, soon found out about these letters.[108] He befriended the expert who had been given the job of deciphering them, and attempted to persuade him not to.[109] Van Male also obtained copies of the letters, which he sent to the Archduke, who confirmed that they were genuine.[110] The Archduke refused to bribe the expert, however, because he was convinced that the cipher was too strong to be broken. When Naunton discovered what Van Male was doing, he applied pressure to the expert, who finally deciphered the letters in late September, although Van Male, if his own account is to believed, had significantly delayed this.[111]

Charles Carter doubted that the letters were ever genuinely deciphered, and suggested that the expert may have simply made the deciphered letters up.[112] Manuscript summaries of the letters appear to have circulated fairly widely, however.[113] They give a detailed account of the contents of five deciphered letters written in June and July: two from the Spanish ambassador in Vienna, the Count of Oñate, to the Archduke; one from Oñate to the Duke of Bavaria; one from Maximillian to Ferdinand and another from Ferdinand to the Elector of Mainz.[114] The upshot of the letters was that Spinola would invade the Palatinate, while the Dukes of Saxony and Bavaria would put down the rebellions in Upper Austria and Bohemia. The Imperial ban on Frederick is also discussed at length, and the complex and detailed discussion of Imperial diplomacy they contain suggests that they were genuine.[115]

There was no guarantee that James would bother to read these intercepted letters. James disliked poring over diplomatic dispatches, and could not always be trusted to read long letters. Trumbull's hopes of royal gratitude for tracking down the printer of *Corona Regia* in 1624 were undermined by James's unwillingness to read his letter, which he said was as big as a Bible, and Trumbull's allies at court frequently advised him to shorten his dispatches.[116] By failing to correctly judge the length of the King's attention span, diplomats ran the risk of having their carefully crafted words summarised through an intermediary who might not have their best interests at heart. Trumbull was particularly worried that the unwelcome warnings he gave about Spinola's preparations for the invasion of the Palatinate in 1620 were going unheeded, complaining that his superiors 'damne my *lett*res to a pitt of perpetuall oblivion, for after they are once on that syde the Seas, I very seldome heare any more newes of them'.[117]

The 'intercepted' letters which James received were not a reliable way of influencing royal policy, because they were open to a variety of interpretations and James tended to believe only those that he wanted to be true. James would often simply dismiss intercepted letters as forgeries, as the reception of the letters warning of an invasion of the Lower Palatinate in the summer of 1620 shows. The Venetian ambassador wrote that the letters had made a significant impact, and had forced Spinola to delay the invasion of the Palatinate by several weeks.[118] In fact, the effect of the deciphered letters might have been considerably smaller than this. They were only decoded in late September, when Spinola had already begun his invasion.[119] The commission that went along with the letters had been sent to James, via Naunton, in August, but it is unlikely that James believed it was genuine. Even those like Beaulieu who were predisposed to believe in their authenticity still had to be reassured that there was no 'artifice or deceite' involved, since it was entirely possible that the Dutch were simply trying to drag James into a conflict over the Palatinate in order to distract Spain from the upcoming recommencement of the Eighty Years' War in 1621.[120] When another letter arrived which had supposedly been written by the Archduchess to Spinola, the Venetian ambassador told his superiors that the King would probably think it a fake, and ignore it accordingly.[121] The fact that an 'intercepted' packet of letters had become a well-established fictional device further militated against their credibility.[122] James had no way of knowing whether a letter was genuine or fraudulent, and his suspicions must have been increased when the letters told him things that he did not want to hear.

English diplomats were not merely conduits of information from their host countries. They could also play an independent role in shaping decision-making through their own provision of foreign news and advice on policy. Gathering information from abroad was arguably a resident ambassador's primary purpose. As Robert Cecil told Trumbull in 1610, 'Your part is to observe and advertise, and mine to make use for the best of His Majesty's service of what I receive from you'.[123] Carleton was reprimanded by Cecil in 1611 for suggesting that since he had little news of consequence to send from Venice, he should not write so regularly. Cecil insisted that he should write weekly, and include news even if it had no bearing on English interests.[124] Cecil encouraged Trumbull to develop and maintain a network of correspondence that stretched across Europe. 'It is a special part of a minister of your employment to have his eyes cast afar off as well as near, and I commend it much in you'.[125] Diplomats could often rise in the King's service by providing advice, although as we shall see, in the 1610s and 20s James made it quite clear to some of his diplomats that advice over certain issues, and particularly the Spanish match, was not welcome. Even if diplomats did not offer direct advice, they could still provide news that strongly implied that a particular course of action should be taken. Trumbull often sent information about the Spanish Netherlands and the Palatinate that made his own views clear. In 1624, for instance, Trumbull reported that the Archduchess was 'more afraid of Mansfelts invadeing some parte of flanders, or succouring Breda' than his marching to the Palatinate in 1624.[126] He did not need to say which policy he would recommend.

Diplomats were often worried that they would be accused of improper behaviour if they provided advice and commentary designed to influence the King, and these fears set limits to their behaviour. They were particularly vulnerable to attempts by those who were closer to the King's ear to undermine them, and the necessity of maintaining good relations with their hosts meant that they were frequently accused of behaving in a partisan or disloyal manner. These accusations, as well as the protestations of innocence they provoked, demonstrate that the idea that diplomats were in league with foreign princes and were manipulating the King were plausible. The King was alert to the possibility that the sympathy many of his diplomats and secretaries felt for Frederick's and Elizabeth's cause and their advocacy of an anti-Habsburg foreign policy might distort the flow of diplomatic information, and the distrust this engendered had severe consequences both for their ability to carry out their diplomatic duties and for their hopes of promotion at home.

Some English diplomats like Trumbull and Carleton were accused of being partisans of Frederick and the Dutch. Even before the political temperature was raised by the outbreak of the Thirty Years' War, Sir Thomas Studder had accused Trumbull of working for one or two of the King's anti-Spanish councillors rather than for the government as a whole.[127] Studder claimed that Trumbull had no credit in the Archdukes's court, that he published numerous libels against the Howards, and thought that Archbishop Abbot, Lord Chamberlain Pembroke and Sir Ralph Winwood, were 'the only true and loyall counsellors' James possessed.[128] Trumbull took legal action against Studder, who was imprisoned and finally banished from the Spanish Netherlands in 1617, but not before he could write another letter to Winwood accusing Trumbull of exploiting the matter of *Corona Regia* to create conflict between the King and Catholic princes. Studder accused Trumbull of sending copies of the libel to France and Germany so that James received it from several countries, conveying the false impression that it was being widely disseminated and read.[129] Trumbull needed powerful friends at court to fend off these attacks, and when false reports were spread about him again in 1619, both Archbishop Abbot and James Hay, Viscount Doncaster, spoke up in his favour. Abbot reassured Trumbull that 'if any ill reports bee brought hither from that side the sea against you, you may bee assured that here be some that thinke as well of you as they can thinke ill'.[130]

Trumbull and Carleton were strong supporters of Frederick and Elizabeth, and found it difficult to maintain a neutral tone in their dispatches following the invasion of the Lower Palatinate and the Battle of White Mountain in 1620.[131] Trumbull complained to Carleton that:

> wee are all but Cyphers, and a Charlatane of Spaine, or a Pantalon of the Archd*uke* haue more creditt at home, then all his ma*iesties* servants abroad. They shall haue power to be beleeued in all things; and what wee wryte is either neglected, or esteemed as a fable.[132]

In 1622, he excused himself for failing to provide news of negotiations for a truce in the Palatinate on the basis that he had been 'branded for a Palat*inian*' and was not trusted with such information.[133]

Trumbull's and Carleton's allies at court frequently advised them to adopt a dispassionate tone when providing information that might otherwise seem calculated to incite James's anger against Spain. George Abbot praised Trumbull for letting him know about the increasing number of English Catholics who were flooding in to the Spanish Netherlands, but warned him not to write 'too violently' of such things to the King, who was 'pressed with cares enough touching the affaires of his owne three kingdoms'. A calm letter that stuck to the facts would demonstrate the trustworthiness of the writer. Expressions of bitterness and outrage would be counter-productive because James would dismiss the letter as ideologically biased. 'An advise written quietly and without passion is better considered of, then when it beginnes with perturbation', he wrote, 'which argueth the zeale of the writer, but remembreth not the person of the receiver'.[134]

Trumbull was also advised to moderate his expressiuns of concern for the Protestant cause, since the King might see such complaints as implicitly critical of his own pacific diplomacy.[135] It might also damage their chances of promotion in a court in which pro-Spanish councillors appeared to be in the ascendant. In 1621 Trumbull wrote that he had been 'taxed with passion for their [i.e. Frederick and Elizabeth's] service' and thereby 'traduced by my enemyes to be a fyerbrand of sedition'.[136] Castle's advice was for Trumbull to 'apply yor selfe to the quallity of the tymes; & not so openly as you doe, to espouse the quarrell of Bohemia'.[137] After warning Trumbull against 'ouergreiuing and passionating yorself about that publicke misfortune [i.e. the plight of Frederick]', Beaulieu wrote that 'it is not onely a losse of teares, and a prejudice of health, but an open danger also that priuate men doe incurre into, at these tymes by taking on and interessing themselues too much in the faultes and proceeding of states'.[138] A few years later, Beaulieu advised his friend 'not to expresse in yor letters any passion' about Charles and Buckingham's potentially dangerous trip to Madrid but divert his energies instead to 'good wishes and prayers' for their success.[139]

Trumbull and Carleton were particularly vulnerable to accusations that they encouraged Frederick to prolong the war, either by supplying news which would give him an excuse to rejoin it, or by failing to adequately communicate James's displeasure if he did so. James could only credibly negotiate a peaceful settlement between the various warring parties on the continent if he could guarantee Frederick's cooperation. Unfortunately, the King exercised only partial control over his son-in-law, who frequently committed acts of war which undermined negotiations.[140]

In 1621, James complained that Carleton was failing to convey his displeasure about Frederick's continued attempts to regain the Palatinate by force. Carleton appeared to be softening the King's rebukes and warnings, and this would only encourage Frederick to commit further warlike acts in future rather than conforming himself to James's own peaceful diplomacy. James hoped that the excuses Carleton made on Frederick's behalf were not representative of the way he spoke to the Elector himself.[141] Carleton was quick to defend himself against this charge and assured him that whenever the Elector disobeyed James, Carleton was 'the first that accuse him' of doing so.[142] This was not entirely true. Carleton wanted James to maintain his support for Frederick and if possible increase it, so he was naturally inclined to soften any unwelcome messages that passed between the two in order to maintain harmonious relations. He was not the only English diplomat to do so. In 1621, Sir Francis Nethersole had brought several messages from Frederick, but omitted those which were most likely to anger James.[143] Carleton's position was that of a mediator between James and Frederick rather than a straight-forward representative of his King. There was also the question of propriety and politeness. It was one thing for James to write a belligerent message to Frederick, and quite another for Carleton to deliver the same words in person. Unfortunately for Carleton, his enemies at court were not sympathetic to his predicament. By 1623, they were telling the King that he was 'so partiall for the king and Queen of Bohemia and the States' that he was 'in hart but little his maiesties seruant'.[144]

Trumbull similarly came under attack in 1621 when he informed Frederick that Spinola had refused to consent to a renewal of the truce in the Palatinate. Trumbull's 'vnfrendes' claimed that this action had encouraged Frederick to renew war and to send an ambassador into England with a presumptuous letter requesting James's support.[145] Carleton tried to reassure his friend that he should not worry about a 'chiding out of England' because Carleton had heard the news from other letters at about the same time, so it could not have been kept secret from Frederick any more than 'fier can be hid when it flameth'.[146] Such matters had to be dealt with delicately if Trumbull and Carleton wanted to avoid being used as scapegoats for Frederick's actions.

Some regarded Carleton as an apologist for Dutch misbehaviour, and he was accused of making representations in the United Provinces without James's authorisation while failing to fully inform the King about Dutch news.[147] When Carleton was directed to seek redress for the Amboyna massacre, for instance, John Chamberlain told his friend that 'you are taxed to be somwhat *tepido* in the busines'.[148] Chamberlain's own view was that in response to the massacre, the royal navy should 'arrest the first [East] Indian ship that comes in our way, and hang up upon Dover cliffes as many as we shold find faultie or actors in this busines, and then dispute the matter afterwards'.[149] Carleton complained that he was accused of sympathising with Dutch views simply because he lived in the Republic. He bemoaned the division in Protestant Europe between 'those of our partie which seeke faire and peaceable wayes' and those who thought 'nothing can serue but *vim vi repellere* [force should be met with force]: amongst which kinde of people it is my fortune to liue, and thereby am brought into ill predicament with others, as yf I did participate of theyr humor'.[150]

Trumbull was also thought to be far too close to the Dutch, and in 1621 he was accused of receiving a Dutch pension. Trumbull was horrified by this damaging accusation, and protested his innocence. 'My conscience is cleare, my harte vpright towards the king our master, and my hands neate from all manner of corruptions', he wrote, and if he had accepted money from anywhere but the exchequer, 'then all the evill fall vpon me and my children, that may light vpon any man livinge'.[151] Carleton told him not to worry too much, because although some might attempt to wound his reputation, their accusations were absurd. Anyone who thought Trumbull received a Dutch pension was 'not onely a knaue but a foole', because secrecy was so lax in the Republic that no-one could hope to conceal such an arrangement.[152]

Trumbull did his best to anticipate and preclude accusations that his information was biased, and he often gave advice while denying that he was doing so. He began one passage on the possibility of continuing negotiations for the restitution of the Palatinate with the words 'I presume not to diue with my shallowe brayne into that deepe mistery', before providing a detailed analysis of the European situation, suggesting that the Emperor was not interested in peace with Frederick.[153] In 1621, Trumbull assured Calvert that 'my desyer is not ... to spane [i.e. to wean] his maiestie to any vnseasonable ressentment nor to exceed the limitts of his commands the bredth of a heire'.[154] In 1624, he finished a relation of his efforts to secure justice over *Corona Regia* by insisting that he did not 'nor ever had the least thought or presumption to counsel or propose anything'.[155]

When Trumbull received news or requests that might be interpreted as partisan, he sometimes asked intermediaries to conceal his part in passing them on to James. In 1622 the Duke of Bouillon asked him to pass on a message to James, urging him to declare himself in favour of Frederick. Trumbull asked Sir Thomas Edmondes to relay the message, but asked that unless James approved of the overture, Trumbull's part in forwarding it should be concealed, lest James's anger turn 'to my vtter ruyne'.[156] He was anxious to present himself as a neutral conduit for information. When he passed on reports of preparations in the Spanish Netherlands for an invasion of James's kingdoms, he assured Conway that 'I wente not abroad to fetch these newes; but proteste vpon my Allegeance to his mai*est*ie they were brought home vnto me, and I haue not (meaninge those that concerne his mai*est*ies Realmes) thervnto added so much as one sillable'.[157] Both Trumbull and Carleton were also alert to the possibility that they might be accused of colluding with each other to present James with a unanimous view of European affairs. In 1623 Carleton warned that their dispatches had recently interpreted the news so similarly that it might seem 'as yf it had bin by consent betwixt vs'.[158] James clearly suspected that his diplomats might relay disinformation from Frederick or the Dutch that was designed to create conflict with Spain.

Trumbull's and Carleton's predicament was not unique. Diplomats from all sides were accused of being too friendly with the government of the countries to which they were sent. John Digby was the King's ambassador in Spain, but his critics claimed he was really the King of Spain's ambassador in England.[159] In the early 1620s he tried to counter such suggestions by associating himself with the King's limited actions in support of Frederick – despatching money on his behalf – in an attempt to repair his public reputation.[160] George Abbot thought that Sir Francis Cottington, another ambassador to Spain, was also 'too addicted to the place where hee liveth'.[161] Gondomar's enemies in England would have been surprised to hear that his Spanish colleagues thought he was suspiciously Anglophile.[162] Diplomats inevitably faced accusations of disloyalty because their success as negotiators and news gatherers depended on securing the trust of their hosts as well as that of their distant master. As a result, they were anxious to avoid being seen to provide biased information to the King.

CONCLUSION

Historians have demonstrated that James was not simply sidelined during the last few years of his reign. The King managed to stave off war with Spain and maintained the final say over foreign policy decisions until his death. As this chapter has tried to show, the reversionary interest nevertheless gained control over the machinery of information gathering during this period, and attempted to use it to create conflict with Spain, with some success. There is no doubt that James recognised the usefulness of Charles's and Buckingham's sabre-rattling in eliciting concessions from Spain, but this diplomatic weapon was becoming rather difficult to control during his final years, and it is not always clear precisely where the balance of power lay.

Even when James appeared to be firmly in charge, before Charles and Buckingham returned from Madrid, Secretaries of State and diplomats could play an important role in shaping the formation and realisation of policy, as Calvert's palming of letters in 1623 shows. There was no simple distinction between the often biased or misleading information and advice that James was fed by diplomats, secretaries and others, and the decisions that he derived from them. The gap between James's opinions and intentions on the one hand, and his ambassadors' presentation of them abroad on the other, meant that ministers and diplomats could play an important role in shaping the interpretation and results of his policies. Participation in foreign policy decision-making was somewhat wider than historians have hitherto allowed. While James's ministers and diplomats did not conspire to force his hand in quite the same way that Elizabeth's sometimes tried to, some of the same political tricks were being played.

The episodes in which secretaries and diplomats delayed or altered his instructions shed further light on the distinctive, if not unique, features of James's style of rule. While the King did not always directly encourage or orchestrate the 'excusable disobedience' of his servants, he was rather relaxed about it when it happened, and it allowed him to disavow policies or create different impressions about his intentions among a variety of audiences. Charles, who expected a more rigid form of obedience, had a rather different attitude. In 1626, Charles complained to the Earl of Mar that the Scottish Privy Council had recently disobeyed him by ignoring an order to raise troops, adding that 'ye durst not have doun so to my father'. Mar replied that on the contrary, the Scottish Privy Council had delayed ill-advised orders sent on James's authority 'a hudrith tyms ... and he hes givin us thanks for itt quhen ve have informed him of the trueth'.[163] While James remained the ultimate arbiter of decisions about foreign policy, he tended to steer the ship of state with a deliberately loose grip.

NOTES

1 For Elizabeth's relationship with her councillors, see in particular Christopher Haigh, *Elizabeth I* (London, 1988), ch. 4; Simon Adams, 'Eliza enthroned? The court and its politics' in Christopher Haigh (ed.), *The Reign of Elizabeth I* (Basingstoke, 1984), pp. 55–77; Patrick Collinson, 'The monarchical republic of Queen Elizabeth I' in Patrick Collinson (ed.), *Elizabethan Essays* (London, 1994), pp. 41–2.

2 'A Treatise of the office of a Councellor and Principall Secretarie to her Matie ... Instructions for a Principall Secretarie observed by R:B: [Beale] for Sr Edwarde Wotton', 1592, Add. 48149, fol. 4v; 8r–v. Bacon made similar comments in his essay 'Of Cunning'. See James Spedding (ed.), *The Works of Francis Bacon* vol. VI (London, 1858), p. 429.

3 Haigh, *Elizabeth I*, pp. 70–4; Gary Schneider, *The Culture of Epistolarity: Vernacular Letters and Letter Writing in Early Modern England 1500–1700* (Newark (NJ), 2005), p. 78.

4 Patrick Collinson, 'Elizabeth I (1533–1603)', *Oxford Dictionary of National Biography*, Oxford University Press; online edn www.oxforddnb.com/view/article/8636 (accessed 25 June 2012).

5 D. H. Wilson viewed James as powerless and decrepit in his last years. See D. H. Wilson, *James VI and I* (London, 1956), pp. 378–447.

6 See Thomas Cogswell, *The Blessed Revolution: English Politics and the Coming of War, 1621–1624* (Cambridge, 1989), pp. 57–65, 70–6, 181–8, 314–16; Pauline Croft, *King James* (Basingstoke, 2003), pp. 125–8; Roger Lockyer, *Buckingham: the Life and Political Career of George Villiers, First Duke of Buckingham, 1592–1628* (London, 1981), pp. 216–17, 223–4.

7 Conrad Russell, 'The foreign policy debates in the House of Commons in 1621', *The Historical Journal* 20 (1977), pp. 289–309; Simon Adams, 'Foreign policy and the parliaments of 1621 and 1624' in Kevin Sharpe (ed.), *Faction and Parliament: Essays on Early Stuart History* (Oxford, 1978), pp. 139–72; Thomas Cogswell, 'England and the Spanish match', in Richard Cust and Ann Hughes (eds), *Conflict in Early Stuart England: Studies in Religion and Politics 1603–1642* (Harlow, 1989), pp. 107–33; Thomas Cogswell, 'Phaeton's chariot: the parliament-men and the continental crisis in 1621', in Julia Merritt (ed.), *The Political World of Thomas Wentworth, Earl of Strafford, 1621–1641* (Cambridge, 1996), pp. 24–46.

8 W. B. Patterson, *King James VI and I and the Reunion of Christendom* (Cambridge, 1997), pp. 297–338.

9 For the events leading up to the creation of the Protestant Union, see Geoffrey Parker, *The Thirty Years' War* (London, 1984), pp. 22–4.

10 For early relations with France, see Maurice Lee, *James I and Henri IV: An Essay in English Foreign Policy, 1603–10* (London, 1970).

11 See in particular Simon Adams, 'The Protestant Cause: Religious Alliance with the West European Calvinist Communities as a Political Issue in England' (DPhil, University of Oxford, 1973).

12 For the Spanish Match, see Cogswell, 'England and the Spanish match', pp. 107–33.

13 Peter Lake, 'Anti-popery: The structure of a prejudice', in Richard Cust and Ann Hughes (eds), *Conflict in Early Stuart England: Studies in Religion and Politics, 1603–1642* (Harlow, 1989), pp. 72–106; Anthony Milton, 'A qualified intolerance: the limits and ambiguities of early Stuart anti-Catholicism', in Arthur Marotti (ed.), *Catholicism and Anti-Catholicism in Early Modern English Texts* (Basingstoke, 1999), pp. 85–115.

14 For the middle path James's foreign policy trod, see Simon Adams, 'Spain or the Netherlands? The dilemmas of early Stuart foreign policy' in Howard Tomlinson (ed.), *Before the English Civil War: Essays on Early Stuart Politics and Government* (London, 1983), pp. 79–102.

15 For the Thirty Years' War, see Parker, *Thirty Years' War*; Peter H. Wilson, *Europe's Tragedy: A History of the Thirty Years' War* (London, 2009).

16 For James's attempts at mediation, see Patterson, *Reunion of Christendom*, chs 9–10; Arthur White, 'Suspension of Arms: Anglo-Spanish Mediation in the Thirty Years' War, 1621–25' (PhD, Tulane University, 1978).

17 For Frederick's intransigence, see Brennan Pursell, *The Winter King: Frederick V of the Palatinate and the Coming of the Thirty Years War* (Aldershot, 2003).

18 For the Parliament of 1621, see Robert Zaller, *The Parliament of 1621* (London, 1971). For foreign policy debates in Parliament, see Russell, 'Foreign policy debates', pp. 289–309; Adams, 'Foreign policy', pp. 139–72; Cogswell, 'Phaeton's chariot', pp. 24–46.

19 Andrew Thrush, 'The personal rule of James I, 1611–1620', in Thomas Cogswell, Richard Cust and Peter Lake (eds), *Politics, Religion and Popularity in Early Stuart Britain* (Cambridge, 2002), p. 94.

20 Girolamo Lando to the Doge and Senate, 30 October 1620, CSPV vol. XVI, p. 458.

21 Simon Contarini and Girolamo Soranzo, extraordinary, and Alvise Corner, ordinary ambassadors in Spain, to the Doge and Senate, 20 May 1622, CSPV vol. XVII, p. 323.

22 Zaller, *Parliament of 1621*, p. 137.

23 For the second session of the Parliament of 1621, see Richard Cust, 'Prince Charles and the second session of the Parliament of 1621', *English Historical Review* 122:496 (2007), pp. 427–41.

24 John Castle to William Trumbull, 11 April 1622, Add. 72275, fol. 137r. Chamberlain to Carleton, 13 April 1622, McClure vol. II, p. 432. The muster was repeated a few months later. See Castle to Trumbull, 9 August 1622, Add. 72276, fol. 3v.

25 For the end of the Spanish match negotiations in the Autumn of 1623 and early 1624, see Cogswell, *Blessed Revolution*, pp. 107–13; Brennan Pursell, 'The end of the Spanish match', *The Historical Journal* 45:4 (2002), pp. 699–726. For the Parliament of 1624, see Robert Ruigh, *The Parliament of 1624: Politics and Foreign Policy* (Cambridge (MA), 1971).

26 Garrett Mattingly, *Renaissance Diplomacy* (London, 1955), pp. 226–7; F. M. Evans, *The Principal Secretary of State: A Survey of the Office from 1558 to 1680* (Manchester, 1923), p. 61.

27 The turnover of Secretaries of State during James's later years was quite rapid. Sir Ralph Winwood died in office in 1617, but Sir Thomas Lake, Sir Robert Naunton and Sir George Calvert were all cast out of office for various reasons.

28 'The State of a Secretaries Place and the Perill Written by the Earle of Salisbury', Harl. 305, fol. 369r.

29 Roy E. Schreiber, 'Naunton, Sir Robert (1563–1635)', *Oxford Dictionary of National Biography*, Oxford University Press; online edn www.oxforddnb.com/view/article/19812 (accessed 29 May 2012). The King hoped to raise the spectre of a French alliance to encourage the Spanish to complete the match.

30 Williams to Buckingham, 30 August 1623, *Cabala, mysteries of state, in letters of the great ministers of K. James and K. Charles* (1653), p. 81. Williams also wrote that in the matter of unpopular concessions to English Catholics, 'I keep off the King from appearing in it, as much as I can, and take all upon my self, as I believe every servant ought to do in such Negotiations'. See Williams to Charles, 14 May 1623, in John Hacket, *Scrinia reserata, a memorial offer'd to the great deservings of John Williams* (1693), p. 128.

31 Williams to Buckingham, 18 September 1623, SP 14/152 fol. 61r.

32 Naunton to Carleton, 23 October 1619, SP 84/92, fol. 190r.

33 Conway to Trumbull, 15 April 1624, SP 77/17, fol. 101r.

34 Conway to Trumbull, 13 September 1624, Add. 72279, fol. 37r.

35 Wolley to Trumbull, 5 November 1624, Add. 72331, fol. 40v.

36 Wolley to Trumbull, 24 December 1624, Add. 72331, fol. 54v.

37 Trumbull to Conway, 27 December 1624, SP 77/17, fols. 437v–8r.

38 Trumbull to Conway, 27 December 1624 (abstract), SP 77/17, fol. 441v.

39 Buckingham to Aston, 16 January 1625, SP 94/32, fol. 6r.

40 [John Coke?] to Carlisle, 16 June 1624, SP 78/72, fol. 293r.

41 Carlisle to Conway, 23 June 1624, SP 78/72, fol. 313v.

42 See S. R. Gardiner, *History of England: from the Accession of James I to the Outbreak of the Civil War, 1603–1642* vol. V (London, 1883), pp. 79–88.

43 'The proceeding in the busines of the Spanish shipps beseiged in Lieth and Abertine by the Hollanders', Stowe 133, fols. 149r–v.

44 Dudley Carleton Jnr. to Carleton, 3 May 1623 (o.s.), SP 84/112, fol. 103v.

45 *Ibid.*, fol. 104r.

46 Tillières to Puysieux, 26 May 1623, PRO 31/3/57, fol. 215r.

47 Carleton Jnr. to Carleton, 3 May 1623 (o.s.), SP 84/112, fol. 104r.

48 'Proceeding in the busines of the Spanish shipps', Stowe 133, fols. 149v–50r.

49 *Ibid.*, fol. 150r.

50 *Ibid.*

51 Carleton Jnr. to Carleton, 3 May 1623 (o.s.), SP 84/112, fol. 105r. It was later alleged that Calvert had delayed the letter at the request of the French ambassador, who was presumably keen to prevent any conflict with the Dutch that might push England and Spain closer together. See Carleton Jnr. to Carleton, 24 April 1624, CSPD 1623–25 (1859), p. 223.

52 Carleton Jnr. to Carleton, 3 May 1623 (o.s.), SP 84/112, fol. 105v.

53 *Ibid.*

54 *Ibid.*, fols. 105v–6r.

55 Carleton Jnr. to Carleton, 25 May 1623, SP 84/112, fol. 171v. Others appear to have distrusted Conway. In April, a post had refused to depart for Spain unless the order to do so was signed by the King. Conway said that if the King had to sign everything, his work would never be done. See Conway to Richard Bingley, 1 April 1623, CSPD 1619–23 (1858), p. 547.

56 Carleton Jnr. to Carleton, 3 May 1623 (o.s.), SP 84/112, fols. 105v–6r.

57 Cogswell, *Blessed Revolution*, p. 90.

58 Buckingham to James, 30 July 1623, David M. Bergeron (ed.), *King James and Letters of Homoerotic Desire* (Iowa City, 1999), p. 196.

59 Carleton Jnr. to Carleton, 25 May 1623, SP 84/112, fol. 171v. A document which attempted to justify Carleton's actions appears to have been annotated by Conway, who was keen to find fault with his conduct. See 'Proceeding in the busines of the Spanish shipps', Stowe 133, fols. 149r–152v.

60 Carleton Jnr. to Carleton, 25 May 1623, SP 84/112, fol. 171v.

61 Chamberlain to Carleton, 30 May 1623, McClure vol. II, p. 499. Here McClure incorrectly identifies 'the white mule' as Buckingham, as he does in Chamberlain to Carleton, 25 June 1625, McClure vol. II, p. 626, in which Chamberlain says that some Members of Parliament have been complaining that the war effort has been mismanaged, and hints that the 'white mule' has been 'misleading and carieng his rider awrie'. The 'white mule' was Conway, not Buckingham. See Albert Marshall, 'Sir Dudley Carleton and English Diplomacy in the United Provinces, 1616–1628' (PhD, Rutgers University, 1978), p. 224. This nickname seems to have originated in an obscure story about the 'cardinal's [i.e. Wolsey's?] muleteer' – see Carleton to Chamberlain, 14 May 1623, SP 84/112, fol. 137r. Wolley's letters are also full of complaints about Conway's duplicity and inefficiency. See Wolley to Trumbull, 27 May 1624, Add. 72330, fol. 102r–v and Wolley to Trumbull, 23 July 1624, Add. 72330, fol. 130v, in which Wolley expresses relief that Conway appears to be trying to give up the secretaryship, which 'he doth as ill performe as euer any did I thinck before him'.

62 Carleton Jnr. to Carleton, 20 September 1623, SP 84/114, fol. 120r–v.

63 Carleton Jnr. to Carleton, 24 April 1624, CSPD 1623–25 (1859), p. 223. Calvert hung on to his office until after the death of James, but was eventually dismissed when he refused to take the oath of allegiance. See Michael Questier (ed.), *Stuart Dynastic Policy and Religious Politics, 1621–1625* (Camden 5th Series, vol. 34, 2009), p. 80. It is worth noting that both Lake and Cranfield were accused of 'palming' letters when their enemies were searching for reasons to have them dismissed from office. See William Lord Roos to James I, 1 June 1618, CSPD 1611–18 (1858), p. 542; Henry Goodere to [Carleton], 18 April 1624, CSPD 1623–25 (1859), p. 217.

64 Carleton Jnr. to Carleton, 3 May 1623 (o.s.), SP 84/112, fol. 104v.

65 Conway to Carleton, 15 May 1623, SP 84/112, fol. 125r.

66 Conrad Russell, *Parliaments and English Politics 1621–1629* (Oxford, 1979), p. 9.

67 Zuane Pesaro to the Doge and Senate, 15 November 1624, CSPV vol. XVIII, p. 485.

68 See for instance Williams to Buckingham, 27 October 1621, *Cabala*, pp. 60–1; Williams to Buckingham, 1 September 1621, *Ibid.*, pp. 62–3; Williams to Buckingham, 14 October 1621, *Ibid.*, p. 82. Kevin Sharpe argued that Williams may also have been motivated

by factional loyalty when he delayed patents for office. See Kevin Sharpe, 'The Earl of Arundel, his circle and the opposition to the Duke of Buckingham, 1618–28' in Sharpe (ed.), *Faction and Parliament*, p. 216.

69 Williams implied that a petition to release a Catholic, which Calvert had forwarded to him, might not have had James's approval, and asked that similar documents come straight from the King or Buckingham in future. See Williams to Buckingham, 22 July 1621, in *Cabala*, pp. 56–7.

70 Laura Stewart, 'The political repercussions of the Five Articles of Perth: a reassessment of James VI and I's religious policies in Scotland', *Sixteenth Century Journal* 38:4 (2008), pp. 1031–2.

71 Schneider, *Culture of Epistolarity*, pp. 77, 79. It is possible, of course, that James connived at Balmerino's behaviour in order to create plausibly deniable ambiguity about his religious intentions when he succeeded to the English throne.

72 See the example of Sir Theodore Turquet de Mayerne, James's physician and occasional diplomatic agent. See Hugh Trevor-Roper, 'Mayerne, Sir Theodore Turquet de (1573–1655)', *Oxford Dictionary of National Biography*; online edn www.oxforddnb.com /view/article/18430 (accessed 29 July 2012).

73 Maurice Lee characterised the Jacobean diplomatic service as 'a group of overworked and underpaid men who lived comfortless, penurious, tedious, occasionally dangerous lives in their country's service'. See Maurice Lee, 'The Jacobean diplomatic service', *The American Historical Review* 72:4 (1967), p. 1264. See also Vivienne Larminie, 'The Jacobean diplomatic fraternity and the Protestant cause: Sir Isaac Wake and the view from Savoy', *English Historical Review* 121:494 (2006), pp. 1300–26.

74 Charles Carter, 'The ambassadors of early modern Europe: Patterns of diplomatic representation in the early seventeenth century', in Charles Carter (ed.), *From the Renaissance to the Counter-Reformation: Essays in Honour of Garrett Mattingly* (London, 1965), p. 282.

75 Marshall, 'Carleton and English diplomacy', pp. 37, 93, 157.

76 Larminie, 'The Jacobean diplomatic fraternity', pp. 1300–26.

77 Lando to the Doge and Senate, 26 February 1621, CSPV vol. XVI, p. 575.

78 Sidney Lee (ed.), *The Autobiography of Edward, Lord Herbert of Cherbury* (2nd edn, London, 1906), p. 123.

79 Castle to Trumbull, 15 October 1618, Downshire vol. VI, p. 546.

80 See Lawrence Stone, *An Elizabethan: Sir Horatio Palavicino* (Oxford, 1956), pp. 66–90; Geoffrey Parker, *The Dutch Revolt* (New York, 1977), pp. 169–92.

81 Charles Carter, *The Secret Diplomacy of the Hapsburgs, 1598–1625* (New York, 1964), p. 151.

82 Thomas Wilson, 'Collection of proceedings on the claim for 100m. from Flanders', SP 77/14, fol. 258v.

83 Naunton to Trumbull, 13 November 1620, Add. 72304, fol. 85r.

84 Digby to Trumbull, 15 April 1621, Add. 72285, fol. 20r.

85 Trumbull to Calvert, 29 October 1622 (o.s.), SP 77/15, fol. 355 r–v.

86 Privy Council to Trumbull, 31 August 1625, Add. 72371, fol. 89r–v; 'Coppie of a Remonstrance presented to the Infanta by William trumbull … for repayment of such monnyes as are due to his said Maiestie, by the States and Townes, of Brabant, Flanders etc', 11/21 October 1625, Add. 72371, fols. 103r–4v.

87 For Trumbull's investigation into the authorship of *Corona Regia*, see Winfried Schleiner (ed.), *Corona Regia* (Geneva, 2010), pp. 13–24. See also Imran Uddin, 'William Trumbull: A Jacobean Diplomat at the Court of the Archdukes in Brussels, 1605/9–1625' (PhD, University of Leuven, 2006).

88 Trumbull to Secretary of State, 30 June 1620 (o.s.), SP 77/14, fol. 148v; Trumbull to Doncaster, [?] September 1623, Eg. 2595, fol. 197v; Trumbull to Buckingham, 3 May 1624 (o.s.), SP 77/17, fol. 116v.

89 Bennet to Trumbull, 22 July 1617, Downshire VI, p. 236; Digby to Trumbull, 15 April 1621, Add. 72285, fol. 20r; Trumbull to Doncaster, [?] September 1623, Eg. 2595, fol. 197v.

90 Giovanni Lionello to the Doge and Senate, 22 June 1617, CSPV vol. XIV, pp. 530–3.

91 Trumbull to Doncaster, [?] September 1623, Eg. 2595, fol. 197v.

92 Castle to Trumbull, 20 May 1624, Add. 72276, 92v.

93 For rumours of plots against James around the time of Henri's assassination, see J. P. Sommerville, *Politics and Ideology in England 1603–1640* (Harlow, 1986), pp. 197–8.

94 Downshire vol. V, pp. xcii–xviii.

95 Lando to the Doge and Senate, 3 September 1620, CSPV vol. XVI, pp. 386–7.

96 Trumbull to Calvert, 14/24 March 1622, SP 77/15, fols. 52r–3r; Trumbull to [Carleton], 12/22 March 1622, SP 77/15, fol. 50r–v.

97 Carleton to Trumbull, 1 April 1622 (n.s.), Add. 72273, fol. 12r; Calvert to Trumbull, 22 March 1622, Add. 72268, fol. 141r.

98 Beaulieu to Trumbull, 27 July 1620, Add. 72253, fol. 135r.

99 *Ibid.*

100 Thomas Edmondes to Trumbull, 23 December 1617, Downshire vol. VI, pp. 351–2.

101 Valaresso to the Doge and Senate, 25 November 1622, CSPV vol. XVII, p. 509.

102 Carleton to Naunton, 18 July 1620, SP 84/96, fol. 39r–v. See also Carter, *Secret Diplomacy*, pp. 137–47.

103 For the invasion of the Lower Palatinate, see Parker, *Thirty Years' War*, pp. 55–61.

104 A copy of the letter in question can be found in Carleton to Naunton, 2 June 1620, SP 84/95, fol. 177r. For the capture of this letter, see also Lando to the Doge and Senate, 10 August 1620, CSPV vol. XVI, p. 352; Carleton to Trumbull, 29 July 1620, Add. 72271, fol. 118r.

105 Naunton to Carleton, 10 August 1620, SP 84/96, fol. 97r. The decipherer was Thomas Phelippes, Walsingham's former code master.

106 Naunton to Trumbull, 13 August 1620, Add. 72304, fol. 79r.

107 Lando to the Doge and Senate, 10 August 1620, CSPV vol. XVI, p. 353; Beaulieu to Trumbull, 3 August 1620, Add. 72253, fol. 136r; 'Diary of Walter Yonge', Add. 28032, fol. 25r.

108 Carter, *Secret Diplomacy*, pp. 137–47. Carter repeats Van Male's suspicion that the enciphered letters had been intercepted by English agents, and that they were merely pretending that the Dutch had intercepted them in order to avoid blame, but Carleton's letters indicate that this was not true.

109 *Ibid.*, pp. 137–8.

110 *Ibid.*, p. 139.

111 *Ibid.*, p. 141. The Venetian ambassador also wrote that they were deciphered at this time. See Lando to the Doge and Senate, 25 September 1620, CSPV vol. XVI, p. 418.

112 Carter, *Secret Diplomacy*, pp. 139, 146–7.

113 'A Collection of the materiall poynts in the intercepted dispatche of the Conde de Onate to the Archduke Alberto, July 1620 deciphred by Phillips', EL 6900 (unfoliated). See also 'Main points from intercepted despatch of Count of Oñate, the Spanish Ambassador, to the King of Spain, 1 August 1622', SP 80/5, fol. 249; 'A collection of the main points contained in the intercepted dispatch of the count de Onate, July 1620', Cotton Vespasian C/XIII, fol.220v; Lando to the Doge and Senate, 16 October 1620, CSPV vol. XVI, p. 443.

114 Van Male only refers to the expert as 'Vincentio' – see Carter, *Secret Diplomacy*, pp. 138–9.

115 The tone of this correspondence contrasts with the uncharacteristically undiplomatic language used in another cache of letters supposedly captured by Mansfeld in October 1621, which were later published as *Cancellaria Hispanica*. These later letters, unlike those discussed above, were not enciphered, which casts further doubt on their credibility. See Pursell, *Winter King*, p. 150. Others have argued that they were genuine. See Parker, *Thirty Years' War*, p. 67. Trumbull, Carleton and even James himself believed they were. See Trumbull to Walter Aston, 14/24 December 1621, Add. 36445, fol. 302v; Carleton to Aston, 3/13 December 1621, Add. 36445, fol. 293r; John Digby to Aston, 23 December 1621, Add. 36445, fols. 319r–20r. *Cancellaria Hispanica* was itself an answer to an earlier publication, the *Anhaltische Kanzlei*, which presented itself as a transcription of letters between Frederick and Charles Emmanuel, Duke of Savoy, detailing their scheming prior to the Elector's acceptance of the Bohemian throne. See White, 'Suspension of Arms', pp. 26–7, 159–60.

116 Wolley to Trumbull, 22 May 1624, Add. 72330, fol. 98r; Castle to Trumbull, 18 March 1625, Add. 72276, fol. 145r.

117 Trumbull to Carleton, 10 July 1620 (n.s.), SP 77/14, fol. 144r.

118 Lando to the Doge and Senate, 25 September 1620, CSPV vol. XVI, p. 418. Whether this is true or not, the Archduke does seem to have delayed the invasion, fearing it would spark war with the Dutch and English. See White, 'Suspension of arms', pp. 113–14.

119 Trumbull to Naunton, 7/17 September 1620, SP 77/14, fols. 208r–9r.

120 Beaulieu to Trumbull, 3 August 1620, Add. 72253, fol. 136r. Carleton had forwarded another 'intercepted' letter in July which indicated that the Dutch simply wanted to draw James into war with Spain and leave him to fight it alone. Carleton says he would 'never fayle to conceale nothing from his ma*iesties* knowledge be it good or bad pleasing or displeasing (for in so doing I should make my self more a servant vnto others then to his ma*iesty*'. See Carleton to Naunton, 2 July 1620, SP 84/96, fol. 2r.

121 Surian to the Doge and Senate, 12 September 1620, CSPV vol. XVII, p. 414.

122 This practice went back to Elizabethan times, if not before. See Alan Stewart and Heather Wolfe (eds), *Letterwriting in Renaissance England* (London, 2004), p. 152. Polemics such as Thomas Scott's *Vox Populi*, of course, purported to be based on transcripts of official documents. For Scott's work, see Peter Lake, 'Constitutional consensus and puritan

opposition in the 1620s: Thomas Scott and the Spanish match', *The Historical Journal* 25 (1982), pp. 805–25.

123 Robert, Earl of Salisbury to Trumbull, 1 February 1610, Downshire vol. II, p. 229.

124 Christian Henneke, 'The Art of Diplomacy under the Early Stuarts, 1603–42' (PhD, University of Virginia, 1999), pp. 201–2.

125 Salisbury to Trumbull, 1 February 1610, Downshire vol. II, p. 229.

126 Trumbull to Conway, 27 December 1624, SP 77/17, fol. 437r.

127 Studder to [?], 28 June 1617 (n.s.), Downshire vol. VI, p. 206. For Trumbull's conflict with Studder, see Uddin, 'Trumbull', pp. 101–5. Trumbull's and Carleton's friends at court often tried to hide the fact that they corresponded with them because it caused 'jealousy'. See James Hay, viscount Doncaster to Carleton, 21 July 1620, CSPD 1619–23 (1858), p. 167; Wolley to Trumbull, 22 May 1624, Add. 72330, fol. 98v.

128 Digby to Trumbull, 16 September 1615 (o.s.), Downshire vol. V, p. 339; Jean Thymon to William Trumbull, 22 October 1615, Downshire vol. V, p. 355.

129 Uddin, 'Trumbull', p. 102; Studder to [Winwood], 28 June 1617, Downshire vol. VI, pp. 206–8.

130 George Abbot to Trumbull, 1 August 1619, Add. 72242, fol. 85v; Doncaster to Trumbull, 22 June 1619, Add. 72287, fol. 77v.

131 For the invasion of the Lower Palatinate and the Battle of White Mountain, see Parker, *Thirty Years' War*, pp. 55–61. For the Battle of White Mountain, see Wilson, *Europe's Tragedy*, pp. 284–307. Even before these events, Carleton was warned that 'to be zealous in the cause of Bohemia is thought a fault in the eyes of those that govern', while Edmondes cautioned Trumbull about being too 'expressyue' in his dispatches. See Nethersole to Carleton, 18 January 1620, CSPD 1619–23 (1858), p. 113; Edmondes to Trumbull, 20 March 1620, Add. 72288, fol. 120r.

132 Trumbull to [Carleton], 6/16 November 1620, SP 77/14, fol. 237r–v.

133 Trumbull to [?], 12/22 July 1622, SP 77/15, fol. 205r.

134 Abbot to Trumbull, 29 March 1616, Add. 72242, fol. 49r.

135 For James's peaceful diplomacy, see Robert Zaller, 'Interest of state': James I and the Palatinate', *Albion* 6:2 (1974), pp. 144–75; Patterson, *Reunion of Christendom*, pp. 293–338.

136 Trumbull to [Carleton], 13/23 July 1621, SP 77/14, fol. 387r–v.

137 Castle to Trumbull, 22 February 1622, Add. 72275, fol. 128r.

138 Beaulieu to Trumbull, 23 February 1621, Add. 72254, fol. 15r. Trumbull to Secretary of State, 5/15 January 1621, SP 77/14, fol. 264r may well have been the particular dispatch which provoked this advice.

139 Beaulieu to Trumbull, 12 March 1623, Add. 72255, fol. 21r.

140 Pursell, *Winter King*.

141 Digby to Carleton, 16 November 1621, SP 84/103, fol. 243r–v.

142 Carleton to Digby, 24 November 1621, SP 84/103, fol. 303r–v.

143 White, 'Suspension of arms', pp. 174–5.

144 Carleton Jnr. to Carleton, 3 May 1623 (o.s.), SP 84/112, fols. 105v–6r.

145 Trumbull to [Carleton], 1/11 September 1621, SP 77/14, fol. 446r; See also Pursell, *Winter King*, pp. 146–9.

146 Carleton to Trumbull, 6/16 September 1621, Add. 72272, fol. 60r–v. Carleton appears to have learnt his lesson by December the following year, when Trumbull sent him letters indicating that the sequestration of Frankenthal would permanantly divide the Palatinate between the Spanish and Austrian Habsburgs. Carleton assured Trumbull that these had not been shown to Frederick. See Carleton to Trumbull, 5 December 1622, Add. 72273, fol. 99r–v.

147 Marshall, 'Carleton and English diplomacy', p. 6; Henry Savile to Carleton, 18 April 1619, CSPD 1619–23 (1858), p. 37.

148 Chamberlain to Carleton, 26 February 1625, McClure vol. II, p. 602.

149 Chamberlain to Carleton, 24 July 1624, McClure vol. II, pp. 569–70. For the Amboyna massacre, see Karen Chancey, 'The Amboyna massacre in English politics, 1624–1632', *Albion* 30 (1998), pp. 583–98.

150 Carleton to Trumbull, 6/16 September 1621, Add. 72272, fol. 59r.

151 Trumbull to [Carleton], 13/23 July 1621, SP 77/14, fol. 387r. Interestingly, it was also rumoured that Conway had bought the secretaryship in 1623 with Dutch money. See Cogswell, *Blessed Revolution*, p. 90.

152 Carleton to Trumbull, 2 August 1621, Add. 72272, fols. 43v–4r.

153 Trumbull to Conway, 30 January 1624, SP 77/17, fol. 20r–v. Trumbull to Conway, 3/13 October 1624, SP 77/17, fols. 360v–361r is written in a similar vein.

154 Trumbull to Calvert, 14/24 June 1621, SP 77/14, fols. 347v–8r.

155 Trumbull to James, 7 May 1624, SP 77/17, fol. 186r.

156 Trumbull to Edmondes, 6 July 1622 (o.s.), Stowe 176, fol. 232r.

157 Trumbull to Conway, 21 July 1624 (o.s.), SP 77/17, fol. 264v.

158 Carleton to Trumbull, 20 November 1623, Add. 72274, fol. 72r.

159 Chamberlain to Carleton, 26 February 1620, McClure vol. II, pp. 291–2. Digby defended himself against these accusations during the Parliament of 1626. See William B. Bidwell and Maija Jansson (eds), *Proceedings in Parliament 1626* vol. IV (Rochester (NY), 1996), p. 164.

160 Beaulieu to Trumbull, 15 December 1620, Add. 72253, fol. 167r; Beaulieu to Trumbull, 13 November 1621, Add. 72254, fol. 63r–v.

161 Abbot to Trumbull, 14 March 1618, Add. 72242, fol. 67r.

162 See J. H. Elliott, *The Count-Duke of Olivares: The Statesman in an Age of Decline* (London, 1986), p. 210.

163 Henry Paton (ed.), *The Manuscripts of the Earl of Mar and Kellie* HMC vol. 60(London, 1904), pp. 145–6.

Chapter 2

Secrecy, counsel and 'outward shows'

INTRODUCTION

The effectiveness of the mechanisms through which James controlled the expression of opinion, and particularly of print, have attracted considerable debate. Older accounts stressed the strength and oppressiveness of the censorship regime.[1] This view has been challenged by Sheila Lambert, who has pointed to the gap between the theory and practice of censorship, suggesting that James and Charles were unable and often unwilling to impose strict controls.[2] More recently, historians have presented a more balanced view. While acknowledging that early Stuart governments did not exert a totalitarian control over the press, Cyndia Clegg and Anthony Milton have challenged the notion that they were entirely toothless. Although the official burning of books did not prevent copies from circulating surreptitiously, they served a 'performative' function in drawing attention to their illicit status.[3] The government were unable to impose a blanket control over printing, but they were able to suppress religious works effectively within scholarly communities.[4] While historians have tended to focus on print censorship, attention has also been paid to illicit speech. Thomas Cogswell has drawn attention to James's crackdown on speeches and sermons that criticised his foreign policy in the early 1620s.[5] Adam Fox and David Cressy have explored the records of individuals prosecuted for spreading rumours or expressing scurrilous opinions about James and his government.[6]

Historians who have explored Jacobean censorship have tended to focus on the effectiveness or otherwise of the regime's attempts to punish and suppress illicit words and opinions, especially those which expressed discontent at James's pacific foreign policy, his pursuit of a Spanish bride for his son, and his toleration of Catholics. This approach has missed a vital step in the process through which royal intentions and policies came to generate discontent. In order for opposition to royal policies to develop, the public first had to know what those royal policies were. If accurate information was 'the key to all "opposition" to royal policies', as Thomas Cogswell has argued, then James had an obvious interest in preventing information which might provoke discontent from entering the public domain in the first place.[7] This chapter intends to shift our focus away from formal censorship to secrecy, to look at how James attempted to conceal information, and how effective these attempts were.

The King did not simply conceal information about his policies from ordinary subjects. The factional divisions of the later 1610s and 1620s meant that James was often reluctant to share information with many of his own councillors. A consideration of such issues allows us to reconsider the 'crisis of counsel' that is said to have occurred in the 1620s. The effectiveness of the Tudor Privy Council has been contrasted with a Council that we are told was largely bypassed during James's later years.[8] Kevin Sharpe argued that the Council ceased to function as an independent advisory body during the period of Buckingham's ascendancy, and particularly after the death of James in 1625.[9] It was only during the 1630s that Charles resumed conciliar govern-ment.[10] This chapter will question the extent and chronology of this 'crisis of counsel' while also examining the unintended consequences of James's unwillingness to share information.

James's habit of masking his intentions and withholding information about his policies created opportunities for him to mislead a variety of audiences about what he intended to do. The final part of the chapter examines what contemporaries often called James's 'outward shewes', the informal gestures and speeches that he used to hint at his intentions and motivations, thus engaging with debates about public relations and image-making. Historians have traditionally argued that James and Charles paid much less attention to their public image than Elizabeth did.[11] Elizabeth's ability to court popularity through the adroit use of public ceremonial and display has long been recog-nised, but her accessibility has traditionally been contrasted with James's and Charles's remote style. James and Charles, we are told, did not enjoy public spectacle and felt less need to explain their actions.[12] Kevin Sharpe and Mark Kishlansky have recently challenged this picture by arguing that the early Stuarts were much more willing to engage in public display and ceremonial than was once thought.[13] We now have a much richer understanding of the ways in which James and Charles presented favourable images of royalty, as well as how these were contested by their sometimes sceptical and unruly subjects. At the same time, historians have recently explored the ways in which councillors, favourites and others attempted to create or harness public opinion in order to pressure the monarch into taking a particular course of action. Richard Cust and Thomas Cogswell have drawn attention to the efforts of MPs and favourites to appeal to a political nation apparently well versed in national events, as well as shedding light on royal attitudes towards these bids.[14] Peter Lake and others have highlighted attempts by courtiers, favourites and religious minorities to harness and call into being various 'publics' as weapons in domestic politics.[15]

Historians have tended to base their assessment of James's success at public relations on the extent to which he participated in public ceremonies, including coronations, civic entries and royal progresses. While historians once emphasised James's dislike of crowds and drew contrasts with Elizabeth's more popular style, Kevin Sharpe recently argued that James was much more adept at public display than was previously thought.[16] The fundamental assumption of both strands of opinion is that the court was a private place, and that engagement with the public happened outside of it. In fact, as James knew well, the court was a goldfish bowl, and the things that he said and did there had a habit of leaking out to the wider political nation. The theatrical gestures and informal pronouncements that James made at court were in fact his primary means of shaping wider perceptions about himself and his policies.

THE RATIONALE FOR SECRECY

The political pressures James faced during the late 1610s and 1620s, when he balanced himself between Spain and many of his own anti-Spanish subjects, made it necessary to conceal his intentions. Relations with Spain regularly swung between periods of friendliness and animosity as a result of events on the continent and the progress of negotiations. During some periods, the Spanish match seemed as good as concluded, but at others it seemed that James might lead Protestant Europe against the Habsburgs. The King was occasionally obliged to make belligerent declarations in order to placate domestic anger at Frederick's plight and to frighten the Spanish into making concessions, but opponents of the match could never tell whether these gestures were meant in earnest or were merely intended to extract concessions. As the Venetian ambassador wrote, James instinctively followed a middle course. 'He does not desire enemies, from his hatred of war', he wrote, 'or close friends so that he may not suffer trouble on their account'.[17] While James did feel that foreign policy was for him alone to decide, his unwillingness to reveal his ultimate intentions was as much a tactical political decision as a principled defence of the prerogative.[18] The result of this ambiguous policy, as we shall see, was that when James finally came to close with one side or the other, he was so distrusted that first Spain, then Parliament and the anti-Habsburg European powers demanded exorbitant terms as security for an alliance.

James could not share his plans with his loyal subjects without also alerting those who would oppose them, both at home and abroad. James was concerned that if the terms of the Spanish match were widely known, they would provoke expressions of discontent in England which would in turn undermine the progress of negotiations when news of them reached Spain. If James decided to support Frederick by force of arms, on the other hand, the success of his military plans would rely on the element of surprise. Knowledge of an impending attack by James's forces would allow his enemies to prepare their defences. In a speech to the Parliament of 1621, he told members that military options to reclaim the Palatinate could not be discussed by a multitude, 'for so my designs may be discovered beforehand'.[19] Samuel Calvert echoed his master's speech by reminding the Commons that 'it is a strange thing for a king to consult with his subjects what was he means to undertake. This were means for all his enemies to know what he intends to do'.[20] Calvert had other motives, of course, since James's sabre-rattling strategy relied on Parliament expressing a general intention of supporting military action without being too specific about whether the enemy would be Spain or the Emperor. James hoped to scare the Spanish into a more compliant attitude in negotiations over the match and the restoration of the Palatinate, but naming them as an enemy would be provocative and counter-productive. Nevertheless, debates on military strategy in Parliament would inevitably spread across Europe, and preventing foreign enemies from discovering the details of James's intentions was a sufficiently compelling reason to close down discussion on its own. With the court split between supporters and opponents of the Spanish match, James worried that not just Members of Parliament, but also his own councillors and diplomats, might leak information about his plans and intentions.

The need to keep state business secret meant that James was increasingly unwilling to share information with his own ministers and ambassadors during his later years, particularly if they opposed his pacific policies. The King had always kept his representatives abroad at arm's length, and diplomats of all persuasions complained that his secretaries failed to keep them informed. In 1610, for instance, Francis Cottington wrote that he had not received any letters from England for over a month.[21] Nevertheless, James appears to have become much more distrustful and unwilling to share information with diplomats who opposed the Spanish match in the early 1620s. He was particularly concerned that they would try to undermine the match or his attempts to end the war in the Palatinate by peaceful diplomacy. John Digby advised James that if he wanted to negotiate peace, he must reduce his ambassadors 'to such a conformity that that which his faithfull ministers have established in one part, bee not overthrown by the malice or artifice of the attempts of others in other parts'.[22] One of the most effective ways to prevent any mischief was to keep anti-Spanish diplomats in the dark about his intentions.

William Trumbull's support of the Protestant cause and his opposition to Spain meant that James did not take him into his confidence. Trumbull frequently complained that he no longer knew what the King wanted. After the breakdown of the peace conference that was held in Brussels in 1622, he wrote that he had only received echoes and vague indications about what James wished to do. As a result, he had been forced to stay indoors, not wanting to face the embarrassment of being unable to answer the questions that Isabella's ministers or other foreign ambassadors would ask him.[23] A few months later he protested that when he visited the Archduchess or her ministers, he was forced to declare his ignorance of affairs which seemed to be discussed and known about by everyone but himself, and begged Calvert to put himself in Trumbull's place and ask 'what service either I, or any other can doe his ma*ie*stie, or howe they may gayne creditt in forrayne, that haue none at all in their own Country'.[24] He claimed to have received no letters from Secretaries of State between August and December 1623, and a further period of silence continued into 1624.[25] Trumbull was soon reduced to making increasingly desperate requests for instructions and information from home, and was so far from the King's confidence that when he heard a rumour that James had declared war on Spain, he was unsure whether it was true or false.[26]

Trumbull was so ignorant of the King's intentions, and so worried about giving his hosts the wrong impression about them, that he was sometimes unable to gather any news himself. In 1624 he complained that:

> I fynde myself reduced into such straytes, that I knowe not on w*h*ich syde to tourne me, what countenance I shall carry, what Language I may speake, or what I am to doe, or leaue undonne... And untill I shall haue y*o*ur Lordshi*p*s answere, necessity will compell me, to keepe within my shell, and forbeare to walke the Streetes, for the preventinge of all errors, and avoydinge of offences in my discourse... Every word I speake, and euery gesture of my body are observed with ruinous eyes, and Glosses many tymes made therevpon, in a contrary sense, moode, and figure. None dare nowe frequente my house, but Artificers, nor I visitt any of my freinds, that are well affected.[27]

Diplomats were not so much passive readers of news as agents of news exchange, forming links between interdependent domestic and foreign news networks, and they acted as a major motor of news circulation in Europe. They were only able to pass information about European events on to their superiors and friends at home because they could repay their foreign correspondents with information about English affairs. Diplomats could not expect to gather privileged information abroad if they had none from home to exchange, and an ambassador who did not know what was going on at home was no use to his host. Francis Cottington was rumoured to have been recalled from Spain in 1617 in part because he did not seem to know what was happening, either in the Spanish or the English court.[28] By keeping his diplomats abroad ignorant of his intentions, James reduced their ability to discover what was happening on the continent. His unwillingness to share information with his diplomats may have inadvertently limited the range of news and council he received in return.

James's tendency to withhold information from his diplomats meant that they relied on well-placed informants at home to find out what was going on. Some of their most important sources were the minor functionaries at court. Bureaucrats like John Beaulieu and John Castle had access to sensitive diplomatic dispatches and warrants, and were willing to share these documents with the likes of Trumbull in exchange for friendship and foreign news. In spite, or rather because, of James's attempts to conceal diplomatic information, the regime was often very leaky.

John Beaulieu, for instance, had access to some of the most sensitive and privileged information in government, and he was able to obtain copies of James's correspondence even before he became French Secretary, a position which involved drafting the King's letters to foreign princes. He sometimes passed on the contents of these letters to Trumbull before the originals had even been sent. When Frederick sent James a letter in which he requested financial and diplomatic help in 1619, Beaulieu was able to tell Trumbull that he had been denied any assistance, 'although the answere be not yet gonne nor signed by his Ma*ie*stie'.[29] He gave a detailed account of another letter to Frederick despite having been 'commanded to keepe the contents thereof very secret, which I hope my letter will not speake after me'.[30] Sometimes Beaulieu would go further than a mere summary, and send Trumbull actual copies of the letters he drafted. He sent Trumbull a copy of one of the King's letters to Frederick, but entreated his friend to 'keepe for a while the copie thereof to yorself', because the original had not yet been sent.[31] When in 1620 Louis XIII made an offer to support James's pacific diplomacy, Beaulieu sent Trumbull a copy of the King's answer, which had not yet been delivered to the French ambassador.[32] Beaulieu had access to some high level correspondence, and the trust he placed in Trumbull in keeping secret the information he passed on was a testament to their close friendship.

John Castle was another minor functionary who nevertheless had access to sensitive information. Through the influence of his uncle Edward Reynolds, Castle became Deputy Clerk of the Privy Seal some time before 1620, at which time he was promoted to full clerk, although he appears to have lost this position with the death of Reynolds in 1623.[33] This position allowed Castle to inform Trumbull about significant grants made to ministers and courtiers. In 1618, for instance, he was able to tell his friend how little money had been set aside for the bishops who were to attend the Synod of Dort, because he had dispatched the warrant himself.[34] On another occasion in 1623, he told Trumbull:

> Whatsoeuer the vulgar prattle the Duke of Buckingham is in the same grace he was afore. I haue visible marks of it for I haue passed him a lease of the customes of

Ireland for 7 yeares in reuerccon after his former; and also the manor of Newby in yorkeshire of the value of £112 *per annum* of old rent.[35]

Thomas Locke, Keeper of the Privy Council Records, who corresponded with both Trumbull and Carleton, was also well placed to pass on official documents. In 1622, for instance, he passed on a list of Count Mansfeld's demands which he had picked up from the council table after the privy councillors had left.[36]

John Chamberlain's access to official correspondence, as well as the private letters of prominent courtiers, reveals that such documents circulated well beyond bureaucratic and diplomatic circles. In 1616, Chamberlain revealed that Lady Somerset's pardon had been signed, and that he had 'had yt in my hand before yt went to the seale'.[37] Chamberlain had presumably gained access to this document through his close friendship with Secretary Winwood. Even when Chamberlain did not obtain copies, he nevertheless managed to discover and summarise the contents of various other private or semi-private letters, such as some written by Lord Roos during his self-imposed exile.[38]

Trumbull was careful to make sure that sensitive information he received from these correspondents would not be repeated in any copies of their letters that he forwarded to friends on the continent. An anonymised extract from one of John Beaulieu's letters, which Trumbull sent to James Hay, Viscount Doncaster, demonstrates this point. The original letter from Beaulieu begins 'I wrote vnto you the laste weeke what was come to my knowledge since my late returne out of the Countrie, and accompanied my *lettre* with a copie of the Treatie with Holand'.[39] In the original, someone has underlined the second part of the sentence, referring to the copy of the treaty, and this section does not appear in the extract in the hand of Trumbull's secretary, which was sent to Doncaster.[40] A passage of uncontroversial but private news has also been underlined in Beaulieu's original, and is similarly absent from the extract sent to Hay. It seems highly likely that Trumbull underlined any sections that were either private, or had the potential to endanger his correspondent or himself, in this case by revealing that he received sensitive documents like the treaty, before passing them on to Wolley, who was then instructed to draft an extract of the original letter which omitted any underlined passages. Even though Doncaster, whose patronage and trust Trumbull was trying to secure, held political and religious views which were similar to his own, Trumbull was still careful to protect his correspondent's identity and to sanitise the letters he forwarded.

English diplomats also shared sensitive European news with their friends abroad and at home, often before James himself had been informed. Trumbull sometimes sent Carleton letters and other documents addressed to James that the King had not yet seen.[41] He almost always included an instruction not to discuss these letters until the King had read them himself, since he knew that to do so any earlier would be highly dangerous. Trumbull also sent Carleton documents which he asked to be kept secret from Frederick, since they risked provoking him to resume military action, for which Trumbull might take the blame.[42]

The motive for passing on such letters was often that they would provide the recipient with ammunition to answer any accusations that their hosts might make against James's actions, or those of his allies or servants. In 1621, for instance, Trumbull passed on letters Sir Horace Vere had sent to James justifying his recent conduct in the Palatinate, which threatened to break the truce James was trying to uphold. Trumbull sent Vere's letters to Sir Walter Aston in Madrid because he knew that Vere's conduct would be 'layd in your dishe by way of recrimination' by the Spanish, and he therefore wished to 'fournishe you with some matter of reply, or excuse'.[43] As with the letters which diplomats received from minor officials like Beaulieu, these favours attempted to correct deficiencies in the Jacobean regime's own provision of information to its representatives abroad.

Correspondents were concerned that the information contained in their letters, and indeed the letters themselves, would be out of their control once sent, and they often put constraints on who their friends could share news with. Carleton often asked Chamberlain to keep information secret until he had heard it from others. Because Carleton was often privy to information known to few, it would be relatively easy to identify him as the source of any leak, so he was particularly keen to prevent certain items from going any further than Chamberlain. He frequently asked Chamberlain not to share the copies of speeches and letters of other correspondents that he sent with his own, and on at least one occasion asked Chamberlain to burn them.[44]

The quality of news Carleton provided to Chamberlain calls into question the applicability of traditional distinctions between private, diplomatic information and public news. There was little difference between the quality of the information Carleton sent to Chamberlain and the Secretary of State, and indeed as Carleton became more and more busy in the early 1620s, his letters to Chamberlain became shorter versions of his official dispatches.[45] This raises intriguing questions about the extent to which the government necessarily had a more accurate sense of European affairs than news-hungry laypeople like Chamberlain.

SECRECY AND COUNSEL

James was reluctant to share information with some of his diplomats, and this often led them to surreptitiously share information with each other and with minor officials at court. James was also increasingly selective about the information he shared with his councillors at home. In part, this was because the discussions of the Privy Council and the advice James was given were often widely reported and discussed. The publication of policy was often seen as one of the Privy Council's proper functions, and at times it acted as a forum for promulgating decisions that had already been worked out in private. A tract attributed to Sir Robert Cecil revealed that while the Council could discuss and make decisions about normal business, weighty or sensitive affairs were decided in meetings between James and Cecil alone. When these matters came to be discussed in the Privy Council, 'it is likened to conference of Parents and solemnization of Matrimonie, the first Matter, the second Order, and indeede the one the Acte, the other the Publication'. There is no sense that Cecil believed that this was an unusual or inappropriate way for the Council to be used.[46] Privy Councils could be forums for publicising the King's outward intentions while very different policies were pursued in secret. According to Sir Roger Wilbraham, James sometimes wrote letters to the Irish Privy Council which instructed them to act harshly against the crown's opponents, perhaps to overawe them, to preserve the illusion of royal rigour and to satisfy those who wished to pursue a hard line, while at the same time secret letters to the Lord Deputy instructed him to take a more practical, moderate approach.[47]

Councillors might independently attempt to publicise their advice to James, however, and the wider dissemination of conciliar discussions was not always simply in the King's interests. Buckingham's comments in favour of the Protestant cause in 1620, or Pembroke's advice against dissolving the Parliament of 1621, were widely reported.[48] By giving advice against the Spanish match and in favour of military intervention on the continent, privy councillors might hope to increase public pressure on James, or at least send a powerful message to potential allies and enemies abroad. James was reluctant to involve the Privy Council in the Spanish match treaty in 1623, for instance, because he was worried that they would refuse to swear to uphold it and thus undermine his authority.[49] Divisions in the Privy Council could be as damaging to James's reputation abroad as his disputes with Parliament. The appearance of consensus and solidarity was harder to maintain when news of the disagreements that inevitably arose with and between his councillors circulated more widely.

James's secrecy created the impression among some observers that he simply ignored his Privy Council. The Venetian ambassador, Girolamo Lando, noted as early as 1621 that referring matters to the council was merely a way for James to drag them out.[50] Business was brought before the council 'not for decision, but simply for ceremony, or to raise difficulties'.[51] According to this view, James tended to encourage self-censorship by precluding discussion of certain topics and making it clear in advance that advice would not be welcome. In 1620, for instance, James told his council that he would never accept advice to declare war, but only on how money might be raised to maintain it.[52] Similarly, after the dissolution of the Parliament of 1621, he let it be understood that any councillors who advised him to call Parliament again would incur his anger.[53] According to Lando, even when his councillors sparked up the courage to offer him advice, James usually did the opposite of what they suggested.[54]

Observers believed that members of the Privy Council were often frightened to raise certain topics with James. When James made a strong declaration in favour of Frederick in front of his Privy Council in the autumn of 1620, the Venetian ambassador believed that anti-Spanish councillors could finally speak their minds. 'Matters had reached such a pass', Lando wrote, 'that even the ministers esteemed most sincere, sound and zealous maintained a reserve about freely expressing their opinions contrary to the royal favour and inclination, and ultimately every one was afraid to speak'.[55] The following year, when James made another similar declaration, Lando reported that 'the King has spoken strongly against the Spaniards ... as usual he cries out against them and afterwards caresses them'.[56] When the optimism created by James's declaration had petered out, Lando once again reported that councillors who supported Frederick were keeping their mouths shut, 'his Majesty having arrived at such a pass that he cannot endure any one to express opinions differing from his own'.[57]

Although James shared the contents of dispatches with Charles, Buckingham and a handful of pro-match councillors, ministers who opposed the match were thought to be shut out. Most of them simply couldn't be trusted with information about a foreign policy they opposed. In 1621 James remarked that no ambassador from the Palatinate was needed in England, since the majority of his ministers behaved like Frederick's representatives anyway.[58] The result, as Lando wrote, was that 'the old ministers and those who look upon matters otherwise than he desires, know little or nothing now of the king's proceedings, as he avoids all except two or three strong partisans of Spain'.[59] 'Those of the highest birth, experience and authority, councillors of twenty years standing', he said, knew least about James's negotiations.[60] These perceptions were not limited to the likes of the Venetian ambassador. The belief that the Spanish faction, and the Spanish ambassador in particular, knew more about James's intentions than the rest of his privy council was widespread. As the author of 'Tom Tell Troth' wrote, it was thought that Gondomar 'knowes your secretts before the greatest parte and most faithfull of your Counsell'.[61]

How accurate was the perception that James ignored his Privy Council? Answering this question is complicated by the fact that we have limited knowledge of what really occurred in Council meetings. The *Acts of the Privy Council* does not record the Council's debates and discussions.[62] It cannot always be relied upon even as a record of the decisions the Council made. According to Lord Keeper Williams, an act of the Council ordering the imprisonment of the Earl of Southampton was published even though the councillors never so much as mentioned him during their meeting, yet this order is recorded in the published *Acts*.[63]

Nevertheless, the Privy Council does appear to have been involved in discussing a wide range of important business in the early 1620s, including local administration, defence and economic problems. Foreign policy was also discussed, particularly where it intersected with the Council's responsibility for trade. A number of meetings were held with Dutch commissioners in an attempt to settle ongoing trade disputes.[64] The Council also discussed measures for the defence of the Palatinate.[65] The perception that James or Buckingham simply ignored or bypassed the Privy Council was not entirely accurate.

The Privy Council was not the only legitimate forum for advice, and James could receive information through many other less formal channels. It was not necessarily the Privy Council's job to even debate important matters of policy. The functions of the Council varied from reign to reign, but it often acted merely as an administrative body, while an inner ring of trusted councillors dealt with more sensitive matters of state.[66] Even those who criticised Buckingham's supposed subversion of the Council during Charles's reign stressed that it should only act independently over small matters, with important business being decided by the King.[67]

Discussions about sensitive matters of policy were increasingly secret, but this does not mean that they did not take place. There is evidence to suggest that the Privy Council, or a committee thereof, regularly discussed the match but that no written record of its deliberations was kept. When the normal business of the Council was finished, the clerks, and perhaps some members of the Council, were sometimes asked to leave. Sir Albertus Morton was reported to have resigned as Clerk of the Privy Council in 1623 because he 'had not the patience to indure to be put out and avoide when any Spanish business came in question'.[68] The practice of excusing clerks from secret discussions appears to have started as soon as James acceded to the throne, and marked a break with Elizabethan practices. In 1605, Samuel Calvert wrote that the clerks were not 'admitted that Liberty which was never denied in the Queen's time, to be present at most Councills'.[69]

While James may not have discussed the most sensitive and important matters of foreign policy with the Privy Council as a whole, this does not mean that his Councillors were entirely ignored. Instead he relied on a series of select committees, often drawn from the Privy Council, to deal with individual issues. Some of these councils had a public role. A war council was created after the Battle of White Mountain, and this signalled James's willingness to intervene in the European war while also drawing up estimates that reminded MPs of the realities of war finance.[70] In most cases, however, the entire purpose of these councils was to give advice in secret, and there may not have been any written record of their meetings.[71] While we know that they existed, we know little about their membership or when they met, and even less about the content of their discussions. A commission was drawn up to advise on the Spanish match in April 1620, for instance, and Digby appears to have addressed letters to members of a select council for German affairs when he went on a diplomatic mission to the Emperor in 1621.[72] James also called a select committee to discuss concessions towards Catholics at the height of the Spanish match negotiations in 1623.[73] Another war council was created during the Parliament of 1624.[74] Even these smaller councils could not always be relied upon. In December 1623, Chamberlain wrote that the commission for foreign affairs 'shalbe somwhat abridged in number, for though they be sworn to secresie yet some things are found to be vented and come abrode that were better kept close'.[75] To some extent, the perception that James ignored his Privy Council was simply an unintended consequence of his relative success in keeping the deliberations of his councillors secret.

James consulted select committees during this period, and the Privy Council still played an important role in discussing and advising on a variety of matters. Nevertheless, there was a great deal of truth to the perception that James excluded many of his councillors from the most important and sensitive area of his foreign policy, the marriage of his son. James was understandably reluctant to share details of these negotiations with individuals who opposed the marriage alliance. In the particular circumstances of Charles and Buckingham's trip to Madrid in 1623, as we shall see, James conducted negotiations almost entirely by himself, although he excluded both the supporters and the opponents of the match during this period. James's secretive behaviour was not without precedent, of course. Royal marriages were regarded as one of the most exclusive areas of the *arcana imperii*. Although Elizabeth I consulted with a select committee over the Anjou match, she did not allow the Privy Council to discuss it and severely punished individuals who wrote or published tracts against it.[76] What was perhaps new in the 1620s was the degree to which James's subjects felt the need to know about and discuss the match, and their willingness to justify such discussions. Discourses about the Spanish match, in particular, were defended on the basis that the marriage would have important consequences for the commonwealth as a whole.[77]

James was forced to involve the Privy Council in swearing to uphold the terms of the marriage treaty in July 1623, and he called the select committee to advise him whether to consider new Spanish terms the following January.[78] Nevertheless, the restriction of information and counsel resumed once the French match treaty negotiations began. Privy Councillors were so ignorant of the progress of the French match that when negotiations were concluded in November 1624 they had to send their servants out to discover why bells were being rung and bonfires were being lit to celebrate.[79] In practice matters of policy were largely decided by the Prince, the Duke and Conway, and members of the former Spanish faction were shut out.[80] Like the opponents of the marriage in 1620–23, members of the Spanish party could not be trusted with information about the direction of foreign policy. When Charles asked a group of councillors to support the war in early 1625, the Earl of Arundel sourly replied that because they were not informed about any of the decisions being made, they could not offer advice or support.[81] Sir William Walter's complaint in the Parliament of 1626 that 'all the council rode on one horse' was an indictment of this style of rule, yet it was slightly out of date.[82] It was only after the former supporters of the match had been excluded from office under Charles that the Privy Council once again became a powerful advisory body. From 1626, councillors repeatedly moderated the actions of Charles and his more hawkish advisers, even manoeuvring the King into calling Parliament in 1628.[83] The 'crisis of counsel' did not simply coincide with the years of Buckingham's ascendancy, and neither can it be entirely blamed on him. At different times, and for different reasons, James, Charles and Buckingham all sought to exclude the Privy Council from decision-making to some extent. Nevertheless, the Privy Council or committees thereof continued to advise on a range of domestic and foreign issues throughout the period. It was really the mixture of delicate marriage negotiations abroad and factional conflict at home that led to a reluctance to share information and a consequent narrowing of the range of advice. There was a 'crisis of counsel', but it was largely limited to the period 1623–25.

James's secretive behaviour in the early 1620s had unintended consequences. If James received advice about sensitive matters from small, secretive committees, it was reasonable for observers who were not privy to such discussions to assume that he received little or no counsel at all. The perception that James did not receive a proper range of counsel, whether it was justified or not, was potentially damaging. It was a commonplace of early modern political theory that the willingness to listen to counsel was one of the things that distinguished legitimate princes from tyrants.[84] If James did not receive adequate counsel at court, it was necessary to advise him of the true state of affairs through other means. Speeches in Parliament or tracts which opposed the King's policies were justified on the basis that the proper sources of counsel had been silenced or were being ignored.[85] Speaking freely and giving honest advice were conceived of as a duty rather than a right, and even comparatively humble individuals could think of themselves as active councillors rather than the passive subjects James would often prefer them to be.[86] Secrecy did not quell discussion about sensitive matters, instead it excited the imaginations of observers and made wild rumours about James's intentions and the future course of politics much more plausible. As we shall see, James's secrecy about the terms of the dispensation for the marriage between Charles and the Infanta in 1623 encouraged paranoid speculation about the Pope's demands.

'OUTWARD SHOWS'

By creating ambiguity about his intentions and by restricting access to information, particularly about the Spanish match, James created opportunities to mislead a variety of audiences about his intentions and the likely course of future events. Contemporaries often referred to his informal hints and theatrical gestures as 'outward shewes' which might or might not reflect his true intentions. How then were these 'outward shewes' interpreted by James's subjects, and did his sometimes ambiguous and manipulative behaviour ultimately undermine his authority?

James often presented himself as an honest and transparent monarch, and it is perhaps telling that he felt the need to do so. In *Basilikon Doron*, he advised his son to be 'pleine and sensible in your language', since it was 'a pointe of imbecilitie of spirit in a King to speake obscurely, much more vntruely, as if he stoode [in] awe of any in vttering his thoughts'.[87] As he wrote in the published declaration that explained his reasons for dissolving the Parliament of 1621, monarchs could hardly conceal their intentions, because they were under constant public scrutiny. 'The great actions of Kings are done as vpon a stage', as he wrote, 'obuious to the publike gazing of euery man'.[88] He went on to claim that he had

> euer affected such sinceritie and vprightnes of heart, as were Wee all transparent, and that men might readily passe to Our inward thoughts, they should there perceiue the selfe-same affections, which Wee haue euer professed in Our outward words and Actions.[89]

Kevin Sharpe's study of Stuart public politics and presentation largely endorsed this view, portraying James as an interventionist monarch who 'eschewed mystery' and 'preferred to be direct, unequivocal, even confrontational in order to tackle problems'.[90] By explaining his actions and intervening in political debate, as Sharpe argued, James inadvertently encouraged public discussion of the *arcana imperii*. While there is some truth to Sharpe's analysis, however, it ignores the distinction between explaining a policy retrospectively and revealing one's plans in advance. While James sometimes justified his previous actions (often reluctantly), he preferred to keep his *intentions* as unclear as possible, and he was far from being the transparent and unequivocal monarch he claimed to be.

Monarchs like James who created ambiguity about their intentions found it easier to divide and rule. Both sides of every political or religious debate could be fed with hopes that James would finally support them, as well as being kept in fear that he would desert them in favour of the other party. This strategy was a legacy of the King's rule in Scotland, as well as being a basic point of sensible policy. James had spent much of his childhood as a political football cast between contending factions, and his reign there was successful in large part because he was eventually able to play various political and religious groups off against each other. Before his succession to the English throne, James gave Catholics the impression that he might convert, while at the same time allowing reform-minded Protestants to believe that he would support their agenda.[91] James's ambiguous stance allowed observers to interpret his speech and actions as they wished. As John Holles wrote, 'No man knows the Kings hart, who hyds his resolution from all men, and with suche artifice, that every man forgeth, and figureth it as clowds in the ayre, according to his imagination, and appetite, sum one shape, sum another'.[92] Godly Protestants or Catholics, supporters or opponents of the Spanish match; all could emphasise different aspects of James's behaviour and hope that the King would come down on their side in the end. Royal actions that appeared to contradict one side's hopes and wishes could be dismissed as temporary concessions to the other. James's style of rule relied as much on the audience's favourable interpretation as the King's own skills.

While his published writings were an important form of political communication, James also prized the spoken word. James was a coiner of memorable phrases as well as a writer of weighty treatises. The man who declared 'no bishop, no king' clearly knew how to craft a sound bite, but other pithy turns of phrase sometimes found their way in to contemporary newsletters. After the dissolution of the Parliament of 1621, for instance, Mead reported that James had promised to govern 'according to the commonweale, but not according to the common will'.[93] When he adjourned the Parliament in April 1621, the King declared that he had been on the throne for eighteen years but had now lived to see himself enthroned in the people's hearts.[94] James's informal speech was as quotable as his official speeches and proclamations. A volume of aphorisms and table-talk attributed to him was published in 1643.[95]

Set-piece speeches were comparatively rare. Most of the time, observers relied on the off-the-cuff comments and declarations James made during the normal course of the day at court in order to understand his inner thoughts and intentions. From the point of view of observers, casual and apparently spontaneous comments were shorter, more easily remembered and more relevant to the transient political concerns of the day. They were also potentially more suggestive of the King's real thoughts and intentions than carefully considered speeches. As Bacon wrote, rulers needed to watch what they said during unguarded moments. 'Short speeches ... fly abroad like darts, and are thought to be shot out of their secret intentions. For as for large discourses, they are flat [i.e. dull] things, and not so much noted'.[96]

James was well aware that he was subject to constant scrutiny and that his people made false inferences based on his outward behaviour and informal speech. As he wrote in the third book of *Basilikon Doron*:

It is a trew old saying, That a King is as one set on a stage, whose smallest actions and gestures, all the people gazingly doe behold: and therefore although a King be neuer so præcise in the discharging of his Office, the people, who seeth but the outward part, will euer iudge of the substance, by the circumstances; and according to the outward appearance, if his behauiour bee light or dissolute, will conceiue præ-occupied conceits of the Kings inward intention.[97]

James's day-to-day speech came under particular scrutiny during the crisis over the Palatinate and the Spanish match. Frederick's assumption of the Bohemian crown in 1619 put pressure on the King to declare his support for the Protestant cause, and this pressure was greatly increased with the invasion of the Palatinate and the defeat at the Battle of White Mountain in 1620. The marriage negotiations were proceeding slowly, and belligerent statements in favour of Frederick might encourage the Spanish to speed things up. James made various informal speeches and gestures during this period designed to raise expectations that he would support military action to restore his son-in-law's lands and titles.

Hopes that the King would support Frederick appear to have reached a peak in March 1620, when the King made a visit to Paul's Cross.[98] The visit was heavily trailed beforehand. Beaulieu told Trumbull that

Vpon Sonday next his Maiestie is to go to Powles Crosse, in the afternoone, when mylord of London (whose turne it was to preache at Whitehall) shall make a sermon; and after it, as men doe presume, some publick exhortation or declaration, about these businesses of Bohemia before his Maiestie.[99]

The Archdukes's ambassador, Van Male, repeated the rumour that some of James's councillors were encouraging him to use the occasion to make a public declaration in favour of Frederick.[100] Sir Francis Nethersole reported that while Protestants believed James would publicly pray for Frederick and exhort his subjects to contribute money to his cause, Catholics believed he was merely going to hear the Bishop of London preach on the virtues of the Spanish match.[101] Speculation about James's imminent public declaration may have encouraged optimistic rumours to circulate in Bohemia that twenty-four tons of gold had been gathered in London to be sent to Frederick.[102] Castle was quick to disabuse Trumbull of any such notion – James's real aims, he wrote, were much less dramatic:

If you haue heard that his Maiesties sollemne going to Paules Crosse on sonday next, hath ane designe to open him in his resoluccons for Bohemia, you will grosly erre to beleeue it. I dare be confident to assure you that his purpose is no other then to value himselfe towards the Cittizens; & to viewe with his owne eyes the ruynous estate at Paules church, to the end he may take some order for contribuccons to amend & raise it.[103]

Castle's prediction proved true, and despite public expectations, the King made no resolution in support of Frederick when he visited St Paul's. Beaulieu reported that 'the people did expect much greater matters of that extraordinarie appearing of his Maiestie in that place; whose end therein some think was other then did appeare'.[104]

Gondomar, the Spanish ambassador, had only recently returned to England when James made his visit to St Paul's. Gondomar arrived to the sound of drums beating in the streets of London, calling men to the colours of a volunteer force that was being sent to aid the Palatinate.[105] The Palatine envoy, the Baron Dohna, had convinced James to allow him to raise troops in England, to be supported by funds raised by Dohna himself. These troops would defend the Palatinate, which was under threat of attack from forces led by Spinola from the Spanish Netherlands. It is possible that James encouraged rumours that he would declare his support for Frederick at St Paul's because it might induce the Spanish government, through Gondomar, to take the threat of English intervention seriously, and to accelerate negotiations for a Spanish match as a result. James was keen to show the Spanish how much domestic pressure he was facing to support Frederick and to raise fears that he had finally lost patience with Spain.

The suspicions surrounding James's underwhelming visit to St Paul's in March 1620 continued when the King ordered the collection of a contribution to repair the Cathedral. Beaulieu wrote that while some thought the money would be diverted to Dohna's fund for Frederick, others were 'of a cleane contrarie opinion that it is a plott of some Spanish partisans, to lessen and crosse by that meanes the other beneuolence'.[106] If there really was a plan to hinder the collection for Frederick by raising money for St Paul's, it appeared to be a success. In late April, Beaulieu reported that far more had been raised in the city for the Cathedral than for Bohemia.[107]

James's sabre-rattling was potentially at its most convincing during the summer of 1620, when he was in possession of a military force. Despite his unwillingness to commit to his son-in law's cause, progress was made during the summer of 1620 with the appointment of Sir Horace Vere to command the troops raised by Dohna. In addition, a fleet led by Sir Robert Mansell was being prepared to suppress the North African pirates, although it could easily by diverted to attack Spanish shipping. As Trumbull reported, there were rumours in the Spanish Netherlands of an imminent English attack.[108] The Archdukes's subjects were particularly worried that Spinola would weaken their defences by taking a large force to attack the Palatinate. The Dutch lobbied James to declare that he would attack the Spanish Netherlands if Spinola invaded the palatinate, but Carleton advised against it, since Gondomar would easily tell by the lack of military preparations in England that this was a bluff.[109] By August, when Spinola's army had departed, Trumbull reported that if an army were to attack the Spanish Netherlands, they would have found little resistance, and that the inhabitants ('I know not by what fatall instinckt') were in terror of an English invasion.[110]

By September, when Spinola had successfully invaded parts of the Lower Palatinate, fear had turned into scorn. Trumbull complained that:

> So much is our reputation blasted; by our irresolution, and cunctation [i.e. delay] (bewitched as wee are with the Spanishe charmes) that euen the shaddowes of Princes dare tread vpon vs ... your *Lordship* cannott comprehend, nor I expresse with howe scornefull termes, and intollerable disdaine they speake here, of our Prince, and Country, that beeing Iustly prouoked by this proude attempt of Spinola, doe yet lye snorting in the lethargicall sleepe, which hath seased on the vitall parts of our State.[111]

Trumbull felt personally humiliated by James's failure to prevent the invasion, and hid away indoors, ashamed to show his face in public.[112]

In early October, James made a characteristically belligerent but vague statement in favour of Frederick, declaring that he would engage his forces on Frederick's behalf, that he would not suffer the ill treatment of his children's patrimony and would exact reparation for the damage Spinola had done.[113] For Lando and others who opposed Spain, it seemed as if the tide had finally turned. 'Every one applauds the king's resolution', he wrote. 'All the wrath and impatience of the people is now converted into love and affection. In a moment all things have changed marvellously'.[114] For those who trusted to James's wisdom and experience, the declaration seemed to confirm that he had long planned to support Frederick and had merely been biding his time.[115]

If the declaration was merely meant to safely vent public anger about the invasion of the Palatinate and encourage the Spanish to accelerate the pace of marriage negotiations, however, it appears to have been successful. By the end of the month letters had arrived from Spain reporting that the marriage articles had been approved there.[116] The publication of the declaration was delayed, creating speculation about how forceful James's words had really been. When Gondomar expressed concern that the common people held 'strong notions' about the strength of the declaration, Buckingham reportedly told him that 'he ought not to pay much attention to what is said by the common people; who are naturally talkative and enlarge upon everything'.[117]

Frederick's defeat at the Battle of White Mountain was a crushing blow for those who had hoped that James would support his son-in-law. The news sparked three days of celebrations in Brussels during which bonfires were lit by Trumbull's door and fireworks fired over his roof, leading him to complain that 'so much is our reputation crestfallen in these parts' that it was interfering with his ability to pursue suits at the Archdukes's court.[118] James made another change of political course by sending out warrants for the calling of a new Parliament, and by making further comments in favour of Frederick. Once again, Castle worried that the King's fair words in support of the Protestant cause were merely for popular consumption:

> his resoluccons are strong & hott for the Palatinate that he will dislodge the vsurper thoughe it should be to be done with the hazard of his person. When the parliament shalbe once sett downe; wee shall see that he giveth not wordes.[119]

Buckingham echoed James's sentiments. In a meeting of the Privy Council he declared that 'as he had received all he had from his Ma*ies*ties most gracious favour & bounty, so he was ready to spend it all in the cause of the k*ing* of Bohemia'.[120] Castle was willing to give Buckingham the benefit of the doubt, but he gave only a qualified welcome to these brave words. 'If this were his speeche, I know not how this Realmes or the people, can honor & love him sufficiently. I will beleeve he vttered it, vntill I know more'.[121]

Reports of James's behaviour at court, filtered and retold through a series of observers, communicated the gist of his words but did not always capture the theatrical manner in which they were made. The Parliament of 1621 gave James an impressive new sabre to rattle, as Thomas Cogswell has argued, but also provided a larger public forum to display his skill as a political 'performer'. Roger Lockyer speculated that James might have staged an encounter during the first session. Concerned that Buckingham would be attacked for his involvement in procuring monopolies, James went to the House of Lords and with the favourite beside him, made a long speech defending Buckingham's actions, adding that he would nevertheless turn against him if he was guilty of corruption. 'If he prove not himself a white crow', James told the assembled lords, 'he shall be called a black crow'. At these words, Buckingham dramatically fell to his knees and declared that he would be content to call himself a black crow if could not clear himself. 'Bearing in mind the close relationship between the king and his favourite', as Lockyer argued, 'and the love of plays and acting which they shared, it is probable that this little scene had been previously rehearsed'.[122]

James was also adept at stage-managing encounters with foreign ambassadors. In 1621 he held an audience with the Dutch ambassadors, who had come to settle differences over trade. While he was speaking to the ambassadors, James contrived to have a crowd of angry merchants enter the room, who demanded that the Dutch representatives satisfy James before they left the country.[123] James's skill in such matters seems partly to justify the famous comment that he was 'the wisest fool in christendom, meaning him wise in small things, but a fool in weighty affairs'.[124] Similar comments were made of James during his reign. Commenting on James's outward shows during Charles and Buckingham's trip to Madrid, the Venetian ambassador wrote that 'the king has peculiar skill in such arts for small matters, good only for evil'.[125]

There were other examples of royal performances during the Parliament of 1621. When he adjourned it in April, James reportedly 'shed joyful tears' after telling the assembled members that thanks to their work, he had been enthroned in his people's hearts.[126] He also drew his sword, jokingly threatening to kill the speaker, before knighting him as a mark of respect for the House.[127] His later tearing up of the Commons' Protestation, in a dramatic ceremony before his Privy Council, was also an intensely theatrical occasion.

James had dissolved the Parliament of 1621 before a third subsidy was enacted, and called for a benevolence to be collected to replace it. A public meal with Charles in early 1622 provided another opportunity for royal performance. James declared that those who created disharmony in Parliament deserved to be spat out, but that he was much consoled by his subjects' readiness to contribute towards the benevolence. Lando wrote that 'this was manifestly pronounced with the object of inviting them to do so'.[128]

RESPONSES TO 'OUTWARD SHEWES'

Historians have argued that the renewed interest in Roman historians such as Tacitus helped to foster a sceptical, analytical attitude towards politics.[129] While this attitude towards the news may have been a more general cultural phenomenon in the early modern period as a whole, it could also be encouraged by specific political contexts and styles of rule. James's ambiguous behaviour forced newsletter writers to seek the truth behind the outward appearance of political events, and a suspicious and sceptical attitude towards the news was entirely justified during James's later years. Nevertheless, as we shall see, observers may have gone too far in attributing complicated, intentional explanations for political actions.

James's ambiguous behaviour baffled many of his subjects. Holles described James's political trajectory as he lurched between a Dutch and Spanish alliance as a 'waterman's walk', likening it to the unsteady gait of a Thames boatman who had become used to the motion of the water. These unpredictable changes of course, as Holles complained, 'distract us poore cuntrimen in our future speculation', and this was precisely their point.[130] According to the Venetian ambassador, even James's closest councillors, let alone observers in the country, found his plans difficult to understand or predict. 'His Majesty's operations seem to contradict each other', he wrote, 'so that the leading ministers of his Council themselves say openly and swear that they cannot understand them'.[131] Only pro-Spanish councillors knew what James intended to do, according to Lando. The rest were subject to paranoid rumours that he would convert to Catholicism, that he would impose new taxes, and that he would use Spanish forces to suppress dissent. 'Even the greatest cherish these fears and suspicions; but actually they are merely shadows based upon appearances and it is possible to surmise anything with the king's taciturnity'.[32]

These frequent changes of course created the impression among some observers that James was simply fickle and indecisive. The King held single-minded perserverance in great esteem. In a proclamation of 1614, he wrote that there was:

> nothing that doth more adorn the true majesty and greatness of sovereign princes than to be constant in their well-grounded resolutions... and by their policy and lawful power, to scatter and beat down all difficulties and undue oppositions, until they have conducted their actions to a good and happy end.[33]

Although the King prized decisiveness, however, many observers thought he did not practise it. Some believed that he could not make his mind up, and would rather go hunting than resolve difficult disputes. In 1610, as the Great Contract was being debated, Calvert wrote that James was 'so distracted with variety of opinion' that 'he cannot resolve that he desires, which is the cause that, as often as he can, he absents himself the town'.[34] Some saw him as was fickle, changeable and suggestible:

> His Majesty promises and ordains various things moved by his own affections, inclinations and prudence; then shortly afterwards, being dissuaded and turned the other way, by three or four, I do not know how, he withdraws and changes them'.[35]

Many believed that James's decisions were rarely irreversible, and a large gap existed between a statement or a promise and the reality that eventually unfolded. Decisions to wage war or to punish corrupt servants as well as promises to remunerate or promote long-serving servants were all merely the first step in a long drawn-out process of mediation, negotiation and compromise. Policies were always provisional until they had been enacted. Decisions like whether to send Sir Horace Vere and his troops to the Palatinate in 1620, for instance, were 'not very ripe fruit, but rather flowers, exposed to a variety of accidents, which, however, should either bear fruit or wither away very soon'.[36] To Lando, the English decision-making process was as changeable as the weather. 'They readily change their minds from one moment to another, just as the air does here, which in a single day gives examples of all four seasons of the year'.[37] Dramatic last-minute reversals were always a possibility. It was reported that the decision to dissolve the Parliament of 1621 was delayed at the eleventh hour when the Earl of Pembroke vehemently interceded with the King to have it extended.[38]

Observers often complained that James would make an apparently resolute declaration in favour of a policy but then delay implementing it or slowly draw back from it altogether. There is some justice to these claims. Like Elizabeth, James preferred to delay decisions rather than risk committing himself to irreversible actions which might have unforeseen consequences. As the Earl of Clarendon wrote, James was 'very quicksighted in discerning difficulties and raising objections, and very slow in mastering them and untying the knots he had made'.[139] James was particularly reluctant to take any action over the invasion of the Palatinate, leading the Venetian ambassador to write that 'all operations here partake of the nature of the cold climate and are generally very slow and late'.[140] When James backtracked on his promises, he often pretended to have forgotten making them in the first place. When he attempted to tone down an initially bellicose declaration drawn up in favour of Frederick in 1621, he pretended that he had never given any hint of abandoning negotiation, despite the fact that he had himself reviewed and corrected the pugnaciously worded first draft.[141] 'In this fashion matters continue to fluctuate to the confusion of every one', as the Venetian ambassador complained, 'and very frequently they say things which afterwards they deny having said'.[142]

Although some failed to understand why the King appeared to favour a Spanish match and did so little to redress the grievances of his deposed son-in-law, many trusted the King's wisdom and experience during these difficult times. When observers reported what appeared to be political or diplomatic errors, the polite convention was to suggest that James's inscrutable plans had just been misunderstood. Trumbull, ended a report in which he expressed scepticism about James breaking with Spain by admitting that 'these thinges are misteryes to me; and beyond the reach of my weake capacity, and therefore I leaue them to better and deeper Iudgementes'.[143] James's defenders often insisted that those who opposed his policies couldn't possibly understand what was really going on. As Robert Tisdale asked the King's critics in 1623, 'Think you then to diue the Hearts of Kings, / That Heau'n hath made vnsearchable? you want wings / To soare the height, Plumbline to reach the Deepe / Of the Kings Tunnell'.[144] The Earl of Kellie responded to doubts about the wisdom of James's complicated diplomacy in 1624 by reassuring the Earl of Mar that 'his Majestie is wysse and knows better how to doe in sutche a besines, better then onye man can think or imagin, his experience is soe great'.[145] James was keen to give the impression that he was party to secret knowledge. When the Venetian ambassador reminded him that Spinola was on the march in 1620, James's reply was enigmatic. 'I know quite well what I am about', he said. 'All these troubles will settle themselves, you will see that very soon. I know what I am talking about'.[146]

There was a sometimes fragile sense that the King ultimately knew his business and must have something up his sleeve, that apparent reverses might be tactical feints in a greater game. According to the Venetian ambassador, leading councillors clung to the belief that 'some great conception of his own is reposing in the depths of his mind, though as yet undiscovered, and time alone will suffice to disclose it'.[147] James cautioned his subjects against judging his policies before they had reached fruition, and he responded to a libel questioning the wisdom of his peaceful diplomacy by writing 'I should be sorry you should see / My actions before they be / Brought to the full of my desires'.[48] The author of 'tom tell troth' conceded that 'all wise Princes have ever reserved to themselves certayne cases of state which the common people call *arcana imperii*'.[49] Nevertheless, the good purposes of these other princes eventually became apparent, 'whereas your Maiesties courses are not only inscrutable but diametrically opposite to poore mans understanding. And so far from giving vs any hope of good effects heereafter as they doe already fullfill the vtmost of our feares'.[50]

Many were willing to give James the benefit of the doubt, but these sentiments increasingly faded. Foreign and domestic observers, and even James's own diplomats, doubted that he would carry out any of his threats. In December 1619, James was said to have 'vsed lately divers speeches of bad impression towards the Spanish nation', lamenting that 'there was no sinceritie or good meaning in their harts'.[51] According to Castle, some thought the King's words were '*ad faciendum populum* [for the purpose of persuading the people], in this tyme that so much expectaccon is had that his Maiestie should doe somewhat in the Cause of Bohemia'.[52] Someone close to James informed Carleton in 1619 that 'though he [James] be slow he will be sure; and that our frends in all parts will haue contentment in his resolution', but even though Carleton was 'content to be deceaued for a time', he still suspected that James had only spoken in such terms because it was '*gratum auribus nostris* [pleasing to men's ears]'.[53] Castle chose to believe that the King's anti-Spanish sentiments were genuine, rather than a sop to those of his subjects who hoped for direct action to aid Frederick, but his assessment was tinged with doubt. 'I will beleeue that his Maiestys words and conceptions agree together', he wrote, 'and that in the depth of his great wisdome, knowinge them to be Mountebancks, he will never matche that Princely propp of our hopes into their bloud'.[54] Other observers were more emphatic. 'If he sometimes appeared wrathful and disposed to draw the sword', the Venetian ambassador wrote, 'it was a fire of straw which quickly disappeared. Sometimes he spoke one way, sometimes another, now he seemed to take a step forward and speak very loud, but simply to alarm the enemy, not to hurt him'.[55]

In particular, diplomats like Trumbull doubted that the House of Commons' declaration to support James with their lives as well as their purses, which the King publicised, would be taken seriously. The declaration owed something to James's own comments the previous year, which were intended to intimidate the Spanish but which he had refused to publish and had gradually retreated from. Trumbull was commanded to present the declaration in the Spanish Netherlands as a spontaneous and unorchestrated initiative of which James had no prior knowledge.[56] While he hoped the declaration might have some effect, he thought that James's sabre-rattling was becoming less and less convincing. 'Menaces, will doe vs small proffitt', he wrote, because in the Spanish Netherlands 'there is such a constante beleef that wee will not vpon any condition engage our selues in a warre, as I should be but deryded for my labour if I should speake of it in this Courte'.[157] While Gondomar appears to have taken the threat of war seriously after Parliament's declaration in 1621, these comments suggest that others on the Spanish side remained unconvinced.[158]

By late 1622 James's credibility had reached such a low level that the Venetian ambassador wrote:

> I may tell your Lordships that matters have reached such a pass here that it might possibly prove less difficult to get the king to decide for war than to induce his subjects to believe the decision. They have been rendered incredulous by past events, and would fear that the pretexts were raised merely as a device for obtaining money, without a thought of doing anything serious.[159]

Scepticism about James's sincerity and his commitment to the Protestant cause continued until the end of the reign. James's declaration in favour of Frederick in 1624, according to William Wynn, was 'tendinge to a warr, in the opinion of most men, yet the wisest sorte believe it is but in (terrorem) of the Spaniard to make him yield the palatinate the sooner'.[160]

James's ambiguous behaviour encouraged the discussion of news. It created a suspicious, analytical attitude towards politics that led observers to search for the real reasons for decisions that were hidden behind public pretexts. Before his visit to Scotland in 1617, James ordered the Scottish Privy Council to quash rumours that he intended to change the form of worship in his northern kingdom, insisting that he merely wanted to visit his native land and reform abuses.[161] Castle was aware that he had weightier motives than he gave out. 'It is much doubted here', he wrote, 'whether the King will attayne to his ends that he covers under the formalities of seeing his countrie'.[162] Given the potential embarrassment that could be caused by the failure of James's attempt to impose his religious policies on the Kirk, some thought that it would be better for the King to stay in England, and to send a commission of bishops and lords to do his work. The 'fruitlessnesse of their paynes and journy would not fall upon so free a censure abroade with the allyes of the King' as James's own failure to impose his will.[163] The practice of giving out a false public rationale for James's trip served to disarm potential opponents of his policies, but it was also a face-saving exercise; if James failed to achieve his aims in Scotland, he could always claim that he had merely travelled there to see his subjects. When the Duke of Lennox and the Marquis Hamilton journeyed to Scotland a few years after James's trip, Beaulieu told Trumbull that the 'pretence' of the trip was to arrange the marriage of Hamilton's son, 'but I conceiue that the differences among those of the ministerie there, for the great contradiction that is made against kings orders, are the cheifest cause thereof'.[164]

The King was clearly not the only one to give out public explanations to hide his real motives. An interesting example from the world of court politics came when Lord Keeper Williams, Bishop of Lincoln, asked to be relieved of the Great Seal in 1624. Williams gave out that he wished to be demoted because his esteemed office kept him from his diocese. The keepership required a 'whole man, and one of an other element', and Williams was unworthy of the position.[165] According to Castle, Williams's pious modesty was really a cover – the bishop was 'actinge of a parte in a Comadie wherein he hath one eye to the people and an other to the Curtaine'.[166] While Williams insisted in public that he wished to spend more time with his flock, the real reason he wanted to give up his office was because as a former supporter of the Spanish match, he feared that Buckingham and Charles might use Parliament to unseat him. His plan, according to Castle, was to 'surrender vpp that before hand with honor, which he feares perchance shalbe taken from him with disgrace'.[167]

The habit of scrutinising the news was difficult to break, and it often led contemporaries to assume they were being deliberately misled when the truth may have been rather more innocuous. The temptation, for contemporaries as well as later historians, was to interpret James's actions in terms of deliberate calculation, and to imagine that subtle motives lay behind his every deed. Castle occasionally doubted the truth of rumours which seemed to exaggerate James's political cunning. When gout in James's hand delayed the signing of a draft French marriage treaty in the summer of 1624, some thought that 'his Maiesty is not so ill in his hand but that he is able to write'.[168] James was lying about his incapacity in order to 'entertayne tyme till it may be knowen what Mendoza [the Spanish ambassador] hath in charge'.[169] The implication seemed to be that James was deliberately leaving the door open for a dramatic reversal in foreign policy if the Spanish were willing to grant concessions, and was lying about his gouty hand in order to cause a delay. Castle was not convinced. The French ambassador was expected soon, and if James was lying about his infirmity, he would quickly discover the truth. The simplest explanation, that James really was unable to sign the treaty, appeared to be the truth.

CONCLUSION

This chapter has attempted to complicate our understanding of the 'crisis of counsel' of the 1620s. The Privy Council, or committees of councillors, was involved in discussions of a wide range of matters, and the period is not marked so much by the collapse of conciliar government as attempts at a more effective degree of secrecy about the discussions that were taking place. James's attempts to conceal information from some of his own councillors and diplomats were not entirely successful, of course, and they were often forced to leak and surreptitiously share news among themselves. The one area of policy in which the range of council really was restricted was Charles's marriage. James, Charles and Buckingham attempted to exclude various councillors from any knowledge of the Spanish and French matches because factional divisions at home would damage delicate negotiations abroad. Ministers and diplomats who opposed the matches were simply not trusted with information about them. As we shall see, this unwillingness to share information or invite counsel was at its height under the unique circumstances of Charles and Buckingham's trip to Madrid in 1623. James, Charles and Buckingham were faced with an increasingly well-informed public who argued for the right to know about marriage negotiations that would affect the entire kingdom. In the circumstances of a growing 'public sphere', secretive behaviour was often interpreted as a narrowing of counsel, and the apparent breakdown of conciliar government at court legitimised the giving of unsolicited advice outside it. The perception that James only listened to the Spanish ambassador and 'evil councillors' encouraged subjects to present advice through Parliament or through printed and manuscript means.

As we have seen, propaganda and image-making were not limited to occasional set-piece ceremonies, speeches, paintings and proclamations. James's habit of concealing his intentions and restricting access to information about policy created opportunities to mislead foreign and domestic observers about his intentions through gestures and informal pronouncements. The dissemination and interpretation of news about the King and his intentions were going on all the time, and this broadens our conception of propaganda and image-making while challenging both the distinction between the 'private' court and the 'public' world outside it, and our assessment of the relative 'public relations' skills of early modern monarchs like Elizabeth and James. While James's ability to manipulate opinion through 'outward shows' may enhance our assessment of his style of rule, his ambiguous behaviour did much to undermine trust between the King, his subjects and foreign powers. James's 'outward shows' led observers to assume that he was dissimulating even when he was not. In order to further explore the perceptions of James's subjects, however, it is necessary to investigate the ways in which information was distorted as it spread from the centre to the kingdom at large.

NOTES

1 See Frederick Siebert, *Freedom of the Press in England 1476–1776: the Rise and Decline of Government Controls* (Urbana (IL), 1952).

2 Sheila Lambert, 'The printers and the government, 1604–1637', in Robin Myers and Michael Harris (eds), *Aspects of Printing from 1600* (Oxford, 1987), pp. 1–29; Sheila Lambert, 'State control of the press in theory and practice: The role of the Stationers' Company before 1640', in Robin Myers and Michael Harris (eds), *Censorship & the Control of Print in England and France 1600–1910* (Winchester, 1992), pp. 1–29. See also

Jason McElligott, 'A couple of hundred squabbling small tradesmen'? Censorship, the Stationers' Company, and the state in early modern England', in Joad Raymond (ed.), *News Networks in Seventeenth Century Britain and Europe* (Abingdon, 2006), pp 85–102.

3 See Cyndia Clegg, *Press Censorship in Jacobean England* (Cambridge, 2001), particularly pp. 68–77.

4 Anthony Milton, 'Licensing, censorship, and religious orthodoxy in early Stuart England', *The Historical Journal* 41:3 (1998), pp. 625–51.

5 Thomas Cogswell, *The Blessed Revolution: English Politics and the Coming of War, 1621–1624* (Cambridge, 1989), pp. 20–34.

6 David Cressy, *Dangerous Talk: Scandalous, Seditious, and Treasonable Speech in Pre-Modern England* (Oxford, 2010); Adam Fox, 'Rumour, news and popular opinion in Elizabethan and early Stuart England', *The Historical Journal* 40:3 (1997), pp. 597–620.

7 Thomas Cogswell, 'England and the Spanish match', in Richard Cust and Ann Hughes (eds), *Conflict in Early Stuart England: Studies in Religion and Politics 1603–1642* (Harlow, 1989), p. 128.

8 John Guy, *Tudor England* (Oxford, 1988), pp. 157, 457.

9 Kevin Sharpe, 'The Earl of Arundel, his circle and the opposition to the Duke of Buckingham, 1618–28' in Kevin Sharpe (ed.), *Faction and Parliament: Essays on Early Stuart History* (Oxford, 1978), p. 227. See also Kevin Sharpe, 'Parliamentary history 1603–1629: In or out of perspective?' in Kevin Sharpe (ed.), *Faction and Parliament*, pp. 38–42.

10 Kevin Sharpe, 'Crown, parliament and locality: Government and communication in early Stuart England', *The English Historical Review* 101:399 (1986), p. 337. See also John Guy, 'The rhetoric of counsel in early modern England' in Dale Hoak (ed.), *Tudor Political Culture* (Cambridge, 1995), p. 306.

11 For Elizabeth's skill at public relations, see Christopher Haigh, *Elizabeth I* (London, 1988), ch. 8; Malcolm Smuts, 'Public ceremony and royal charisma: The English royal entry in London, 1485–1642', in A. L. Beier, David Cannadine and James Rosenheim (eds), *The First Modern Society: Essays in English History in Honour of Lawrence Stone* (Cambridge, 1989), pp. 65–93; David Cressy, *Bonfires and Bells: National Memory and the Protestant Calendar in Elizabethan and Stuart England* (London, 1989), pp. 50–66, 120.

12 Tim Harris, '"Venerating the honesty of a tinker": The King's friends and the battle for the allegiance of the common people in Restoration England', in Tim Harris (ed.) *The Politics of the Excluded, c. 1500–1850* (Basingstoke, 2001), pp. 198–200. Maurice Lee criticised James's enjoyment of court masques as 'the wrong kind of theater'. See Maurice Lee, *Great Britain's Solomon: James VI and I and his Three Kingdoms* (Urbana, 1990), p. 151.

13 *Kevin Sharpe, Image Wars: Promoting Kings and Commonwealths in England, 1603–1660* (London, 2010); Mark Kishlansky, 'Charles I: a case of mistaken identity', *Past & Present* 189 (2005), pp. 61–9. Mary Morrissey has also shown that James was able to use sermons preached at St Paul's Cross to present a favourable image of his reign. See Mary Morrissey, 'Presenting James VI and I to the public: Preaching on political anniversaries at Paul's Cross', in Ralph Houlbrooke (ed.), *James VI and I: Ideas, Authority, and Government* (Aldershot, 2006), pp. 107–21.

14 Richard Cust, 'Politics and the electorate in the 1620s', in Cust and Hughes (eds), *Conflict in Early Stuart England*, pp. 134–67; Thomas Cogswell, 'The people's love: The Duke of Buckingham and popularity', in Thomas Cogswell, Richard Cust and Peter Lake (eds), *Politics, Religion and Popularity* (Cambridge, 2002), pp. 211–34; Thomas

Cogswell, '"Published by authoritie": Newsbooks and the Duke of Buckingham's expedition to the Ile de Ré', *Huntington Library Quarterly* 67:1 (2004), pp. 1–25. See also Richard Cust, 'Charles I and popularity', in Cogswell, Cust and Lake (eds), *Politics, Religion and Popularity*, pp. 235–58.

15 Peter Lake and Steven Pincus, 'Rethinking the public sphere in early modern England', in Lake and Pincus (eds), *Politics of the Public Sphere in Early Modern England* (Manchester, 2007), pp. 1–30; Peter Lake and Michael Questier, 'Puritans, papists and the "public sphere": The Edmund Campion affair in context', *Journal of Modern History* 72 (2000), pp. 590–2; Peter Lake, 'The monarchical republic of Queen Elizabeth I' (and the Fall of Archbishop Grindal) revisited' in John F. McDiarmid (ed.), *The Monarchical Republic of Early Modern England: Essays in Response to Patrick Collinson* (Aldershot, 2007), pp. 129–47. See also Paul Hammer, 'The smiling crocodile: The Earl of Essex and late Elizabethan "popularity"', in Lake and Pincus (eds), *Public Sphere*, pp. 95–115. For the 'public sphere', see also Jürgen Habermas, *The Structural Transformation of the Public Sphere: An Inquiry into a Category of Bourgeois Society* (Boston, 1989); Craig Calhoun (ed.), *Habermas and the Public Sphere* (Cambridge (MA), 1992).

16 See Sharpe, *Image Wars*, pp. 89–123.

17 Valaresso to the Doge and Senate, 19 January 1624, CSPV vol. XVIII, p. 195. The saying that James wanted moderate enemies rather than friends was said to be a favourite of Gondomar's. See Relation of England of Girolamo Lando, 21 September 1622, CSPV vol. XVII, p. 449. Since I will make extensive use of the Venetian ambassadors' letters in this and other chapters, it is worth noting that they are not completely reliable. The ambassadors were often ill-informed about matters in the country, and tended to describe ideological divisions in crude terms. Nevertheless, it is noticeable that successive Venetian ambassadors tended to make very similar judgements about James and his behaviour, and these were consistent not only with the views of other ambassadors, such as Tillières, but also with many of the other newsletter writers who are quoted here. As Conrad Russell argued, when it came to court news the Venetian ambassadors were likely to be as reliable as any other source. See Richard Cust, *The Forced Loan and English Politics, 1626–1628* (Oxford, 1987), pp. 10–11.

18 Lee, *Great Britain's Solomon*, p. 263.

19 Robert Ruigh, *The Parliament of 1624* (Oxford, 1971), p. 231.

20 Simon Adams, 'Spain or the Netherlands? The dilemmas of early Stuart foreign policy', in Howard Tomlinson, (ed.), *Before the English Civil War: Essays on Early Stuart Politics and Government* (London, 1983), p. 82.

21 Francis Cottington to Trumbull, 7 December 1610 (o.s.), Downshire vol. II, p. 404.

22 Robert Zaller, *The Parliament of 1621* (London, 1971), p. 144.

23 Trumbull to Calvert, 17/27 October 1622, SP 77/15, fol. 338r–v.

24 Trumbull to Calvert, 8/18 December 1622, SP 77/15, fol. 420r.

25 Trumbull to Conway, [?] December 1623 (o.s.), SP 77/16, fol. 387r; Trumbull to Conway, 11/21 April 1624, SP 77/17, fol. 84r; Trumbull to Calvert, 7/17 May 1624, SP 77/17, fol. 138r.

26 Trumbull to Conway, 13/23 July 1624, SP 77/17, fol. 244r; Trumbull to Conway, 15/25 July 1624, SP 77/17, fol. 251r; Trumbull to Conway, 21 July 1624 (o.s.), SP 77/17, fol. 263r; Trumbull to Carleton, 16/26 August 1624, SP 77/17, fol. 283r.

27 Trumbull to Conway, 11/21 April 1624, SP 77/17, fols. 84v–5r.

28 Castle to Trumbull, 27 December 1617, Downshire vol. VI, p. 357. For Cottington's complaints that he received little news from England, see Martin J. Havran, *Caroline Courtier: The Life of Lord Cottington* (London, 1973), pp. 21, 56.

29 John Beaulieu to Trumbull, 15 October 1619, Add. 72253, fol. 63r.

30 Beaulieu to Trumbull, 22 September 1619, Add. 72253, fol. 57r.

31 Beaulieu to Trumbull, 6 March 1616, Add. 72252, fol. 95v.

32 Beaulieu to Trumbull, 10 March 1620, Add. 72253, fol. 100r.

33 Castle to Trumbull, 2 October 1619, Add. 72275, fol. 88v; Castle to Trumbull, 4 June 1622, Add. 72275, 141v; Castle to Trumbull, 15 October 1624, Add. 72276, fol. 123v.

34 Castle to Trumbull, 15 October 1618, Downshire vol. VI, p. 546.

35 Castle to Trumbull, 31 October 1623, Add. 72276, fol. 62v.

36 Thomas Locke to Carleton, 15 June 1622, in Thomas Birch (ed.), *The Court and Times of James I* (London, 1849), pp. 314–15.

37 John Chamberlain to Carleton, 20 July 1616, McClure vol. II, p. 17.

38 Chamberlain to Carleton, 1 April 1618, McClure vol. II, pp. 153–4.

39 Beaulieu to Trumbull, 16 September 1619, Add. 72253, fol. 59r.

40 'Extract of another lettre written from London the 16 of September 1619', Eg. 2593, fols. 46v–7r. This letter is printed as 'Extract of a Letter from [?], 16 September 1619', in Birch (ed.), *Court and Times of James I* vol. II, pp. 188–90, where it is tentatively but incorrectly attributed to Thomas Murray. 'Extract of a Letter from [?], 17 September 1619' in pp. 188–90 of the same volume is a copy of 'Extract of a letter written from London the 17 of September 1619', Eg. 2593, fol. 46r–v', which in turn is taken from Castle to Trumbull, 17 September 1619, Add. 72275, fol. 84r.

41 Trumbull to [Carleton], 30 July 1620 (o.s.), SP 77/14, fol. 180v; Trumbull to [Carleton], 10/20 December 1622, SP 77/15, fol. 430r.

42 Trumbull to [Carleton], 15/25 November 1622, SP 77/15, fol. 388r–v; Carleton to Trumbull, 5 December 1622, Add. 72273, fol. 99r–v.

43 Trumbull to Walter Aston, 2/12 October 1621, Add. 36445, fol. 254r–v.

44 Carleton to Chamberlain, 13 February 1618, Lee, p. 254.

45 See Lee, p. 20.

46 'The State of a Secretaries Place and the Perill Written by the Earle of Salisbury', Harl. 305, fols. 370r–v.

47 Harold Spencer Scott (ed.), *The Journal of Sir Roger Wilbraham* (Camden Miscellany vol. X, London, 1902), p. 97.

48 Roger Lockyer, *Buckingham: The Life and Political Career of George Villiers, first Duke of Buckingham, 1592–1628* (London, 1981), pp. 83–4; Joseph Mead to Martin Stuteville, 10 January 1622, Harl. 389, fol. 127r.

49 Conway to Buckingham, 17 July 1623, Harl. 1580, fol. 307r.

50 Lando to the Doge and Senate, 10 April 1621, CSPV vol. XVII, p. 14.

51 Relation of England of Girolamo Lando, 21 September 1622, CSPV vol. XVII, p. 441; Lando to the Doge and Senate, 11 February 1622, CSPV vol. XVII, p. 229.

52 Lando to the Doge and Senate, 2 October 1620, CSPV vol. XVI, p. 424.

53 CSPV vol. XVII, p. xlvii.

54 Valaresso to the Doge and Senate, 25 November 1622, CSPV vol. XVII, p. 510.

55 Lando to the Doge and Senate, 8 October 1620, CSPV vol. XVI, p. 429.

56 Lando to the Doge and Senate, 17 September 1621, CSPV vol. XVII, p. 132.

57 Lando to the Doge and Senate, 4 June 1621, CSPV vol. XVII, pp. 60–1.

58 *Ibid.*, p. 60.

59 Lando to the Doge and Senate, 11 February 1622, CSPV vol. XVII, p. 229.

60 Lando to the Doge and Senate, 14 January 1622, CSPV vol. XVII, p. 210.

61 'Tom Tell Troth or a Free Discourse touchinge the Murmurs of the tyme directed to his Maiestie by way of humble advertisement', Bod. MS. Tanner 73, fol. 202r.

62 As Richard Cust has argued, this is likely to give us a false impression that Council meetings were marked by harmony and consensus. See Cust, *Forced Loan*, pp. 8–9.

63 Williams to Buckingham, 22 July 1621, *Cabala, Mysteries of State, in Letters of the Great Ministers of K. James and K. Charles* (1653), p. 56; APC vol. 38, p. 21.

64 APC, vols 38–9 *passim*.

65 *Ibid.*

66 'The Marian court and Tudor policy-making', Early modern seminar, University of Cambridge, May 1998 (www.tudors.org/undergraduate/68–the-marian-court-and-tudor-policy-making.html); Natalie Mears, 'The "Personal Rule" of Elizabeth I: Marriage, Succession and Catholic Conspiracy, c. 1578–c. 1582' (PhD, St. Andrews, 1999), pp. 92–3.

67 William Davenport's commonplace book, Cheshire Archives ZCR 63/2/19, fol. 44r.

68 Chamberlain to Carleton, 4 January 1623, McClure vol. II, p. 472.

69 J. Vernon Jensen, 'The staff of the Jacobean Privy Council', *Huntington Library Quarterly* 40:1 (1976), p. 32.

70 Lando to the Doge and Senate, 8 January 1621, CSPV vol. XVI, p. 517.

71 Interestingly, Bacon argued that small 'cabinet councils' were in fact less secretive than ordinary ones, because their members could expect more 'glory' from divulging their proceedings. See Francis Bacon, 'Of counsel' in James Spedding (ed.), *The Works of Francis Bacon* vol. XII (London, 1857–74), pp. 146–51.

72 Lando to the Doge and Senate, 24 April 1620, CSPV vol. XVI, p. 238; Valaresso to the Doge and Senate, 8 December 1623, CSPV vol. XVIII, p. 164; Cogswell, *Blessed Revolution*, p. 128; Digby to Lords Commissioners for affairs of Germany, Bod. MS. Clarendon 3, fols. 94r–105v.

73 Conway to Buckingham, 1 August 1623, Harl. 1580, fol. 313r.

74 Valaresso to the Doge and Senate, 26 April 1624, CSPV vol. XVIII, p. 280.

75 Chamberlain to Carleton, 20 December 1623, McClure vol. II, p. 535.

76 Mears, 'Personal Rule', pp. 88–90.

77 Both Thomas Alured and the author of the speech attributed to George Abbot made this claim for legitimate discussion in their writings against the match. See Thomas Alured's letter to Buckingham, Sloane 1455, fols. 20r–3v; 'The Coppy of the Archbishop of Canterburyes speech', 27 July 1623, Bod. MS. Tanner 73, fol. 302r.

78 See Cogswell, *Blessed Revolution*, pp. 129–30.

79 Castle to Trumbull, 26 November 1624, Add. 72276, fol. 131v. See also Ruigh, *Parliament of 1624*.

80 Lockyer, *Buckingham*, p. 225.

81 *Ibid.*, pp. 225–6. Arundel made a similar complaint at the first Privy Council meeting of Charles's reign. See Sharpe, 'The Earl of Arundel', p. 227.

82 See William B. Bidwell and Maija Jansson (eds), *Proceedings in Parliament 1626* vol. II (Rochester (NY), 1992), p. 323.

83 Cust, *Forced Loan*, pp. 56, 72–3, 82–4.

84 See for instance Justus Lipsius, *Politica: Six Books of Politics or Political Instruction*, ed. Jan Waszink (Assen, 2004), p. 355.

85 See for instance Thomas Scott, *Vox Populi* (1620) and the anonymous manuscript tract 'Tom Tell Troth', Northampton Record Office, FH69.

86 David Colclough, *Freedom of Speech in Early Stuart England* (Cambridge, 2005). The legitimacy of free speech depended on the context, as Colclough has argued. For the right to counsel, see also Guy, 'Rhetoric of counsel', pp. 293–4.

87 James Craigie (ed.), *The Basilicon Doron of King James VI* vol. I (London, 1944), p. 180–2. It is worth noting that in the manuscript form of this work, James writes that if Henry faces a rebellion, he should nevertheless dissemble in order to gain time. This caveat was not included in the version published in 1603.

88 *His Maiesties declaration, touching the procee[d]ings in the late assemblie and conuention of Parliament* (1621), p. 3.

89 *Ibid.*, p. 4.

90 Sharpe, *Image Wars*, pp. 7, 121.

91 Pauline Croft, 'The gunpowder plot fails', in Brenda Buchanan, Justin Champion, David Cannadine, et al., *Gunpowder Plots* (London, 2005), pp. 14–19; Susan Doran, 'James VI and the English succession' in Houlbrooke (ed.), *James VI and I*, p. 33. These hints were more blatantly contradictory than the deliberately ambiguous signals Elizabeth gave about her intentions prior to the religious settlement of 1558.

92 Holles to John Holles Jnr., [26 March 1616], in P. R. Seddon (ed.), *Letters of John Holles, 1587–1637* (Thoroton Society Record Series, vol. 35), p. 124.

93 Mead to Stuteville, 2 February 1622, Harl. 389, fol. 140v.

94 Newsletter, [?] April 1621, Harl. 389, fol. 45r.

95 Ben Agar, *King James, his apopthegmes, or table-talke* (London, 1643).

96 Francis Bacon, 'Of seditions', Spedding (ed.), *Works of Francis Bacon* vol. VI, p. 131.

97 Charles Howard McIlwain (ed.), *The Political Works of James I* (New York, 1965), p. 43. See also his speech to the Parliament of 1610: 'Kings' actions (even in the secretest places) are as the action of those that are set upon the stage, or on the tops of houses, and I hope never to speak that in private which I shall not avow in public'. J. P. Kenyon, *The Stuart Constitution 1603–1688* (Cambridge, 1986), p. 81.

98 For the visit to Paul's Cross, see Morrissey, 'Presenting James VI and I to the public', pp. 107–21.

99 Beaulieu to Trumbull, 24 March 1620, Add. 72253, fol. 104r.

100 Charles Carter, *The Secret Diplomacy of the Hapsburgs, 1598–1625* (New York, 1964), p. 151.

101 Francis Nethersole to Carleton, 21 March 1620, CSPD 1619–23 (1858), p. 132.

102 Bohdan Chudoba, *Spain and the Empire* (Chicago, 1952), p. 236.

103 Castle to Trumbull, 23 March 1620, Add. 72275, fol. 100r.

104 Beaulieu to Trumbull, 31 March 1620, Add. 72253, fol. 106v.

105 Lockyer, *Buckingham*, p. 83; S. R. Gardiner, *History of England from the Accession of James I to the Outbreak of the Civil War, 1603–42* vol. III (London, 1883), p. 336. For the raising of troops for Vere's expedition, see Simon Adams, 'The Protestant Cause: Religious Alliance with the West European Calvinist Communities as a Political Issue in England, 1585–1630', (D.Phil, Oxford, 1973)', pp. 300–3.

106 Beaulieu to Trumbull, 7 April 1620, Add. 72253, fol. 108r.

107 Beaulieu to Trumbull, 28 April 1620, Add. 72253, fol. 112v. For the collection of the benevolence, see Adams, 'Protestant Cause', p. 296.

108 Trumbull to Secretary of State, 21 June /1 July 1620, SP 77/14, fol. 134r.

109 Carleton to James I, 19 June 1620, SP 84/95, fol. 272r.

110 Trumbull to [Carleton], 8/18 August 1620, SP 77/14, fol. 191v.

111 Trumbull to [Carleton], 11/21 September 1620, SP 77/14, fol. 212r.

112 Trumbull to [Carleton], 4/14 October 1620, SP 77/14, fol. 223r; Trumbull to [Carleton], 5/15 October 1620, SP 77/14, fol. 226r.

113 R. Dallington to the Earl of Rutland, 3 October 1620, in H. C. Maxwell Lyte (ed.), *The Manuscripts of the Duke of Rutland*, HMC 24, i (London, 1888), p. 467. This letter is wrongly dated to 1622. See also Lando to the Doge and Senate, 8 October 1620, CSPV vol. XVI, p. 430.

114 Lando to the Doge and Senate, 23 October 1620, CSPV vol. XVI, p. 450.

115 Lando to the Doge and Senate, 11 October 1620, CSPV vol. XVI, p. 430.

116 Lando to the Doge and Senate, 23 October 1620, CSPV vol. XVI, p. 450.

117 *Ibid.*, p. 451.

118 Trumbull to [Carleton], 19/29 November 1620, SP 77/14, fol. 243r; Trumbull to Carleton, 6/16 November 1620, SP 77/14, fols. 236v–7r.

119 Castle to Trumbull, 9 November 1620, Add. 72275, fol. 110r.

120 *Ibid.* Buckingham appears to have been involved in a similarly stage-managed encounter when he begged Charles to recall Parliament in 1628. See Cust, *Forced Loan*, p. 77.

121 Castle to Trumbull, 9 November 1620, Add. 72275, fol. 110r.

122 Lockyer, *Buckingham*, p. 94. See also Zaller, *Parliament of 1621*, p. 70. A similar episode in the Parliament of 1610 involving Robert Cecil may also have been planned in advance. See G. D. to A. W. at Middelborough, 28 July 1610, Downshire vol. II, pp. 330–1.

123 Lando to the Doge and Senate, 10 April 1621, CSPV vol. XVII, pp. 15–16.

124 Anthony Weldon, *The Court and Character of King James* (1650), pp. 186–7. Weldon's work is not at all the 'entirely one-sided' account of James's reign that it has been presented as. See Pauline Croft, *King James* (Basingstoke, 2003), p. 4.

125 Valaresso to the Doge and Senate, 17 March 1623, CSPV vol. XVII, p. 591.

126 Newsletter, [?] April 1621, Harl. 389, fol. 45r.

127 Croft, *King James*, p. 111.

128 Lando to the Doge and Senate, 11 February 1622, CSPV vol. XVII, p. 230.

129 Peter Burke, 'Tacitism, scepticism and reason of state' in J. H. Burns and Mark Goldie (eds), *The Cambridge History of Political Thought, 1450–1700* (Cambridge, 1991), pp. 479–98; Malcolm Smuts, 'Court-centred politics and the uses of Roman historians, c. 1590–1630' in Kevin Sharpe and Peter Lake (eds), *Culture and Politics in Early Stuart England* (London, 1994), pp. 21–43; J. H. M. Salmon, 'Seneca and Tacitus in Jacobean England' in Linda Levy Peck (ed.), *The Mental World of the Jacobean Court* (Cambridge, 1991), pp. 169–88.

130 Holles to Thomas Darcy, Viscount Colchester, 19 February 1623, in Seddon (ed.), *Letters of John Holles* vol. 36, p. 271.

131 Lando to the Doge and Senate, 3 April 1620, CSPV vol. XVI, p. 222.

132 Lando to the Doge and Senate, 14 January 1622, CSPV vol. XVII, p. 210.

133 James Larkin and Paul Hughes (eds), *Stuart Royal Proclamations Volume I: Royal Proclamations of King James I 1603–1625* (Oxford, 1973), p. 327.

134 Samuel Calvert to Trumbull, 10 June 1610, Downshire vol. II, p. 490.

135 Lando to the Doge and Senate, 22 January 1621, CSPV vol. XVI, p. 535.

136 Lando to the Doge and Senate, 11 June 1620, CSPV vol. XVI, p. 276.

137 Lando to the Doge and Senate, 18 June 1620, CSPV vol. XVI, p. 283.

138 Joseph Mead to Martin Stuteville, 10 January 1622, Harl. 389, fol. 127r.

139 Edward Hyde, Earl of Clarendon, *History of the Rebellion* vol. I (Oxford, 1888), pp. 14–15.

140 Lando to the Doge and Senate, 18 June 1620, CSPV vol. XVI, p. 283.

141 Lando to the Doge and Senate, 22 January 1621, CSPV vol. XVI, p. 535.

142 Lando to the Doge and Senate, 29 January 1621, CSPV vol. XVI, pp. 544–5.

143 Trumbull to [Carleton], 23 January 1624 (o.s.), SP 77/17, fol. 15r.

144 Robert Tisdale, *Pax Vobis* (London, 1623), p. 14.

145 Thomas, Earl of Kellie, to John, Earl of Mar, 12 April 1624, in Paton (ed.), *Manuscripts of the Earl of Mar and Kellie* vol. II, p. 199.

146 Lando to the Doge and Senate, 27 August 1620, CSPV vol. XVI, p. 377.

147 Lando to the Doge and Senate, 3 April 1620, CSPV vol. XVI, p. 222.

148 James Craigie (ed.), *The Poems of James VI of Scotland* (Edinburgh, 1958), p. 183. The anonymous author of a poem written around the same time exhorted his readers to 'rest content / and marke how fruit shewes the event'. See 'O blessed king that heares the poore', Royal 18 A. xxxii, p. 8.

149 'Tom Tell Troth', Northampton Record Office, FH69, fol. 8r.

150 *Ibid.*, fols. 8r–v.

151 Castle to Trumbull, 8 December 1619, Add. 72275, fol. 93v.

152 *Ibid.*

153 Carleton to Trumbull, 9 November 1619, Add. 72271, fol. 41r.

154 Castle to Trumbull, 8 December 1619, Add. 72275, fol. 93v.

155 Relation of England of Girolamo Lando, 21 September 1622, CSPV vol. XVII, p. 441.

156 Trumbull to Carleton, 16/26 June 1621, SP 77/14, fol. 350r. This may well have been true, but the emphasis on this point implies that James worried that observers might believe that the declaration was contrived.

157 *Ibid.*

158 Lee, *Great Britain's Solomon*, p. 276.

159 Valaresso to the Doge and Senate, 23 September 1622, CSPV vol. XVII, p. 460.

160 William Wynn to John Wynn, 31 March 1624, NLW 9059E/1206.

161 James I to the council of Scotland, 15 December 1616, CSPD 1611–18 (1858), p. 414.

162 Castle to Trumbull, 6 March 1617, Downshire vol. VI, p. 128.

163 *Ibid.* For James's trip to Scotland and the Articles of Perth, see Laura Stewart, 'The political repercussions of the Five Articles of Perth: A reassessment of James VI and I's religious policies in Scotland', *Sixteenth Century Journal* 38:4 (2008), pp. 1013–36.

164 Beaulieu to Trumbull, 3 July 1619, Add. 72253, fol. 49v.

165 Castle to Trumbull, 20 May 1624, Add. 72276, fol. 92r.

166 *Ibid.*

167 *Ibid.*

168 Castle to Trumbull, 2 July 1624, Add. 72276, fol. 107r–v.

169 *Ibid.*

Chapter 3

———◆———

Political rumours

INTRODUCTION

Contemporaries sometimes imagined themselves as ships trying to navigate a sea of news and rumour, ultimately at the mercy of the elements. During a particularly quiet period, John Castle wrote that he had little news to report, 'for there is nothinge, but deepe sylence and a dead Sea'.[1] In another letter he complained that 'if the occurrence beyond the Seas rise which no more tyde then ours here at home, there is surely then a dead water for the affaires of all Christendome'.[2] Sir Giles Mompesson echoed this sentiment when he wrote that 'we are fallen in these partes, into a dead calme, there is not the least breath of newes stirring'.[3] The tide of news ebbed and flowed, and a lack of news left the information-hungry stranded and listless.

Calm seas could quickly be whipped up by storms of rumour. In 1620 William Trumbull complained to Doncaster that he was 'so tossed here, vpon the wynde of vncertaine, and contradictory rumors' about the Palatinate 'as I know not what to wryte to your Lordship'.[4] Beaulieu similarly complained of being 'tossed to and from by the vncertaine wynds of common rumors' about events in Germany.[5] A few months later he apologised for repeating a false rumour in his previous newsletter, but thought that because it had been generally believed, Trumbull would forgive him for being 'carried awaye with the violence of that streame'.[6] During Charles's and Buckingham's trip to Madrid, Richard Corbett described the 'Flouds' of rumours that ran down the nave of St Paul's cathedral.[7] The stream of rumour could be as unstoppable as a flood, and like a storm that suddenly gathered at sea, turbulent, unpredictable and potentially treacherous.

The imagery of rumour drew much of its power from its association with popular rebellion. According to the ancients, rumour or 'fame' had been brought forth as a revenge on the Gods for defeating the Giants, and as such it represented an alternative form of rebellion.[8] The representation of fame

in Virgil as a terrifying winged beast with many tongues had a great influence over early Stuart writers.[9] As Bacon wrote, rumours were 'preludes of
seditions to come ... seditious tumults, and seditious fames, differ no more
but as brother and sister'.[10] The problem for governments was that rumour
was a mode of political discourse that even the poorest members of society
could freely engage in. Shakespeare likened it to a pipe that was so easy to
learn that even 'the blunt Monster, with vncounted heads, / The still-discor-
dant, wavering Multitude / Can play vpon it'.[11] According to the official rhetoric,
ordinary people were emotional and gullible, they lacked judgement and were
always eager for change and novelty, and so were particularly likely to credit
slanders and seditious rumours that might undermine proper obedience to
authority. Rumour could indeed play a part in rebellions. Rumours that the
monarch had died, that a pretender to the throne had emerged, or that the
authorities planned to impose new taxes or religious policies could encourage
or legitimise rebellion, and naturally monarchs attempted to suppress them.[12]
Tudor governments introduced or reinforced laws against rumours and
seditious words, although as David Cressy has pointed out, they were not easy
to enforce and punishments were not always harsh in practice.[13]

The association between rumour and rebellion was very strong, and to
some extent it is still with us. Historians and psychologists alike have tended
to represent rumour as an uncontrollable popular force, a means for us to
understand the sometimes paranoid and febrile political ideas of ordinary
people. The classic experimental work was done by Gordon Allport and Leo
Postman in the 1940s.[14] Allport and Postman showed a test subject a picture
of an ambiguous everyday scene and asked them to describe it to another
subject from memory, without being able to refer back to the original image.
The second subject passed on what they had been told to a third and so on in
a slightly more sophisticated version of 'Chinese whispers'. The descriptions
given at each stage were then compared, and were shown to undergo a process
of 'sharpening and levelling' as they passed from person to person, becoming
shorter, more memorable and less ambiguous as they went. Details were
progressively lost, and reports become easier to grasp and retell.[15] Subjects
increasingly imputed meaning to events and motives to the people depicted
in the scenes, turning ambiguous images into recognisable stories. Only
those distortions which harmonised with common cultural stereotypes were
likely to be passed on, and the final test subject's description simplified and
exaggerated the original picture in line with their prejudices.[16] A knife held by
a white man in the original picture, for instance, had magically jumped into a
black assailant's hand by the end of one experiment. The sociologist Tamotsu
Shibutani extended Allport's and Postman's work, arguing that because every
participant in a rumour chain helped to distort and shape its meaning, the
act of creating or spreading a rumour was futile. The content of a report

deteriorated quickly in the act of repeatedly passing it on. Rumours that were spread on purpose would only survive this process if the community in which they circulated was already receptive to their message, under circumstances in which they would have sprung up spontaneously anyway. It was as difficult to control a rumour as it was to control a lynch mob.[17]

Like psychologists and sociologists, historians have tended to highlight the uncontrollable, protean nature of false reports, and have used rumours to try to understand the politics of ordinary people. Adam Fox has shown how scurrilous rumours reveal a 'sophisticated awareness of current events' which 'suggest that even humble people were participating in the arguments that anticipated the civil war'.[18] In an illuminating article about rumours that circulated during the reign of Henry VIII, Ethan Shagan argued that rumours were 'the stuff of popular politics'.[19] Since every person who passed on a rumour was free to add their own gloss and manipulate its content and meaning, rumours were 'free from government control, or indeed from any control at all'.[20] One might attempt to plant or spread a rumour, but there was no way of controlling how it would subsequently be distorted as it passed from person to person. 'Inventing a rumour', as Shagan argued, was 'the most insignificant of acts'.[21]

Historians who have tended to rely on the court records of individuals who were prosecuted for spreading seditious rumours risk repeating elite stereotypes about the unsophisticated, emotional and gullible multitude. As we shall see, despite the outward fear and disdain elites expressed for 'vulgar rumours', in practice they were increasingly willing to rebut, exploit and spread rumours for their own political purposes during this period. Rumours were not simply the popular form of discourse that historians have tended to present them as. Instead, they often came about through a dialogue between elite and popular politics.

This chapter will begin by examining the collective 'Chinese whispers' process through which many political rumours formed, a process that in many ways supports the view of rumour as an uncontrollable, plebeian mode of discourse. Despite the low regard in which rumours were often held, writers nevertheless included them in their newsletters, and the chapter will consider why this was the case. It will assess their value in providing information about popular opinion, and the explanatory functions they served. As we shall see, rumours could often mitigate the impact of bad news, and the chapter will explore a number of case studies where this seems to have occurred, looking particularly at rumours surrounding some of the battles and sieges that occurred on the continent. Finally, the chapter will examine examples where individuals played an important role in deliberately spreading rumours. In particular, we will explore attempts to damage the Spanish match by reporting that the Infanta had married an alternative suitor, or that the Spanish were preparing to invade James's kingdoms. As we shall see, the King himself was often as susceptible to false rumours as the rest of his subjects.

THE FORMATION AND FUNCTIONS OF RUMOURS

Many of the false reports preserved in manuscript newsletters during this period seem to confirm that rumours were collectively constructed by ordinary people, rather than being deliberately spread. Their development often matched the gradual process of distortion described by Allport and Postman. Sometimes rumours could be started by a simple misunderstanding. In Paris in 1612 a soldier drew his sword on a captain of the guard named Rouët near the Louvre. The soldier fled without a fight, but was was pursued by bystanders who cried out that he had tried to kill Rouët. Others misheard this and thought that someone had tried to kill le Roi, the King, Louis XIII. A rumour quickly spread that Louis was dead, and the Paris crowds could not be appeased until he showed himself publicly, an incident which demonstrated the potential power of ordinary subjects when inflamed by false reports.[22]

A less dramatic, more incremental form of this process of distortion can be observed in contemporary newsletters, particularly those of Joseph Mead and his London correspondents. These writers often mixed people's names up if they sounded similar, and this created false rumours about who did what to whom. In 1621, when Bacon fell from power, Mead wrote that Sir Thomas Lee had been granted custody of the great seal, when the real recipient was almost certainly Sir James Ley, who presided over the Lord Keeper's trial.[23] When writers were confused about the names of individuals in the news, they more often substituted a famous or topical person for a more obscure one. Mead attributed an anti-Catholic speech given by Sir Robert Phelips in the Parliament of 1621 to his father, Sir Edward Phelips. Sir Edward had been a speaker of the House of Commons, and although he had died in 1614 his name was probably better known at the time.[24] A London newsletter writer similarly reported that Heneage Finch, who had recently been made recorder of London and had taken a leading role in the prosecution of Sir Giles Mompesson, had been questioned for writing a controversial book, *The Worlds Great Restauration*. In fact the author was Sir Henry Finch, who had not been the subject of recent public discussion to the same extent.[25] The names of offices were also confused. It was reported in 1623 that Owen Gruffith had been made a privy councillor, when in fact he only became extraordinary clerk of the Privy Council.[26] The habit of leaving gaps for names in newsletters testifies to the fact that some elements of reports were more memorable than others. While newsletter writers always communicated the gist of a story, they often left blank spaces for the names of individuals to be filled in later. Names can be found written in a later hand, but sometimes writers were unable to discover them before sending their letters, and they have been left blank.[27] Specific names were harder to remember than the narrative essence of a report, and it is easy to see how false rumours could be born when a name that came easily to mind was substituted for another.

Observers sometimes suspected that rumours based on mistaken identity rested on even more tenuous connections than having similar names. In 1621, Sampson Price had been imprisoned for giving an anti-Spanish sermon. Around the same time, Lewis Bayly, Bishop of Bangor, was imprisoned for opposing the Book of Sports. Mead was certain that Price had been imprisoned, but described the news about Bayly as a rumour. The former report had given rise to the latter, he thought, simply because both were Welsh clergymen, and so easily confused with each other.[28]

The names of places were also frequently muddled up. The battles and sieges of the Thirty Years' War exposed James's subjects to a host of unfamiliar place names, and their knowledge of central European geography was often severely stretched. In 1621, Bethlem Gabor was reported to have marched into Breslau in Silesia, an unlikely destination as it was north east of Prague and far from his own territories in Transylvania. This rumour was explained by the fact that Breslau sounded similar to Brno in Moravia, where he actually was.[29] Similar mistakes often arose from a more speculative form of inference. When Spinola was reported to have captured a town near Worms, a rumour circulated that he had taken Pfeddersheim, as this was the largest and most prominent town nearby, when in fact he had taken Westhoven, which was smaller and more obscure.[30]

These small mistakes demonstrate the beginnings of the process through which false rumours could emerge. As reports travelled further and passed from person to person, trivial errors multiplied and serious distortions arose. The accuracy as well as the volume of political news decreased the further away one was from London.[31] Beaulieu apologised for his lack of news in one letter, explaining that he had only recently returned from a stay at Downham Hall in Suffolk. 'In that wilde corner', as he wrote, 'all the world might go upside downe afore it should be heard of'.[32] Mead excused the poor quality of news he passed on about the Parliament of 1621 on the basis that he was 'farre from London & haue nothing but mine eares to help me'.[33] James's trip to Scotland in 1617 represents a rare natural experiment in the distorting effects of distance. As the King travelled further north, news about court appointments became progressively more uncertain. John Holles wrote that while news from the court at Huntingdon in Cambridgeshire was reasonably accurate, 'Lincoln, and Nuark tell us odd tales' about court appointments.[34]

As news reports travelled, they were simplified and exaggerated. The summaries that individuals made of newsletters allow us to see this process in action. The extracts were often much more emphatic than the original letters on which they were based. A letter from Frankenthal sent in 1621 stated that there was 'much talk of the king of Denmarks purpose to come in person' to the Palatinate, but the extract stated that 'the King of Denmark will come in person with an armie'. Caveats and qualifications in the original, which merely reported speculation about Christian IV's intentions, were not preserved.[35] The news often became more dramatic, and elements of conflict were amplified. In 1621, Mead reported a fairly mundane story about how Lord Keeper Williams had asked James to appoint officers of the court of Chancery who had served under his predecessor, Thomas Egerton. Being new to the office, Williams hoped these experienced officials would allow him to learn the ropes. In the process of retelling, this story became much more vivid and theatrical. Williams was said to have begged on his knees for the King to appoint the officers so that he could not be blamed in future for the misdeeds of individuals he had not personally nominated. Charles was also said to have clashed with Williams over the appointments.[36] The low copying fidelity of oral reports meant that only the more dramatic details or distortions were likely to be remembered long enough to be communicated to others.

Some individuals were aware of the ways in which rumours became exaggerated and distorted as they passed from person to person. In Venice, Fulgenzio Micanzo wrote that he had already received reports about Somerset's trial, 'Fame bringing them hither amplified by passing many hands' and transforming them into rumours that he had poisoned Prince Henry and treasonably plotted against James.[37] In 1618, Micanzo reported that rumours were circulating in Venice that the Spanish match had been concluded, 'perhaps out of the Custome of fame *quae vires acquirit eundo* [which gathers strength as it goes]'.[38]

The distortions inherent in the process of oral communication meant that speculation about the likelihood of an expected event could quickly be transformed into definitive (if false) information that it had already occurred. One of the most common ways in which this phenomenon manifested itself was in the false reports that prominent individuals had died, where in fact they were merely ill.[39] The expectation that a ruler *might* die was simplified through the process of transmission into the rumour that he or she *had* died. When Queen Anne fell ill in November 1618, for instance, Chamberlain reported that 'yt was geven out all this towne over that the Quene was dead on Thursday', when in fact she lived until March the following year.[40] Rumours of the long-expected death of Emperor Mathias circulated so often that observers became increasingly sceptical about them. When news reached London of Mathias's death in 1619, Chamberlain wrote that he 'hath ben dead here I know not how often ... and for some other reasons I suspend my beleefe'.[41] There may have been a collective assumption that the most likely reason why a prominent individual was being spoken about was because they had died. Rumours that the Prince of Orange had survived an assassination attempt were sparked when thieves tried to steal his purse in 1624.[42] When contemporaries heard vague reports that something or other had happened to a monarch, general or statesman, they might naturally assume that he had become topical for this reason.

While a long illness made it plausible that some individuals might die in their beds, others met a more violent end. When the Prince of Condé was arrested in 1616, it was rumoured that he had been stabbed to death, which was certainly believable considering the political instability in France during Louis XIII's minority – Marie de Medici's chief minister, the Marshal d'Ancre, was after all stabbed to death the following year.[43] Generals were sometimes reported to have died, and those who lived by the sword, as the Count of Bucquoy or Bethlen Gabor did, were occasionally falsely rumoured to have died by it.[44]

On several occasions, the shutting of the ports led contemporaries to speculate that James might have died, and this present-tense speculation quickly transformed into past-tense rumour. The death of a monarch was always a potentially dangerous moment in Tudor and Stuart England. Ships were barred from coming or going when a monarch died, presumably to prevent foreign powers from interfering with the succession. As a result, when the ports were closed in March 1619, it was thought that James, who was seriously ill, had died.[45] Trumbull reported that 'the dolefull bruite of shutting our Portes, for some disaster befallen his maiestie, continueth here among the vulgar' in the Spanish Netherlands.[46] Carleton was ordered to contradict these rumours in the Dutch Republic.[47]

Rumours were often simply created when observers drew false inferences, or when speculation was passed on as fact. Contemporaries were aware of the thin line, which rumour constantly crossed, between speculation and seemingly conclusive information. In 1619, Trumbull reported a rumour that the Elector Palatine had forcibly taken Frankfurt, which Trumbull said 'doth proceed from an apprehenccon that he may doe it'.[48] Similarly, Dudley Carleton Jnr. passed on a rumour that Prince Charles had been captured in France during his journey to Madrid in 1623, but conceded that the report was 'grounded onely upon the possibility thereof'.[49] The distinction between 'may do' and 'has done' was too fine to survive the process of oral transmission.

Newsworthy rumours might be included in letters even when there was plenty of reliable information to report. Nevertheless, writers were much more likely to resort to passing on rumours during quieter periods. News did not flow in a steady stream, and the dramatic series of events of the late 1610s and early 1620s was punctuated by periods in which writers struggled to fill their letters. In one letter Chamberlain explained that 'we were never at so low ebbe for matter of newes specially publicke', as a result of which, observers like him were 'even faine to set ourselves a worke with the poorest entertainments that you have lightly [i.e. perhaps] seene or heard of'.[50] John Beaulieu began one letter to Sir Thomas Puckering by saying that he would 'rather entertaine you with rumours and vncertainties' than write nothing at all.[51]

The modern 'silly season' had its early Stuart analogue during the summer, when the absence of the King and court from London led to a scarcity of news. 'If I shoulde faile in my correspondence for a fortnight or 3. weekes', Castle wrote in the summer of 1624, 'yor losse would be little consideringe the barrennesse of this place, and the custome of the Courte in tymes of Progresse, which medleth with little busines, and begetts as little alteraccon'.[52] Beaulieu similarly complained that the absence of the court 'maketh … this place like a desart'.[53] Rumours were particularly rife during this period. In the summer of 1619, Chamberlain wrote that he 'never knew a more empty and barren time for newes then this vacation hath ben, so that they are faine almost every weeke to coyne great battells in Bohemia'.[54]

At other times, the expectation of a significant political event, such as the return of Charles from Madrid, could stifle discussion of other matters and leave writers with little to report. 'I haue very Little matter worthy a letter', Trumbull wrote in September 1623, when Charles was on his way home from Madrid, 'the expectaccon of his Highness arriuall hauing bred a generall silence in all businesses of the Publick'.[55] Similarly, the expectation of a new Parliament tended to force other issues off the agenda. Beaulieu wrote in February 1624 that 'all matters are fallen so calme vpon the expectation of the parlament … as there is nothing at all stirring here amongst vs'.[56] The return of Charles or the calling of a Parliament tended to reduce the supply of news because James deferred decisions about other, more routine matters, which were the ordinary subjects of news, until the dust from such major political events had settled. Writers were reluctant to write when news was subject to daily change and contradiction. Castle apologised to the Earl of Bridgewater for his recent silence in 1640, saying that he was 'desirous to write when rumors were a little more settled, and not vpon the confusion of advertisements, which are full of uncertaynty'.[57] While this principle no doubt helped writers to preserve their reputation for accuracy, a lack of news only left their correspondents with more room for speculation and rumour.

Newsletter writers faced formidable problems in sifting fact from fiction, and news that turned out to be true was at first often treated as rumour. Apparently implausible news, such as that Charles and Buckingham had left England to go to Madrid, was initially disbelieved. Even false rumours had some value if they roughly approximated the truth. Initial reports were often inaccurate, but they could still be close to the mark and give some indication of what had happened. Trumbull believed that one could not discount rumours entirely. 'As I dare not take vulgar bruits for current money', as he wrote in one of his despatches, 'so I may not contemne them altogether, seeinge hetherto (those that were the most vnlikely) haue proued but too true'.[58] The truth could take time to emerge, but that did not mean that rumours, which at least had the virtue of circulating rapidly, were without merit. As Beaulieu wrote about reports from La Rochelle in 1623, 'of these things, as they proue to be true, you shall sooner be informed by the immediate rumour thereof then by the Echo of my relations'.[59] Rumour was a first draft of news, necessarily imperfect, but often suggestive of the truth.

Rumours performed another important function in simplifying and explaining complex news and the motives of political actors. Continental observers who struggled to understand the reasoning behind James's marriage negotiations with Spain and his tolerant attitude towards Catholics were partly satisfied by rumours that the King had secretly converted to Catholicism.[60] English Catholics hoped these reports were true. Lord Evers was reportedly imprisoned for alleging that both James and Charles had secretly converted.[61] James tried to quash these rumours, reassuring a gathering of bishops that he would remain a Protestant and drawing attention to his anti-papal writings in a poem in which he also asked his subjects why they would 'push me downe to hell / By makinge me an Infidell'.[62] Intermittent reports about rebellions against James that circulated on the continent in 1621–22 simplified and exaggerated domestic conflict and discontent over his foreign policy in a similar way.[63] In 1621 the citizens of Vienna discussed rumours that 'there should be some commotion in England'. The rebellion was supposedly led by Charles, who had 'shewed great discontent of late' at his father's pacific policies.[64] The following year, a pamphlet was published in Spain alleging that James had been imprisoned and the crown had been passed to Frederick.[65]

False rumours could also provide useful information about the status of popular opinion. It was useful to know what people thought, even if they were deluded. Carleton included rumours about affairs in Germany in his letters to Aston because he believed it was 'somtymes of vse to see how cleare the waters run as well in their severall streames as their fountaynes'.[66] The significance of many reports was not that they were true but that many people wanted them to be. Sir Francis Crane wrote that the credit given to rumours of Spinola's departure from the siege of Bergen-op-Zoom in 1622 indicated that 'wee woulde haue it so' even if there were no grounds for belief.[67] When a German gazetta reported that the estates of Moravia had kidnapped the Duke of Bouillon, intending to use him as a bargaining chip in peace negotiations with the Habsburgs, Trumbull mentioned that while it didn't report the 'truth of those things', the gazetta nevertheless indicated 'the passions of the Authors'.[68] The inclusion of false rumours also allowed correspondents to contrast idle reports with their own more accurate information, and demonstrated their judgement in being able to distinguish between the two.

Although ordinary people shape the content of false reports, rumours do not offer an entirely reliable means of studying popular opinion. Rumours were the lowest common denominator of political discourse, since the process of oral communication tended to strip them of nuances and caveats while retaining or exaggerating frightening, salacious and memorable elements. Mainstream popular discussion of politics may have been much more moderate, careful and sceptical than the content of these rumours would seem to imply. Nor does the wide dispersal of a rumour necessarily mean that it was believed. False reports were often transmitted precisely because observers did not believe them. The newsworthiness of a rumour stemmed less from its actual content than from the fact that it was supposedly being spread by other malicious or gullible people. More incredible and exaggerated rumours were more newsworthy, and thus more likely to spread, because individuals thought they were false and that they represented particularly blatant examples of disinformation or popular credulity. This implies that we should be careful in drawing broader conclusions about popular opinion based on the success of rumours.

Historians have recently suggested that the variability of reports led to a 'sceptical crisis' in which individuals were so worried about the inaccuracy of reports that they began to question the possibility of gaining any knowledge at all about the world.[69] Jacobean newsletter writers certainly complained of the difficulties they faced in sifting truth from falsehood amid the multiplicity of conflicting news. As Wolley put it, there were sometimes so many 'eydle and forged reports' that 'no man knoweth what to beleeue'.[70] Monarchs and diplomats would of course suppress information and mislead the people. Members of rival confessions would also spread damaging lies. John Wolley described the interpretation of the news by Catholics as an attempt to mould reality to their own purposes. After the invasion of the Palatinate in 1620, he complained that the citizens of Brussels 'make Counte Henry de Nassau, dead of sickness ... Frankental was conquered long since by ther calculation'.[71]

Newsletter writers also thought that in this uncertain news culture, people tended to simply believe what they wanted to believe. In the earlier stages of negotiations for the Spanish match, for instance, Chamberlain had doubts about how quickly it would be concluded, 'the Lady beeing yet scant eleven yeares old', but reported that authoritative news was difficult to come by since 'every man hopes or feares as he is affected'.[72] In 1624 Wolley felt unable to confirm or deny reports that the French match had been concluded since 'some men speake as they heare, and others as they would haue it'.[73]

Nevertheless, during this period newsletter writers appear to have believed, perhaps naively, that the truth was discoverable in principle, and there is little evidence that they doubted the possibility of obtaining knowledge about events in the end. Wishful thinking and partisan interpretation were not universal impediments to uncovering the truth, because they were always ascribed to other people but very rarely to the observer themselves. News and rumour were ultimately different things, even if they were initially difficult to distinguish. The 'truth' would emerge eventually, but the process was gradual and fitful. Many news diarists annotated reports by writing 'proved true', or 'a false report' in the margin or between the lines, indicating that news only attained the status of fact over a period of time, as further information either verified or discredited it.[74] If a report was repeated, it could usually be trusted, but if nothing more was heard of it, it could safely be ignored. Simon Digby affirmed that 'I dare giue no credit to Rumors, till I heare them seconded some days after', and Joseph Mead concluded a lurid murder report by telling his correspondent that 'if you hear of it again, you may believe it; but I suspect it, because some who came from London, on Tuesday, could not tell of it'.[75] Both Carleton and Trumbull accepted that time was 'the mother of truth'.[76]

THE MOMENTUM OF EXPECTATIONS

One of the most important psychological functions of false rumours was that they could often mitigate the impact of unpleasant news. They helped individuals to gradually accept a situation in which their hopes and expectations about the likely course of national and international events had been dashed. This phenomenon is particularly apparent in the rumours that surrounded the dramatic events on the continent that James's subjects were so eager to hear about during this period. The contradictory reports that circulated about Frederick's defeat at the Battle of White Mountain, some of which suggested that his losses had been exaggerated, or even that he had retained control of Prague, offer an interesting case study of this phenomenon. The Battle of Fleurus and the siege of Berghen-op-Zoom, which were viewed very differently in the Dutch Republic and the Spanish Netherlands, demonstrate how widely rumours about the same events could differ, and how both sides could create reports which reduced the impact of their own defeats. Finally, rumours that the Queen of Bohemia had died following the Battle of White Mountain show how the momentum of recent events could shape the plausibility of rumours.

Battles were inherently unpredictable and uncertain events, and their outcome was often not immediately clear to the participants. It was possible, for example, for part of an army to be routed and to spread reports of defeat even though the remainder of the army had turned the tide. It is also possible that many of the false reports about the outcome of battles were spread on purpose. False expectations about a battle's likely outcome might be raised by the common practice of exaggerating troop numbers.[77] After a battle had occurred, both sides were often keen to claim victory if the outcome was anything less than decisive. In 1620 Carleton heard various reports of defeats suffered by the Emperor in Austria, 'but aduertisements out of those parts are so diuers that it is hard to know what to belieue. for as they haue there *pila minantia pilis* [spear opposed to spear], so hether they send *scripta minantia scriptis* [writing opposed to writing]'.[78] False reports of this nature could be remarkably resistant to falsification. Some of the Parliamentarian victories invented by Civil War propagandists survived in the historiography as genuine battles right into the twentieth century.[79]

The rumours that circulated in England about the outcome of battles on the continent were not inaccurate in an even-handed way. Contemporaries were much more likely to invent or exaggerate Protestant victories than Catholic ones. The news diarist William Whiteway was told that Tilly, rather than the Duke of Brunswick, had been defeated at Stadtlohn, and recorded news of a dramatic victory by Bethlen Gabor a month after the Prince had made peace with the Emperor.[80] Some of these reports can be put down to wishful thinking. Carleton told Trumbull in 1622 that in the United Provinces, although 'some uncertaine reports' had circulated of the Protestant defeat at Wimpfen, 'we were deaf of that eare', unwilling to believe unwelcome news.[81] False reports of Protestant victories would be correspondingly more likely to survive the filtering process of oral communication.

The Battle of White Mountain, which took place outside Prague in October 1620, was a disaster for Frederick. He fled Prague in the face of victorious Imperial troops, who later re-established Habsburg control over Bohemia and forced him and his family into exile in the United Provinces.[82] Although the outcome of the battle was decisive, however, this was unclear in the first few weeks after it was fought.[83] Simonds D'Ewes enquired after the result of the Battle of White Mountain on a daily basis, 'with rumour attributing victory first to one side, then to the other'.[84] Some reports indicated that Frederick had either died in the battle or had been taken prisoner.[85] Benjamin Buwinkhausen at Stuttgart, and Henry Bilderbeck at Cologne, however, wrote that Frederick's defeat was not as decisive as the Habsburgs pretended.[86] John Beaulieu was initially under the impression that the battle had been a draw. The source for this news was said to be a letter supposedly written by Frederick to James, telling the King that although there had been losses on both sides, Frederick still controlled Prague and did not expect any more Habsburg offensives that year.[87] Ferdinand was said to have lost more troops than Frederick, and some thought that false news of his defeat was spread 'to dishearten the people; and disolue the princes [i.e. the Protestant Union] in the Palatinat'.[88] Even if Frederick had lost the battle, Prague was thought to be so secure that some thought its capture could only have been achieved by witchcraft, and the Emperor was said to have paid sorcerers and necromancers to put a plague on the Bohemian army.[89]

The truth soon became apparent. Beaulieu apologised for passing on 'such pleasing, though most grosse lyes' about the battle to Trumbull.[90] His only excuse was that the rumours were 'so *gene*rally taken vp and beleeued ... for three or fower dayes, as that you would excuse me, if you were here, for being carried away with the violence of that streame'.[91] Even when Frederick's defeat had become certain, rumours nevertheless emerged that although he had initially lost Prague, the Imperial soldiers had pillaged the city so ruthlessly that 'the townsmen rose, and drave them out and kept the towne for the king of Bohemia'.[92] Odds of twenty to one were offered in the Dutch Republic if the report proved false.[93] This story was accompanied by further rumours that both the Pope and the Emperor were dead.[94] At the same time, news arrived of a prophecy that Frederick would retake Prague in or before 1623 and be crowned Emperor.[95] As the war went on, optimism gave way to pessimism. In 1624, when dire rumours about Protestant defeats circulated, Trumbull wrote that although he was 'not lightly carryed away by such rumors ... I haue continually observed, euer since that fatall and dismall battell of Prague, that all Prognostications howe vnlikely soeuer; against those of our party, haue in the end proued too true'.[96]

The reports about the Battle of White Mountain demonstrate the erratic way in which the truth about events emerged, but also that conflicting rumours served a purpose for observers who struggled to work out what had happened. There was a continuum of opinion about the outcome of the battle in the weeks and months after it was fought, providing reports to suit the hopes of all sides. Some believed the initial news about Frederick's defeat, but opinion quickly moved to the opposite extreme when rumours circulated suggesting that the severity of his losses had been exaggerated, that the battle had been a draw or even a strategic victory, or that the Emperor himself had suffered a dramatic reversal when the citizens of Prague massacred his troops. The pendulum of rumour swung from one side to the other before finally settling on the truth, and these extreme reports set the plausible limits of the outcome of the battle, calibrating expectations by suggesting the truth might lie somewhere in between.

The rumours about the outcome of the Battle of White Mountain also indicated that when expectations of victory met with a sudden reversal, reports that moderated the severity of defeat quickly spread to cushion the impact. Rumours which suggested that Frederick's defeat at White Mountain was not as bad as first thought, and even that the battle was effectively a Protestant victory, provided consolation and allowed individuals to come to a realisation of the unpalatable truth by degrees. The formation and spread of these rumours was not a deliberately orchestrated process – rather they spread through wishful thinking and a collective attempt to reconcile new information with previous expectations.

Divergent reports that circulated about the outcome of the Battle of Fleurus and the siege of Bergen-op-Zoom in 1622 show how widely expectations could differ, and provide further evidence that rumours could satisfy psychological needs. In the Dutch Republic, the battle was seen as a strategic Protestant victory, while the Spanish siege of Bergen was thought to be doomed to failure. In the Spanish Netherlands, on the other hand, the battle was seen as a decisive defeat for Mansfeld's troops, while the success of the siege was viewed as inevitable. The commentary and speculation that circulated about these events also show how willing the people were to believe false rumours which flattered their hopes and expectations, and how reluctantly they adapted to news which ran to the contrary.

The immediate background to the battle were the defeats suffered by Frederick's forces at Wimpfen and Hochst in the Summer of 1622, after which the Elector dismissed his commanders and left the Palatinate, returning to the United Provinces.[97] Mansfeld thereafter accepted a commission from the Dutch, marching through the Spanish Netherlands in order to relieve the town of Bergen-op-Zoom, which Spinola's forces had besieged in July.[98] In late August, Cordoba tried to block Mansfeld's path at Fleurus in Brabant. Historians have tended to view the battle as a strategic victory for Mansfeld and Brunswick, because although the Spanish inflicted heavy losses, they failed to prevent their opponents from continuing on their way to relieve Bergen-op-Zoom.[99]

From the Spanish Netherlands, Trumbull reported that Mansfeld had been decisively defeated at Fleurus, and his forces subsequently destroyed.[100] This also appears to have been how the battle was reported in Spain.[101] Carleton, on the other hand, from his vantage point in the Dutch Republic, was quick to retort that these reports were mere 'vanities'.[102] As far as Carleton was concerned, the battle was a victory for the Protestant side, and a complete rout of Cordoba's forces had only been prevented by the refusal of two regiments of Mansfeld's horse to fight because of lack of pay.[103] Even the seemingly conclusive evidence of Mansfeld's defeat – the parading of some of his troops' captured colours through Brussels – could be given a positive spin. Carleton wrote that Cordoba's troops had been forced to fight hard for the colours, which had not been given up in retreat.[104] The Infanta's subjects had 'no great cause to brag' about their capture, as they had been unable to pursue the regiments which lost them.[105]

Trumbull was initially uncertain of the progress of the siege of Bergen, which Mansfeld was now on the way to relieving.[106] He told Carleton that although he would like to give him an accurate account of the siege, 'in truth all things that come from both sides are so exaggerated, minted or disguised, by the measure of the passion or the affection of the relaters as I can not discerne where I may settle my beleeue'.[107] There was no doubt, however, about which way the people of Brussels inclined. According to Trumbull, the prevailing opinion there was that Spinola's victory was inevitable. In September, he reported that one of the forts guarding the town had already been taken by Spanish forces, which were so powerful that many were asking 'What rampartes, or humane forces are able to resiste their fury?'[108] A few days later, Trumbull reported that confidence in Spinola was so high that 'Within lesse then a moneth wee make accompt to singe Masse in Bergen'.[109] Mansfeld's attempts to attack Spinola's supply convoys, by contrast, were described as 'feeble'.[110] Looking back on the siege a month later, Trumbull conceded that even he had believed the town would fall to Spinola's troops, and that others had gone so far as to think that not only Bergen, but all of Brabant would be cleared of Dutch troops 'for all ensewinge ages'.[111] These optimistic reports were repeated in Trumbull's correspondence with friends in London[112]

Opinion in the United Provinces, as Carleton reported, could not have been more different. The passage to Bergen was 'not easy to be shutt up, or rather impossible' and the Spanish army 'could hardly haue found such another rock in the countrey to breake yourselues uppon'.[113] The attacks on the town were ineffectual, according to Carleton, and the Spanish side could not 'brag of one foote of ground wonne uppon vs since their first sitting downe there'.[114] The fighting was so one sided it sounded almost like a game for the Dutch. 'We fling plentie of Granados into your trenches ... all this, with losse of few or no liues of our men; whilest yours, hitherto, haue gotten nothing but blowes'.[115] Trumbull's and Carleton's views may have been influenced by printed propaganda spread by either side, although they do not mention this.

When the siege was finally raised by the combined forces of Mansfeld and the Dutch, forcing Spinola to retreat, opinion in the Spanish Netherlands took some time to adjust. Trumbull reported that the fires seen in the besieging camp had led to rumours that the siege had been raised, but interestingly, this was supplemented by a report that while Spinola himself had departed, he had left Cordoba behind him with four regiments of infantry to defend the trenches.[116] This mitigating report seemed to answer a similar need as those that suggested that Prague had remained in Frederick's control after the Battle of White Mountain. Such rumours offered some grounds for hope, drawing out the process of coming to terms with a significant defeat. Rather than reversing expectations in an abrupt and painful manner, such rumours allowed contemporaries to arrive at the unpalatable truth by degrees. Expectations about Spinola's imminent victory in the Spanish Netherlands, just like English expectations of Frederick's victory, were difficult to turn around once they had gathered momentum.

Rumours were not assessed by unchanging standards of credibility but became more or less believable depending on the pattern of recent events and expectations about the likely course of the future. Confidence in Spinola's eventual victory at Bergen-op-Zoom in 1622 was so high that it appeared to encourage unrelated rumours, which Carleton was quick to correct, that either Steenwijk or Deventer in the Dutch province of Overijssel had been yielded to the Spanish.[117] When the siege failed, optimism gave way to pessimism, and Trumbull seemed to be expressing a more general view when he said that Spinola's retreat meant that 'the hande begins to tourne, and the dyce are in some sorte changed'.[118] Just as Spinola's expected success had made rumours about the capture of other Dutch towns plausible, the failure of the siege seemed to encourage rumours that the Spanish army would mutiny and that Tilly had died during the siege of Mannheim.[119] When events were unfolding favourably for one side or another, it was expected that they would continue to do so, and wishful-thinking rumours were more likely to be entertained. When things were going badly, rumours of unrelated disasters were taken more seriously. The credibility of rumours was judged on the basis of the direction of recent events, even if the causal link between the rumour and the event was tenuous or non-existent.

The rumours that circulated in early 1621 that Elizabeth of Bohemia had died reveal that the links between a report and its immediate context were not always so slender. After the Battle of White Mountain, Elizabeth had been forced to flee Bohemia while heavily pregnant. It was soon rumoured that she had died in childbirth. Trumbull had heard that Elizabeth had given birth to a 'monster', and he begged the Secretary of State to 'contradict these (I hope) Romishe fictions'.[120] The rumour, which had 'flowen with a swifte wing all ouer these parts of Europe' so staggered Sir Edward Villiers when he heard it in Flanders, that he was unsure whether to continue on with his diplomatic mission to Frederick.[121] Trumbull speculated that the rumour might have been spread on purpose. The report of Elizabeth's death, it was hoped, had been raised 'to coole the heate of our intended Parlament', or to 'disharten' it.[122]

The rumours of Elizabeth's death seemed to fit the recent pattern of Protestant disasters. Carleton worried that they might be true since 'all ill newes of late dayes are too much verified'.[123] By expecting the worst, Carleton and others could psychologically cushion themselves against the impact of bad news. The credibility that recent events lent to rumours of Elizabeth's death might also have encouraged the circulation of similar rumours that James, Charles and the Duke of Brandenburg had also died.[124] It might seem that contemporaries were committing the equivalent of the 'hot hand' fallacy in which a gambler assumes that the chances of winning a current bet are affected one way or another by previous wins or losses, when in fact each bet is independent.[125] This appears to have been what was happening when rumours of Tilly's death achieved a greater degree of credibility after the relief of Bergen-op-Zoom. There was a potential link, however, between Elizabeth's supposed death in childbirth and the Battle of White Mountain, because the stress caused by her flight might have caused her to miscarry. As Carleton realised, the rumour of her death might have arisen 'vppon presumption of what is vsual to great-bellied woemen in such trauayle of body and affliction of minde'.[126] The drawing of links between rumours and events which appear at first unconnected could represent a valid attempt to assess their credibility and make sense of the pattern of events.

DELIBERATE RUMOUR-MONGERING

While these case studies allow us to confirm and extend elements of existing psychological and historical research, the spontaneous and uncontrollable model of rumour only tells part of the story. Psychologists, sociologists and historians have tended to exaggerate the extent to which rumours became distorted by the process of oral communication, and underestimate the role individuals played in deliberately spreading rumours. Popular rumours were seized upon and exploited by elites, and they created opportunities for individuals from the top to the bottom of the social scale to engage in politics and even to shape the perceptions of the King.

Many of the inaccuracies in the existing model of rumour formation can be traced to the influential experiments of Allport and Postman. There are important differences between the way these experiments were designed and the reality of how rumours were spread and scrutinised. Participants in Allport's experiments did not have an opportunity to question or clarify the descriptions that were passed on to them. The descriptions of images shown to participants were passed on in a linear 'Chinese whispers' fashion, whereas in everyday life individuals compare reports from multiple sources. The overall effect is to exaggerate the distorting effects of oral communication.[127] Perhaps the biggest difference between these experiments and the reality of how news was discussed was that the test participants did not have any stake or particular interest in the truth or falsehood of reports. In Early Stuart England, individuals who were regularly gulled by false reports could expect to be subjected to public ridicule. Sir Henry Wotton was sufficiently convinced by Tommaso Cerronio's story about a plot to assassinate James I that he sent the Italian to England, perhaps expecting hearty thanks for his efforts, but his credibility was damaged when Cerronio's story was exposed as nonsense. The false rumours surrounding the early return of Prince Charles from Spain also had consequences for those who believed them. Charles had still not returned when Simonds D'Ewes noted in his diary:

> the first rumour in England that the prince was come ... was a false rumour and yett it tooke such effect that Sr Edward Montague, latelye made Lord Montague, went in to Northamptonshire, and ther spread it, causing bonfires to bee made in severall places, and in the verye towne of Northampton, of which hee was after-wards heartilye ashamed.[128]

The consequences of spreading false rumours could be more severe than a loss of face. William Whiteway noted in his news diary that following one report of Charles's return, 'ballads were made of it, but it prooved false, the ballad-singers were sent to prison'.[129]

In general, observers were not as credulous as the examples of rumour discussed above might seem to suggest. Trumbull, Carleton and their correspondents rarely reported rumours that later turned out to be false as though they were beyond doubt at the time. In most cases, they identified uncertain reports as such and surrounded them with caveats and qualifications. They most often suspended their belief rather than committing themselves to anything. When a rumour spread that the Palatine ambassador had convinced James to recognise Frederick as the King of Bohemia, for instance, Castle told Trumbull that he would 'beleeue it shalbe so, when I heare it is done'.[130] In 1620 he told Trumbull that 'yf any of yor private freinds putt you in hope of a Parliament to be convened this wynter, you may beleeue it as I haue ever done the accomplishment of the Spanish Match – which is *cum dide scientia*' [when knowledge is spread].[131] Such sentiments demonstrated a newsletter writer's usefulness to their correspondent in sorting fact from fiction.

While the formation of rumours is usually presented as a collective process, some individuals had much more influence over it than others. Even if rumours made use of ideas that were already present in the popular mind, those who created or spread them could certainly influence the timing of an outbreak. Rumours were also much more likely to take flight if they originated from a credible source who had privileged access to information. Rumours were not infinitely malleable, and individuals could influence their form and content. Pithy constructions or memorable details tended to be retained as a rumour was repeated.[132] The designation of a Spanish fleet as a 'Catholic Armado', for instance, or the observation that it was 'as big as that of '88' tended to be repeated by successive speakers and writers even if other details were forgotten. Even after they had started to circulate, rumours could also be given greater currency and legitimacy when repeated by prominent individuals. Reports that Buckingham had poisoned James were given a fresh burst of life when MPs hinted that they were true during impeachment proceedings against the Duke in the Parliament of 1626.

Elites outwardly condemned 'vulgar' rumours, but this masked a willingness to pass them on. Trumbull sometimes used slightly disparaging terms when repeating rumour and speculation. In 1624 he wrote that 'Our criticks and curious observers' had been discussing Spanish war plans, that 'our discoursers, and contemplatyue Spirittes' had been discussing the arrival of the Duke of Neuberg in Brussels, and that 'our speculatiues' thought James could do nothing to restore the Palatinate without the help of Bethlen Gabor. By passing on the conjectures of others, Trumbull distanced himself from the act of rumour spreading while simultaneously engaging in it.

RUMOUR AND ENGLISH FOREIGN POLICY

Many of the rumours that spread more widely originated as deliberate attempts to shape the perceptions of the King. A colourful cast of foreign ambassadors, merchants, sailors, travellers and charlatans hoped to be brought before the King so that they could persuade him that the Infanta had married an alternative suitor or that the Spanish were planning to invade his kingdoms. Such startling reports offered a very direct way for relatively humble people to engage in politics at the highest level, and demonstrated that the King himself was potentially vulnerable to rumours that circulated among his less well-informed subjects.

Throughout the Spanish match negotiations, foreign ambassadors and other individuals attempted to persuade James that the Infanta had already been married. In the summer of 1622, persistent reports circulated that the Infanta had or would soon be married to the Duke of Florence rather than Charles, thus breaking the match.[33] These reports seem to have circulated widely in Italy from as early as February, but were seized on by the Venetians, who instructed their ambassador in England to pass them on.[34] Lando encouraged 'well disposed ministers' in James's court to tell the King about these rumours, but they were reluctant to anger him by spreading unwelcome and uncertain news.[35] Valaresso, Lando's replacement, reported that James had now heard of the rumours and was 'beginning to despair of the Spanish marriage'.[36] When he brought the issue up with James directly, the King exclaimed that the Spanish were 'the most rascally men in the world' if they were carrying out parallel marriage negotiations in Italy.[37] By repeating rumours that were common currency, the Venetian ambassadors could distance themselves from the accusation that they were deliberately trying to hinder the match by claiming that they were merely passing on what they had heard.

These rumours were given a new lease of life in September when 'a certaine factor belonging to one of our spanish Marchants' who claimed to have been in Spain recently 'made report that the match betweene the Infanta & the Florentyne was absolutely finished'. The man was committed to the Gatehouse by the Privy Council, and others who were thought to have passed on the rumour were questioned.[38] There is a sense that these rumours could not only damage the prospects of the match by persuading James that the Spanish were acting in bad faith, but could also provide ammunition to those who opposed the match anyway and would be encouraged to claim that there was no smoke without fire. The punishment and questioning of those who circulated rumours of a Florentine match in September 1622 suggests not only that James resented being personally misled, but also that he didn't want the rumours to circulate more widely.

Rumours of marriage negotiations between the Infanta and one of Ferdinand's sons had an even longer and more tangled history. Rumours that an

Austrian match had been concluded circulated as early as 1617, and Digby was forced to delay his embassy for Spain until the truth could be ascertained.[139] When he reached Madrid, he was told that although the Austrians had approached the Spanish over a possible match, their offer had been declined out of respect for Charles.[140] In September 1620, the Austrians again proposed that the Infanta should be married to Ferdinand's eldest son.[141] A few months later, the Venetian ambassador relayed information from his colleague in Madrid that the conclusion of the marriage was imminent.[142] It was even rumoured that Ferdinand had gone to Italy in person to meet with the Infanta.[143] Later that spring, the English ambassador in France, Sir Edward Herbert, was told that Philip III had always intended an Austrian match. When he passed this information on, James accused him of trying to undermine the match by relaying disinformation that had obviously been planted by either the French government or the pro-French faction at court, who wished to undermine the match.[144] This rumour also found its way into Chamberlain's letters, who expressed his perplexity at the difference between reports coming from France and Spain.[145] In July 1621, it was said that the Emperor was trying to 'traverse' the Spanish match, and had sent a picture of his eldest son to Spain.[146] Sir Griffin Markham, a Catholic refugee in the Spanish Netherlands who had taken part in the Bye plot in 1603, was thought to be on his way to Madrid to advance the Austrian match.[147] Since the Infanta did indeed eventually marry Ferdinand III, it is likely that these rumours were at least partly true.[148] It is also possible that the Spanish ultimately found these reports useful in their dealings with the English. As James ultimately hoped that Spain would provide military support against their Austrian Habsburg cousins to restore the Palatinate, the prospect of a rival suitor made it clear to him that the alternative to a Spanish match was an even closer alliance between Spain and Austria.

James was reportedly 'much moved' by these rumours, and in September 1621 he expressed 'great agitation and passion in his bedchamber ... swearing and declaring that everyone was betraying him and adding that he would never believe any one again'.[149] Despite Spanish denials, these rumours lingered for some time. In February 1622 a captain who had recently returned to England told James that the Austrian match had been concluded, but because his ears had been 'so often beaten' with similar reports, he did not believe them.[150] Similar rumours were still circulating at the height of Anglo-Spanish negotiations, when Charles and Buckingham were in Madrid. Beaulieu reported that allegations that the Infanta had been promised to Ferdinand's son 'much increase our doubt of their [i.e. Spanish] intentions'.[151]

Interestingly, while the representative of anti-Habsburg powers sometimes tried to sabotage the match, in some circumstances they tried to encourage the belief that it had been concluded. Although France and Venice did not wish to see England allied to their most powerful enemy, the competing priorities of

European politics sometimes produced cross-currents of rumour. As early as 1617, when formal negotiations were just opening, Carleton complained that the French ambassador was trying to sow discord between the Dutch Republic and England by suggesting that the match had nearly been concluded.[152] Later in the year, news of the conclusion of the match, which oddly enough, was supposed to have been mediated by the King of Denmark, found its way into an Italian gazetta.[153] In early 1621, the Venetian ambassador in Spain thought that rumours of the imminent conclusion of the match were being circulated in order to dissuade Louis XIII from intervening in the Valtelline for fear of provoking an Anglo-Spanish alliance against him.[154] Rumours of the conclusion of the match were reportedly spread by the Spanish in April 1624 in order to delay English war preparations.[155] Far from being the preserve of the 'vulgar multitude', rumour and misinformation were used by the diplomatic and political elite as weapons in a battle for perceptions that was played out on an international scale.

James was also assailed by sporadic reports that his putative Spanish allies were in fact preparing to invade his kingdoms. These rumours are often overlooked by historians of the period. They are indicative of wider apprehensions about Spanish intentions which formed the backdrop to domestic opposition to the Spanish match. The threat of invasion was also an additional factor for James to weigh in the balance when considering whether or not to intervene militarily in the Palatinate.

In October 1618 Thomas Lorkin reported a general 'apprehension of the Spaniards', which was provoked by the sudden disappearance of Spanish merchants from London, a lack of gunpowder, and the transportation of ordnance to Spain. Although James was not 'willing to discover [i.e. reveal] any fear', Lorkin wrote, 'wise men think he is not free from apprehension'.[156] Early in 1619, several commentators noted that a large armada was being prepared in Spain which was thought to be 'greater then that in [15]88', and Chamberlain reported that the 'Spanish preparations sounds lowde here at last'.[157] James appeared to take the threat seriously, ordering the preparation of a fleet that would eventually sail in 1620 under the command of Sir Robert Mansell, ordering an increase in the size of the Middlesex militia, and directing Lieutenants and Sheriffs to muster the trained bands in the provinces.[158] The threat appears to have been taken seriously enough for Philip to send a declaration, protesting that the fleet was intended for North Africa rather than England, but this does not appear to have completely dispelled public fears, and the atmosphere remained jittery.[159]

Fears of invasion revived in 1622, with the gathering of another Spanish fleet. These rumours, like those of an alternative match for the Infanta, were often started or reinforced by sea captains, merchants and others who had recently returned from the continent, who claimed to have witnessed preparations and who perhaps expected a reward for raising the alarm. A Scottish man had come from Spain spreading news of the fleet, but although 'everyone talked' of an invasion attempt, 'the King would noe wayes beleeve it', and the man in question was imprisoned.[160] Fear and uncertainty continued throughout the summer, with some expressing surprise that no preparations were being made to resist the fleet, and others pointing to a new commission given to Mansell to protect home waters.[161] Observers were aware that a large Spanish fleet was putting to sea, and although the Spanish ambassadors declared that it was not intended for England, some feared that James was being deceived.[162] Tensions appear to have reached a peak when the fleet finally appeared on the coast in early October. According to Castle, who was at Hampton Court, the arrival of the fleet had 'putt this Court into a great deale of businesse'. The Spanish ambassador was keen to 'free his Maiesty of all Iealoucies', insisting that it was intended to free ports in Flanders blockaded by the Dutch. In addition, Digby had written from Spain, passing on promises that 'from hence forward there shall be no shippes sent this way, but his Maiesty shall haue an account of their purpose'. These assurances succeeded in making the court 'less apprehensiue then at the first alarm', although some thought that the Spanish might divert the fleet and attack James's kingdoms at the last moment, and at one point it was said to be on the coast of Ireland.[163]

These rumours show how real the fear of sudden attack was in the years after the outbreak of the Thirty Years' War. Despite ongoing negotiations for a match – and Sir Edward Coke reminded the Parliament of 1621 that the great armada of 1588 had been dispatched while peace negotiations were still going on – mutual suspicions remained.[164] While on the surface James remained unperturbed, some thought he was inwardly troubled by reports of a possible attack, and interpreted some of his actions, such as preparing Mansell's fleet in 1619, as belying his true fears. Above all, these rumours point to the ways in which all sides could hope to provoke James's fears and shape his perceptions of foreign nations during this uncertain period.

These and other rumours could be spread for a variety of political reasons. Excited reports about James's conversion to Catholicism circulated in 1621 partly because the papal nuncio to Milan had been fed with hopes that he had been chosen to lead a delegation to England tasked with securing the King's return to the fold. The Spanish had allowed the nuncio to believe that he would be appointed to this role because they wanted to secure his support in the dispute about the Valtelline.[165] Sometimes the intended audience was rather larger. Inhabitants of the Spanish Netherlands frequently suspected that false news of the arrival of the annual Spanish treasure fleet, which carried silver from the new world to pay Spanish troops, were deliberately given out to prevent mutinies.[166] Some even suspected that news of the return of the fleet was given out in 1624 to dissuade James from setting out an English fleet to intercept it.[167]

CONCLUSION

Adam Fox has argued that rumours of Spanish invasion and internal conspiracy circulating among ordinary people in 1628 demonstrated a 'rather different and more elastic conception of what was possible in politics, let alone plausible, than is usually reckoned upon in historical discussions of political opinion'.[168] The evidence presented in this chapter suggests that much the same could be said of those at the very top of the political order, including James himself. James was assailed by reports of invasion fleets, assassination plots and alternative matches. His own diplomats and secretaries could not be trusted to provide him with impartial information. This all contributed to the uncertain and sometimes paranoid atmosphere in which information was assessed and decisions were made.

Beset by conflicting reports and biased sources, James like his subjects, had little better guide to the truth or falsehood of reports than his own hopes and prejudices. James dismissed reports that Philip III had never intended the Spanish match to go ahead on the basis that Gondomar and Digby had assured him they were false.[169] When the Venetian ambassador told him about rumours that the Spanish were negotiating a match with Ferdinand, he found James 'unwilling to believe what he did not wish and perhaps taking pleasure in deceiving himself in hoping always for the best'.[170] With no stable standards of verification, it was tempting for James to simply believe what he wanted to believe.

On occasion, rumours were spread for selfish financial reasons rather than as a political weapon. Reports about new recusancy laws in England were spread in Venice by English Catholic refugees who hoped to coax alms and pensions out of sympathetic patrons.[171] The sellers of a pamphlet titled 'A Declaration of the Catholicks of England to their King' tried to drum up business by boasting that after James had read it, he had granted a toleration of Catholicism and allowed a Mass to be said in St Paul's Cathedral.[172] Premature reports of Charles's return from Madrid in 1623 originated from an unscrupulous individual who used the pretext of spreading the good news to steal a post horse.[173] Rumours of an English victory at the Ile de Ré were spread by a Dutchman who landed in Portsmouth and wished to secure a warm welcome there, perhaps in the form of a free drink, by bearing good news.[174] These rich and diverse examples suggest that creating and spreading a rumour was far from an insignificant or futile act. Ordinary people did distort and appropriate rumour, but rather than springing up spontaneously, many rumours were started or bolstered by individuals for a wide range of political or private reasons.

James himself was not above engaging with false reports. His publication of a declaration on the dissolution of the Parliament of 1621 indicated that he increasingly felt the need to justify and explain his actions in order to prevent rumour and misinformation from circulating.[75] James also used rumours as an excuse to elicit information or to disguise the source of an accusation. In 1619, for instance, he instructed Trumbull to tell the Archdukes that 'flying reportes and rumours' that Spinola intended to attack the Palatinate had reached his ears.[76] In fact, the King had been given this information by Trumbull, Carleton and others. James told Trumbull to inform the Archdukes that he did not personally believe these reports, but would appreciate it if they could confirm or deny them. Rather than directly accusing Spinola of preparing to attack the Palatinate, James was using the existence of these rumours as a subtle way to let the Archdukes know that he was aware of the possibility of an attack, with the implication that he might make preparations to counter it. If James extracted a denial and Spinola later invaded, he could justify his own inaction in the affair by claiming the Archdukes had misled him. James was using rumours in his political manoeuvres while maintaining a public stance of ignoring them.

Political rumours were almost always a mixture of elite and popular discourse. The garbled accounts of the Thomas Overbury poisoning scandal that circulated in England and on the continent provide an interesting example of this. During his investigation of the scandal, Sir Edward Coke vaguely hinted that he had uncovered a larger popish conspiracy as great as that of 1588 or 1603. As Alastair Bellany has pointed out, this encouraged and legitimised pre-existing speculation about Catholic plotting at court.[77] Coke had an important influence on the form, content and timing of these rumours, but they were only successful because they chimed with popular conceptions. News of the conspiracy also became distorted as it travelled, and observers in Paris, Cologne and Rome were under the impression that Somerset had poisoned the late Prince Henry and had tried to murder James himself.[78] This misunderstanding was probably a consequence of the fact that while James was well known throughout Europe, most people were unlikely to have heard of Overbury. As the story of the scandal passed from person to person, any distortions which simplified the complex story of the Overbury poisoning by introducing the familiar trope of a plot against the King would be more likely to be remembered and passed around. Despite the disdainful attitude towards vulgar rumour that educated men often expressed, rumour was a means for individuals from both the top and the bottom of the political hierarchy to influence the other, and they offer us one of the few means available to describe and analyse the connections between the worlds of popular and elite politics.

There are reasons to believe that rumour and innuendo were becoming increasingly acceptable weapons of political warfare in the 1620s. A number of political manuscript tracts which presented rumours supposedly circulating among the common people were written during this period.[79] Frequent parliamentary sessions during this period provided opportunities to exploit and legitimise popular reports.[180] In the Parliament of 1626, Samuel Turner attempted to give flesh to abstract debates about grievances by raising six accusations against the Duke of Buckingham, all of which were based on 'common fame'. These included charges that Buckingham protected Catholics and was responsible for the defeat at Cadiz.[181] Common rumours of this kind were sufficiently authoritative to serve as accusations against the Duke, even though (or because) supporting evidence was difficult to produce. Buckingham defended himself by arguing that rumours were 'too subtle [i.e. insubstantial] ... for me to contest with ... but as fame is subtill, soe its often and especiallie in accusations, false'.[182] The difficulty of contending with rumours was doubtless one of the things that made them such appealing political weapons. Buckingham may also have worried that some mud would eventually stick if enough was thrown, and the repetition of rumours against him would lead observers to assume that some variation of the story must be true. While not all of these accusations were convincing, other charges based on common rumours, such as that Buckingham had poisoned James, were hinted at in the later impeachment proceedings against him. Whether or not Buckingham's enemies believed these charges to be true remains a mystery, but either way, it is significant that they were willing to make political use of a mode of discourse that was almost universally associated with the seditious multitude. The encouragement and exploitation of common rumours was to reach its height during the Long Parliament, when at critical moments, Pym and his allies sought to excite popular fears by evoking the threat of internal Catholic conspiracy and foreign invasion.[183]

NOTES

1 John Castle to William Trumbull, 6 December 1622, Add. 72276, fol. 19r.

2 Castle to Trumbull, 2 August 1621, Add. 72275, fol. 119r.

3 Giles Mompesson to Trumbull, 24 April 1623, Add. 72365, fol. 106r.

4 Trumbull to James Hay, Viscount Doncaster, 21 September/1 October 1620, Eg. 2593, fol. 230r.

5 John Beaulieu to Trumbull, 11 February 1620, Add. 72253, fol. 142r.

6 Beaulieu to Trumbull, 7 December 1620, Add. 72253, fol. 165r.

7 Thomas Cogswell, *The Blessed Revolution: English Politics and the Coming of War, 1621–1624* (Cambridge, 1989), pp. 46–7.

8 See Francis Bacon, 'Of fame' in James Spedding (ed.), *The Works of Francis Bacon* vol. XII (London, 1860), pp. 283–4.

9 See Virgil's *Aeneid*, book IV. For a detailed investigation of the representation of rumour in ancient and early modern literature, see Philip Hardie, *Rumour and Renown* (Cambridge, 2012).

10 Francis Bacon, 'Of seditions and troubles' in Spedding (ed.), *Works of Francis Bacon* vol. XII, pp. 123–30.

11 *Henry IV Part II* (I.i.18–23).

12 See in particular Geoffrey Elton, *Policy and Police* (Cambridge, 1972), ch. 2; Keith Thomas, *Religion and the Decline of Magic* (London, 1971), pp. 478–83.

13 David Cressy, *Dangerous Talk: Scandalous, Seditious, and Treasonable Speech in Pre-Modern England* (Oxford, 2010), pp. 265–7.

14 Gordon Allport and Leo Postman, *The Psychology of Rumor* (New York, 1947).

15 *Ibid.*, pp. 75, 86. For criticisms of the experiments of Allport and Postman, see Tamotsu Shibutani, *Improvised News: a Sociological Study of Rumor* (New York, 1966), pp. 5–7. For a more recent study of the phenomenon of rumour, see Jean-Nöel Kapferer, *Rumors: Uses, Interpretations and Images* (New Brunswick, 1990).

16 Allport and Postman, *Psychology of Rumor*, pp. 99–156.

17 Shibutani, *Improvised News*, p. 199.

18 Adam Fox, 'Rumour, news and popular opinion in Elizabethan and early Stuart England', *The Historical Journal* 30:3 (1997), p. 597.

19 Ethan Shagan, 'Rumours and popular politics in the reign of Henry VIII', in Tim Harris, (ed.), *The Politics of the Excluded, c. 1500–1850* (New York, 2001), pp. 30–1, 38.

20 *Ibid.*

21 *Ibid.*, p. 35.

22 Beaulieu to Trumbull, 15 September 1612, Downshire vol. III, p. 368.

23 Joseph Mead to Martin Stuteville, 24 March 1621, Harl. 389, fol. 41r. Ley's custody of the great seal was only temporary.

24 Mead to Stuteville, 10 February 1621, Harl. 389, fol. 14v.

25 Newsletter, [?] April 1621, Harl. 389, fol. 45r.

26 Owen Wynn to John Wynn, 3 September 1623, NLW 9058E/1137.

27 See for instance the report on Sir Henry Montague in the Diary of Walter Yonge, Add. 28032, fol. 39v, or Chamberlain's report on 'Sir [Edward] Mallerie' in Chamberlain to Carleton, 1 December 1621, McClure vol. II, p. 413.

28 Mead to Stuteville, 14 July 1621, Harl. 389, fol. 108v. In fact, Price was born in Shrewsbury. Both reports were true.

29 Newsletter from London, 23 February 1621, Harl. 389, fol. 19r.

30 Newsletter from London, 2 March 1621, Harl. 389, fol. 28v; Extract from a letter of Dr Burges to [Mead], 26 February 1621, Harl. 389, fol. 24r.

31 For the distorting effect of distance, see Adam Fox, *Oral and Literate Culture in England, 1500 – 1700* (Oxford, 2001), p. 355.

32 Beaulieu to Trumbull, 10 September 1619, Add. 72253, 55r.

33 Mead to Stuteville, 24 February 1621, Harl. 389, fol. 21r.

34 John Holles to Lord Norris, 9 April 1617, in P. R. Seddon (ed.), *Letters of John Holles 1587–1637*, vol. I, (Thoroton Society Record Series vol. 31, 1975), p. 156. Much of the news – that the Earl of Montgomery was a Privy Councillor, that William Compton was made

Earl of Northampton, and John Digby made Viscount Sherborne, was not so much inaccurate as premature.

35 Mead to Stuteville, 24 February 1621, Harl. 389, fol. 21r.

36 Mead to Stuteville, 14 July 1621, Harl. 389, fol. 108r.

37 Fulgenzio Micanzo to William Cavendish, 17 June 1616, in Roberto Ferrini (ed.), *Lettere a William Cavendish* (Rome, 1987), p. 57.

38 Micanzo to Cavendish, 12 January 1618, in Ferrini (ed.), *Lettere*, p. 74.

39 For modern examples of this type of rumour, see Kapferer, *Rumors*, p. 221.

40 Chamberlain to Carleton, 21 November 1618, McClure vol. II, p. 185.

41 Chamberlain to Carleton, 10 April 1619, McClure vol. II, p. 228.

42 Carleton to Trumbull, 1 July 1624, Add. 72274, fol. 104r.

43 John Luntius to Trumbull, 8 September 1616, Downshire vol. V, p. 587. For the murder of d'Ancre, see Sharon Kettering, *Power and Reputation at the Court of Louis XIII: The career of Charles d'Albert, duc de Luynes (1578–1621)* (Manchester, 2008), pp. 76–81.

44 David Underdown (ed.), *William Whiteway of Dorchester: His Diary 1618 to 1635* (Dorset Record Society 12, 1991), p. 29; Trumbull to [Carleton], 12/22 September 1621, SP 77/14, fol. 461r.

45 Trumbull to [Robert Naunton], 25 March 1619 (o.s.), Harl. 1581, fol. 152r–v; Trumbull to Buckingham (copy), 12/22 April 1619, Add. 72379, fol. 40r. Carleton was directed to contradict these reports abroad. See Naunton to Carleton, 1 April 1619, CSPD 1619–23 (1858), p. 32.

46 Trumbull to [Naunton], 25 March 1619 (o.s.), Harl. 1581, fol. 152r–v.

47 Naunton to Carleton, 1 April 1619, CSPD 1619–23 (1858), p. 32. An apprentice, Matthew Mason, was punished for spreading stories of a portent which signified dramatic changes in the kingdom, which may have fed in to these rumours. See Meeting of the Privy Council, 11 April 1619, APC vol. 36: 1618–19, p. 419; 'A warrant to the Treasurer of Bridwell', 30 April 1619, APC vol. 36: 1618–19, p. 437.

48 Trumbull to James Hay, Earl of Doncaster, 10/20 July 1619, Eg. 2592, fol. 218r.

49 Carleton Jnr. to Carleton, 13 March 1623 (n.s.), SP 84/111, fol. 159r.

50 Chamberlain to Carleton, 10 April 1618, McClure vol. II, p. 155.

51 Beaulieu to Puckering, 31 March 1630, Harl. 7010, fol. 151r.

52 Castle to Trumbull, 30 July 1624, Add. 72276, fol. 111r.

53 Beaulieu to Trumbull, 3 August 1620, Add. 72253, fol. 136r.

54 Chamberlain to Carleton, 23 August 1619, SP 14/110, fol. 35r.

55 Castle to Trumbull, 18 September 1623, Add. 72276, fol. 60r.

56 Beaulieu to Trumbull, 6 February 1624, Add. 72255, fol. 115r.

57 Castle to Bridgewater, 3 September 1640, EL 7857.

58 Trumbull to Secretary of State, 27 January/6 February 1621, SP 77/14, fol. 274v.

59 Beaulieu to Trumbull, 7 November 1623, Add. 72255, fol. 89r.

60 Cogswell, *Blessed Revolution*, p. 34. For persistent rumours of James's conversion circu-

lating on the continent, see Ferrini (ed.), *Lettere, passim.* Contemporary prophesies alluded to a possible change in religion. See Alastair Bellany and Andrew McRae (eds), 'If 88 be past then thrive', 'Early Stuart libels: an edition of poetry from manuscript sources', *Early Modern Literary Studies Text Series I* (2005) http://purl.oclc.org/emls/texts/libels (accessed 29 July 2012). English Catholics may have been responsible for spreading some of these rumours on the continent. See Michael Questier, *Stuart Dynastic Policy and Religious Politics, 1621–1625* (Cambridge, 2009), p. 25.

61 Mead to Stuteville, 28 September 1622, Harl. 389, fol. 233r.

62 Newsletter from London, 8 March 1622, Harl. 389, fol. 157r; James Craigie (ed.), *The Poems of James VI of Scotland* (Edinburgh, 1958), p. 189.

63 Girolamo Lando to the Doge and Senate, 21 May 1621, CSPV vol. XVII, p. 53; Simon Digby to Trumbull, 21 November 1621 (o.s.), Add. 72286, fols. 56v–7r; John Digby, Earl of Bristol to Trumbull, 4 January 1622, Add. 72285, fol. 75v; Beaulieu to Trumbull, 11 October 1622, Add. 72254, fol. 161v.

64 Simon Digby to Trumbull, 21 November 1621 (o.s.), Add. 72286, fols. 56v–57r.

65 London newsletter, 17 May 1622, Harl. 389, fol. 190v. See also 'Extract of "A moste true Relation", 1621', Harl. 295, fol. 294r.

66 Carleton to Walter Aston, 17/27 November 1623, Add. 36446, fol. 232r.

67 Francis Crane to Trumbull, 5 October 1622, Add. 72364, fol. 48r.

68 Trumbull to Secretary of State, 5/15 January 1621, SP 77/14, fols. 264v–5r.

69 Brendan Dooley, 'News and doubt in early modern culture or, are we having a public sphere yet?', in Brendan Dooley and Sabrina Baron (eds), *The Politics of Information in Early Modern Europe* (London, 2001), p. 276; Mark Knights, *Representation and Misrepresentation in Later Stuart Britain: Partisanship and Political Culture* (Oxford, 2004).

70 John Wolley to Trumbull, 13 October 1624, Add. 72331, fol. 33v.

71 Trumbull to Secretary of State, 28 September 1620 (o.s.), SP 77/14, fol. 220r–v.

72 John Chamberlain to Dudley Carleton, 7 March 1618, McClure vol. II, p. 147. See also Wolley to Trumbull, 10 October 1623, Add. 72330, fol. 63r.

73 Wolley to Trumbull, 22 October 1624, Add. 72331, fol. 35v.

74 See for instance Mary Anne Everett Green (ed.), *Diary of John Rous* (Camden 1st Series, vol. 66, 1856); Diary of Walter Yonge, Add. 28032.

75 Simon Digby to Trumbull, 14 July 1621 (o.s.), Add. 72286, fol. 18v; Mead to Stuteville, 9 June 1621, Thomas Birch (ed.), *The Court and Times of James I* vol. II (London, 1849), p. 258.

76 Carleton to Trumbull, 1 August 1622 (n.s.), Add. 72273, fol. 44r; Trumbull to George Calvert, 2/12 November 1622, SP 77/15, fol. 370r; Trumbull to Secretary of State, 31 December 1623 (o.s.), SP 77/16, fol. 383r; Trumbull to Edward Conway, [?] February 1625, SP 77/18, fol. 23r.

77 See Shibutani, *Improvised News*, pp. 192–3. The size of Spinola's army in 1620 was thought to have been deliberately exaggerated. See Trumbull to Secretary of State, 10 August 1620, SP 77/14, fol. 193v–r; Carleton to Naunton, 23 August 1620, SP 84/96, fol. 136r.

78 Carleton to Trumbull, 8 April 1620, Add. 72271, fol. 84r.

79 Ronald Hutton, *Debates in Stuart History* (Basingstoke, 2004), p. 42.

80 Underdown (ed.), *William Whiteway*, pp. 50, 53. For the Battle of Stadtlohn, see Geoffrey Parker, *The Thirty Years War* (London, 1987), p. 68.

81 Carleton to Trumbull, 12/22 May 1622, Add. 72273, fol. 24r.

82 For the Battle of White Mountain, see Parker, *Thirty Years' War*, pp. 55–61; Peter H. Wilson, *Europe's Tragedy: A History of the Thirty Years' War* (London, 2009), pp. 284–307.

83 The dislocations of war appear to have made it difficult to send posts across Germany during this period, and this almost certainly created the conditions in which false rumours about the battle could flourish. By 1 December, no posts had arrived from Francis Nethersole in Prague for the previous three weeks. See Locke to Trumbull, 1 December 1620, Add. 72299, fol. 36r.

84 J. O. Halliwell (ed.), *The Autobiography and Correspondence of Sir Simonds D'Ewes*, vol. I (1845), p. 154.

85 Trumbull to Aston, 18/28 November 1620, Add. 36444, fol. 233v.

86 Trumbull to [Carleton], 8 December 1620 (n.s.), SP 77/14, fol. 247r.

87 Beaulieu to Trumbull, 30 November 1620, Add. 72253, fol. 161r. This letter may have been written in the brief interval between the loss of the battle and Frederick's escape from Prague.

88 Naunton to Trumbull, 1 December 1620, Add. 72304, fol. 87r; the Earl of Leicester to the Countess of Leicester, 26 November 1620, William A. Shaw and G. Dyfnallt Owen (eds), *Report on the Manuscripts of the Viscount De L'Isle*, HMC 77, v (London, 1962), p. 422.

89 Mead to Stuteville, 3 February 1621, Harl. 389, fol. 9r–v. Prague was indeed well fortified, and Frederick's army was largely intact; his final defeat was largely due to a collapse in morale. See Wilson, *Europe's Tragedy*, p. 306. It should also be remembered that the war had very much gone against Ferdinand until 1620 – Vienna was besieged twice. See Parker, *Thirty Years War*, pp. 51–2, 55–6.

90 Beaulieu to Trumbull, 7 December 1620, Add. 72253, fol. 165r.

91 *Ibid.*

92 Underdown (ed.), *William Whiteway*, pp. 31–2. See also Mead to Stuteville, 9 February 1621, Harl. 389, fol. 11r; Dr Meddus to Mead, 16 March 1621, Harl. 389, fol. 27v.

93 Newsletter, 16 March 1621, Harl. 389, fol. 27v.

94 William Wynn to John Wynn, 18 February 1621, NLW 9057E/938; newsletter from London, 23 February 1621, Harl. 389, fol. 18v

95 Mead to Stuteville, 24 February 1621, Harl. 389, fol. 21r.

96 Trumbull to [Carleton], 16/26 January 1624, SP 77/17, fol. 11v.

97 For the campaign in 1622, see Parker, *Thirty Years War*, pp. 64–8.

98 For the battles of Wimpfen and Hochst, see William P. Guthrie, *Battles of the Thirty Years' War: from White Mountain to Nordlingen, 1618–35* (Westport, (CT), 2002), pp. 95–9.

99 Parker, *Thirty Years War*, pp. 67–8.

100 Trumbull to Carleton, 23 August 1622 (n.s.), SP 77/15, fol. 263r.

101 Digby to Trumbull, 16 September 1622 (o.s.), Add. 72285, fol. 83r.

102 Carleton to Trumbull, 29 September 1622 (o.s.), Add. 72273, fol. 60r.

103 *Ibid.*, fol. 60v.

104 *Ibid.*, fols. 60v–1r.

105 Carleton to Trumbull, 5 September 1622 (n.s.), Add. 72273, fol. 65r.

106 For the siege of Berghen, see Wilson, *Europe's Tragedy*, p. 339.

107 Wolley to Trumbull Jnr., 25 August/4 September 1622, Add. 72330, fol. 22r.

108 Trumbull to [Carleton], 3/13 September 1622, SP 77/15, fol. 271r.

109 Trumbull to [Carleton], 7/17 September 1622, SP 77/15, fol. 280r.

110 Trumbull to [?], 17/27 September 1622, SP 77/15, fol. 295r.

111 Trumbull to [Carleton], 1/11 October 1622, SP 77/15, fol. 321r.

112 Castle to Trumbull, 24 September 1622, Add. 72276, fol. 11v.

113 Carleton to Trumbull, 8/18 August 1622, Add. 72273, fol. 56v.

114 Carleton to Trumbull, 12 September 1622 (n.s.), Add. 72273, fol. 71v.

115 Carleton to Trumbull, 3 October 1622 (n.s.), Add. 72273, fol. 79r–v.

116 Trumbull to Calvert, 26 September 1622, SP 77/15, fol. 315r–v; Trumbull to [Carleton], 27 September/4 October 1622, SP 77/15, fols. 313v–4r.

117 Trumbull to [Carleton], 17/27 September 1622, SP 77/15, fol. 295; Carleton to Trumbull, 3 October 1622 (n.s.), Add. 72273, fol. 79r–v.

118 Trumbull to [Carleton], 1/11 October 1622, SP 77/15, fols. 320v–1r.

119 Trumbull to Calvert, 20/30 October 1622, SP 77/15, fol. 345r. Some isolated mutinies did occur – see Trumbull to [Carleton], 10/20 December 1622, SP 77/15, fol. 431r; Trumbull to Calvert, 20/30 October 1622, SP 77/15, fol. 345r.

120 Trumbull to Secretary of State, 5/15 January 1621, SP 77/14, fol. 264r.

121 Trumbull to Secretary of State, 18/28 January 1621, SP 77/14, fol. 269r; Lockyer, *Buckingham*, p. 86. For Villiers's mission, see Arthur White, 'Suspension of Arms: Anglo-Spanish Mediation in the Thirty Years' War, 1621–25' (PhD, Tulane University, 1978), pp. 149–51.

122 Trumbull to Carleton, 5 January 1621 (n.s.), SP 84/98, fol. 137r; Trumbull to Carleton, 5/15 January 1621, SP 84/99, fol. 16r.

123 Carleton to Trumbull, 9 January 1621, Add. 72272, fol. 1v.

124 Trumbull to Carleton, 3/13 January 1621, SP 84/99, fol. 11v; Trumbull to Aston, 6/26 January 1621, Add. 36445, fol. 1v.

125 For the 'hot hand' fallacy, see Thomas Gilovich, *How We Know What Isn't So* (New York, 1991), pp. 11–16.

126 Carleton to Trumbull, 9 January 1621, Add. 72272, fol. 1r.

127 The results of larger studies have sometimes contradicted and sometimes supported Allport's and Postman's conclusions. See M. L. De Fleur, 'Mass communication and the study of rumor', *Sociological Inquiry* 32 (1962), pp. 51–70.

128 Elisabeth Bourcier (ed.), *The Diary of Sir Simonds D'Ewes, 1622–1624* (Paris, 1974), pp. 158–9.

129 Underdown (ed.), *William Whiteway*, p. 54. The false alarms with which people had been deluded even affected their behaviour when Charles really did return. Simonds D'Ewes recorded that when the Prince landed, 'in all places in the Kingdome distant from London, few or noe bonefires weere made, in regarde they had been deluded before, and soe beleeved not now', an instance of 'rumour fatigue' similar to that which developed in response to Spanish invasion scares later in the decade. See Bourcier (ed.), *Diary of Sir Simonds D'Ewes*, pp. 162–3.

130 Castle to Trumbull, 11 February 1620, Add. 72275, fol. 97r.

131 Castle to Trumbull, 21 October 1620, Add. 72275, fol. 108r.

132 Thomas Cogswell demonstrated that well-turned phrases derived from a propaganda pamphlet about the ill-fated Ile de Ré expedition in 1627 were unconsciously repeated by observers. Thomas Cogswell, 'The people's love: The Duke of Buckingham and popularity', in Thomas Cogswell, Richard Cust and Peter Lake (eds), *Politics, Religion and Popularity* (Cambridge, 2002), p. 230.

133 London newsletter, 12 July 1622, Harl. 389, fol. 214r; Mead to Stuteville, 13 July 1622, Harl. 389, fol. 217r.

134 Micanzo to Cavendish, [?] February 1622, Ferrini (ed.), *Lettere*, p. 150; Micanzo to Cavendish, 15 July 1622, *Lettere*, pp. 192–3; Beaulieu to Trumbull, 28 June 1622, Add. 72254, fol. 122r; Locke to Mead, 12 July 1622, Birch (ed.), *Court and Times*, p. 321; Locke to Carleton, 13 July 1622, CSPD 1619–23 (1858), p. 424.

135 Lando to the Doge and Senate, 18 February 1622, CSPV vol. XVII, p. 241.

136 Valaresso to the Doge and Senate, 15 July 1622, CSPV vol. XVII, p. 371.

137 Valaresso to the Doge and Senate, 24 July 1622, CSPV vol. XVII, pp. 379–80.

138 Castle to Trumbull, 20 September 1622, Add. 72276, fol. 9r. See also Beaulieu to Trumbull, 20 September 1622, Add. 72254, fol. 154r; Locke to Carleton, 11 September 1622, CSPD 1619–23 (1858), p. 446.

139 Trumbull to Ralph Winwood, 27 August 1617, Downshire vol. VI, p. 268; Trumbull to Winwood, 26 September 1617, Downshire vol. VI, p. 296; John Bennet to Trumbull, 21 August 1617, Downshire vol. VI, p. 259; Thomas Locke to Trumbull, 14 August 1617, Downshire vol. VI, p. 255.

140 Beaulieu to Trumbull, 21 October 1617, Downshire vol. VI, p. 314.

141 S. R. Gardiner, *History of England from the Accession of James I to the Outbreak of the Civil War, 1603–42* vol. III (London, 1883), p. 377.

142 Beaulieu to Trumbull, 8 February 1621, Add. 72254, fol. 11v.

143 Diary of Walter Yonge, Add. 28032, fol. 40r.

144 Christian Henneke, 'The Art of Diplomacy under the Early Stuarts, 1603–42' (PhD, University of Virginia, 1999), pp. 140–2. This is another indication that James was aware of the ways in which the diplomatic information he was fed might be distorted.

145 Chamberlain to Carleton, 23 April, 1621, McClure, vol. II, pp. 365–6.

146 Trumbull to [Carleton], 3/13 July 1621, SP 77/14, fol. 373r.

147 Trumbull to [Carleton], 10/20 August 1621, SP 77/14, fol. 423r.

148 The Emperor certainly approached the Spanish about a marriage alliance in the autumn of 1624, and may have done so earlier. See J. H. Elliott, *The Count-Duke of Olivares: The Statesman in an age of decline* (London, 1986), p. 218.

149 Lando to the Doge and Senate, 17 September 1621, CSPV vol. XVII, pp. 132–3.

150 Beaulieu to Trumbull, 22 February 1622, Add. 72254, fol. 91r. See also George Roberts (ed.), *The Diary of Walter Yonge* (Camden 1st Series, vol. 41, 1848), p. 53.

151 Beaulieu to Trumbull, 27 June 1623, Add. 72255, 53v.

152 Carleton to Winwood, 6/16 February 1617, SP 84/76, fols. 132r–4r. See also Albert Marshall, 'Sir Dudley Carleton and English Diplomacy in the United Provinces, 1616–1628' (PhD, Rutgers University, 1978), p. 69.

153 News from Antwerp, 4 December 1617, Downshire vol. VI, p. 332.

154 Corner to the Doge and Senate, 19 February 1621, CSPV vol. XVI (1619–21), p. 569. During the winter of 1621–22 there were rumours in France that an Anglo-Spanish invasion fleet was on its way. See A. Moote, *Louis XIII, the Just* (London, 1989), p. 134.

155 'An Extract out of an Advertisement received 21 April 1624', *Calendar or State Papers Ireland*, James I, vol. 5: 1615–25, p. 486.

156 Thomas Lorkin to Thomas Puckering, 20 October 1618, in Birch (ed.), *Court and Times* vol. II, p. 93.

157 Underdown (ed.), *William Whiteway*, p. 25; Lorkin to Puckering, 26 January 1619, in Birch (ed.), *Court and Times* vol. II, p. 128; Chamberlain to Carleton, 16 January 1619, McClure vol. II, p. 208. For invasion scares during the Elizabethan period after 1588, see Paul E. J. Hammer, *Elizabeth's Wars* (Basingstoke, 2003), pp. 215–16 and *passim*.

158 Beaulieu to Trumbull, 28 January 1619, Add. 72253, fol. 6r; Beaulieu to Trumbull, 18 February 1619, Add. 72253, fol. 14r.

159 Lorkin to Puckering, 16 February 1619, in Birch (ed.), *Court and Times* vol. II, p. 137.

160 Bourcier (ed.), *Diary of Sir Simonds D'Ewes*, p. 67. Locke to Trumbull, 29 March 1622, Add. 72299, fol. 67r; Locke to Carleton, 30 March 1622, CSPD 1619–23 (1858), p. 366.

161 Roberts (ed.), *Diary of Walter Yonge*, p. 58; Castle to Trumbull, 9 August 1622, Add. 72276, fol. 3r–v.

162 Francis Nethersole to Carleton, 28 September 1622, CSPD 1619–23 (1858), p. 451.

163 Castle to Trumbull, 3 October 1622, Add. 72276, fol. 13r–v; Beaulieu to Trumbull, 4 October 1622, Add. 72254, fol. 160v; Beaulieu to Trumbull, 11 October 1622, Add. 72254, fol. 161v.

164 Wallace Notestein, Frances Relf and Hartley Simpson (eds), *Commons Debates 1621* vol. III (London, 1935), pp. 466–7.

165 Giacomo Vendramin, Venetian Resident at Milan, to the Doge and Senate, 17 November 1621, CSPV vol. XVII, p. 165.

166 Trumbull to [Thomas Edmondes], 12 October 1609, Downshire vol. II, p. 152; Trumbull to Aston, 20 June 1624, Add. 36447, fol. 104r. John Throckmorton reported similar rumours about English troops in Dutch pay. See John Throckmorton to Viscount Lisle, 4 February 1616, in Shaw and Owen (eds), *Manuscripts of the Viscount De L'Isle*, p. 394.

167 Valaresso to the Doge and Senate, 14 June 1624, CSPV vol. XVIII, p. 344.

168 Fox, 'Rumour, news and popular opinion', p. 616. These rumours are also discussed in Cressy, *Dangerous Talk*, pp. 136–7.

169 Lando to the Doge and Senate, 25 June 1621, CSPV vol. XVII, p. 72.

170 Valaresso to the Doge and Senate, 24 July 1622, CSPV vol. XVII, pp. 379–80.

171 Isaac Wake's interview with the Doge, 13 January 1625, CSPV vol. XVIII, p. 543.

172 Mead to Stuteville, 7 July 1621, Harl. 389, fol. 105r.

173 Holles to the Earl of Somerset, 16 September 1623, in Seddon (ed.), *Letters of John Holles*, p. 282.

174 Beaulieu to Puckering, 21 August 1627, Harl. 7010, fol. 30r.

175 See *His Maiesties declaration, touching the procee[d]ings in the late assemblie and conuention of Parliament* (1621).

176 Naunton to Trumbull, 17 September 1619, Add. 72304, fol. 41r; Conway and Weston to Secretary of State, 22 July 1620, SP 77/14, fols. 163r–4r.

177 Alastair Bellany, *The Politics of Court Scandal in Early Modern England: News Culture and the Overbury Affair, 1603–1660* (Cambridge, 2002), p. 183.

178 De Gueretin to Trumbull, 22 January 1616, Downshire vol. V, p. 408; Henry Bilderbeck to Trumbull, 24 January 1616, Downshire vol. V, p. 409; 'News from Rome', 6 January–5 February 1616, Downshire vol. V, pp. 389–40. See also Micanzo to Cavendish, 17 June 1616, in Ferrini (ed.), *Lettere*, p. 57.

179 See 'Tom Tell Troth or a Free Discourse touchinge the Murmurs of the tyme directed to his Maiestie by way of humble advertisement', Bodleian MS. Tanner 73, fols. 199r–204r; 'The Teares of the oppressed people of England', 1623, Bodleian MS. Tanner 73, fol. 304r–v. Anonymous letter to James, Harl. 1581, fols. 395r–397r. 'O Blessed King that Heares the Poore', Royal 18 A. xxxii, along with James's own 'The wiper of the Peoples teares', 'Early Stuart libels: an edition of poetry from manuscript sources', Alastair Bellany and Andrew McRae (eds), *Early Modern Literary Studies Text Series I* (2005), http://purl.oclc.org/emls/texts/libels (accessed 29 July 2012), were intended to answer some of the popular fears and complaints expressed through these rumours. For an earlier example of this genre, see 'Aduertisements of a Loiall subiect to his Gratious Soueraigne draun from obseruacons of the peoples speeches written by an unknown Author in Anno 1603', Harl. 35, fols. 46or–62v. For a later one, see 'Obseruations on the generall Murmurations, theire reasons, and Votes of the most and best affected of your Maiesties Subiectes', Sheffield Archives, Str P 40/91.

180 The Parliament of 1614, of course, had been undermined by rumours of parliamentary 'undertaking'. See Stephen Clucas and Rosalind Davies, *The Crisis of 1614 and the Addled Parliament* (Aldershot, 2003), p. 5.

181 'Queries against the Duke of Buckingham, grounded on public fame, and delivered into the House of Commons by Dr. Turner', [11 March] 1626, SP 16/22, fol. 99r.

182 'Notes of a speech or personal declaration made or intended to be made in the House of Lords', [May 1626], SP 16/524, fol.31r.

183 Edward Hyde, Earl of Clarendon, *History of the Rebellion* vol. I (Oxford, 1888), p. 327.

Chapter 4

Rumour in court politics

INTRODUCTION

Many of the rumours that circulated around the kingdom began life as attempts to manipulate the perceptions of the King. Occasions on which individuals tried to shape the King's policies with dramatic reports about the Spanish match or the threat of invasion were comparatively rare, however. What role did more routine rumours about goings on at court play in politics, and what role, if any, did observers at the periphery play in shaping day-to-day politics at the centre? A consideration of these issues requires a closer analysis of one of the most important forums in which rumours were fomented and used as political weapons, the court.

The court has been relatively overlooked compared to the attention historians have lavished on Parliament.[1] Much of the relevant historiography has in one way or another explored the relationship between the court and other political arenas rather than investigating it in its own right.[2] Historians who have studied the court exclusively have tended to analyse either the broad ways in which its personnel and organisation shifted between the reigns of James I and Charles I, or the specific details of individual courtiers' lives and political battles.[3] This chapter will take a different approach by analysing the role that news and rumour played in shaping political reality at court.

The court was the source of news about a wide range of topics, including reports about the behaviour of the King, his ministers and foreign diplomats, news of Star Chamber trials and court scandals, as well as foreign news. While these topics frequently punctuated and sometimes monopolised the news, however, the 'who's up and who's down' of court appointments and demotions were the mainstay of political discussion. While 'matter of state' could extend to foreign policy or constitutional and religious issues, for court-watchers like John Holles it had a slightly less lofty definition: 'what factions be up, what down, the reasons thereof, their references, their aspects, what forrein feeding they have, what domestik', and such news was 'courtiers merchandise'.[4] Such information was not just of interest to those engaged in the incessant jockeying for patronage and office at the centre. Provincial observers also filled their newsletters and diaries with reports about court appointments.[5] The rise or fall of an individual courtier could alter the balance of factions and signal changes in royal policy, with consequences that would be felt well beyond the court. These reports also had a more practical and immediate significance for ambitious diplomats or members of the provincial elite, who needed to identify the most influential patrons to help them secure the central or local offices they sought.

One of the problems that historians have faced in trying to reconstruct court politics is that courtiers often had little need or inclination to write down reports about court affairs, particularly if they were politically dangerous. The best and most voluminous material for uncovering this largely oral arena are the newsletters written by relatively minor figures at court to friends in the provinces, and particularly to diplomats abroad. Agents and ambassadors like William Trumbull and Sir Dudley Carleton were themselves engaged in the quest for office at home, and in many ways can be used by historians as proxies for the much larger number of courtiers in England who left relatively little evidence of their activities. The precise limits of the court have always been difficult to pin down, because it encompassed an ill-defined and shifting body of councillors, bureaucrats and suitors.[6] The engagement in court politics of diplomats who knew many of the leading courtiers personally, and had their own friends and enemies around the King, indicates that the borders of the court effectively extended overseas.

Newsletters written to diplomats and others from court often contained reports that individuals had been, or would soon be, elevated to profitable positions, or that they had been, or would soon be, disgraced. A flavour of this sort of rumour is given by the newsletter writer John Chamberlain, who wrote in 1621 that:

> All the last weeke Sir Richard Weston was Secretarie (as far as common fame could make him) insomuch that yt was saide not to be in dooing, but don, but now the report cooles again and he is yet where he was as likewise Sir John Suckling, who was in all haste to be chauncellor of the Exchequer.[7]

This chapter will examine the ways in which these rumours shaped political reality at court. As we shall see, false reports about appointments could have a self-fulfilling potential, and could improve a courtier's prospects of promotion, while reports of their imminent disgrace could make their fall from power all the more likely. While some of them appear to have been spread deliberately, others grew out of the same processes of mishearing, wishful thinking and false inference as other rumours. These reports can tell us much about the role of perceptions and 'outward shewes' in court politics, as well as the ways in which relatively lowly courtiers could influence the King's decisions. Successful courtiers needed to harness both the court 'voice' and the perceptions of the King, particularly when the former could influence the latter. In order to examine these rumours, however, it is important to understand the uncertain political atmosphere that made them plausible during the later years of James's reign.

THE UNCERTAINTIES OF COURT POLITICS

Seemingly unlikely rumours about promotions and demotions flourished during the latter part of James's reign in large part because his court was a particularly unpredictable political arena. Observers struggled to explain the factionalism and instability that characterised the 1610s and 1620s. A verse poem written around 1623, 'Fortunes wheele' captures the sense of bewilderment many felt when looking back over the reign. The author charts the spectacular rise and fall of men like the Earls of Somerset and Suffolk, Sir Edward Coke, Sir Thomas Lake, Sir Francis Bacon, Sir Robert Naunton, Sir Henry Yelverton and others, punctuating every dramatic reversal with the refrain 'Fortunes wheele, is quicklie turnde aboute'.[8] John Chamberlain expressed a similar sentiment in 1620, when he noted the large number of senior figures demoted and in many cases imprisoned in recent years. It seemed to him as though 'we live of late under some rolling planet', as he wrote,

> for yt is observed that in lesse than five yeares most of our principall officers have ben displaced or disgraced, as a Lord Chauncellor, a Lord Treasurer, a Lord Chamberlain, a Lord Admirall, a master of the horse, a secretarie, a master of the wards, a Lord Cheife Justice and an Atturny generall.[9]

The high turnover of ministers during the later years of James's reign contrasts with the relative continuity of personnel under Elizabeth. While historians once thought that Elizabeth's court was a place of intense rivalry, it has more recently been argued that her ministers were more often divided against the Queen than among themselves.[10] The relative ideological unanimity of her inner circle, at least until the 1590s, meant that ministers rarely tried to unseat factional rivals.[11] Elizabeth was loyal to her councillors, and men like Burghley, Walsingham and Hatton died in office.[12] This relative stability continued during the early part of James's reign in England, with Robert Cecil and other Elizabethan ministers remaining in power. Factionalism was also much less intense under James's successor. Charles was quick to defend his ministers, and managed to establish a fairly stable set of senior councillors in the 1630s.[13] Richard Weston was the first Lord Treasurer to die in office since Cecil.

Not all of the blame for the instability at court can be placed on James himself. The King was not directly responsible for the court scandals that led to the fall of Somerset or Sir Thomas Lake, although it could be said that his complacent attitude toward corruption did help to create the circumstances that eventually led to the disgrace of men like Suffolk.[14] Unlike Elizabeth, James also faced pressure to sacrifice ministers to Parliament, although his son responded to similar demands in a very different way. Charles was stubbornly loyal to prominent figures like Buckingham, even when it might have been politically expedient to let them go. In the 1630s, he made it clear that he would stand by his officials come what may, and this did much to dampen the factional conflict that might otherwise have led to their dismissal. Courtiers learnt that it was useless or counter-productive to try to supplant ministers in whom Charles had placed his trust.[15]

James was outwardly reluctant to sacrifice ministers, and reportedly warned Charles and Buckingham that they were making a rod for their own backs in sanctioning parliamentary impeachments.[16] In practice, however, he did not dig his heels in to the same extent as his son, and tended to simply let his servants sink or swim. Ministers were never entirely secure in their positions during the latter part of his reign, and they served in the knowledge that the King would not defend them if they overstepped the bounds of their authority or if their enemies at court or in Parliament uncovered a sufficiently serious scandal to remove them from power. When leading ministers were accused of corruption, James allowed justice to take its course, although he frequently reduced the fines and punishments that Parliament or Star Chamber imposed. James drew the line at attacks on Buckingham, but his strategy to protect the favourite during the Parliament of 1621 simply involved sacrificing another minister, Sir Francis Bacon.[17]

James often appeared indecisive about court appointments, and this contributed to the general atmosphere of uncertainty at court. The King often seems to have delayed his decisions, particularly when lots of candidates were jockeying for an office. When the Secretaryship of State became available after the death of Robert Cecil in 1612, Thomas Edmondes was told that 'the great and several canvassings which are made hinder his Ma[iest]ty From resolving, by which unhappiness the public in the meantime doth suffer'.[18] It is possible that James's apparent dithering was a deliberate tactic. Louis XIV famously said that when he bestowed an office he made one hundred discontented persons and one ingrate. By delaying decisions about appointments, James could mitigate some of this discontent. While they waited, candidates could negotiate among themselves and agree to stand aside in return for later favours, while others might drop out of the running through the sheer expense of attending the court, thus narrowing the potential pool of candidates and making James's decision easier.

Even after a position had been verbally promised, James could still be persuaded to change his mind while the bureaucratic formalities were still underway. When John Williams was created Lord Chancellor in 1621, he was apparently so worried that his rivals might meddle with the sealing of his warrant that he waited from ten in the morning until seven at night for it to be done. At the last moment, some Privy Councillors persuaded James to delay it once again.[19] His position was still not clear a few days later, when it was reported that the Great Seal was given to him and taken away again three times in the same day.[20]

The gap between the promise of an office and its actual bestowal could be large enough to create genuine confusion in the minds of courtiers who thought that their appointment was a done deal. William Trumbull, who was repeatedly promised a reversion of a clerkship but repeatedly disappointed, was only too aware of this.[21] Suitors had a powerful incentive to spread news of a royal promise of promotion as widely as possible at court because it would both discourage competitors for the office in question and put pressure on James to keep his word. It is easy to imagine how false rumours about appointments could be generated by clients' attempts to convince others that the promises they received were reliable and that their promotion was assured.

While James was liable to sacrifice prominent officials, he was lenient in his punishments, and this generated further speculation and uncertainty at court because disgraced ministers could often hope to be restored to power. James was particularly kind to those who had been impeached by Parliament. He never collected the £40,000 fine imposed on Francis Bacon by the Parliament of 1621, and released his former Lord Chancellor after only three days in the Tower. He also significantly reduced the fine imposed on Lionel Cranfield by the Parliament of 1624. James was equally merciful to those who fell in scandals outside of Parliament. The Earl of Suffolk and his wife only spent ten days in the Tower after being found guilty of corruption in 1619, and almost the first thing to be discussed after their £30,000 fine was imposed was how much it would eventually be reduced by.[22] Individuals who had fallen from power often had reason to hope that they would not only be treated leniently, but that they might be forgiven and welcomed back into the King's service. Sir Robert Naunton was suspended as Secretary of State in January 1621, but rumours that he would be restored continued to circulate until he was finally replaced by Sir Edward Conway two years later.[23]

DISINFORMATION ABOUT APPOINTMENTS

James's style of rule fuelled speculation at court and created an uncertain atmosphere in which false rumours about appointments and demotions could be deliberately spread and used as political weapons. Speculation that a courtier would be promoted to a powerful and profitable position often seems to have been generated by the candidates for office themselves. Although John

Castle thought Sir Henry Wotton would not be made provost of Eton in 1624, he told Trumbull that Wotton 'tells his friends every day he shall shortly haue his grant'.[24] In Wotton's case, such assurances were well-placed, since he was indeed made provost, but the same could not be said for Oliver St John, First Viscount Grandison, who 'assured his friends' that he would be made master of the Court of Wards in 1624.[25]

At other times, the friends and dependants appear to have talked up a candidate's chances. Following the downfall of Secretary Naunton, Castle noted that 'The freinds of Sir Iohn suckling give out that he out that he shall be qualified with the secretaryship out of hand'.[26] Months later, it was rumoured that Naunton, who was supposed to have been replaced, would soon be restored to the secretaryship. Buckingham had recently visited him at home, Castle wrote, and the King had also sent him encouraging messages. 'But for the bruite howe he h[ath] been twice with the king within these few dayes', he added, 'hold it to be forged by some of his owne'.[27]

The mutually supporting relationship between prominent courtiers and their dependants and allies helps to explain the circulation of these rumours. Patrons had an interest in attracting support by creating a sometimes false sense of inevitability about their prospects of promotion. A public display of confidence in one's own chances would inspire a similar confidence in others, and would encourage friends and clients, who might expect some reward for their support, to speak up on their behalf. If a courtier was indeed elevated to an important and profitable position, their friends and clients could expect to rise in their wake. Clients could enjoy practical benefits from such expectations, for instance by securing credit on the basis that they would soon be promoted along with their patron. Clients who looked to powerful figures for offices, titles and pensions therefore had their own incentive to talk up the chances of their patrons, sometimes to the extent of creating the false impression that they had already been granted an office.

False rumours about the bestowal of an office could create a vital window of opportunity during which candidates could work to obtain a post that their rivals assumed had already been granted. When Trumbull applied for the reversion of a clerkship of Chancery in 1622, he was told that it had already been granted to Sir Francis Cottington. 'Men hand tricks for their freinds as trappes for their foes,' Castle wrote, 'and perhapes the naminge of Cott is but an artifice to diverte you vpon an other subiecte, whilest the meanes be wrought to procure him this which you nowe seek[e].'[28] Such reports encouraged competitors to accept an apparent *fait accompli* and give up hope of obtaining the office they sought, thus making it easier for the unscrupulous rumour-monger to claim their prize. Even if a rival remained confident about their chances, false rumours might be enough to scare off their friends and intermediaries. When Holles failed to obtain the treasurership of the household in 1616, he blamed intercessors, who being 'frighted with a few false fyers, or discouraged with sum impediments, will quit a faisable work, and so give place to a latter cummer'.[29]

The competition for the position of principal secretary of state in 1617 demonstrates the political benefits that rumours about appointments could confer. When Ralph Winwood died in 1617, Thomas Lake, his fellow secretary, attempted to take control of foreign dispatches, which Winwood had usually handled while Lake accompanied the King on his hunting trips. If Lake could take over the execution of foreign business as soon as possible, he would be able to present himself as the *de facto* principal secretary, which would discourage competitors for the post and make it all the more likely that the King would finally grant it to him. It was soon rumoured that Lake had already been granted the lodging and diet that went with Winwood's position, as well as a warrant for £1,400 per year to pay for espionage, creating the impression that his actual appointment as principal secretary was a mere formality. The fact that the details of this rumour, down to amounts of money, were so specific, surely added to its persuasive power, but Chamberlain nevertheless reported that 'yt falls not out so.'[30] Carleton appears to have been on the receiving end of a similar manoeuvre when he made his own bid for the vacant secretaryship. Buckingham convinced him to give up on his campaign for the position by telling Carleton that the King had already decided to give the office to someone else, thus clearing the field for his own preferred candidate, Sir Robert Naunton.[31] Spreading such rumours was not a risk-free strategy. Reports about the good progress suits were making could discourage some competitors, but as Bacon wrote, they could also 'quicken and awake' others who saw the prize slipping out of their grasp.[32]

Rumours of a courtier's imminent rise could yield other political benefits. In August 1617, Edward Coke was battling with his estranged wife, Lady Hatton, for custody of their daughter, Frances. Coke, who was out of favour with the King, wanted to marry Frances to Buckingham's elder brother to secure his return to grace, but his wife had attempted to derail the match. When it became clear that James supported the match, observers took it as a sign that Coke would soon return to royal favour. It was said that James now spoke favourably of Coke, and that he could 'no longer be spared from the helm'.[33] It was rumoured that Coke would be restored to the King's Bench, and was 'uppon composition with the Chancelor of the Excheker to be under Tresorer'.[34] Although these rumours did not intimidate Lady Hatton, who was 'well acquainted with his wonted artifice', they appear to have led other courtiers to comply with his wishes.[35] Coke was able to flex his muscles, controlling access to Lady Hatton and his daughter, and committing a woman for slanderous words against the prospective bridegroom in large part because rumours of his forthcoming promotions 'doth authoryse [him] in what he goes aboute'.[36] Rumours about a courtier's standing with the King could have a very immediate and practical effect on their ability to get things done.

In some cases it seems that candidates wished to spread the word that they had been granted a post merely so that they could claim a consolation prize if their bid ultimately failed. Following the death of the Earl of Salisbury in 1612, a candidate for the vacant secretaryship claimed that Thomas Lake was attempting 'to engage the king as much as he may and intrude himself as far as he can into the execution of the place that his friends may pretend that he hath the more wrong done him, if he be excluded in the end'.[37] The more a candidate was 'in voice' for a particular place, the more of a sense of expectation and entitlement they could drum up. Even if this was not enough to secure the post they wanted – and the King was after all the final arbiter of such things – they could nevertheless claim some sort of compensation, because a lesser request would look modest in the context of an earlier royal denial. Castle had precisely this strategy in mind when he advised Trumbull, who had recently failed to secure the provostship of Eton, to take the opportunity to ask for his arrears to be paid instead. 'Hauing not satisfied you about Eton', he wrote, 'perhaps his M*aiesty* may be the rather inclined nowe in the freshnesse of the businesse to do you this other fauor'.[38] As Bacon put it, 'the reparation of a denial, is sometimes equal to the first grant; if a man show himself neither dejected nor discontented. *Iniquum petas ut aequum feras* [ask for what is unreasonable so that you may obtain what is just] is a good rule'.[39]

It is also possible that rumours about appointments might have been spread by the King himself as part of an informal consultation exercise. Political writers like Justus Lipsius recommended that rulers should pay attention to the general reputation of a candidate for office, because although a courtier might succeed in deceiving the King about their virtues and abilities, they would not be able to deceive everyone else.[40] By floating the idea of an appointment in advance, James would encourage other courtiers to express their opinion about a candidate, allowing the King to gain a more informed view of their suitability for a position. Contemporaries were aware that this method of consultation could be used in other contexts. Fulgenzio Micanzo wrote that rumours that James had secretly become a Catholic may have been spread with the King's tacit approval as a means to test the waters of public opposition before converting. Such manoeuvres put Micanzo 'in mynd of a trick often used by the Spanyards and Romans who when they meane to doe some extravagant Act use to divulge it for done that they may know what men say of it, & to know what opposition it is like to meet withall'.[41] A similar technique was said to be used in the world of publishing. It was a common practice when publishing controversial books 'first to divulg the title and contents, to observe how the world tasts such a subject, and to give occasion unto others to bring in more intelligence ... and after follows the worke it self'.[42] The King may have informally suggested promotions in order to see if they would meet with any opposition at court, and it is possible that some of the false reports about appointments originated in this way.

RUMOURS OF DISGRACE

Rumours about promotions at court clearly had a self-fulfilling potential. Reports that a courtier had been granted an office could discourage competitors and clear the way for their actual instatement. By building up a sense of entitlement and momentum about their candidacy, courtiers could improve their chances of securing the office they desired, or at the very least enhance their chances of claiming some sort of compensation from James. Nevertheless, rumours could cut both ways, and could be used to damage as well as to boost a courtier's position. Reports that a powerful individual would fall or had already fallen from power could make their disgrace all the more likely.

Reports of the imminent fall of Lionel Cranfield, Earl of Middlesex, in 1623 provide an example. During Charles's and Buckingham's trip to Madrid, Cranfield had attempted to supplant the favourite in James's affections by promoting his brother-in-law, Arthur Brett, as a replacement. A showdown between Buckingham and Cranfield was expected. Shortly before Buckingham returned, it was reported that Cranfield's profligacy 'had greatly displeased his Maiestie' and that he would be stripped of his white staff, which would be given to alderman Cockayne, 'a man of tryed wisdome; who should give £10000 and remitt £10000 more which his Maiesty oweth him'.[43] Castle assured Trumbull that the whole thing was a mere 'bubble, raised by the ill willers of the Lord Tresorer, whereof he hath purchased so great a number that no man affordeth him almost a good worde'.[44] The specific sums of money detailed in these rumours deserve attention. They give the rumour an air of specious plausibility that a more vague report would lack. Such concrete sums seem to imply that the rumour must surely be true, particularly as the total sum Cockayne was said to offer was the same as that which had successfully secured the treasurership for Montagu in 1621.

Rumours of a courtier's imminent fall from power could encourage their enemies to make accusations of wrongdoing that they would otherwise be too frightened to make. It was often better to withhold evidence that implicated a minister in corruption or other crimes while it seemed likely that they would continue in power. Rumours that a minister had fallen out of favour or was likely to be disgraced would encourage their enemies to make accusations without fear of retaliation. Rumours that a courtier faced disgrace also had the potential to deter their clients from speaking out on their behalf, and might encourage them to switch sides. As Bacon noted, the defection of just one courtier could be a tipping point in factional battles. 'The traitor in faction', as he wrote, 'lightly goeth away with it; for when matters have stuck long in balancing, the winning of some one man casteth them, and he getteth all the thanks'.[45] New clients, looking for a patron to attach themselves to, would not wish to link their fortunes to a man whose influence appeared to be on the wane. Men like Middlesex owed their offices to James, but in a sense they were powerful because people thought they were powerful. They were able to secure the cooperation of other courtiers and officials because of the expectation that they would stay in office. When their fall was thought to be imminent, this authority abruptly disappeared, and all-powerful ministers quickly found that their enemies came out of the woodwork. During Cranfield's impeachment, Castle wrote that the 'glorious tree of the Middlesex Earle is hewinge downe', adding that 'every man nowe hath a hatchett' to cut at him.[46]

Even relatively minor courtiers could benefit from the disgrace of a senior minister, because their fall would often create a chain of vacancies. The promotion of an individual to a vacant position would open up their old office, and filling it would create another vacancy in turn. When it was reported that George Abbot had been deposed in 1621 for accidentally shooting and killing a gamekeeper, for instance, observers were quick to speculate about the reshuffle that would ensue. Lord Keeper Williams, it was thought, would replace Abbot as Archbishop, and Viscount Mandeville would be made Lord Keeper in his place, which would make room for Lionel Cranfield to become Lord Treasurer, which would potentially create vacancies further down the line.[47] The prospect of opening vacancies at court created a powerful incentive for rivals and candidates from the top to the bottom of the ladder of office to spread and believe rumours about the impending end of a minister's political career. As Robert Beale wrote, when they tried to supplant prominent individuals, courtiers tended to 'looke rather to some parte of the spoile or praie, then eyther to iust matter, or the seruice of God, Prince or Countrie'.[48] John Holles, as usual, had a more vivid way of putting it. The disgrace of his patron, the Earl of Somerset, created speculation about promotions among members of the victorious rival faction, leading him to remark bitterly that 'at the hewing down a great oke, all the neabors gather chipps'.[49]

If a minister fell as part of a corruption scandal and a fine was imposed, royal creditors could also hope to recoup some of their money from the exchequer. Diplomats were often told about these rare windfalls so that they could make a claim for their arrears. John Castle provided early information about Cranfield's fine in 1624, letting Trumbull know whether any of the money had been set aside to pay particular creditors. He warned his friend that Lord Fielding and Sir Henry Goodere were already asking for some of the money.[50] Trumbull staked his own claim as quickly as he could, but not before other diplomats with debts to pay had done the same.[51] Although it should be remembered that these punitive fines were often remitted, they may well have given some courtiers an additional incentive to hope for, and perhaps pass on rumours about, the fall of a corrupt minister.

Individuals may have had reason to fear offending powerful courtiers under normal circumstances, but once they were disgraced, these worries appear to have largely evaporated. Chamberlain wrote of Sir John Bennet's fall from grace that 'as when the cocke is once turned the water followes apace, so some men that perhaps otherwise wold have ben silent, now they see him going are content to give him his full loade'.[52] It was foolish to slander a minister when he had the power to strike back, but when he fell from office enemies both within and outside the court could do so in relative safety. Castle gave a much more damning opinion of Sir Thomas Murray when he left office in 1622 than he would have while Murray was the Prince's Secretary, describing him as 'rather a Pedant then a statesman & more cunning in contriving his faction, then able for the publike', adding 'this is the smell which he hath left behinde him'.[53]

A dead politician could also be criticised with impunity. When Lord Chief Justice Montagu was prematurely rumoured to be dead, Chamberlain wrote that he 'will recover [i.e. put right] many slanders that wold have run on him yf he had died', such as that he had accepted bribes from a notorious cutpurse.[54] When Lord Chancellor Egerton died in 1617, Chamberlain wrote that he 'left but an indifferent name beeing accounted too sowre, sever and implacable, a great ennemie to parlements and the common law, only to maintain his owne greatnes, and the exorbitant jurisdiction of his court of chauncerie'.[55] It is difficult to imagine Chamberlain expressing such sentiments when Egerton was alive, and these political obituaries are often the most candid feature of a correspondent's letters. This might help to explain why the majority of the libels against Buckingham circulated in the months immediately after his assassination.[56]

The habit of slandering disgraced or dead ministers was shared by the lower reaches of society. As Chamberlain wrote, 'when men are downe the very drunkards make rimes and songes upon them'.[57] Courtiers frequently complained that if their conduct was in any way questioned, the common people assumed that they were guilty of high crimes. Bishop Williams complained that accusations that he had mishandled Chancery business had generated false rumours in the city that he had been placed under house arrest.[58] Holles similarly wrote that when he was questioned about misbehaviour, the people assumed that he had been convicted of a crime.[59] Courtiers worried about their broader reputation and about what was being said about them in city and country. It is likely that they were not merely concerned with preserving their honour but also with the practical political effects such rumours might have if they were repeated at court.

False rumours that a candidate for office had died could also be used to damage their chances of promotion. In 1635 Thomas Wentworth was trying to secure the position of Lord Treasurer. When George Goring joked in Queen

Henrietta Maria's presence that Wentworth had been assassinated in Ireland, the report was taken literally by bystanders, and news of the Lord Lieutenant's death quickly spread.[60] The timing of these rumours was highly suspicious, and they may have represented a deliberate attempt by Wentworth's rivals to disable him. Such rumours would necessarily only work in the short term, as dispatches from Ireland would soon indicate that reports of his death were premature. Nevertheless, at critical moments, such as when the decision to appoint a treasurer was being made, a short-term effect might be all that was needed. Even these reports could be turned to Wentworth's advantage, however. Because courtiers might conceal their true opinions about a minister while he was alive, rumours of his death provided opportunities to distinguish friend from foe. Wentworth's friend John Okehampton promised to make good use of rumours of his death by 'discerninge the hidden affections of your frends and enimyes to you'.[61]

Even when false rumours of a minister's death were disproved, they could nevertheless reinforce the impression that they were in poor health and perhaps not up for the job, providing a seemingly charitable pretext for their dismissal. Arthur Chichester, another Lord Deputy of Ireland, was rumoured to have died in 1614, and this might well have contributed to the decision James made to replace him, citing concerns about his welfare.[62]

Rumours about the ill health of Thomas Egerton, the Lord Chancellor, show that these and similar reports had the potential to hasten a courtier's political decline by encouraging their enemies to attack. Egerton had for some time been locked in conflict with Edward Coke. In February 1616, according to Holles, Coke seized the opportunity of Egerton's ill health, 'which he supposed would end him', to support an attempt to bring a *praemunire* indictment against the Chancellor.[63] Coke had 'seased upon my Lord Chancellor ... supposing him uppon his death bed, and thence never to have risen again to have resented' this attack, but unfortunately for Coke, Egerton still had over a year yet to live.[64] When Egerton heard of Coke's move against him, 'choler, and comfort revyved him', and he struck back.[65]

Rumours of a courtier's death were sufficiently damaging that victims of misinformation went to some lengths to counteract them. According to Chamberlain, Francis Bacon's illness in 1619 had 'raised a rumor, as yf he were like enough to have a Lord Keeper for his coadjutor, or rather to have the place executed by commission when his health will not suffer him to follow yt'.[66] This rumour had the potential to damage Bacon's career, since rivals could claim he was too ill to perform his duties effectively. 'To disperse such mists', therefore, he travelled to the King, who had also been ill recently, 'to see and congratulate his Majesties happie recoverie'.[67] This public display of vitality, neatly juxtaposed with the King's own sickness, was intended to dispel these damaging reports.

Rumours sometimes took on a more subtle form than the suggestion that a minister had died or would shortly lose his office. In March 1622, Castle reported a 'fable' concerning Sir Robert Naunton, who was trying to work his way back into royal favour after being suspended from the secretaryship in 1621. If Naunton could be restored, so the rumour went, he would 'make a suite to his Ma*ie*sty that he may goe to Rochell'.[68] The suggestion was that Naunton was rather too committed to the Protestant cause in Europe, and that this might be in conflict with his loyalty to James. This rumour clearly had the potential to damage the chances of Naunton's suspension being lifted, and Castle wrote that it was being spread by 'some that worke at his disgrace'.[69]

Rumours that a patron had lost the power to promote suits were also dangerous. An episode involving Sir Henry Yelverton's promotion to Attorney General in 1617 provides a good example. Given Buckingham's powerful position as a patronage broker, observers at court naturally assumed that Yelverton had sought the favourite's intercession with the King in seeking the position, but in fact Yelverton had secured it without his help. Yelverton was asked to draw up his own warrant for the attorneyship, but took some time in doing so, and this led to rumours that the delay in filling the position was due to a decline in Buckingham's influence over appointments. With his ability to secure the fruits of office called into question, Buckingham complained bitterly to Yelverton about the delay, and urged him to complete the warrant as soon as possible.[70] The problems Buckingham experienced in securing the release from prison of the Earl of Oxford in 1624 also 'bred a whispering that his favor and fortune declined, yt beeing observed that he had prevayled in litle or nothing since his comming out of Spaine'.[71]

When a courtier's position hung in the balance, their allies often spread exaggerated rumours about their imminent return to power. In December 1616, at the nadir of his court career, the friends of Sir Edward Coke were putting it about that the case brought against him in Star Chamber would be quashed, that he would soon be made a baron, and, for good measure, that he was a likely to be made Lord Treasurer if the position became vacant.[72] Some observers who 'studdie Ragioni di stato, and carrie the pollitiques of Iustus Lipsius in their pockett' believed that James had never wished to disgrace Coke, but had temporarily taken him down a peg in order to give superficial satisfaction to his enemies.[73] James would soon demonstrate his clemency by 'exalting him as highe in grace and honor as euer before'.[74] Similarly, when the Earl of Bristol returned from Madrid in 1624 to face the wrath of Buckingham, with whom he had fallen out the year before, it was reported that 'some that favor him w[ould] haue the worlde vnderstand, that his danger is blowen over. They say the duke & he shall be reconciled at his comming to Court'.[75] The fall of men like Coke and Bristol was not a trivial matter for their clients. At stake was the loss of a patron – someone their entire career might depend on. The effect would be felt not just by clients and other relative small-fry, but also by friends and equals who stood to lose powerful allies.

Rumours that a patron would soon enjoy a dramatic reversal of fortunes, and would be restored to a position of favour, would encourage the patron's friends to speak up on his behalf, and dissuade his enemies from joining in the attack. No-one wanted to risk undermining someone who might soon be in a position to exact revenge. As we have seen, correspondents were reluctant to commit hostile opinions about individual ministers and courtiers to paper until it was clear that they were past hope of recovery. If courtiers found their way back into favour, they would remember those who had spoken against them. Holles lamented the fact that Coke's return to favour in 1617 allowed him to revenge himself against the opponents who had appeared against him during his recent period of disgrace.[76] In most circumstances, and given the unpredictable nature of the King's affections, it was much safer for most courtiers to stay out of it. Campaigns of disinformation, deliberately orchestrated by a minister's friends, could slow down the momentum of attacks and give them a chance to rebuild their positions. Sometimes only the rumour of a dramatic reversal of fortunes, it seems, was enough to recapture the court's attention and reverse a narrative of seemingly inevitable political decline. A big lie would be more effective than a little one.

MISINFORMATION

Given their potential to shape reputations and alter the balance of power at court, it would be tempting to assume, as contemporaries often did, that they were spread deliberately. In many cases, however, there are grounds for arguing that some of what appeared as deliberate rumour-mongering was mere speculation and wishful thinking passed on as fact. In trying to understand the complex processes of rumour transmission, contemporaries often misinterpreted misinformation as disinformation. In some cases, candidates for positions at court might have genuinely, if incorrectly, believed that they had been granted offices. In others, the desire to flatter a candidate by prematurely addressing them by a title they hoped to receive might have produced false rumours that they had received it. More broadly, there was a tendency for speculation and wishful thinking to be distorted by the process of oral transmission into more definite, although false, reports. While this evidence qualifies the forgoing discussion of deliberate rumour-mongering at court, it remains the case that false rumours, whether 'accidental' in origin or deliberately spread, had the power to shape political reality at court.

The source material used to understand court politics during this period may lead us to exaggerate the political cunning of courtiers and their ability to use underhand tactics such as the spreading of false rumours. Most of the court insiders who left large collections of newsletters were losers in the quest for office. John Holles tied his fortunes to Somerset just before the Earl was brought down. William Trumbull failed to gain any significant office despite years of lobbying, and even though Carleton capitalised more effectively on the rise of Buckingham, his real reward did not come until Charles's reign. It may have consoled such individuals to believe that their enemies at court used deceitful tactics.

Patrons and intercessors were responsible for many of the false rumours about appointments at court. It was in their interests to exaggerate their ability to obtain the fruits of patronage in order to attract clients, and in the process they sometimes appear to have misled naive courtiers into believing that they were in line for a promotion. When deluded courtiers expressed misplaced confidence about their chances, it generated rumours that they might be granted a position or that they had already been granted it.

Historians are familiar with the fact that individuals competed to secure the support of powerful patrons at court, but there was also competition among patrons for clients, particularly when they sought allies in their political battles. Rival patrons made exaggerated promises about the gifts and offices they would secure in exchange for a client's support. During the period of rivalry between Somerset and Buckingham in 1615, for instance, Holles wrote that the leaders of the new faction 'like skillfull shopp keepers magnify their ware beyond the worth, to draw on chapmen'.[77]

Even when factional rivalry was less intense, courtiers needed to be on their guard against patrons who promised much but delivered little. Castle often warned Trumbull against being fed with false hopes when dealing with 'those which professe in Court to do greatest miracles for you'.[78] Echoing the commercial imagery Holles had employed, he exhorted Trumbull to 'rely not upon hopes and faire words', that were 'borne and dye in the breath ... the Court is the Markett of such wares'.[79] Similarly, Wolley wrote that while Secretary Conway was able to 'fill any one with complimenting words enough ... for performance he neuer intends any such thing'.[80]

It was not necessary to secure offices for clients in order to gain their political support; one merely needed to keep them in hope. James was constantly surrounded by a tiresome stream of intercessors trying to obtain this or that office, monopoly or pension. Patrons risked their own credit if their requests irritated the King, and clients often had no way of knowing whether or not their intercessors had actually spoken to James on their behalf. Patrons could often expect to be handsomely rewarded for their attempts to intercede with the King even if they failed to obtain offices for their clients.[81] When Trumbull asked Philip Herbert, first Earl of Montgomery, to help him to obtain the provostship of Eton in 1623, he offered to obtain an expert Flemish gardener for the Earl as a token of his thanks. Montgomery failed to secure the position for Trumbull, but requested the gardener anyway.[82] In more extreme cases, patrons may simply have accepted gifts from clients without bothering to perform any mediating service at all. When Castle heard that an unnamed mediator had failed to procure a reversion of a chancery clerkship for Trumbull in 1622, he told his friend that 'I doubt there may be some abuse in the answere delivered':

> I give you not this advise without some grounde, placed on myne owne experience. for I knewe once when this very person havinge been ingaged by an inwarde freind of myne to move his Maiestie in his favour, retourned answere at the last that the suite was denyed; and yet my freind presently after, procured it by an other way.[83]

These deceitful practices were not unique to James's reign. Francis Bacon noted in his essay on suits that 'some embrace Sutes which neuer mean to deale effectually in them, But if they see there may be life in the matter by some other meane, they will be content to winne a thank or take a second reward'.[84] Clarendon praised Thomas Coventry as a man who would 'never suffer any man to depart from him with an opinion that he was inclined to gratify him when in truth he was not', suggesting that some courtiers were willing to do the opposite in the 1630s.[85] While Charles tended to make up his own mind about appointments, however, James gave the impression of being more persuadable, and this may have made the false promises of intermediaries more plausible during his reign.[86]

Premature rumours of court appointments might also have originated from a desire to flatter. In 1616, Castle reported that Sir Henry Montagu was the most likely candidate for the position of Chief Justice of the King's Bench, and that some were already calling him by that title two months before it was actually granted.[87] When it was first rumoured that Sir Lionel Cranfield would be made Earl of Middlesex in 1622, petitioners immediately began addressing him as such, even though the official ceremony had not taken place.[88] It made sense for suitors to ingratiate themselves as early as possible with someone who seemed likely to be elevated to a powerful position. To use a title prematurely was a way of expressing a flattering confidence that the King would shortly recognise their talent and suitability. It is easy to imagine how these sentiments of confidence could be misinterpreted as congratulations for a position that had already been awarded.

The hierarchies and responsibilities of office were rarely clearly delineated, and this might have created further uncertainty over the use of titles from which false rumours might grow. Sir Lewis Lewkenor, the Master of Ceremonies, was offended when Trumbull used that title to address Sir John Finet, the Assistant of Ceremonies. If Lewkenor was offended with Trumbull, Finet said, he should be offended with many others, not least the King, who had called him master of ceremonies when he knighted him.[89]

Correspondents were quick to seize on any outward indications that might help them to predict which offices might be granted to which courtiers, and it is likely that observers sometimes simply jumped to the wrong conclusions. Rumours of a courtier's promotion could be created by something as simple as a visit from the favourite. Buckingham's visit to Thomas Lake's house in 1618 made many people believe that his prosecution would 'receive a more favourable issue than was imagined'.[90] Rumours that Sir Edward Coke would be made a Lord Treasurer were similarly bolstered when Buckingham visited his house in 1619.[91]

Candidates were aware that observers both within and outside the court interpreted the buying and decoration of a new house as an indication of their political prospects. Many thought that Sir Richard Weston would become Lord Treasurer in 1624 because he had moved in to a new house, and was (rather optimistically) soon 'busie in tricking and trimming yt up' in preparation.[92] Such purchases could end with embarrassment. Thomas Edmondes bought a new house in 1609, presumably in the hope of gaining the role of Secretary of State, but was forced to return to his old house in Blackfriars when his hopes of promotion were dashed.[93] Moving out of an expensive house confirmed a courtier's disgrace. When Sir George Calvert began letting out his house in St Martin's Lane in 1624, Trumbull wrote that 'Your *Lordship* in your wisedome can Iudge of the sequence', namely that Calvert's time as Secretary of State was over.[94]

Rumours about appointments were often not so much false as premature, and they often seem to have originated from speculation and negotiations for positions rather than being deliberately manufactured. The rumour that Sir Edward Conway had been sworn Secretary of State in 1622 was false, but it certainly indicated that he was a candidate for the post, and in fact he did become secretary two years later.[95] Although Holles added 'quid non?' to reports circulating in 1616 that George Villiers would soon be ennobled, the favourite was indeed made an Earl the following year.[96] The specific details included in reports that Cockayne would be made Lord Treasurer in place of Cranfield in 1624 might have originated in very real, if speculative, negotiations carried out by the candidate and his allies. Rumours that Cockayne would pay £10,000 and cancel the same amount of royal debt may not simply have been invented by Cranfield's enemies, but may instead have echoed offers Cockayne or his friends were making behind the scenes.[97]

THE COURT 'VOICE'

As we have seen, James's court was particularly rumoursome during the latter part of his reign in England. Rumours about court appointments and demotions were powerful political weapons because they could be self-fulfilling. Rumours that a courtier had been granted an office could discourage competitors and clear the way for their actual instatement. By informally taking on the duties of a post and building up a sense of entitlement and momentum about their candidacy, courtiers could improve their chances of securing the office they desired, or at the very least allow them to claim some sort of compensation from James. The expectation of a courtier's promotion also provided more immediate, practical benefits by enhancing their authority and forcing rivals to comply with their wishes. At the same time, speculation about a minister's impending fall from power could encourage their enemies to join attacks against them. Such rumours were not always deliberately spread by Machiavellian courtiers. As we have seen, they could circulate for a number of reasons, and were often an echo of speculation and wishful thinking rather than a deliberate attempt to mislead.

Historians of Jacobean politics have tended to focus their attention on the powerful courtiers who tended to dominate contemporary commentary. The evidence presented here suggests that even the relative small-fry who attended court could have a collective influence on appointments and demotions. Historians have long recognised that the King was more the final arbiter of decisions about appointments and punishments than the sole decision-maker. James delegated the role of patronage broker to others, most obviously Buckingham, although the King always had the final say, and rejected his favourite's candidates when he appointed Calvert as Secretary of State in 1619 and John Williams as Lord Keeper in 1621. Moreover, there was always a maze of personal interests, privileges and precedents to negotiate when the King wished to make an appointment. Since offices were regarded as pieces of property and were bought and sold, James or Buckingham could not always simply dispense with a minister without compensating them, and men like Calvert could hang on to their offices in the hope of selling them long after they had ceased to perform their ministerial functions. The impact of a particular appointment or demotion on the balance of factions also had to be considered. The King did not have complete freedom of manoeuvre.

James was known to collect gossip and rumour from courtiers that he was close to, and his interest was not purely for entertainment.[98] The general reputation of candidates for office surely played a part in his decisions. Indeed, the language with which observers described the rise and fall of courtiers sometimes implied that the collective preferences of their peers affected their political chances. The general opinion and preference of the court was the court 'voice'. To 'voice' could mean to express a preference or vote, as well as simply to report information orally, and it is perhaps significant that observers sometimes used language associated with elections and parliamentary votes to describe the competition for office.[99] The candidate who had the court 'voice' was not simply the individual James was thought to favour most, but referred to the person who had the general support of other courtiers. John Throckmorton made a clear distinction between the two when he wrote that while James's gracious behaviour towards Winwood in 1612 had created an *opinion* that he would be appointed Secretary of State, 'he hath already the voice'.[100] James could certainly ignore the court's preferred candidate. In 1611, for instance, he appointed George Abbot to the see of Canterbury even though 'most voices run upon Winchester'.[101] Nevertheless, the preferences of the court and the information courtiers provided about a candidate's conduct and reputation formed part of the context for royal decision-making. The King was forced to pay at least some attention to collective beliefs about a candidate's chances of promotion, not least because as we have seen, courtiers who were denied a position that they were generally thought to be in line for would often try to claim some sort of compensation from the King.

Discussion of court appointments was not limited to the court itself. Holles wrote in 1616 that Villiers's expected promotions were being 'babbled' about in London as well as Whitehall.[102] Speculation outside the court could have an indirect influence over the competition for office, since rumours about vacancies gave candidates an excuse for applying for them. In 1618 Sir Henry Carey was moved by rumours circulating outside the court that Viscount Wallingford would soon be forced to relinquish the mastership of the Court of Wards. Although Carey expressed doubts about 'what fate dependes uppon that voice, or what vertewe there is in the people's ydle predictions to bringe events to passe', he nevertheless took the opportunity to lobby Buckingham for the position.[103]

The public disgrace of failing to secure an office could also act as a powerful disincentive to applying for it (or at least being seen to) in the first place. It could be politically damaging, not to mention embarrassing, to be denied a position after campaigning for it. In 1617, George Abbot privately advised Carleton's friends not to name him as a possible successor to Ralph Winwood as Secretary of State 'least they rather hurte you then helpe you'.[104] Since James might not be inclined to give Carleton the position, Abbot argued, 'to haue your name tossed about is but to bring you on the stage and to haue you putt of with disgrace'.[105] Courtiers' political fortunes depended not only on gaining access to the King and maintaining his favour, but also in shaping the perceptions of a wider audience at court and even outside of it.

NOTES

1 A. Courtney, 'Court Politics and the Kingship of James VI and I, c. 1615–c. 1621' (PhD, University of Cambridge, 2008), pp. 1–6 contains a particularly useful discussion of this point.

2 Much of the scholarship on this subject, including Perez Zagorin, *The Court and the*

Country (New York, 1970), Geoffrey Elton, 'Tudor government: The points of contact III: The court', *Transactions of the Royal Historical Society*, 5th series, 26 (1976), pp. 211–28; and Linda Levy Peck, *Court Patronage and Corruption in Early Stuart England* (Boston (MA), 1990), has tended to focus on the relationship between court and country and the role of court patronage in maintaining political ties. Linda Levy Peck (ed.), *The Mental World of the Jacobean Court* (Cambridge, 2005) is an important exception. There is of course a great deal of excellent work on the links between court politics, news culture and foreign policy.

3 Neil Cuddy, 'The revival of the entourage: The bedchamber of James I, 1603–1625', in David Starkey (ed.), *The English Court: From the Wars of the Roses to the Civil War* (Harlow, 1987), pp. 173–225 and Kevin Sharpe, 'The image of virtue: the court and household of Charles I, 1625–42', *Ibid.*, pp. 226–60. For biographies of courtiers, see Roger Lockyer, *Buckingham: The Life and Political Career of George Villiers, First Duke of Buckingham, 1592–1628* (London, 1981); Linda Levy Peck, *Northampton: Patronage and Policy at the Court of James I* (London, 1982); Menna Prestwich, *Cranfield: Politics and Profits under the Early Stuarts* (Oxford, 1966); Martin J. Havran, *Caroline Courtier: The Life of Lord Cottington* (London, 1973); Roy E. Schreiber, *The First Carlisle: Sir James Hay, First Earl of Carlisle as Courtier, Diplomat and Entrepreneur, 1580–1636* (Philadelphia (PA), 1984); Michael Alexander, *Charles I's Lord Treasurer, Sir Richard Weston, Earl of Portland 1577–1635* (Chapel Hill (NC), 1975). The approach of many of these biographies has been to rehabilitate the reputations of individuals previously seen as mere venal courtiers and to portray them as reformers.

4 John Holles to John Holles Jnr., [4 March 1616], in P. R. Seddon (ed.), *Letters of John Holles 1587–1637* vol. I, (Thoroton Society Record Series vol. 31, 1975), p. 118.

5 See for instance the newsletters of Joseph Mead, Harl. 389–90, or the news diary of Walter Yonge, Add. 28032 *passim*.

6 For some definitions of the court, see Neil Cuddy, 'Reinventing monarchy: The changing structure and political function of the Stuart court, 1603–88', in Eveline Cruickshanks (ed.), *The Stuart Courts* (Stroud, 2000), pp. 60, 62.

7 Chamberlain to Carleton, 28 July 1621, McClure, p. 392.

8 'Fortunes wheele. or Rota fortunæ in gyro' (Alastair Bellany and Andrew McRae (eds),'Early Stuart libels: an edition of poetry from manuscript sources', *Early Modern Literary Studies Text Series* I (2005), http://purl.oclc.org/emls/texts/libels (accessed 29 July 2012). The image of the wheel of fortune was of course much older than this poem.

9 John Chamberlain to Dudley Carleton, 4 November 1620, McClure vol. II, p. 325.

10 John Neale, 'The Elizabethan political scene', in John Neale, *Essays in Elizabethan History* (London, 1958), pp. 59–84; Simon Adams, 'Eliza enthroned? The court and its politics', in Christopher Haigh (ed.), *The Reign of Elizabeth I* (Basingstoke, 1984), pp. 55–6.

11 Janet Dickinson has recently argued that even the factionalism of the 1590s has been exaggerated. See *Court Politics and the Earl of Essex, 1589–1601* (London, 2012).

12 Adams, 'Eliza enthroned?', pp. 61–70.

13 Richard Cust, *Charles I: a Political Life* (Harlow, 2005), pp. 178–82.

14 See for instance James's response to the commission of enquiry into naval affairs in 1608. A. P. McGowan (ed.), *The Jacobean Commissions of Enquiry 1608 and 1618* (London, 1971), p. xv.

15 Kevin Sharpe, *The Personal Rule of Charles I* (New Haven, 1992), pp. 178–9. Whether Charles's loyalty to his ministers was ultimately in his or their interests is a different question. As Conrad Russell wrote, 'His [Charles's] determination to save his servants may do him credit, but his servants never seem to have been much the better for it'. Conrad Russell, *The Causes of the English Civil War* (Oxford, 1990), p. 187.

16 Edward Hyde, Earl of Clarendon, *History of the Rebellion* vol. I (Oxford, 1888), p. 28.

17 James dramatically told the Parliament of 1621 that he would not defend Buckingham if accusations of corruption against him were substantiated, although Roger Lockyer has suggested that this performance was rehearsed and that James acted to protect his favourite. See Lockyer, *Buckingham*, p. 94. The harsh punishment of Henry Yelverton, who was imprisoned for his speech against Buckingham, made it clear that further attacks on the Duke would not be tolerated. See Conrad Russell, *Parliaments and English Politics 1621–1629* (Oxford, 1979), p. 111.

18 Thomas Edmondes to Trumbull, 28 January 1613, Downshire vol. IV, p. 27.

19 Joseph Mead to Martin Stuteville, 23 June 1621, Harl. 389, fol. 98v.

20 Mead to Stuteville, 30 June 1621, Harl. 389, fol. 100r. Williams complained that rumours about the probationary nature of his office were circulating at court, which were intended to 'scare away my men, and to put a disgrace upon me'. He asked Buckingham to draw up a declaration stating the true terms of his appointment. See Williams to Buckingham, 27 July 1621, *Cabala, Mysteries of State, in Letters of the Great Ministers of K. James and K. Charles* (1653), p. 56. Nevertheless, the speeches he made on being sworn Lord Keeper and first sitting in Chancery repeatedly referred to his office as being probationary. See 'Speech made by John Williams when he was sworn Lord Keeper', 9 October 1621, Bod. MS. Tanner 73, fol. 75r–v.

21 John Digby to William Trumbull, 21 December 1621, Add. 72285, fol. 73r–v; Digby to Trumbull, 4 January 1622, Add, 72285, fol. 75r; Trumbull to Conway, 5/15 January 1624, SP 77/17, fol. 2v.

22 Castle to Trumbull, 8 December 1619, Add. 72275, fol. 93v.

23 Castle to Trumbull, 14 June 1622, Add. 72275, fol. 147v; Castle to Trumbull, 11 October 1622, Add. 72276, fol. 15v.

24 Castle to Trumbull, 9 July 1624, Add. 72276, fol. 109v.

25 Castle to Trumbull, 28 May 1624, Add. 72276, fol. 95r.

26 Castle to Trumbull, 29 March 1622, Add. 72275, fol. 130r.

27 Castle to Trumbull, 11 October 1622, Add. 72276, fol. 15v.

28 Castle to Trumbull, 28 June 1622, Add. 72275, fol. 149v.

29 Holles to the Countess of Harford, 6 August 1616, in Seddon (ed.), *Letters of John Holles* vol. I, p. 138.

30 Chamberlain to Carleton, 8 November 1617, McClure vol. II, p. 113.

31 Buckingham to Carleton, 2 December 1617, SP 84/81, fol. 2r; Edward Harwood to Carleton, 20 December SP 14/94, fols. 119r–20r, Harwood to Carleton, 22 December 1617, SP 14/94, fol. 110r.

32 Francis Bacon, 'Of suitors', in James Spedding (ed.), *The Works of Francis Bacon* vol. XII (London, 1857–74), pp. 249–51.

33 Holles to Thomas Lake, 6 August 1617, in Seddon (ed.), *Letters of John Holles* vol. II, p. 188.

34 Holles to the Earl of Suffolk, 9 August 1617, in Seddon (ed.), *Letters of John Holles* vol. II, p. 190.

35 Holles to Lake, 6 August 1617, in Seddon (ed.), *Letters of John Holles* vol. II, p. 188.

36 Holles to the Earl of Suffolk, 9 August 1617, in Seddon (ed.), *Letters of John Holles* vol. II, p. 190.

37 F. M. Evans, *The Principal Secretary of State: A Survey of the Office from 1558 to 1680* (Manchester, 1923), p. 66. Lake was indeed given a barony when he failed to secure the principal secretaryship in 1617.

38 Castle to Trumbull, 6 June 1623, Add. 72276, fol. 44r.

39 Francis Bacon, 'Of suitors', in Spedding (ed.), *Works of Francis Bacon* vol. XII, p. 251.

40 Justus Lipsius, *Politica: Six books of politics or political instruction,* Jan Waszink (ed.) (Assen, 2004), p. 357.

41 Fulgenzio Micanzo to William Cavendish, 2 August 1623, in Roberto Ferrini (ed.), *Lettere a William Cavendish* (Rome, 1987), p. 248.

42 Warren Townshend to Trumbull, 5/15 January 1618, Downshire vol. VI, p. 364. James himself tended to publish prose and poetry anonymously or in manuscript form and only later admitted authorship.

43 Castle to Trumbull, 12 September 1623, Add. 72276, fol. 58v.

44 *Ibid.*

45 Francis Bacon, 'Of faction', in Spedding (ed.), *Works of Francis Bacon* vol. XII, pp. 254–5.

46 Castle to Trumbull, 16 April 1624, Add. 72276, fol. 82r.

47 Mead to Stuteville, 15 September 1621, Harl. 389, fol. 118r.

48 Robert Beale, 'A Treatise of the office of a Councellor and Principall Secretarie to her Matie ... Instructions for a Principall Secretarie', Add. 48149, fol. 9v.

49 Holles to Holles Jnr., 7 January 1616, in Seddon (ed.), *Letters of John Holles* vol. I, p. 102.

50 Castle to Trumbull, 30 July 1624, Add. 72276, fol. 112v.

51 Castle to Trumbull, 20 May 1624, Add. 72276, fol. 92v; Thomas Cogswell, *The Blessed Revolution: English Politics and the Coming of War, 1621–1624* (Cambridge, 1989), p. 273.

52 Chamberlain to Carleton, 2 May 1621, McClure vol. II, p. 308.

53 Castle to Trumbull, 25 October 1622, Add. 72276, fol. 18r.

54 Chamberlain to Carleton, 19 April 1617, McClure vol. II, pp. 71–2.

55 Chamberlain to Carleton, 29 March 1617, McClure vol. II, p. 65.

56 Kevin Sharpe, *Image Wars: Promoting Kings and Commonwealths in England, 1603–1660* (London, 2010), p. 129.

57 Chamberlain to Carleton, 23 November 1616, McClure vol. II, p. 40.

58 Williams to Buckingham, 21 September 1621, *Cabala*, p. 74.

59 John Holles to the Duke of Lennox, 25 July 1617, in Seddon (ed.), *Letters of John Holles*, pp. 178–9.

60 Julia Merritt, 'Power and communication: Thomas Wentworth and government at a distance during the personal rule, 1629–1635', in Julia Merritt (ed.), *The Political World of Thomas Wentworth* (Cambridge, 1996), p. 128.

61 John Okehampton to Thomas Wentworth, 14 March 1635, Sheffield Archives, Str P 14, p. 330.

62 John McCavitt, 'Chichester, Arthur, Baron Chichester (1563–1625)', Oxford Dictionary of National Biography, Oxford University Press, 2004; online edn www.oxforddnb.com/view/article/5274 (accessed 10 May 2012).

63 Holles to Holles Jnr., 23 February 1616, in Seddon (ed.), *Letters of John Holles* vol. I, p. 116.

64 Holles to Holles Jnr., [4 March 1616], in Seddon (ed.), *Letters of John Holles* vol. I, p. 118.

65 Holles to Holles Jnr., 23 February 1616, in Seddon (ed.), *Letters of John Holles* vol. I, p. 116.

66 Chamberlain to Carleton, 24 April 1619, McClure vol. II, p. 233.

67 *Ibid.*

68 Castle to Trumbull, 23 March 1622, Add. 72275, fol. 131v.

69 *Ibid.*

70 Lockyer, *Buckingham*, p. 41; Courtney, 'Court Politics', pp. 134–8.

71 Chamberlain to Carleton, 3 January 1624, McClure vol II, p. 538.

72 Castle to Trumbull, 8 December 1616, Downshire vol. VI, p. 63.

73 Castle to [?], 26 March 1616, Harl. 7002, fol. 400r.

74 *Ibid.*

75 Castle to Trumbull, 30 April 1624, Add. 72276, fol. 86v.

76 Holles to Lake, 6 August 1617, in Seddon (ed.), *Letters of John Holles* vol. II, p. 189.

77 Holles to Lord Norris, 31 May 1615, in Seddon (ed.), *Letters of John Holles* vol. I, p. 71.

78 Castle to Trumbull, 8 March 1624, Add. 72275, fol. 90r.

79 Castle to Trumbull, 18 November 1616, Add. 72275, fol. 68r.

80 John Wolley to Trumbull, 17 July 1624, Add. 72330, fol. 125r.

81 For the gifts and payments a patron could expect in return for their intercession, see Peck, *Northampton*, pp. 70–3.

82 Castle to Trumbull, 9 May 1623, Add. 72276, fol. 36v; Castle to Trumbull, 24 May 1623, Add. 72276, fol. 39v.

83 Castle to Trumbull, 24 September 1622, Add. 72276, fol. 11r.

84 Francis Bacon, 'Of suitors', in Spedding (ed.), *Works of Francis Bacon* vol. XII, p. 250.

85 Clarendon, *History of the Rebellion* vol. I, p. 58.

86 Brian Quintrell, 'The Church triumphant? The emergence of a spiritual lord treasurer, 1635–1636', in Merritt (ed.), *Political World of Thomas Wentworth*, pp. 81–108.

87 Castle to Trumbull, 26 September 1616, Downshire vol. VI, p. 17. As we have seen, the Infanta was already being referred to as 'Princessa' 'by way of anticipation' during negotiations in 1623. See Aston to Trumbull, 3 August 1623 (n.s.), Add. 72245, fol. 123r.

88 Thomas Locke to Trumbull, 12 July 1622, Add. 72299, fol. 84r.

89 John Finet to Trumbull, 12 November 1616, Downshire vol. VI, p. 43.

90 Thomas Lorkin to Thomas Puckering, 5 January 1618, in Thomas Birch (ed.), *The Court and Times of James I* (London, 1849), p. 120.

91 Chamberlain to Carleton, 2 January 1619, McClure vol. II, p. 197.

92 Chamberlain to Carleton, 21 August 1624, McClure vol. II, p. 577.

93 Beaulieu to Trumbull, 9 February 1610, Downshire vol. II, p. 285.

94 Trumbull to Carleton, 16/26 August 1624, SP 77/17, fol. 283r.

95 Castle to Trumbull, 28 June 1622, Add. 72275, fol. 149v.

96 Holles to Holles Jnr., 7 January 1616, in Seddon (ed.), *Letters of John Holles* vol. I, p. 102.

97 Castle to Trumbull, 12 September 1623, Add. 72276, 58v.

98 According to Anthony Weldon, Thomas Lake 'would tell Tales, and let the King know the passages of the court'. See Anthony Weldon, *The Court and Character of King James* (1650), p. 56. For Somerset's role as a conduit for court news, see Alastair Bellany, *The Politics of Court Scandal in Early Modern England: News Culture and the Overbury Affair, 1603–1660* (Cambridge, 2002), p. 32.

99 See 'voice, v.'. OED Online. March 2012. Oxford University Press. 14 May 2012, www.oed.com/view/Entry/224335?rskey=lnekRD&result=2&isAdvanced=false (accessed 29 July 2012). It is worth noting that it could also refer to a single vote given in Parliament.

100 John Throckmorton to Trumbull, 7 July 1612, Downshire vol. III, p. 325.

101 John Sanford to Trumbull, 22 February 1611, Downshire vol. III, p. 28.

102 Holles to Holles Jnr., 7 January 1616, in Seddon (ed.), *Letters of John Holles* vol. I, p. 102.

103 Henry Carey to Buckingham, 14 October 1618, in S. R. Gardiner (ed.), *The Fortescue Papers*, (Camden 2nd Series, vol. 1, 1871), p. 56.

104 Abbot to Carleton, 3 November 1617, SP 105/95, fol. 13r.

105 *Ibid.*

Chapter 5

───────◆───────

Managing the news during Prince Charles's trip to Madrid, 1623

INTRODUCTION

Charles's and Buckingham's trip to Spain in 1623 has been much studied. Historians have tried to understand what motivated the Prince and Duke to travel to Madrid and why the negotiations they conducted there for a Spanish match ultimately broke down.[1] While contributing to debates about the rationale for the trip and the reasons for its failure, the primary aim of this chapter is to use these events as a case study of the management of information. James's efforts to keep the trip to Madrid secret, to restrict access to information about the negotiations they conducted there and also to present a misleadingly optimistic impression of the progress they were making provide an illuminating and well-documented case study of the methods by which he attempted to conceal and manipulate diplomatic news. While a great deal of attention has been paid to the course of negotiations in Madrid, events in England have largely been overlooked.[2] This chapter demonstrates that while events in Spain were important, the success of the match also relied on the King's ability to shape the perceptions of the Spanish ambassadors and his own subjects at home.

This case study allows us to address a number of questions that have been raised by previous chapters. The first set of questions relates to James's secretive behaviour, his reasons for restricting information and counsel and the consequences of doing so. As we have seen, the 'crisis of counsel' of the 1620s has been somewhat exaggerated. The Privy Council continued to deal with a wide variety of domestic and foreign business, and James still received advice from secretive committees. Nevertheless, James, Charles and Buckingham largely excluded the Council from the Spanish and French match negotiations. Information was restricted to a small number of trusted ministers and ambassadors, and the Privy Council as a whole was often unaware of the progress of negotiations. The question of precisely why James felt the need to behave in such a secretive manner remains to be answered. Did it represent a principled defence of the *arcana imperii*, or did James and others have more specific political reasons for restricting access to this information? What would have happened if he had taken a wider range of advisers into his confidence, and what were the consequences of failing to do so? Finally, what role did James's secretive and ambiguous behaviour play in generating rumours? An understanding of these phenomena and their interactions is only possible by placing them in the context of a detailed political narrative.

The discussion of secrecy and 'outward shewes' in previous chapters has largely relied on the observations of foreign ambassadors and minor courtiers who were forced to guess at James's real intentions and motivations. It is possible that they misinterpreted the King's actions, exaggerating both the extent to which he restricted access to information and his habit of manipulating the expectations of those around him. The separation of James from his son and favourite meant that all three were forced to commit to paper information that they would normally reserve for face to face discussion. By analysing their own correspondence as well as the observations of outsiders, we can come to a fuller understanding of how accurate perceptions about James's secrecy and attempts to manage the news really were.

Under normal circumstances, James's ability to manipulate expectations was limited because a large number of people in court and country had access to foreign news. Any claims he made about the progress of negotiations for the Spanish match or the likelihood that he would intervene in the Thirty Years' War might be contradicted by well-informed ambassadors and courtiers. During their trip to Madrid, however, Charles and Buckingham largely conducted negotiations in secrecy and only shared information with James. For much of the time, English ministers were almost totally ignorant of the progress of the match. This near-monopoly of information from Madrid gave James the opportunity to shape perceptions without much fear of contradiction. This case study therefore allows us to study the nature and extent of the King's 'outward shewes' under almost ideal circumstances.

The chapter will first examine the rationale for the trip to Madrid, and the role that concerns about secrecy might have played in James's decision to allow it to go ahead. It will then consider the methods by which news about the departure of Charles and Buckingham was kept secret, and how effective these were, before examining the ways in which James restricted access to information from Madrid, and the consequences of his behaviour. James's control over the flow of information from Madrid allowed him to present a misleadingly optimistic impression of the progress of negotiations there. By analysing the preparations James made for the return of Charles and the Infanta, and the commentary and speculation that surrounded them, this chapter will examine why James may have wished to imply that the negotiations would soon be successfully concluded, and where the balance between deliberate manipulation and false inference lay. The King's ability to manage perceptions was put to the test during these crucial negotiations. The legacy of his political trickery, as we shall see, was that observers tended to assume that he was scheming and manipulating even when he was not. The sceptical and often cynical reaction of foreign ambassadors and others to his behaviour show how his attempts to manage the news could backfire in ways which could potentially damage negotiations and undermine royal authority.

THE JOURNEY TO MADRID AND THE RATIONALE FOR SECRECY

Charles and Buckingham had a variety of reasons for travelling to Madrid in 1623. The outbreak of the Thirty Years' War in 1618 gave the Spanish marriage negotiations a new urgency. James hoped that a large dowry would help to reduce his debts. A dynastic alliance with the most powerful Catholic power in Europe would also counterbalance the marriage of his daughter, Elizabeth, to the Protestant Elector Palatine, increasing James's influence with both sides of the confessional divide. After Frederick accepted the Bohemian crown, James had reason to hope that the continuing marriage negotiations would dissuade Spain from assisting the Emperor against his son-in-law. The invasion of the Palatinate by a Spanish army in 1620, which formally fought in the Emperor's name, showed that this was not the case. James now hoped that the conclusion of the match would lead Spain to exert pressure on the Emperor to restore Frederick to his lands and titles. As we have seen, the threat of an alternative match between the Infanta and the Emperor's son had hung over the Spanish match negotiations for years, and James realised that the alternative to an Anglo-Spanish marriage would be an even closer alliance between the Habsburgs. The slow progress of negotiations created suspicions that the Spanish were merely stringing James along in order to prevent him from supporting Frederick by force of arms, and that they had no intention of completing the match. The trip to Madrid can partly be explained by Charles's and Buckingham's desire to cut through the continual delays in negotiations and discover whether the intentions of the Spanish were sincere.[3]

Other international considerations may also have played a part in Charles's and Buckingham's decision. Persistent rumours that the Dutch and Spanish were seeking to renew their truce raised fears that James would no longer be able to play the two off against each other.[4] The King would find it harder to negotiate with the Dutch over trade and fishing disputes if they were no longer locked in a struggle for survival with Spain.[5] At the same time, Spain was more inclined to an English alliance, and more willing to pay for it with a large dowry, while the war with the Dutch continued. There were also worries that the Spanish would ask the Dutch to expel Frederick and Elizabeth as a condition for peace, leaving them nowhere to go but across the Channel.[6] This was a dismal prospect for James. The couple would act as a powerful focus for opposition to the King's peaceful diplomacy if they came to England. Hints of Anglo-Spanish military cooperation against the Dutch, which James had been dropping for some time, were probably aimed at preventing any rapprochement between Spain and the Republic.[7]

The match could also have an impact on French politics. Louis XIII was preparing for an all-out assault on James's Protestant allies in France, the Huguenots. An attack on La Rochelle was being prepared, and James feared that the destruction of Huguenot independence would deprive him of an important diplomatic lever in his dealings with Louis. Charles's and Buckingham's trip was successful in diverting French attention. Fearing a joint Anglo-Spanish attack, Louis moved ordnance and ammunition intended to be used against La Rochelle to the Channel coast.[8] As Kellie wrote, 'the greatest reasone that theis of the religion are now in quyet is the Prince his goeing to Spaine, and the feare of that freindshipe makes him [Louis] desire to have all his subjects in quyetnes and of one mynd'.[9]

The idea to travel in person to Madrid seems to have come from Charles, but the Prince then had to convince James to go along with his plan. Clarendon's account of this process of persuasion, if it is to be believed, can tell us much about the internal politics of secrecy.[10] According to Clarendon, James initially agreed to the trip to Madrid, perhaps simply to appease Charles's impatience. The King knew that preparations for a fleet to transport Charles could not be kept secret, and foreknowledge of the trip would create opportunities for both Spanish negotiators and English councillors to obstruct the journey and dissuade the Prince from embarking on it.[11] It was only after the King had agreed to the trip in principle that Charles and Buckingham met with James in private and revealed their intention of travelling secretly by land, thus calling the King's bluff. James objected that the journey would be dangerous, and that the Spanish would use the opportunity of the Prince's presence to extract greater concessions.[12] Since the trip relied on secrecy, James could scupper Charles's and Buckingham's plans by revealing them to others. It was perhaps with this in mind that he called for Sir Francis Cottington to join them, telling Charles and Buckingham that the veteran diplomat would be able to advise them about the preparations necessary for their journey, and the best route to take. When told about the trip, however, Cottington was horrified, and repeated James's objections against it. Buckingham attempted to silence Cottington, while James tried to defend him on the basis that he had simply offered honest advice. In the end, James reluctantly consented to the trip, while Cottington remained silent about it. If Clarendon's account is correct, secrecy about the trip, and attempts to leak information about it, were vital to its success from the very beginning.

Once James had committed to supporting the trip, it became crucial to keep it a secret. The attempt to cut through delays in Madrid relied on an element of surprise which would be lost if Spanish negotiators were forewarned about the journey. The trip was highly dangerous. Charles might be attacked by robbers and bandits on the roads that led to Madrid. There was also a possibility that Louis XIII, who was keen to prevent any alliance between England and Spain, might try to detain them as they travelled through France.[13] As James wrote, his chief fear was that 'upon the first rumour of your passing, he [Louis] should take a pretext to stop you'.[14] John Chamberlain wrote that there were 'daungers enough every way', along the road, and he could 'hardly conceave how they should passe thorough Fraunce undiscovered'.[15] Many feared that word of their trip would spread before them, and John Beaulieu hoped that they would 'preuent and forerunne all newes of their passing'.[16] Charles and Buckingham had little choice but to travel under assumed names, wearing false beards. Their suspicious appearance led the mayor of Canterbury to arrest them, and they were forced to reveal their true identity before resuming their disguises and continuing on to Dover.

The farcical attempts by Charles and Buckingham to conceal their identities risk distracting us from other, potentially more effective methods by which news of the trip was suppressed. Before he left, Charles sent one of his equerries to Newmarket with his horses, as though he intended to follow them.[17] Endymion Porter and Francis Cottington, who were to accompany Charles and Buckingham to Madrid, went ahead of them and closed the ports on James's orders, thus preventing ships from leaving for the continent until it was too late for the news of the journey to precede them.[18] They remained closed for ten days.

Efforts to maintain secrecy in 1623 were not entirely successful. Rumours that Charles might leave the country circulated before his departure.[19] In January, when rumours circulated that the match had been concluded, Chamberlain wrote that the Prince was expected to travel in person to meet his new bride.[20] It was separately rumoured that Buckingham would travel by sea to meet the Infanta.[21] Plans for a voyage to Spain had clearly been considered for some time. The overland journey to Madrid the following month was shocking and disconcerting, but some sort of trip involving Charles or Buckingham had been expected.

The attempt to block English ports was no guarantee of secrecy. Chamberlain reported that the French ambassador had sent news of the journey to France before the ports were shut, 'having gotten notice of yt [the journey] by some meanes or other'.[22] Suspicions were raised when Louis issued a proclamation that appeared to forbid the hiring of any post horses, which Charles would use to travel south.[23] Even if Louis was not forewarned about the journey, James realised that a messenger from the ambassador's household might still sail from some 'blind creek' bearing news of Charles's departure, even if the ports themselves were closed.[24] He wrote to Louis asking him to allow Charles to pass unhindered through France, sending Carlisle to explain that the trip was 'the wilfull conceate of a young man'.[25] James also tried to reassure the French ambassador about the implications of an Anglo-Spanish alliance by implying that a French match was still possible. If matters didn't work out in Madrid, he said, Charles could stop by in La Rochelle and visit the French King on his return journey.[26] The Venetian ambassador believed that this suggestion was made 'to slacken the diligence of movements in France to detain the prince'.[27]

The closing of the ports in February 1623 had unintended consequences. It was rumoured that the Prince himself had died, because the last Dutch ship to leave England had brought news that he had gone missing. The Prince, it was assumed, had been murdered in his coach, and the ports stopped to prevent his murderer from escaping.[28] It was also rumoured that James's subjects had risen up in rebellion and taken him prisoner.[29] As these rumours gathered momentum, they clearly picked up related ideas that happened to be lying in their path. Sir Dudley Carleton thought that the details of Charles's supposed assassination had sprung from recent reports of a plot to murder the Prince of Orange in his coach.[30] The plotters were themselves said to be influenced by François Ravaillac, who had stabbed Henri IV of France to death – in his coach.[31] When contemporaries built explanations for uncertain events like the disappearance of Charles, they made use of ideas that were fresh in contemporary imagination and came quickly to mind, as well as borrowing from historical example.

Given the fears about the Prince's safety, there was some relief when Charles and Buckingham arrived in Madrid in March. At first, all appeared to go well. Many in Spain assumed that Charles had come to convert to Catholicism, and he was warmly welcomed.[32] The temporal articles of the marriage treaty had been agreed, and Charles and Buckingham merely had to wait for a papal dispensation to arrive. There were signs that the years of delay were finally coming to an end. Philip III had probably never intended to complete the match. Philip IV was also reluctant to bring the marriage to a conclusion and had tried to extricate himself from the negotiations, but had slowly come to the view that the match should be allowed to go ahead, although his favourite, Olivares, opposed it. Dynastic concerns tipped the balance in favour of the marriage. If Charles died without producing an heir, the crown would pass to Frederick and Elizabeth, who were implacably opposed to Spanish interests.[33] As James wrote, 'I think they have reason there, if they love themselves, to wish you and yours rather to succeed unto me, than my daughter and her children'.[34]

Although news from Madrid was initially promising, James, Charles and Buckingham were anxious to keep details of their negotiations secret, even from their own councillors. Writing from Madrid soon after their arrival, Buckingham complained that the letters he and Charles wrote to the King were being widely read in England.[35] They both implored the King to 'advise as little with your Council in these businesses as you can', and repeated this request on a regular basis.[36] In April they warned James to keep the terms of the papal dispensation secret, since knowledge of them would 'beget disputes, censures and conclusions there to our prejudice', and when Cottington returned from Spain in June, he was instructed to pass on another request for James to conceal the news he brought.[37] Later in the negotiations, they asked him to 'speak nothing, for if you do, our labour will be the harder here'.[38]

While James, Charles and Buckingham may have shared a principled commitment to protecting the *arcana imperii,* there were also practical political reasons for their secrecy in 1623. James could not trust many of his own councillors with information about the negotiations. He rightly suspected that some of them wished to derail the match, and during the early 1620s he moved to prevent any act of sabotage while assuring the Spanish that opposition was limited to a few malcontents.[39] According to the Venetian ambassador, in 1621 James told his Privy Councillors that he was determined to conclude the marriage, hoping that this would warn his 'patriot' ministers against any attempt to prevent it.[40] A few months later, Digby informed the resident ambassador in Spain, Sir Walter Aston, that those who opposed the match now realised that the King would not be persuaded against it and were deliberately using Parliament to create the impression in Spain that it was an unpopular policy.[41] Information could be inadvertently leaked by even James's closest and most trusted councillors, let alone by those who opposed the match, and news from Madrid could spread widely and rapidly. When James shared the contents of a dispatch with his secretaries in July, Conway wrote that their contents 'quickly ran through Court and city, and will fly through the kingdom'.[42] The best policy under such circumstances was for James to keep the contents of his correspondence with Charles and Buckingham almost entirely to himself.

James was particularly anxious to suppress news of the toleration of English Catholics that the Spanish negotiators were demanding. During the summer of 1622, James had suspended penal laws against Catholics, and had issued directions to preachers which ordered them to avoid contentious topics. While he was willing to allow a *de facto* tolerance, however, a *de jure* toleration would be undesirable and probably impossible to achieve. Lord Keeper Williams warned that the announcement of concessions towards Catholics could provoke a 'mutinie' among James's more zealous subjects.[43] The King rightly worried about how his anti-Catholic subjects would react to any concessions he might make, and how this response would be perceived in Madrid.

Actions by James's subjects that fell short of rebellion could also be highly damaging to his authority and the success of the match. By attacking Spanish ambassadors, writing libels against the match or rioting against Catholics, ordinary subjects could demonstrate the unpopularity of the match and the religious concessions that it would entail.[44] In his poetry James implicitly acknowledged the power of his subjects to 'marr or patch' the marriage negotiations, and he exhorted his subjects to 'hold your pratlinge, spare your penne / Be honest and obedient men' because he knew that expressions of anti-Spanish sentiment would not go down well in Madrid.[45] He repeatedly reassured the Spanish that he would punish the authors of anti-match books and speeches.[46]

Knowledge of the concessions that James was willing to offer might also provoke spontaneous local persecution of Catholics which would anger the Spanish negotiators and underline the King's inability to enforce a toleration. Charles worried that local officials in England would impose 'vexacçons ... vppon Catholicks ... against the will of theire prince'. Any delay in negotiations, he said, only served to 'give Courage and boldnesse to such as distaste this marriage in England ... to procure new molestacçons to Catholicks with an hope to Crosse itt'. Local persecution of Catholics would then give the Spanish authorities an excuse to delay the departure of the Infanta indefinitely, since they would argue that James had not kept to his side of the bargain.[47]

James was also keen to conceal his proposal for an Anglo-Spanish partition of the Dutch Republic.[48] Although he had dangled the prospect of joint operations against the Dutch in front of the Spanish before, in 1623 James directed both John Digby and Buckingham to press the issue while Charles was in Madrid.[49] Herbert believed that the Marquis of Inojosa had been dispatched to England to discuss these plans, but advised the King not to agree to an alliance until Charles and the Infanta were safely in England.[50] These offers might help to explain James's belligerent reaction when Dutch ships attacked the Dunkirk vessel that tried to escape from Scottish ports during the summer of 1623. Spain would hardly be impressed by English proposals to invade the Dutch Republic if they could not even protect Spanish ships in their own ports. Many of James's subjects were horrified by the idea that the relationship with the Dutch would now take a decisive turn for the worse, and the author of one pro-match poem sought to reassure his readers that James would not 'breake the prouerbe true / to change an old friend for a newe'.[51] The imminent shift in English foreign policy also caused unease abroad. Louis XIII was so concerned that the match would lead James to abandon the Dutch that he agreed to pay 200,000 crowns in arrears due to French troops in the Republic.[52]

Commercial rivalry with the Dutch made some form of cooperation with Spain an attractive option for James, and Charles was to provide safe passage for Spanish ships and troops operating against the Republic during the early 1630s.[53] Spanish negotiators certainly expected some sort of change in Anglo-Dutch relations in return for their large dowry.[54] Nevertheless, given James's natural aversion to war and his difficulties in raising money, it is highly unlikely that he was serious about a full-blooded military alliance against the Republic, let alone a partition of the Netherlands. While a joint Anglo-Spanish force would have been formidable, it would be unlikely to achieve what Spain alone had been unable to do after decades of conflict. It seems more likely that James's offer was an initial negotiating stance which would bear little relation to the final outcome. In the meantime, the prospect of military cooperation might encourage Philip to conclude the match and dispatch the Infanta. The Venetian ambassador did not believe that James's proposals were made in good faith. 'I have always found the king very slippery', he wrote, 'and apt to speak in different ways for the attainment of his ends'.[55] It is worth noting that Digby chose to ignore James's instructions about cooperation for the time being, writing 'His Majesty's pleasure to be first known' on the back of the letter he received, perhaps thinking it best to wait and see if James would persist with his offer.[56]

Although the Dutch may well have known about the proposed Anglo-Spanish attack (and reportedly didn't believe it was genuine), James did not know that this was the case. Advanced knowledge of his proposal would severely limit his ability to maintain friendly relations with the Dutch if the offer was fake, let alone mount a successful attack against them if it was real. While popular anti-Dutch sentiment certainly existed in England, many of James's subjects would also be hostile to the prospect of a war against their fellow Protestants in alliance with a Catholic power. Inojosa later claimed that James had been so insistent that the matter should be kept secret that 'besides the kinge and the Count of Olivares noe man in Spaine knewe of it'.[57]

The success of negotiations in Spain relied on suppressing information which would arouse opposition at home, and persuading critics to abandon hopes that the match would fail. Even prominent opponents of Spain might acquiesce if they could be convinced that the match was inevitable. As Digby wrote in 1621, 'though many do and will for the present speake freely yet when it is once concluded each one will be glad to hold his peace and submitt himself to [James's] good will and pleasure'.[58] As Charles told Philip, any sign of delays to the match would 'animate those in England that affect not this marriadge, to raise vp new stormes against the Catholicks ... hoping by that meanes to disturb it'.[59] If the match was finally concluded, however, no-one would dare to disobey James, 'for they shall see all their intentions quite cutt off'.[60] Since the success or failure of negotiations was to some extent at the mercy of James's councillors and subjects, it was essential to shape their perceptions of the negotiations by suppressing news from Madrid and presenting the match as a *fait accompli* to which further resistance would be futile. James's behaviour angered those who felt that the match would affect the political and religious course of the kingdom as a whole, and who therefore claimed a legitimate right to know about and discuss the negotiations.[61] The author of an anonymous tract against the match lamented that 'we are growne now soe Contemptible in our Princes eyes that he thinkes vs unworthie of the knowledge of the most important matter that euer happened to our Lande, the Marriage of our prince'.[62] In the absence of news from Madrid, as we shall see, many of James's subjects came to their own conclusions about the progress of negotiations there.

THE PRACTICE AND CONSEQUENCES OF SECRECY

James had a variety of practical political reasons to keep the news of Charles's and Buckingham's trip to Madrid secret, and to conceal details of their negotiations there. But how exactly did the King restrict information about events in Madrid, and how effective were his methods? What were the consequences, intended and unintended, of his secretive behaviour?

Many observers reported that James was virtually the only person in England who knew about the progress of the negotiations. In early June 1623 the Venetian ambassador informed his superiors that 'the King writes the letters with his own hand, and alone receives and reads them, communicating the contents to no one soever'; even senior ministers were 'as much in the dark as the vulgar', and had even asked the ambassador himself if he knew what was going on in Spain.[63] Beaulieu similarly apologised for not being able to tell William Trumbull anything about the negotiations, but said that everyone was in the same boat:

> The truth is, that we are all blynde here in that mysticall busines of the Mariage which is wholy directed and shutt vp in His Maiesties bosome, so as no man els hath any true knowledge of the state and secrett thereof, and we are forced to drawe our conclusions out of the outward shewe and proceedings of the Court.[64]

James was particularly secretive during the most sensitive and important period of negotiations in 1623, but his behaviour was part of an established pattern. As early as 1620, the Earl of Kellie was forced to apologise to the Earl of Mar for not being able to pass on information about a new obstacle the Spanish had raised in negotiations, 'being contramandit bye the Prince himselfe not to speik of it'.[65] In 1621, the Venetian ambassador wrote that James had stopped telling the Privy Council about the status of negotiations in order to 'render everyone dumb'.[66]

James did not have a complete monopoly over news from Madrid during Charles's and Buckingham's trip. Sir Edward Conway and Sir George Calvert both conferred with the King about the negotiations to some extent, or wrote or received letters to and from Spain.[67] Nevertheless, most councillors, even those who supported the match like the Earl of Kellie, were firmly excluded for most of the trip. One of Buckingham's friends in England reassured the

Duke that 'the King is so reserved in the Princes affaires, as that he neither imparts the businesses of Spain, nor his intents therein to any of his privie Councel'.[68] Even Lord Keeper Williams, who was later consulted about the means to satisfy Spanish demands of toleration, was kept in the dark about the terms of the dispensation when it arrived in England.[69] Those who knew about the progress of negotiations, as we shall see, were under strict orders not to talk about them.

To some extent, James's secretive behaviour during this period was similar to that of other English monarchs who negotiated treaties, particularly marriage alliances, with foreign Catholic princes. A similar degree of secrecy surrounded Elizabeth's dealings with the Duke of Anjou. Although Elizabeth had not shared details of the marriage negotiations with her Privy Council, a smaller group was called upon to advise her, and this group included individuals who opposed the match.[70] What surprised and dismayed James's councillors and other observers in 1623 was that he concealed the negotiations from virtually all of his advisers, whether they supported the match or not. The Spanish match negotiations had more in common with the negotiations for a French match in 1624 and the much later Treaty of Dover in 1670, which also involved unpopular demands for Catholic toleration or conversion, although Charles's journey to Madrid and his presence there in 1623 arguably meant that the stakes were even higher.[71]

James was constantly on his guard against attempts by insatiably curious councillors to discover the contents of his diplomatic letters. In January 1623, an unnamed courtier furtively read some of the King's correspondence, providing the basis for the Venetian ambassador's detailed report on the progress of the match.[72] Some of the snooping was almost comical. In April, James complained that the Marquis of Hamilton had tried to read letters from Charles and Buckingham over his shoulder, helpfully offering to decipher any difficult handwriting for the King.[73]

James quickly learned that the only way to prevent such prying was to read the letters in private and then burn them. John Castle reported that a packet of letters that arrived in May was 'burned ... with shew of discontentment'.[74] The King, Chamberlain wrote, 'acquaints no body with any thing comes thence [from Spain], but burnes the letters as fast as he reades them'.[75] The ever-helpful Marquis of Hamilton also burnt a letter from Buckingham in James's presence after the King had read it.[76] Not all of these letters were about the Spanish match. Conway reported that James also burnt letters that Buckingham had written from Madrid about matters of patronage at home.[77] James also wrote many of the letters to Charles and Buckingham in his own hand, and he so distrusted his own Latin secretary that on one occasion he avoided writing to Philip IV, asking Buckingham to pass on his thanks and good wishes verbally instead.[78]

James did not only burn those letters from Madrid that were addressed to him. The Venetian ambassador reported that the King 'recently opened all the letters [from Spain] and burned many addressed to private individuals'.[79] He was clearly worried that private letters carried along with his own official correspondence might give some idea of the state of negotiations. William Wynn complained that he had not received any letters from his brother, Richard, who had gone to join Charles in Madrid. Even though posts arrived every day, 'all the letters to privatt men that come by post, are continuallie suppressed, and burnt, because there should be no intelligence given of what they doe intend to doe in the spanishe busynes'.[80] James's subjects who already lived in Spain or who had travelled to accompany Charles were asked to refrain from writing to England altogether, 'vpon penaltie'.[81] Merchants' letters were also reportedly intercepted, and it was rumoured that letters written in England to correspondents in Spain were being opened and read.[82] The effectiveness of the blackout was remarkable. Kellie was astonished that a courier who arrived in May 'did not bring onye letter but one from the Prince to his Majestie, not onye to onye uther bodye'.[83] The ban on private letters lasted at least until August, when the Earl of Kellie was reporting that couriers from Spain were still bringing 'noe letters to onye but to his Majestie him selfe'.[84]

Couriers who travelled from Spain were in a unique position to speculate about the contents of their packets. These couriers were often servants of Digby, Charles or Buckingham, and their presence in Madrid gave them the opportunity to gather information about the progress of negotiations, even if they didn't know the details of the letters themselves. As a result, they seem to have been routinely questioned by news-hungry people as soon as they arrived in England. James therefore made sure that the couriers who carried letters to and from Madrid in 1623 reported directly to him when they arrived and avoided talking to anyone else. One of Joseph Mead's correspondents reported in May that Walsingham Gresley, one of Digby's servants, had just returned from Spain, 'but neither is he liberall in relating, nor hath any other beene (for ought I heare) in writing'.[85] Similarly, when Peter Killigrew arrived, Chamberlain wrote that 'all that can be got out of him is, that the Prince is well and wishes to be at home'.[86] Observers were forced to glean what little they could about the contents of Charles's letters from the subscription of the packets.[87]

Couriers were often dispatched as soon as they arrived. Kellie reported that a recently arrived courier 'went out of the towin without his butts' soon after arriving, while Beaulieu reported that after reading a letter from Madrid and casting it in to the fire, James would dispatch a courier with a reply 'out of hand'.[88] James no doubt needed to reply to Charles as quickly as possible to maintain the momentum of negotiations in Spain, but the quick turnaround also meant that his couriers had little time to speak with anyone but the King. Diplomats who acted as informal couriers were also ordered to remain silent.

The Earl of Carlisle refused to discuss the progress of negotiations even with his closest friends after his return from Spain in June.[89]

Strenuous efforts were made to ensure that James's English subjects in Madrid had little or nothing to report. Courtiers who had gone to join Charles in Madrid were largely confined to the same house, and most of them hadn't even seen the Prince, having been told that they 'must not much stirr abroad' during their stay.[90] One of the Prince's attendants, Sir George Goring, was so isolated that his only Spanish friend was a young page. 'As for greater folkes I know not them and they see not me. We all liue in mighty state for noebody comes at vs'.[91] The writer of an anonymous tract complained that virtually the only man allowed near Charles was the 'Ruyner of the people', Buckingham.[92] As a result, as Trumbull complained, 'none of our Countrymen that are in the Courte of Spaine, either knoweth or will adventure, to wryte that which commes to their eares'.[93] Correspondents were reduced to basing their reports about events in Spain on information provided by individuals living thirty miles or more away from the Spanish court.[94] The dismissal of the Prince's servants and chaplains may have reflected English concerns about diplomatic leaks rather than being (as some feared) a Spanish plot to isolate the Prince and encourage his conversion to Catholicism.[95]

Secrecy in Madrid was maintained on the orders of Charles and Buckingham, and it was they who instructed couriers who travelled to England to remain silent.[96] They conducted negotiations almost to the exclusion of anyone else, a situation which according to Kellie, made 'most men mervell'.[97] Bristol was consulted, but Cottington was only asked about specific matters on occasion.[98] Aston, who actively suppressed the writing of letters by private individuals, was also reticent about the progress of negotiations in his own correspondence with Trumbull and Carleton, who complained about the bareness of his letters.[99] Aston had good reason to fear that any details he saw fit to share with his diplomatic colleagues would find their way back to England. An anonymised extract of one of Aston's letters survives in Carleton's correspondence.[100]

Restricting the supply of information from Spain increased the demand, and some information did slip through the net. Diplomats and couriers who returned to England from Spain could not always be relied on. Robert Carey was given explicit orders by both Charles and James to keep his mouth shut when he returned to England, but he couldn't help divulging a few details to his niece, who then spread them further.[101] Cottington also let some words slip when he returned later in the month.[102] News that the dispensation had arrived slipped out when Calvert received a letter from Bristol which James did not have the opportunity to intercept.[103] While James could generally silence his own diplomats in Madrid, the representatives of other nations were beyond his control. The French ambassador in Spain passed on information about Spanish diplomatic movements and the terms of the marriage treaty to the English ambassador in France, Edward Herbert.[104] On occasion, the international diplomatic network of information could, as it were, route around any attempt at censorship. Finally, the Spanish ambassadors in London shared news about the negotiations with their English Catholic friends. Conway complained that the details of the proposed toleration were becoming 'as common as the balletts sung in streets'.[105] James asked the Spanish ambassadors to prevent such leaks 'as verie disadvantagious to his Maiestie and to their partie'.[106]

For a long period in May and early June an odd silence descended, and for five weeks no couriers appeared to arrive at all.[107] The absence of news was unexpected, since Charles had promised he would write once a week.[108] Observers advanced a variety of explanations. Some speculated that the King was 'not only hiding the letters but concealing the bearers', although the Venetian ambassador dismissed this explanation as 'a thing both false and practically impossible'.[109] Others believed that the couriers were going to the Countess of Buckingham, who could have passed on news to James during his frequent visits.[110] Tillières admitted that this was mere conjecture, since as so often during these negotiations, even councillors of state and gentlemen of the bedchamber were no better informed than anyone else about what James was doing.[111] Some thought that James was not so much concealing couriers as routing them through France in a devious way:

> Till yesterday we had no newes out of Spaine this moneth or five weekes, for the King had found a way to have advertisement thence without notice of any body the packets beeing sent to our ambassador in Fraunce who sent them away by some servant or messenger of his owne, and stayed those that brought them till aunswer came backe to dispatch them.[112]

In other words, the King was having the letters to and from Spain relayed through Paris, ensuring that Spanish news came from an unexpected direction, via a courier who would have little knowledge of events in Spain, and who was unlikely to be aware of the contents or even the significance of the letters he carried.[113]

While some believed that James was going to great lengths to hide posts from Spain, there were other explanations for the lack of news. One of these was that the couriers were being deliberately delayed in France, where the prospects of an Anglo-Spanish alliance were viewed with dismay. Louis feared that if James allied with Spain, he would cease to support the Dutch, and would use his influence with the Huguenots to encourage them to rise up in rebellion against the French crown.[114] The French had an interest in creating delays which might slow the pace of negotiations, and English lines of communication ran directly through their territory. Conway had noticed in April that posts were taking a long time to arrive, and thought they should be punished for their tardiness since, as Tillières noted, every minute James waited for the arrival of a courier seemed like a day.[115] The couriers may not simply have been lazy, however. Chamberlain wrote that the lack of news from Spain in May 'breedes suspicion that there is some stop or restraint in Fraunce'.[116] In late May, Herbert made an official complaint in France about the 'retardings and delay' of couriers, which elicited a promise for 'better order henceforth'.[117] Nevertheless, Walsingham Gresley, who was on his way to Spain, was detained at Fontainebleau by the French authorities in early June.[118]

While the French authorities may have played a part in slowing couriers, the truth about the silence in May and June was much simpler than most observers suspected. James did not receive any letters during this period because Charles and Buckingham did not send any.[119] Far from concealing couriers, James was as frustrated as anyone by the lack of news.[120] The arrival of the papal dispensation in April had generated a great deal of further activity and uncertainty in Madrid. It demanded toleration for English Catholics and the abrogation of laws against them. The Infanta would be allowed two more years to educate any children, and English Catholics would have free access to her chapel.[121] Philip was asked to secure sufficient guarantees that James would enact and maintain these changes. A junta of Spanish theologians was formed to consider what conditions Philip should demand.[122] As Aston wrote, there was little to report while the junta deliberated, and negotiations over the conditions of the new treaty were unpredictable and fitful.[123] It seems that Charles and Buckingham were reluctant to write when the terms, as Digby wrote, were subject to daily change.[124] They therefore decided to stop writing altogether until they could 'send word at one stroke of the final completion of the negotiations'.[125] Far from deviously hiding dispatches and re-routing couriers, James simply did not receive any letters during this period, but as so often, observers preferred more complex, intentional explanations which highlighted their own ability to see the truth beneath the surface of events. The legacy of James's political trickery was that observers tended to assume that he was scheming and manipulating even when he was not.

Although James exerted a remarkable degree of control over news from Spain, his secretive behaviour backfired. Rather than closing down discussion of the negotiations and its possible terms, his burning of letters and unwillingness to share the news led many of his subjects to assume the worst. Observers tended to assume that James would not destroy letters from Madrid if they contained good news. At one point during the spring Castle told Trumbull that the King had been put in a foul mood by some recent letters 'which it seemes advertise that thinges go not well at Madrid'.[126] 'After he had reade them', Castle added, 'he cast them aside without once looking after them againe, which is not his Custome when he hath any newes that please him'.[127] The lack of news from Spain in May, according to Simonds D'Ewes, 'ioyed the hearts a little of drooping protestants, controuling the late insolent boastings of the popish crue'.[128] The Earl of Kellie wrote that most were 'diffident' about the likely success of the match, and that 'this long sylence confermes them mutche in their opinione'.[129] Observers were able to use the fact that no messengers had arrived to disprove rumours that the match had taken place.[130] Interpretations of James's behaviour were often based on wishful thinking, and anti-Spanish observers tended to interpret either too many couriers or too few as an indication that negotiations were stalling. In January, Chamberlain wrote that the 'continuall messages' between England and Spain in January 'argue that all is not as we wold have yt', and that negotiations were clearly not as settled as James pretended, but the lack of news in May and June was also interpreted as an indication of delays.[131]

In the absence of definite information about the terms of the papal dispensation and marriage treaty, observers tended to assume the worst about the Spanish demands. Williams told Buckingham that he had 'so lock'd up all things in your own Breast, and sealed up his Majesties, that now our very Conjectures (for more they were not) are altogether prevented'. As a result, 'We all think, and the Town speak and talk of the worst, and of very difficult Conditions'.[132] Courtiers guessed that a letter from Charles contained a demand for James to end the Dutch alliance and introduce a full toleration of Catholicism.[133] It was rumoured that the terms of the dispensation included the granting of Virginia and the Bermuda islands to Philip, as well as for Portsmouth, Plymouth and the Isle of Wight to be garrisoned with Spanish troops. James would also be required to pull all English troops out of the Dutch Republic.[134] Charles had reportedly been asked to swear to defend the Pope and recognise his authority, although the Prince had denied this request.[135] Liberty of conscience would be granted to James's Catholic subjects, and a Jesuit college would be opened in England to educate their children.[136] Elizabeth and her children would be forced to live in Brussels as hostages to the safety of the Infanta.[137] The writer of one newsletter even claimed that Philip had demanded 'Scotland and Walles in dowrye'.[138] Not everyone believed such harsh terms, and Mead questioned whether these reports could possibly be true.[139]

English Catholics, who lobbied for better terms when the details of toleration were being negotiated in July, were thought to be the source of some of these rumours.[140] Conway complained that they added 'such inventions and addiccons, as deforme them past knowledge'.[141] Although some Catholics appeared eager to boast and exaggerate about the coming toleration, others feared provoking a backlash. Wynn reported that when rumours circulated about the terms of the dispensation earlier in the summer, all the Catholics denied them.[142]

It is possible that some of these rumoured terms had some basis in fact. Charles reported that Olivares had tried to insert 'new, unreasonable, undemanded' points into the junta's requests in June.[143] The favourite hoped that Charles and Buckingham might accept these terms in their haste to get home, but he was eventually forced to drop them. Some of the rumours circulating in England may have been derived from these initial bargaining positions. Olivares may well have argued that if James was really interested in a military alliance against the Dutch, he wouldn't mind pulling English troops out of the Republic. The request for an English stronghold as security for the safety of English Catholics was certainly real. The papal nuncio had asked for this soon after Charles arrived in Madrid, although the Prince refused.[144] English opponents were likely to ignore these nuances and exaggerate the terms, particularly as James kept many of them secret when he and the Privy Council finally swore to uphold the marriage treaty in July.

'OUTWARD SHOWS' OF CONFIDENCE

James's near monopoly over news from Madrid placed him in a unique position to present his own rather optimistic view of the negotiations. The King was aware that observers who were starved of information from Madrid had to rely on his own reactions to Charles's and Buckingham's dispatches to find out what was happening. The fact that he kept the details of negotiations to himself gave him much more freedom to present a favourable impression of their progress without being contradicted by observers in Spain. James needed to reassure his subjects that Charles was being treated well and would be allowed to return, but he also sensed the opportunity to dampen hostility to the match by presenting it as a done deal to which further opposition would be useless. His outward behaviour during this period appears to confirm Bacon's observation that 'he that will be secret, must be a dissembler in some degree'.[145]

Historians have highlighted the extent of public hostility to the Spanish match. The tracts and libels written against it, and the public celebrations that met Charles when he returned without the Infanta have been well studied. Although many of James's subjects bitterly opposed the marriage, however, the King had reason to hope that a silent majority were more amenable than it sometimes appeared. Newsletter writers occasionally gave the impression that public opinion about the match was fickle. According to Castle, the punishment of an individual for spreading false rumours about the failure of the match in 1622 led to a sudden change in the stream of public discourse. The people were now so afraid of expressing doubts about the match that they went to the opposite extreme. 'Nowe all men in their discourse ... speake as confidently and as far on the other side', he wrote, claiming that the marriage had definitely been concluded, and welcoming the Spanish alliance because it would help James to counteract the commercial threat posed by the Dutch.[146] It is an open question whether this episode demonstrated that opponents of the match were capable of changing their minds, or whether supporters who were normally silent used it as an opportunity to voice their opinions. Castle implied that such talk was merely a temporary reaction to the threat of royal punishment, but it is possible that he was simply reluctant to acknowledge the existence of an underlying strand of popular support for the marriage which was associated with anger at recent Dutch outrages.

The public celebrations James organised to mark Charles's safe arrival in Spain offered further evidence, for those who wished to see it, that the match might not be so unpopular after all. James did his best to publicise the generous welcome Charles was given in Madrid. As the Venetian ambassador sourly noted, James was delighted at the Prince's reception, and wished 'to feed others on the smoke upon which perchance he feeds himself'.[47] A book detailing the Prince's entertainment was printed by authority, and widely read.[48] Humphrey May told Buckingham that news of Charles's reception 'hath much disapointed the censorious wisdeom' of armchair statesmen who thought the trip would be a disaster.[49]

When London failed to express its joy at Charles's arrival in Spain, James ordered that bells be rung and bonfires lit in every street. Some thought these celebrations were muted and thinly attended, but others were not so sure.[50] The Venetian ambassador wrote that since the celebrations, 'people now seem better disposed towards the marriage either from natural flexibility to do the behest of him who commands them, or from a new friendliness corresponding to the honours accorded to their prince or perhaps from necessary dissimulation'.[51] The bonfires were even misinterpreted as celebrations of the marriage itself.[52] James was not to know that the public reaction to Charles's safe return in October without the Infanta would be much more enthusiastic and spontaneous. The public 'iollitye and feasting' which accompanied the ceremony in which James and his councillors swore to observe the terms of the marriage treaty in July gave supporters of the match another hopeful sign. Simonds D'Ewes was disgusted that thousands of Londoners broke the Sabbath to witness this event.[53]

James hoped that news of celebrations in England would be well received in Spain. When verses in praise of the match were composed on behalf of the University of Oxford 'upon our bells and bonfires for the Princes safe arrivall in Spaine', Chamberlain expected them in print 'that the Spanish may see with what applause we are like to receve her [the Infanta]'.[54] It was presumably hoped that this would calm any Spanish fears that English hostility towards the match would make it impossible to achieve; or at least to prevent the Spanish from using domestic opposition as an excuse to either raise their demands or break off negotiations altogether. It is possible that the Spanish ambassadors themselves played along with this conceit. When new ambassadors arrived, it was said that they had enjoyed their reception so much 'that they desired to have all the orations and other exercises and disputations, and that they might be printed'.[55] Both James and the ambassadors had an interest in presenting a positive picture of English support for the match.

The behaviour of anti-Spanish councillors during Charles's and Bucking-ham's time in Madrid suggested that Digby and others were right to suppose that opponents would reconcile themselves to the match if it appeared to be unstoppable. The Francophile Earl of Carlisle, who was sent to Madrid while Charles and Buckingham were there, was known to have opposed the match, and some worried that he would not be welcome in Madrid, but observers were surprised to hear that he had 'wrettin mutche good' about Philip and Spain during his stay.[156] According to James, Carlisle was now '*todos Catillanos* [completely Castilian] and a devoted servant to the Conde d'Olivares'.[157] As a result, he was 'mutche lawched at be sume that knows how mutche he hed bein contrarye to that courss'.[158]

While James's councillors had been almost entirely excluded from negotia-tions since Charles and Buckingham left the country, in July the King finally asked for the Council's advice on whether to accept the Spanish junta's terms.[159] Seeking counsel at this point would allow James to share some of the responsibility for the treaty and allow him to claim that he had the Council's full support. Involving a wider number of councillors would also reassure Spanish negotiators that the fulfilment of the treaty relied on something more solid than royal promises. The councillors were so unused to giving advice, so averse to sharing the burden, or so uncertain about what James wanted that Lord Chancellor Williams had to prod them into giving a response.[160]

James had reason to fear that his Privy Councillors would voice greater opposition to the match when they were called on to swear to uphold the terms of the treaty. He had tried to dissuade the Spanish from insisting on the participation of the Council by arguing that it was not necessary, and that 'his honor and the cause [would] receaue preiudice by theire rufusall' to swear.[161] Opponents of the match on the Council were far from enthusiastic about the treaty. Pembroke was deeply reluctant to participate in the ceremony, and excused himself on the basis of ill health. Some prominent councillors were likely to remain intransigent. The Earl of Oxford, in particular, was considered to be a potential leader of those who were discontented with the negotiations, but he had been kept in the Tower of London following earlier clashes with Buckingham. If the Earl was to be prosecuted in Star Chamber, however, he would have to be set free. As James wrote, Cranfield advised him to suspend the prosecution to keep Oxford out of the way, '"Except", quoth he, "ye would provide a ringleader for the mutineers" – which advice I followed'.[162]

James had good reason to worry that his councillors would refuse to swear to uphold the treaty, but he was surprised and delighted to report that our 'great Primate [Abbot] hath behaved himself wonderful well in this business ... and my Lord Chamberlain [Pembroke] hath gone beyond all the Council, in clear and honest dealing'.[163] Charles's safety was a powerful argument in favour of complying with Spanish demands.[164] By July, James and many of his ministers were beginning to worry that the Prince would be kept in Spain indefinitely, and Abbot seems to have cooperated with James over the oath because he wanted to secure the Prince's return to England on any terms, knowing that concessions to Catholics could be withdrawn later.

A speech written against the match circulated in Abbot's name, and although the Archbishop denied writing it, it was certainly plausible that he might have done. Yet even this document suggests that observers were frustrated with the recent silence of prominent opponents of the match like Abbot. The Archbishop supposedly began the speech by saying that he had been 'so longe silent and I am afraid by my silence to haue neglected the duty of the place it hath pleased god to call mee vnto'.[165] While the main target of the speech was the Spanish match, it can also be read as a veiled criticism of Abbot's apparent willingness to conform to James's wishes during this period. Humphrey May might have been referring to the flexibility of supposedly rigid opponents of the match when he told Buckingham that recent events had led him to 'despise men of slippery and vntenible natures, that are prepared for all occasions, and will never be held by the foote but by a feather'.[166]

When James had sworn to uphold the terms of the treaty in July, he began to negotiate with the Spanish ambassadors in England over the precise terms of any toleration for Catholics.[167] Mutual distrust between James and the Spanish meant that questions of secrecy and publicity were central to these discussions. The King called a select committee to discuss the concessions and how they were to be enacted.[168] The King wanted to delay unpopular moves towards toleration until the Prince and the Infanta were safely in England. In exchange for money he hoped to quietly pardon individual Catholics for their past offences. The Spanish ambassadors, on the other hand, insisted that concessions should be enacted before the Infanta's arrival, and wanted James to issue a much more public proclamation announcing a general pardon, which would be much harder to abrogate. Lord Keeper Williams warned that a proclamation risked provoking a rebellion, and it is possible that the Spanish diplomats hoped to scupper the match by demanding something that James would not be able to deliver.[169] James argued that an order to his judges under the Great Seal would address those who were responsible for enforcing recusancy laws, whereas a proclamation 'was onely to vulgar people whoe had noe interest in the busines, not were capable of any thinge but feare and Rumor'.[170] A proclamation, he said, would actually be less binding than an order, because one proclamation could simply be cancelled by another in future.[171] In practice, the legal status of these documents was beside the point. Private promises and instructions could be broken or reversed much more easily than public declarations. A compromise was worked out, but James realised that Philip would be much more likely to dispatch the Infanta that year if he believed that James was doing everything in his power to satisfy the ambassadors' demands. The King urged Inojosa to tell his superiors in Spain that he was acting in good faith, and asked to see copies of his dispatches.[72] Inojosa promised to help, but his letters did not express the confidence in James's trustworthiness that the King would have liked. As Charles and Buckingham wrote, 'we find that they here believe the Marquis of Onoyosa's intelligence, better than all your Majesty's real proceedings; but we beseech you take no notice to the Marquis of Inoyosa of his juggling (for he has written hither, contrary to his professions), until we wait upon you'.[73]

The Spanish ambassadors had good reason to believe that James would not keep his word. While the Prince was in Spain, Williams drafted a declaration intended to dispel English fears about Catholic toleration. The declaration, which would be published after the Infanta was safely in England, stated that the Treaty would not bring an alteration of religion, and that English Catholics would have no better treatment than if the marriage had not occurred. The document ended with a list of strict rules for the defence of Protestantism, including orders for the enforcement of attendance and the repair of churches.[74] Williams offered to take the blame if James decided to reinforce the recusancy laws.[75]

Even at this late stage in negotiations, the King continued to act with obvious duplicity, giving different audiences mutually exclusive impressions about his wishes and inclinations. While he strove to convince the Spanish that any obstacles to the marriage could be overcome, he could not resist signalling to his anti-Catholic subjects that he secretly agreed with them. The building of a Catholic chapel for the Infanta must have contrasted uncomfortably with James's earlier foundation of Chelsea College, a centre for anti-papal polemic, in 1609.[76] His reluctance to make too many concessions to English Catholics before the successful conclusion of negotiations and the arrival of the Infanta led him to delay work on the chapel for the most trivial reasons, such as that it would disturb some birds who lived on the building site, and contradictory rumours circulated throughout the country about whether or not the chapel was being built.[77] Tillières reported that James had referred to the chapel as a home for the devil, and hinted that the displaced birds would soon return.[78] If the Spanish were wise, Tillières went on to say, they would respond to James's double dealing by insisting on strong conditions upon which he would not be able to renege.[79] One of the Spanish ambassadors, Coloma, certainly did not think that James would abide by the promises he made in 1623, and Charles struggled to convince Olivares that James could be trusted.[80]

Many anti-Spanish observers were deeply sceptical that the match would ever be made. Castle doubted Spanish assurances even when the match looked like going ahead.[81] 'So longe as that which they promise is most proffitable for them', he told Trumbull in 1622, 'so long they will keepe that which they haue promised'.[82] Beaulieu was equally sceptical of the match ever receiving papal approval. 'I euer thought that the Spaniarde would rather haue it in doing then donne, so I doe conceiue that Romish formalitie [i.e. a dispensation] to be their reserued pretence from whence they doe purpose to fetch all their excuses for their future delayes'.[183] When George Gage brought a copy of the Pope's dispensation to the King, Castle refused to believe it was authentic, and reiterated his belief that the Pope's consent to the marriage would be the obstacle whereby the Spanish King could 'easily gett off, and saue his honor'.[184]

James had previously given the impression that the match was as good as concluded, and he often had good reasons for doing so. In 1620, the Venetian ambassador observed that James 'lets it be understood that the marriage is arranged and expresses his displeasure with those who show any signs of not believing it'.[185] In January 1623 James once again confirmed that negotiations were fully concluded.[186] His optimism at this point appeared to be well founded, and James may simply have passed on the news he received from Spain. As Buckingham later alleged, Digby often wrote that the match had been concluded, only to write later that the Spanish had raised new difficulties.[187] When they arrived in Madrid, Charles himself confirmed that negotiations were in as good a state as they had ever been.[188] News that the match negotiations were nearing completion was easily transformed into reports that it had in fact been concluded, but it is unclear where in the chain of communication this distortion occurred.

Although James may genuinely have believed that the match had been, or was close to being concluded in the early 1620s, observers increasingly thought that he was cloaking inward doubts about the negotiations with a public display of confidence and optimism. When Endymion Porter brought news about the negotiations in January 1623, the Venetian ambassador reported that the King 'wrote and laboured a long while in the night and seemed sad; finally he feigned the gout to cover his dissatisfaction, though in public he displayed as much joy as he could'.[189] Cottington's arrival in June led Valaresso to report that 'his Majesty, as usual, keeping the news from every one soever announces that the negotiations are proceeding favourably and the marriage will be completed soon ... But many indications speak otherwise'.[190] In July the Earl of Kellie similarly wrote that James, who 'lewkes for the best of evrye thing' had been 'cloiss in the particulars' of a recent dispatch from Charles and Buckingham, and 'onlye in the generall he sayes to us that are neere him that all things are concludit'.[191] James's behaviour tended to confirm individuals in their existing views. Those who wished to believe that the match was concluded were heartened by James's confidence, while those who did not simply refused to believe him. In 1620, when James was trying to convince courtiers that the marriage had been arranged, the Venetian ambassador wrote that 'The ministers who do not want it say, his Majesty says it is arranged just as those who desire it say: We believe it is arranged'.[192]

During Charles's stay in Madrid, observers believed that James was trying to assuage public fears about the Prince's safety by creating the false impression that he would be home soon. The King publicly stated that he would be back by the end of May, although this claim was undermined when Charles sent for his tilting horses, which as Kellie wrote, 'argewes noe sudden returne'.[193] James nevertheless persisted in his conceit. 'His Majestie is of that mynd that he lewkes for the Prince before the end of Maye or in the beginning of June', Kellie wrote, 'whitche moste men thinks it will not be soe'.[194] Valaresso dismissed James's claims that Buckingham would return in the next few days by writing that 'with such audacity do they spread all sorts of lies here'.[195]

While the larger attempt to manipulate expectations about the negotiations in Madrid went on, Buckingham engaged in his own private campaign to shape perceptions about his conduct in Madrid. While the success of the match relied in large part on starving English critics of the match of information about the progress of negotiations, as we have seen, Buckingham had his own reasons for suppressing news from Madrid. Buckingham was well aware that he would be blamed if the match failed, and news of his clashes with Olivares would only provide his enemies around the King with evidence that he was mismanaging the negotiations. His attempts to monitor and influence opinion in England in 1623 prefigure his later efforts to garner support for himself and his war policies.[196]

A number of Buckingham's friends kept him informed about how his behaviour in Madrid was interpreted by a variety of audiences in England. One correspondent told him that there were 'contrary opinions in Court and City' about his conduct. While the former admired Buckingham for his loyalty and zeal to religion, 'by the other you are maligned', and it was said that he was deliberately delaying the negotiations.[197] While Protestants thought Buckingham was a papist, Catholics thought him 'the greatest enemy they have'.[198] News of Charles's reception in Madrid provided a temporary respite from criticism. As Williams told him, 'all Discontents are well appeased, and will so remain without doubt, as long as Businesses continue successful'. If the negotiations failed, however, Buckingham would be blamed for taking Charles to Spain.[199] Reports about Buckingham's over-familiarity with Charles and his quarrels with Olivares were particularly damaging to his reputation at home, and rumours about the terms of the dispensation threatened to 'cast a black vayle ouer the beautie and luster of those Councells [i.e. Buckingham's] that guided the iourney thither'.[200] Williams made some effort to establish the source of these reports, but was unable to do so.[201] Other friends and clients attempted to contradict rumours about Buckingham's conduct. 'I have worke enough both in Court, and Cittie', as Viscount Rochford told the Duke, 'to falsifie their reports of you, yea some of them about weomen very base ones, and much tendinge to your great dishonour'.[202] Buckingham even instructed his clients to spread stories which absolved him of any blame for the failure of the negotiations, although these efforts were not entirely successful. As Sir John Hipsley told the Duke, 'I find that all my Lord of Bristols actions are so much extolled that what you command me to say is hardly believed'.[203] When Buckingham was in England, his servants would probably have provided most of their information about court and city opinion, and their attempts to influence it, in person. His absence in 1623 allows us to read about activities that may have been going on regularly when he was at home but for which no written evidence survives.

PREPARATIONS FOR THE INFANTA, AND PUBLIC REACTIONS

What reaction did James's attempts to manage expectations provoke among ambassadors, courtiers and ordinary subjects? An analysis of the preparations James made for the return of Charles and the Infanta provide a way of exploring the often excessively cynical reception of the King's 'outward shewes'.

The preparation and dispatch of a fleet to collect Charles and the Infanta was one of the most publicly visible ways for James to create the impression that the match would be concluded and that the Prince would return soon. Observers were immediately suspicious that James was preparing ships merely to create a sense of activity and urgency. Valaresso wondered why James was making two ships ready to collect the Duke of Buckingham in April, for instance, because several suitable English ships were already in Spanish ports.[204] Salvetti thought that the order to send the tilting horses to Charles had been countermanded 'so as to give hope that the Prince will now return', but that thousands of Londoners still refused to believe that the match would be concluded.[205]

When he finally assembled a fleet, James dispatched it from Greenwich, close to the capital, rather than a larger and more convenient port on the south coast. The geography of communications in early Stuart Britain might help to explain his decision. News of the departure or arrival of a fleet tended to be more immediate and certain if it came from a port close to London. When the English forces returned to Plymouth after their disastrous failure at Cadiz in 1625, 'there were very imperfect relations' about the expedition, according to Clarendon, 'and the news of yesterday was contradicted the morrow'.[206] As with news of the Battle of White Mountain, contradictory rumours allowed people to come to terms with the defeat by degrees. The fleet that brought the remnants of Buckingham's Ile de Ré expeditionary force home in 1627, by contrast, arrived in Portsmouth, 'within such a distance of London that nothing could be concealed of the loss sustained'.[207] 'The effects of this overthrow did not at first appear in whispers, murmurs, and invectives, as the retirement from Cales had done', Clarendon wrote, 'but produced such a general consternation over the face of the whole nation'.[208]

News of the dispatch of a fleet to collect Charles and the Infanta would therefore have the greatest impact on public perceptions if the ships began their journey in a port close to the capital. Although the fleet was expected to travel to Plymouth before leaving for Spain, as the French ambassador wrote, James wanted it to be brought near London first in order to publicise its departure all the more, and to create the impression that he was certain that Charles and the Infanta would return soon.[209] Tillières was scathing about this stratagem, which he considered typical of James's style of rule. By staging an elaborate send-off in Greenwich, James was 'covering an impertinence with an impertinance', deflecting public anger at the huge cost of Charles's trip, which the Spanish dowry would barely recover, by giving the unwarranted impression that everything would soon be settled.[210]

The dramatic farewell James staged for the admirals of the fleet at Greenwich struck some observers as a particularly clumsy and transparent attempt to manipulate public perceptions. The Catholic admirals, led by the Earl of Rutland, gathered before James:

> The King, in a loud voice, urged their departure. He said that the earl ought to be waiting for a wind instead of the wind waiting for him, and the prince might be embarked before the ships reached those ports. These expressions are unskilled artifices, as at that time the king certainly had no news subsequent to what he received a fortnight ago, simply stating that nothing was settled though a settlement was near.[211]

The 'glittering shew' of the admirals' dispatch, and James's dramatic order for Rutland to be gone 'with all speed, and not to expect any countermand for further stay' was widely reported.[212] A libel circulating at the time indicates that the Venetian ambassador was not the only one who believed that Rutland's send-off was intended to mislead the people. Although the dispatch of the fleet seemed to indicate that the match had been concluded, the author of one popular poem wrote that:

> I doubt tis but a rumor
> The Fox hee knowes how for to wincke
> To fitt the peoples humor
> for questionless all doubts were scande
> before our Charles went thether
> and now a nauie is at hande
> to seale the Lorde knowes whether.[213]

The Spanish ambassadors, who wished to avoid raising expectations about the conclusion of the match, were frustrated by these actions. They claimed 'to have suffered prejudice', as Valaresso wrote, 'because by his premature demonstrations the king announced as complete what, according to them, was not even begun'.[214] Events in Madrid did not go according to plan, however. Cottington brought news of further delays in the negotiations, and it now appeared that the Spanish would be unwilling to dispatch the Infanta to England until a toleration of Catholics had been enacted. Charles asked James to 'seeme much discontented, at the delay vntyll the spring, and to giue out, that he wyll rather absolutly breake the business, then any way, to admitt of soe great a distrust, and dishonor to him'.[215] Observers spent the next few months recording repeated delays as the ships waited in the Downs, then at Portsmouth, before finally returning with Charles and Buckingham, but without the Infanta, in September.[216]

The letters Charles and Buckingham wrote from Madrid indicate that perceptions of James's behaviour during the dispatch of the fleet were excessively cynical. Charles and Buckingham had requested the ships themselves, and they repeatedly asked James to send them a peremptory order to return home.[217] In doing so they hoped to put pressure on the Spanish to bring negotiations to a swift conclusion by convincing them that the window of opportunity for a marriage was closing. As one of Buckingham's friends in England advised him, his intention to return to England soon 'will force them [the Spanish] out of their dull pace, and put them upon the rock, from which they cannot escape, except they fulfil your desires'.[218] Buckingham also had his own reasons for wanting to leave Madrid, quite apart from any pressure his and Charles's imminent departure might exert on Spanish negotiators. His friends in England were increasingly worried about the situation at court during his absence. His clients were being attacked while he was away, and he was urged to return to England as soon as possible.[219]

The dispatch of the ships coincided with a period of silence from Madrid. As far as James knew, Charles and Buckingham urgently needed the fleet to be sent. The King also realised that it was expensive to keep the ships in port, and that it would be better to send them on their way before their provisions were consumed or rotted.[220] James dramatically urged Rutland to make haste in public, but he did the same in private letters to the admiral.[221] He only stayed the fleet when Cottington brought news of the junta's terms, which created further delays and led Charles to countermand the order for the ships.[222]

The dispatch of Rutland's fleet was accompanied by elaborate preparations for the Infanta's arrival, which James did his best to publicise. He pestered the Spanish authorities for information about the Infanta's entourage so that he could make the appropriate arrangements.[223] These requests were no doubt intended in part to test Spanish intentions as well as to encourage a sense of momentum and inevitability about the match. A detailed itinerary was also worked out for Charles and the Infanta's journey from Southampton to London.[224] These preparations provided further opportunities to co-opt opponents of the match and create the impression that they would eventually comply with James's wishes. The anti-Spanish Earl of Southampton was required to ensure that the roads would be cleared and improved, and Charles and the Infanta were expected to stay a night at his house.[225]

In early June, James sent some of his most powerful nobles and ministers, including the Duke of Lennox, the Marquis Hamilton, the Earl of Pembroke and Lord Treasurer Cranfield, to Southampton to inspect the lodgings being prepared for Charles and his new bride. The inclusion of Pembroke in this delegation was doubtless intended to create the impression in Spain that James could rely on the reluctant consent, if not the enthusiastic support, of even his most anti-Spanish councillors. Domestic observers were nevertheless highly sceptical about the necessity of the preparations and James's motives in ordering them to be made. 'I have little opinion', as Castle wrote, 'that so many great personages haue no other errand in this Iourney, then preparaccon of lodgings. I thinke there is an other secrett hidden vnder this cover'.[226] Chamberlain was equally surprised that 'so many prime counsaillors' were given this task, when only a few 'herbingers or such like officers' would have done the job.[227] One of Joseph Mead's correspondents was baffled that such a visit should be made when James had not yet received news of the successful conclusion of negotiations. 'I cannot learne', he wrote 'that his Ma*ie*stie hath receiued any Post from spaine these 3 weeks or more (I will not say hath not) which may seeme strange and occasion strange thoughts'.[228] Chamberlain believed that the real reason behind the inspection was to 'shew how diligent and obsequious we are in any thing that concerns her [the Infanta]'.[229] Castle's own opinion was that the journey to Southampton was 'only *ad faciendum populum*; without any other misterie in it, then to have the bruite spreade that things went on well in spayne', and that the Prince would shortly return.[230] The French ambassador wrote that the preparations, which were obviously intended to make the people believe that negotiations were rapidly proceeding towards a successful conclusion, were privately laughed at.[231]

James's public 'performances' in favour of the match generated widespread if short-lived rumours that the match had been concluded. These rumours began before Charles and Buckingham left for Madrid. When Endymion Porter returned from Spain in January 1623, the fact that 'the King was very merry and jocund' gave rise to the rumour that the match was fully concluded.[232] James's reactions to the arrival of couriers in May also led to 'muttering' that the match would soon be concluded, and there were intermittent rumours in spring and early summer that the marriage had taken place.[233] Thomas Locke reported that the lords' visit to Southampton had created 'a great noice as if the Prince would haue bin heere'.[234] Some even believed that the cumulative effect of James's 'outward shewes' had increased support for the match, but this was potentially counter-productive. Valaresso reported that many Protestants had laid their 'great repugnance of old' aside, and seemed better disposed towards the match, but this made the Spanish ambassadors suspicious that they were only supportive because James had given them secret assurances that he would not introduce a toleration of Catholicism.[235]

Rumours of the successful conclusion of the match were necessarily short-lived, however, and for the most part, observers were sceptical and occasionally derisive about James's 'performances'. When presented with reports that the Palatinate would be restored in 1622, or that the marriage was in good forwardness, sceptics responded that they hoped it was 'lawfull not to beleeue vntill we see it', or asked that 'god forgive them their sinnes, that thinke, it will neuer bee'.[236] To Castle, the contrast between James's private feelings and his outward behaviour in 1623 was obvious. 'Howsoever he discourseth openly to the contrary', he wrote, James was not 'inwardly contented' with the progress being made in Madrid, a fact vividly demonstrated by his angry burning of letters.[237] The knowledge that his private reaction to letters would be widely discussed seems to have led James to drop his optimistic facade altogether. In late June, Beaulieu reported that James now received letters from Spain:

> with such a temper and indifferencie, as that fewe men can discerne by any outward demonstration when he be pleased or displeased in his mynde; neither can any man certainly judge by any thinge that appeareth, either of the true state of the business, or of the issue that it is like to haue.[238]

Although Charles was keen to return home, the Spanish junta insisted that the Infanta should stay in Spain while James put his promises for a toleration of Catholics into practice. As Charles complained, this was a clear indication that Philip did not trust English promises, and it also meant that those who opposed the match could attack Catholics to prevent the Infanta from coming. James was particularly worried that Charles would consummate the marriage and that an heir to the throne might be raised in Spain. Charles also realised, crucially, that the completion of the match would not automatically result in the restoration of the Palatinate.

The patterns of scepticism about outward shows continued as the match fell apart. In July Charles ordered preparations to be made for hunting when he returned home 'as though he would be heare before winter'. Many suspected that Charles was merely making yet more outward shows, designed to allay public fears that he would stay in Spain indefinitely. 'Some think they know the meaning of such reports', as Mead wrote, '& haue but litle confidence in them'.[239] After Charles and Buckingham returned from Madrid, observers found it difficult to guess whether James would continue or break negotiations. As the gentleman and councillors in Sir Robert Phelips's 'Discourse by way of Dialogue' both agreed, the matter was 'lockt vpp in the knowledges of a very few, soe that we should as yt were but shoote in the darke to make any coniecture what wilbe done'.[240] The negotiations for a French match that followed the return of Charles and Buckingham were just as secretive as the

Spanish match negotiations. The King continued to restrict information to a small number of councillors, and the Earl of Kellie wrote that in England only James, Charles, Buckingham and to a lesser extent Conway knew the details of negotiations.[241] Privy Councillors were reportedly so ignorant of the progress of the match that when it was concluded in November 1624 they sent their servants out to discover why bells were being rung and celebratory bonfires lit.[242] Couriers from France were dispatched as soon as they arrived in order to avoid curious questioners.[243] 'As potticaries discharge their shopps of corrupted drugs, and suche as be not vendible', as Holles complained, 'so the fagg end of the news is peradventure caste out among us'.[244] Once again, observers suspected that James was being secretive about the French negotiations because they were not going well. 'The more secrecy', as Holles wrote, 'the worse success, neither be the works of darknes prosperous at any time'.[245]

CONCLUSION

As we have seen, the success of negotiations in Madrid relied in large part on keeping secret the controversial concessions James was willing to offer. The King went to extraordinary lengths to suppress information about the match, even from most of his own councillors. Although observers were sometimes excessively cynical about James's 'outward shewes', the weight of evidence does indeed suggest that he used his control over diplomatic information from Madrid to present the match as a done deal, and thereby dissuaded opponents of the match from attempting to undermine it. The King's behaviour had important unintended consequences. His secrecy about the marriage treaty encouraged the circulation of damaging rumours which exaggerated the severity of its terms. James's attempts to manage the news could backfire in ways which undermined royal authority. His behaviour exposed him to ridicule and led many of his own subjects to doubt whether his words could be believed. The impact on the negotiations themselves were perhaps more damaging. The Spanish ambassadors doubted that James's promises about Catholic toleration could be trusted, and his equivocation over matters such as the building of the chapel seemed to justify their fears. Charles's and Buckingham's realisation that the match would not lead to the restitution of the Palatinate undoubtedly played an important part in ending the match, but doubts about James's sincerity, and the resulting decision to delay the dispatch of the Infanta until the King's promises of toleration had been put into practice also contributed to the breakdown of negotiations.

Perhaps the most important consequence of their secretive behaviour was that by concealing the details of negotiations James, Charles and Buckingham deprived themselves of counsel. By taking the direction of negotiations almost entirely into their own hands, they bypassed the system of conciliar government which otherwise acted as a bulwark against royal incompetence and allowed them to escape responsibility for failed policies. James's ability to secure the cooperation and support of his subjects relied in part on maintaining the impression that he knew what he was doing. This belief came under severe strain during this episode. The King's reaction to the news that Rutland's fleet needed to be delayed reveals something of the pressure he felt to maintain the appearance of being in control of events. 'I know not how to satisfy the people's expectation here, neither know I what to say to our Council', he wrote 'for the fleet that stayed upon a wind this fortnight (Rutland and all aboard) must now be stayed, and I know not what reason I shall pretend for the doing of it'.[246] By refusing to take councillors into his confidence about the negotiations, James had become too closely associated with the match, and found it difficult to blame others when things went wrong.[247] Buckingham's attempt to use Digby as a scapegoat for the failure of the match caused further political trouble when the former ambassador joined the attack on the favourite in the Parliament of 1626.

James's lament also raises intriguing questions about the balance of power between actor and audience in the Jacobean theatre of state. In 1624, when James was making bellicose gestures while privately telling the Spanish ambassador that he would not go to war, Wynn wrote that 'his kingcrafte is now vpon the stage and the eyes of the Christian worlde are sett vpon him expectinge woonders at his handes'.[248] Constant exposure to public scrutiny was not always comfortable, to say the least. Theatrical metaphors were entirely appropriate; a demanding audience might heckle an unconvincing performer. Public expectations could be raised and manipulated, but they also needed to be satisfied.

NOTES

1 For the trip to Madrid and negotiations in Spain, see in particular Thomas Cogswell, 'England and the Spanish match', in Richard Cust and Ann Hughes (eds), *Conflict in Early Stuart England: Studies in Religion and Politics 1603–1642* (Harlow, 1989), pp. 107–33; Alexander Samson (ed.), *The Spanish Match: Prince Charles's Journey to Madrid, 1623* (Aldershot, 2006), pp. 51–73; Glyn Redworth, *The Prince and the Infanta: The Cultural Politics of the Spanish Match* (New Haven, 2003); Robert Cross, 'Pretense and perception in the Spanish match, or history in a fake beard', *Journal of Interdisciplinary History* 37 (2007), pp. 563–83; S. R. Gardiner, *Prince Charles and the Spanish Marriage* vol. II (London, 1869), pp. 297–381. See J. H. Elliott, *The Count-Duke of Olivares: The Statesman in an Age of Decline* (London, 1986), pp. 207–14 for a Spanish perspective on the final stages of negotiations. For the end of negotiations, see Brennan Pursell, 'The end of the Spanish match', *The Historical Journal* 45:4 (2002), pp. 699–726.

2 For the important English Catholic dimension to negotiations at home, however, see Michael Questier (ed.), *Stuart Dynastic Policy and Religious Politics, 1621–1625* (Camden 5th Series, vol. 34, 2009).

3 Glyn Redworth argued that the trip was a reckless romantic gesture, but while Charles certainly became infatuated with the Infanta, and the trip was very risky, there were also rational reasons behind the journey. It is an exaggeration to say, as Redworth does, that his evidence 'blows out of the water' Cogswell's argument that Charles and James hoped to discover whether the Spaniards were truly committed to a marriage alliance. See Redworth *Prince and the Infanta*, p. 73.

4 Trumbull to Calvert, 6/16 February 1623, SP 77/16, fol. 50v; Trumbull to Calvert, 20/30 March 1623, SP 77/16, fol. 97v; Kellie to Mar, 27 April 1623, in Henry Paton (ed.), *Supplementary Report on the Manuscripts of the Earl of Mar and Kellie* vol. II, HMC 60 (London, 1930), p. 166; Trumbull to Calvert, 1/11 May 1623, SP 77/16, fol. 164v; Trumbull to Calvert, 27 June 1623, SP 77/16, fol. 212v. The Infanta was formally instructed to explore the possibility of a settlement in October 1624 and again in July 1625. See Elliott, *The Count-Duke of Olivares*, pp. 224, 236.

5 Questier, *Stuart Dynastic Policy*, p. 19. James did say that he would welcome peace in the Low Countries if it was part of a larger settlement that ended the Thirty Years' War, however. See James to Charles and Buckingham, 15 March 1623, in David M. Bergeron (ed.), *King James and Letters of Homoerotic Desire* (Iowa City, 1999), pp. 155–6.

6 Trumbull to [Carleton], 10/20 December 1622, SP 77/15, fol. 431r.

7 Arthur White, 'Suspension of Arms: Anglo-Spanish Mediation in the Thirty Years' War, 1621–25' (PhD, Tulane University, 1978), pp. 105–6.

8 London newsletter, 4 April 1623, Harl. 389, fol. 308r.

9 Thomas, Earl of Kellie, to John, Earl of Mar, 4 May 1623, in Paton (ed.), *Mar and Kellie* vol. II, p. 166.

10 Clarendon claimed that his information came from Cottington. See Edward Hyde, Earl of Clarendon, *History of the Rebellion* vol I (Oxford, 1888), pp. 15–22. Clarendon's account is not entirely reliable. It was written many years after the events in question, and some of his claims, such as that Buckingham initiated the trip and persuaded Charles to go, were probably wrong. See Roger Lockyer, *Buckingham: The Life and Political Career of George Villiers, First Duke of Buckingham, 1592–1628* (London, 1981), pp. 137–8.

11 Clarendon, *History of the Rebellion* vol I, p. 16.

12 *Ibid.*, p. 18.

13 The Jesuits apparently tried to encourage Louis to do this. See Questier, *Stuart Dynastic Policy*, p 40, *n.* 162.

14 James to Charles and Buckingham, 27 February 1623, in G. P. V. Akrigg (ed.), *Letters of James VI and I* (London, 1984), p. 389. A satirical poem of the time asked whether good subjects should 'despaire / For ever seing Englandes heire' if the Prince was detected in France. See 'Since Arthur or his table stood', Harl. 367, fol. 163r.

15 Chamberlain to Carleton, 10 February 1623, McClure vol. II, pp. 481–2.

16 John Beaulieu to William Trumbull, 21 February 1623, Add. 72255, fol. 14r.

17 Elisabeth Bourcier (ed.), *The Diary of Sir Simonds D'Ewes, 1622–1624* (Paris, 1974), p. 119.

18 George Calvert to Trumbull, 7 March 1623, Add. 72268, fol. 161r. This was not the first time that the ports had been blocked. Similar orders were issued at the beginning of each new reign, presumably to prevent news of the previous monarch's death from allowing foreign powers to interfere with the succession. They were also sometimes closed in order to prevent the escape of fugitives.

19 Charles appears to have considered making the trip from as early as May 1622. See Redworth, *Prince and the Infanta*, pp. 51, 53–4.

20 Chamberlain to Carleton, 4 January 1623, McClure vol. II, pp. 471–2.

21 Kellie to Mar, 14 February 1623, in Paton (ed.), *Mar and Kellie* vol. II, p. 150; Valaresso to the Doge and Senate, 20 January 1623, CSPV vol. XVII, p. 548. Glyn Redworth has argued that plans for Charles to go to Madrid had been made during the summer of 1622. See Glyn Redworth, 'Of pimps and princes: Three unpublished letters from James I and the Prince of Wales relating to the Spanish match', *The Historical Journal* 37:2 (1994), pp. 405–7.

22 Chamberlain to Carleton, 10 February, 1623, McClure vol. II p. 481; Beaulieu to Trumbull, 12 March 1623, Add. 72255, fol. 20r. See also Bourcier (ed.), *Diary of Sir Simonds D'Ewes*, pp. 120–1.

23 Bourcier (ed.), *Diary of Sir Simonds D'Ewes*, p. 120.

24 James I to Charles and Buckingham, 27 February 1623 in Akrigg (ed.), *Letters of James*, p. 389.

25 Kellie to Mar, 25 February 1623, in Paton (ed.), *Mar and Kellie* vol. II, p. 152.

26 Alvise Valaresso to the Doge and Senate, 11 March 1623, CSPV vol. XVII, p. 585.

27 Valaresso to the Doge and Senate, 17 March 1623, CSPV vol. XVII, p. 591.

28 Carleton to Calvert (copy), 6 March 1623, SP 84/111, fol. 161r; Trumbull to Calvert, 27 February 1623 (o.s.), SP 77/16, fol. 73r. Charles was also rumoured to have died in the summer of 1625, perhaps reflecting popular fears about the succession. See David Cressy, *Dangerous Talk: Scandalous, Seditious, and Treasonable Speech in Pre-Modern England* (Oxford, 2010), pp. 133–4.

29 Collegio, Secreta Esposizioni Principi, 25 March 1623, CSPV vol. XVII, p. 601.

30 This was not the first time the Prince of Orange was rumoured to have been assassinated. See Joseph Mead to Martin Stuteville, 10 February 1621, Harl. 389, fol. 15v.

31 Carleton to Trumbull, 19 September 1618 (o.s.), Add. 72270, fol. 106r. See also William Davenport's commonplace book, Cheshire Archives ZCR 63/2/19, fol. 29r.

32 For the celebrations in Madrid, see David Sánchez Cano, 'Entertainments in Madrid for the Prince of Wales: Political functions of festivals' in Samson (ed.), *The Spanish Match*, pp. 51–73.

33 Pursell, 'End of the Spanish match', pp. 703–4.

34 James to Charles and Buckingham, 15 March 1623, in Philip Hardwicke (ed.), *Miscellaneous State Papers from 1501 to 1726* vol. I (London, 1778), p. 404.

35 Buckingham to Conway, 8 April 1623, Harl. 6987, fol. 65r.

36 Charles and Buckingham to James, 17 March 1623, in Hardwicke (ed.), *State Papers* vol. I, p. 410.

37 Charles and Buckingham to James, 27 April 1623, in Bergeron (ed.), *Letters of Homoerotic Desire*, p. 190; Charles's instructions for Cottington's journey to England, 7 June 1623, Bod. MS. Clarendon 3, fol. 32r.

38 Charles and Buckingham to James, 15 July 1623, in Hardwicke (ed.), *State Papers* vol. I, p. 427.

39 For courtiers' attempts to mobilise the public to put pressure on Elizabeth I to call off

the Anjou match in 1579, see Susan Doran, *Monarchy and Matrimony* (London, 1996), pp. 164–5; Natalie Mears has questioned whether John Stubbes's *A discouerie of a gaping gvlf* was part of an organised propaganda campaign. See Natalie Mears, 'The "Personal Rule" of Elizabeth I: Marriage, Succession and Catholic Conspiracy, c. 1578–1582' (PhD thesis, St Andrews, 1999), ch. 4.

40 Girolamo Lando to the Doge and Senate, 15 October 1621, CSPV vol. XVII, p. 149.

41 John Digby to Walter Aston, 23 December 1621, Add. 36445, fols. 321v–2r. The Parliament of 1621 passed new recusant legislation, and there were several expressions of hispanophobe and anti-Catholic sentiment, particularly during the prosecution of Edward Floyd, and of course in the request that Charles should be 'timely and happily married to one of our own religion'. Digby almost certainly had the Earl of Southampton in mind when he wrote about a conspiracy to undermine the match. Southampton was later accused of colluding with and directing MPs to oppose James's policies. See 'The Examination of Henry Wriothesley, earl of Southampton', Bod. MS. Tanner 73, fol. 23r–v.

42 Edward Conway to Buckingham, 23 July 1623, in Hardwicke (ed.), *State Papers* vol. I, p. 429.

43 Williams to Buckingham, 30 August 1623, *Cabala, Mysteries of State, in Letters of the Great Ministers of K. James and K. Charles* (1653), p. 80. Williams argued that the granting of individual pardons to Catholics would be better than a more public general pardon. While the former policy would be gradual, a proclamation would make a sudden and dramatic impression that could lead to rebellion.

44 For attacks on the Spanish ambassadors in 1623, see Questier, *Stuart Dynastic Policy*, p. 63.

45 Alastair Bellany and Andrew McRae (eds), 'The wiper of the Peoples teares', 'Early Stuart Libels: an edition of poetry from manuscript sources', *Early Modern Literary Studies Text Series I* (2005), http://purl.oclc.org/emls/texts/libels (accessed 29 July 2012).

46 Digby to Aston, 15 December 1620, Add. 36444, fols. 249v–250r; Digby to Aston, 23 December 1621, Add. 36445, fol. 321v.

47 Charles to Olivares, June 1623, Stowe 143, fol. 62r. Charles was admittedly discussing a hypothetical situation in which the Infanta remained in Spain until James had enacted a toleration, but local persecution could still threaten negotiations while they were taking place. The persecution of Catholics later threatened to scupper the French match. See Conway to Carlisle and Kensington, 7 August 1624, SP 78/73, fol. 15r.

48 Gardiner, *History of England* vol. V, pp. 84–6.

49 *Ibid.*, vol. IV, pp. 273–4; vol. V, pp. 84–6; James to Charles and Buckingham, 15 March 1623, in Akrigg (ed.), *Letters of James*, p. 396.

50 Herbert to Calvert, 30 May 1623 (o.s.), SP 78/71, fol. 161r; Herbert to James, 3 June 1623 (o.s.), SP 78/71, fol. 175r–v.

51 'O blessed king that heares the poore', Royal 18 A. xxxii, p. 8.

52 Herbert to James, 19/29 April 1623, SP 78/71, fol. 121v.

53 For English cooperation with Spain in the early 1630s see Kevin Sharpe, *The Personal Rule of Charles I* (London, 1992), pp. 70–5, 825–47; Caroline Hibbard, *Charles I and the Popish Plot* (Chapel Hill (NC), 1983), pp. 25, 139–40. Charles did however consider war with Spain in the middle of the decade. See Sharpe, *Personal Rule*, pp. 509–36.

54 Digby to Buckingham, 14 March 1620, Bod. MS. Clarendon 3, fol. 82v. Digby wrote that at the very least, it was expected that James would not esteem the friendship of the Dutch more than that of Spain.

55 Lando to the Doge and Senate, 10 December 1621, CSPV vol. XVII, p. 176.

56 Gardiner, *History of England*, vol. V, p. 86. Bristol later refused to answer questions about the offer of cooperation to anyone but Charles. See 'Bristol's answers to questions concerning his diplomacy', Harl. 6798, fol. 209r. When the match negotiations collapsed and Charles and Buckingham sought to conclude an anti-Habsburg alliance with the Dutch, James's earlier offer to partition the Republic became an awkward topic. Rather audaciously, Conway tried to reassure the Prince of Orange by claiming that military cooperation had been Gondomar's idea rather than James's. See Robert Ruigh, *The Parliament of 1624: Politics and Foreign Policy* (Cambridge, (MA), 1971), pp. 38, 191.

57 'Marquis Inijosa his Letter to King James against the duke of Buckingham and his miscariage in Spaine', Harl. 4761, fol. 90r.

58 Digby to Aston, 23 December 1621, Add. 36445, fol. 322v.

59 Charles to Philip IV, June 1623, SP 94/27, fol. 71v.

60 *Ibid.* Charles similarly told Olivares that the match 'being absolutely Concluded none dares attempt [to prevent] itt, because then they shall see all theire proiects and Invenccons ouerthrowne'. See Charles to Olivares, June 1623, Stowe 143, fol. 62r.

61 Both Thomas Alured and the author of the speech attributed to George Abbot made this claim for legitimate discussion in their writings against the match. See Thomas Alured's letter to Buckingham, Sloane 1455, fols. 20r–3v; 'The Coppy of the Archbishop of Canterburyes Speach', 27 July 1623, Bod. MS. Tanner 73, fol. 302r.

62 'The Teares of the oppressed people of England', 1623, Bod. MS. Tanner 73, fol. 304v.

63 Valaresso to the Doge and Senate, 26 May 1623, CSPV vol. XVIII, pp. 22–3; Valaresso to the Doge and Senate, 2 June 1623, CSPV vol. XVIII, p. 27.

64 Beaulieu to Trumbull, 23 May 1623, Add. 72255, fol. 41r.

65 Kellie to Mar, 23 April 1620, in Paton (ed.), *Mar and Kellie* vol. II, p. 99.

66 Lando to the Doge and Senate, 15 October 1621, CSPV vol. XVII, p. 149.

67 See William Wynn to John Wynn, 20 May 1623, NLW 466E/1105; Edward Conway to Buckingham, 23 July 1623, in Hardwicke (ed.), *State Papers* vol. I, p. 429.

68 [Viscount Rochford?] to Buckingham, [1623], in *Cabala*, p. 160.

69 Williams to Buckingham, 9 May 1623, in John Hacket, *Scrinia reserata, a memorial offer'd to the great deservings of John Williams* (1693), p. 126.

70 Mears, '"Personal Rule" of Elizabeth I', pp. 88–90.

71 For the Treaty of Dover, see Ronald Hutton, 'The making of the secret treaty of Dover, 1668–1670', *The Historical Journal* 29:2 (1986), pp. 297–318.

72 Valaresso to the Doge and Senate, 20 January 1623, CSPV vol. XVII, p. 548.

73 James to Charles and Buckingham, 1 April 1623, in Akrigg (ed.), *Letters of James*, p. 403.

74 Castle to Trumbull, 16 May 1623, Add. 72276, fol. 38v. See also Kellie to Mar, 16 May 1623, in Paton (ed.), *Mar and Kellie* vol. II, p. 169. Foreign observers also commented on this incident. See Salvetti's newsletter, 16/26 May 1623, Add. 31112, fol. 369; Tillières to Puysieux, 26 May 1623, PRO 31/3/57, fol. 214r.

75 Chamberlain to Carleton, 17 May 1623, McClure vol. II, p. 497.

76 Hamilton to Buckingham [no date], Harl. 1581, fol. 1r.

77 Conway to Buckingham, 25 June 1623, SP 94/27, fol. 50r.

78 Conway to Buckingham, 1 August 1623, Harl. 1580, fol. 314r.

79 Valaresso to the Doge and Senate, 26 May 1623, CSPV vol. XVIII, pp. 22–3. The burning of private letters was widely reported. See Mead to Stuteville, 17 May 1623, Harl. 389, fol. 326r.

80 William Wynn to John Wynn, 20 May 1623, NLW 466E/1105.

81 Mead to Stuteville, 24 May 1623, Harl. 389, fol. 331r.

82 Transcript of a letter dated 22 May 1623, William Davenport's commonplace book, Cheshire Archives ZCR 63/2/19, fol. 31v; Humphrey May to Buckingham [?], 31 July 1623, Harl. 1583, fol. 272r.

83 Kellie to Mar, 16 May 1623, in Paton (ed.), *Mar and Kellie* vol. II, p. 169.

84 Kellie to Mar, 9 August 1623, p. 176.

85 [?] to Mead, 9 May 1623, Harl. 389, fol. 324v. Similar comments can be found in Bourcier (ed.), *Diary of Sir Simonds D'Ewes*, p. 134 and Kellie to Mar, 14 March 1623, in Paton (ed.), *Mar and Kellie* vol. II, p. 156.

86 Chamberlain to Carleton, 12 July 1623, McClure vol. II, p. 507.

87 *Ibid.*

88 Kellie to Mar, 16 May 1623, in Paton (ed.), *Mar and Kellie* vol. II, p. 169; Beaulieu to Trumbull, 20 June 1623, Add. 72255, fol. 51r.

89 Tillières to Puysieux, 7 June 1623, PRO 31/3/57, fol. 218r.

90 William Wynn to John Wynn, 20 May 1623, NLW 466E/1105.

91 Sir George Goring to Sir Henry Carey, [no date], Kent History and Library Centre, U269/1, Oo114.

92 'The Teares of the oppressed people of England', 1623, Bod. MS. Tanner 73, fol. 304r.

93 Trumbull to [Carleton], 4/14 July 1623, SP 77/16, fol. 221v.

94 London newsletter, 23 May 1623, Harl. 389, fol. 329r. James Howell's detailed letters from Spain were probably fictional. See Agnes Repplier (ed.), *Epistolae Ho-Elianae or the Familiar Letters of James Howell* (New York, 1907).

95 Mead to Stuteville, 24 May 1623, Harl. 389, fol. 331r. For the dismissal of Charles's retinue, see Gardiner, *History of England* vol. V, p. 43. A London newsletter writer believed that the Spanish intended to 'make him [Charles] turne Romanishe'. See transcript of a letter dated 22 May 1623, William Davenport's commonplace book, Cheshire Archives ZCR 63/2/19, fol. 31v.

96 Tillières to Puysieux, 26 May 1623, PRO 31/3/57, fol. 214r.

97 Kellie to Mar, 9 May 1623, in Paton (ed.), *Mar and Kellie* vol. II, p. 167.

98 *Ibid.*

99 Pursell, 'End of the Spanish match', p. 713; Castle to Trumbull, 16 May 1623, Add. 72276, fol. 38v. Aston claimed that he had been too busy to write in detail. See Aston to Trumbull, 1 June 1623 (n.s.), Add. 72245, fol. 115r.

100 'From Madrid the 20 June 1623', SP 94/27, fols. 15v–16r is taken from Aston to Carleton, 10/20 June 1623, SP 94/27, fols. 13r–14v.

101 Tillières to Puysieux, 11 June 1623, PRO 31/3/57, fol. 221r.

102 Tillières to Puysieux, 29 June 1623, PRO 31/3/57, fol. 227v.

103 Conway to Buckingham, 3 May 1623, Harl. 1580, fol. 299v.

104 Herbert to James, 3 June 1623 (o.s.), SP 78/71, fol. 175r.

105 Conway to Buckingham, 17 July 1623, Harl. 1580, fol. 309r.

106 *Ibid.*

107 Beaulieu to Trumbull, 13 June 1623, Add. 72255, fol. 49r; Kellie to Mar, 24 May 1623, in Paton (ed.), *Mar and Kellie* vol. II, p. 171; Beaulieu to Trumbull, 6 June 1623, Add. 72255, fol. 47r.

108 Kellie to Mar, 4 May 1623, in Paton (ed.), *Mar and Kellie* vol. II, p. 166.

109 Valaresso to the Doge and Senate, 30 June 1623, CSPV vol. XVIII, p. 40.

110 Tillières to Puysieux, 19 June 1623, PRO 31/3/57, fol. 225v.

111 *Ibid.*

112 Chamberlain to Carleton, 14 June 1623, McClure vol. II, p. 503.

113 The rumour may have come about because Walsingham Gresley, who was on his way to Spain, was detained by the French and wrote a letter via Herbert to inform Conway about this. See Herbert to Conway, 18/28 May 1623, SP 78/71, fol. 151r; [Conway] to Buckingham, 11 May 1623, SP 94/26, fol. 226r–v.

114 Herbert to James, 23 June 1623 (o.s.), SP 78/71, fol. 191v.

115 Tillières to Puysieux, 11 June 1623, PRO 31/3/57, fol. 222v.

116 Chamberlain to Carleton, 30 May 1623, McClure vol. II, p. 499.

117 Conway to John Coke, 21 April 1623, CSPD 1619–23 (1858), p. 564; Herbert to Calvert, 24 May 1623 (o.s.), SP 78/71, fol. 157r.

118 Tillières to Puysieux, 11 June 1623, PRO 31/3/57, fol. 222v.

119 'Messengers to and from Spain – Feb–May', SP 94/26, fol. 249r; Aston to Trumbull, 1 June 1623 (n.s.), Add. 72245, fol. 115r.

120 Carleton Jnr. to Carleton, 26 May 1623, SP 84/112, fol. 170r.

121 Charles and Buckingham to James, 10 April 1623, in Hardwicke (ed.), *State Papers* vol. I, p. 414.

122 Pursell, 'End of the Spanish match', p. 710.

123 Aston to Conway, 22 May 1623, SP 94/26, fol. 240r.

124 Digby to Trumbull, 13 August 1623, Add. 72285, fol. 117r.

125 Valaresso to the Doge and Senate, 23 June 1623, CSPV vol. XVIII, p. 45.

126 John Castle to Trumbull, 9 May 1623, Add. 72276, fol. 36r.

127 *Ibid.*, The writer of a letter transcribed by William Davenport made a similar observation. 'The letters, that the Kinge receaues from Spaine of late, he burnes them all, soe pleasinge they are to him'. See transcript of a letter dated 22 May 1623, William Davenport's commonplace book, Cheshire Archives ZCR 63/2/19, fol. 31v.

128 Bourcier (ed.), *The Diary of Sir Simonds D'Ewes*, p. 134.

129 Kellie to Mar, 3 June 1623, in Paton (ed.), *Mar and Kellie* vol. II, p. 172.

130 Mead to Stuteville, 3 May 1623, Harl. 389, fol. 322r.

131 Chamberlain to Carleton, 25 January 1623, McClure vol. II, p. 475.

132 Williams to Buckingham, 9 May 1623, in Hacket, *Scrinia*, p. 126. Similar observations are made in a London newsletter, 27 June 1623, Harl. 389, fol. 210r.

133 Tillières to Puysieux, 26 May 1623, PRO 31/3/57, fol. 214r–v.

134 Owen Wynn to John Wynn, 5 [May/April?] 1623, NLW 9058E/1096. Castle to Trumbull, 20 June 1623, Add. 72276, fol. 49v. Similar demands were discussed by the 'common voice' in France. See Herbert to Calvert, 30 May 1623 (o.s.), SP 78/71, fol. 161r.

135 Transcript of a letter dated 22 May 1623, William Davenport's commonplace book, Cheshire Archives ZCR 63/2/19, fol. 31v.

136 Mead to Stuteville, 17 May 1623, Harl. 389, fol. 326r.

137 Diary of Walter Yonge, Add. 28032, fol. 53v.

138 Transcript of a letter dated 22 May 1623, William Davenport's commonplace book, Cheshire Archives ZCR 63/2/19, fol. 31v.

139 Mead to Stuteville, 24 May 1623, Harl. 389, fol. 331v

140 Questier, *Stuart Dynastic Policy*, p. 58.

141 Conway to Buckingham, 17 July 1623, Harl. 1580, fol. 309r.

142 Owen Wynn to John Wynn, 5 [May/April?] 1623, NLW 9058E/1096.

143 Charles and Buckingham to James, 26 June 1623, in Hardwicke (ed.), *State Papers* vol. I, p. 422.

144 Charles and Buckingham to James, 10 April 1623, in Hardwicke (ed.), *State Papers* vol. I, p. 414. See also Gardiner, *History of England* vol. V, p. 22.

145 Francis Bacon, 'Of simulation and dissimulation' in James Spedding (ed.), *The Works of Francis Bacon* vol. XII (London, 1857–74), p. 97.

146 Castle to Trumbull, 20 September 1622, Add. 72276, fol. 9r.

147 Valaresso to the Doge and Senate, 28 April 1623, CSPV vol. XVII, pp. 641–2.

148 Mead to Stuteville, 14 April 1623, Harl. 389, fol. 314r; Diary of Walter Yonge, Add. 28032, fol. 53r.

149 Humphrey May to Buckingham, 23 April [1623], Harl. 1581, fol. 358r–v.

150 Mead to Stuteville, 5 April 1623, Harl. 389, fol. 310r.

151 Valaresso to the Doge and Senate, 14 April 1623, CSPV vol. XVII, p. 630.

152 Bourcier (ed.), *The Diary of Sir Simonds D'Ewes*, p. 129.

153 *Ibid.*, p. 147. D'Ewes gave an account of the ceremony in 'A short view of the 20th of July last past ...' under the pseudonym 'Philanax Patroleinus'. See Add. 4149, fols. 284r–9r.

154 Chamberlain to Carleton, 3 May 1623, McClure vol. II, p. 495.

155 Chamberlain to Carleton, 10 February 1623, McClure vol. II, p. 483.

156 Williams to Charles, 28 February 1623, in Hacket, *Scrinia*, p. 116; Kellie to Mar, 22 April 1623, in Paton (ed.), *Mar and Kellie* vol. II, p. 164.

157 James to Charles and Buckingham, [Late May 1623], in Bergeron (ed.), *Letters of Homoerotic Desire*, p. 166.

158 Kellie to Mar, 22 April 1623, in Paton (ed.), *Mar and Kellie* vol. II, p. 164. Tillières wrote that Carlisle's praise for Spain was against his natural inclinations, but he had done it to please James, Charles and Buckingham. See Tillières to Puysieux, 7 June 1623, PRO 31/3/57, fol. 218r.

159 Conway to Buckingham, 17 July 1623, Harl. 1580, fol. 307v.

160 Gardiner, *History of England* vol. V, p. 67.

161 Conway to Buckingham, 17 July 1623, Harl. 1580, fol. 307r.

162 James to Buckingham, 18 April 1623, in Bergeron (ed.), *Letters of Homoerotic Desire*, p. 165.

163 James to Charles and Buckingham, 21 July 1623, in Hardwicke (ed.), *State Papers* vol. I, p. 428.

164 Conway told Buckingham that Abbot had initially opposed the swearing of the oath, but that James talked him and the rest of the council around, 'care of the Prince his honour and safetie being a violent argument'. See Conway to Buckingham, 17 July 1623, Harl. 1580, fol. 309r.

165 'The Coppy of the Archbishop of Canterburyes Speach', 27 July 162, Bod. MS. Tanner 73, fol. 302r.

166 Humphrey May to Buckingham [?], 31 July 1623, Harl. 1583, fol. 273v.

167 Questier, *Stuart Dynastic Policy*, pp. 60–1.

168 Conway to Buckingham, 1 August 1623, Harl. 1580, fol. 313r.

169 Williams to Buckingham, 30 August 1623, in *Cabala*, p. 80.

170 Conway to Buckingham, 5 August 1623, Harl. 1580, fol. 319r–v.

171 *Ibid.*, fol. 318v. Conway suspected that arguments in favour of a proclamation had been provided to the Spanish ambassadors by the 'ignorant, fearefull, distrustfull Romaine Catholiques that had sought them'. *Ibid.*, fol. 319r.

172 Conway to Buckingham, 1 August 1623, Harl. 1580, fol. 313v.

173 Charles and Buckingham to James, 20 August 1623, in Bergeron (ed.), *Letters of Homoerotic Desire*, p. 197. See also Conway to Buckingham, 5 August 1623, Harl. 1580, fol. 318r.

174 See Hacket, *Scrinia*, pp. 122–3.

175 Williams to Buckingham, 30 August 1623, in *Cabala*, p. 81.

176 Anthony Milton, *Catholic and Reformed: The Roman and Protestant Churches in English Protestant Thought: 1600–1640* (Cambridge, 1995), pp. 32–3.

177 Valaresso to the Doge and Senate, 26 May 1623, CSPV vol. XVIII, p. 23; Thomas Lushington's 'Sermon Preach'd at St Maries in Oxford', Landsdowne 213, fol. 177r.

178 Tillières to Puysieux, 19 June 1623, PRO 31/3/57, fol. 224v.

179 *Ibid.*

180 Gardiner, *History of England* vol. V, p. 56; Charles to Olivares, June 1623, Stowe 143, fols. 62r–3v.

181 Manuscript tracts with titles such as 'The Impossibility of the Match with Spaine' speak for themselves. See Harl. 37, fols. 61r–87v.

182 Castle to Trumbull, 23 March 1622, Add. 72275, fol. 131r.

183 Beaulieu to Trumbull, 3 August 1620, Add. 72253, fol. 136r.

184 Castle to Trumbull, 11 October 1622, Add. 72276, fol. 15r.

185 Girolomo Lando to the Doge and Senate, 17 September 1620, CSPV vol. XVI, p. 401.

186 Valaresso to the Doge and Senate, 27 January 1623, CSPV vol. XVII, p. 555.

187 Clarendon, *History of the Rebellion* vol. I, p. 24.

188 Charles and Buckingham to James, 27 March 1623, in Hardwicke (ed.), *State Papers* vol. I, p. 413.

189 Valaresso to the Doge and Senate, 20 January 1623, CSPV vol. XVII, p. 548.

190 Valaresso to the Doge and Senate, 30 June 1623, CSPV Vol. XVIII, pp. 49–50.

191 Kellie to Mar, 24 May 1623, in Paton (ed.), *Mar and Kellie* vol. II, p. 171; Kellie to Mar, 11 July 1623, in *Mar and Kellie* vol. II, p. 174.

192 Lando to the Doge and Senate, 17 September 1620, CSPV vol. XVI, pp. 401–2.

193 Valaresso to the Doge and Senate, 17 March 1623, CSPV vol. XVII, p. 592; Valaresso to the Doge and Senate, 24 March 1623, CSPV vol. XVII, p. 599; Kellie to Mar, 31 March 1623, in Paton (ed.), *Mar and Kellie* vol. II, p. 160.

194 *Ibid.*

195 Valaresso to the Doge and Senate, 14 July 1623, CSPV vol. XVIII, p. 62.

196 See in particular Thomas Cogswell, 'The people's love: The Duke of Buckingham and popularity', in Thomas Cogswell, Richard Cust and Peter Lake (eds), *Politics, Religion and Popularity in Early Stuart Britain* (Cambridge, 2002), pp. 211–34.

197 [Viscount Rochford?] to Buckingham, [1623], in *Cabala*, p. 159.

198 *Ibid.*, p. 160.

199 Williams to Buckingham, 9 May 1623, in Hacket, *Scrinia*, p. 126.

200 Williams to Buckingham, [August 1623], in *Cabala*, p. 78; Conway to Buckingham, 3 May 1623, Harl. 1580, fol. 299v. See also Williams to Buckingham, 15 June 1623, in Hacket, *Scrinia*, pp. 135–6. The perception that Buckingham masterminded the trip was probably false, of course, and Charles seems to have initiated it. See Lockyer, *Buckingham*, pp. 137–8.

201 Williams to Buckingham, [August 1623], in *Cabala*, p. 78.

202 Henry Carey, Viscount Rochford, to Buckingham, [1623], Bod. MS. Tanner 73, fol. 346r.

203 Sir John Hipsley to Buckingham, 1 September 1623, in *Cabala*, p. 316.

204 Valaresso to the Doge and Senate, 28 April 1623, CSPV vol. XVII, p. 641. The French ambassador also believed that the preparations were made for appearances only. See Tillières to Puysieux, 26 May 1623, PRO 31/3/57, fol. 214r.

205 Salvetti newsletter, 25 April/5 May 1623, Add. 31112, fol. 358–9. See also London newsletter, 9 May 1623, Harl. 389, fol. 324r.

206 Clarendon, *History of the Rebellion* vol. I, p. 49. Most of the fleet did indeed land at Plymouth. See Owen Wynn to Sir John Wynn, 9 February 1626, NLW Wynn MSS

9060E/1389. The flagship landed in Kinsale in Ireland.

207 Clarendon, *History of the Rebellion* vol. I, p. 50.

208 *Ibid.*

209 Tillières to Puysieux, 7 June 1623, PRO 31/3/57, fol. 219r.

210 *Ibid.*

211 Valaresso to the Doge and Senate, 9 June 1623, CSPV vol. XVIII, pp. 33–4.

212 Mead to Stuteville, 30 May 1623, Harl. 389, fol. 333r; London newsletter, 30 May 1623, Harl. 389, fol. 333r.

213 Alastair Bellany and Andrew McRae (eds), 'All the Newes that's stirring now', 'Early Stuart libels: an edition of poetry from manuscript sources', *Early Modern Literary Studies Text Series I* (2005), http://purl.oclc.org/emls/texts/libels (accessed 29 July 2012).

214 Valaresso to the Doge and Senate, 14 July 1623, CSPV vol. XVIII, p. 63.

215 Charles's instructions for Cottington's journey to England, 7 June 1623, Bod. MS. Clarendon 3, fol. 33r.

216 Mead to Stuteville, 21 June 1623, Harl. 389, fol. 342r; London newsletter, 4 July 1623, Harl. 389, fol. 346r.

217 Charles and Buckingham to James, 27 March 1623, in Bergeron (ed.), *Letters of Homoerotic Desire*, p. 190; Charles and Buckingham to James, 27 April 1623, Bergeron (ed.), in *Letters of Homoerotic Desire*; Charles and Buckingham to James, 22 April 1623, in Hardwicke (ed.), *State Papers* vol. I, p. 415; Charles and Buckingham to James, 27 June 1623, in Hardwicke (ed.), *State Papers* vol. I, p. 423; Charles and Buckingham to James, 29 July 1623, in Hardwicke (ed.), *State Papers* vol. I, p. 432.

218 [Viscount Rochford?] to Buckingham, [1623], in *Cabala*, p. 161.

219 *Ibid.*, p. 160. The inability of Buckingham's clients to obtain the fruits of patronage while he was in Madrid was doubtless one of the motivations for encouraging him to return.

220 James to Charles and Buckingham, 10 April 1623, in Hardwicke (ed.), *State Papers* vol. I, p. 414.

221 Conway to Rutland, 29 May 1623, SP 94/26, fol. 251r; Conway to Rutland, 3 June 1623, SP 94/27, fol. 2r.

222 James to Charles and Buckingham, 14 June 1623, in Hardwicke (ed.), *State Papers* vol. I, p. 421; Conway to Rutland, 18 June 1622, SP 94/27, fol. 35r.

223 Kellie to Mar, 27 April 1623, in Paton (ed.), *Mar and Kellie* vol. II, p. 164. For the preparations, see Gardiner, *History of England* vol. V, p. 55.

224 Kellie to Mar, 22 April 1623, in Paton (ed.), *Mar and Kellie* vol. II, p. 163.

225 Bourcier (ed.), *The Diary of Sir Simonds D'Ewes*, pp. 139–40.

226 Castle to Trumbull, 6 June 1623, Add. 72276, fol. 44v.

227 Chamberlain to Carleton, 14 June 1623, McClure vol. II, p. 501.

228 [Dr Meddus] to Mead, 5 June 1623, Harl. 389, fol. 337r.

229 Chamberlain to Carleton, 14 June 1623, McClure vol. II, p. 501.

230 Castle to Trumbull, 20 June 1623, Add. 72276, fol. 51r.

231 Tillières to Puysieux, 11 June 1623, PRO 31/3/57, fol. 222v. The reluctance of the inhabitants of Denmark House to move out so that it could be made ready for the reception of Charles and the Infanta might have also reflected scepticism that such preparations were necessary. See APC, 1621–23, p. 493.

232 Chamberlain to Carleton, 4 January 1623, McClure vol. II, pp. 471–2.

233 [?] to Mead, 16 May 1623, Harl. 389, fol. 328r; Mead to Stuteville, 28 April 1623, Harl. 389, fol. 320r; [?] to Mead, 21 June 1623, Harl. 389, fol. 342v.

234 Thomas Locke to Trumbull, [4] July 1623, Add. 72299, fol. 119r.

235 Valaresso to the Doge and Senate, 16 June 1623, CSPV vol. XVIII, p. 28.

236 Mead to Stuteville, 19 January 1622, Harl. 389, fol. 133v; William Wynn to John Wynn, 8 September 1622, NLW 9058E/1033. See also Castle to Trumbull, 18 July 1623, Add. 72276, fol. 52r.

237 Castle to Trumbull, 11 April 1623, Add. 72276, fol. 26v; Castle to Trumbull, 16 May 1623, Add. 72276, fol. 38v.

238 Beaulieu to Trumbull, 27 June 1623, Add. 72255, 59r.

239 Mead to Stuteville, 18/23 July 1623, Harl. 389, fol. 351r.

240 Robert Phelips, 'A Discourse by way of Dialogue betweene a counsellor of State and Country gentleman who served in the last assembly of the estates in the yeare 1621', Somerset Record Office, DD/PH/227/16, fol. 1v.

241 Kellie to Mar, 12 August 1624, in Paton (ed.), *Mar and Kellie* vol. II, p. 209.

242 See Castle to Trumbull, 26 November 1624, Add. 72276, fol. 131v.

243 Kellie to Mar, 16 October 1624, in Paton (ed.), *Mar and Kellie* vol. II, p. 213; John Holles to the Earl of Somerset, 20 September 1624, in Seddon (ed.), *Letters of John Holles* vol. II, p. 295.

244 John Holles to William Knollys, Viscount Wallingford, 6 February 1625, in Seddon (ed.), *Letters of John Holles* vol. II, p. 297.

245 John Holles to the Earl of Somerset, 2 March 1625, in Seddon (ed.), *Letters of John Holles* vol. II, p. 298.

246 James to Charles and Buckingham, 14 June 1623 in Akrigg (ed.), *Letters of James*, pp. 415–16.

247 An analogy might be drawn with Buckingham in the later 1620s. His allies warned him that if he ignored the Privy Council when formulating military strategy, he would carry all of the blame if it failed. See Thomas Lord Cromwell to Buckingham, 8 September 1625, SP 16/6, fol. 44v.

248 William Wynn to John Wynn, 31 March 1624, NLW 9059E/1206.

Chapter 6

The politics of rumour during Buckingham's illness, 1624

INTRODUCTION

In the later 1620s, as Charles I became embroiled in disastrous wars with Spain and France, his favourite, the Duke of Buckingham, became the subject of various damaging rumours, many of which took on the status of fact. Buckingham was rumoured to be an agent of foreign powers, and was accused of plotting to bring in foreign troops to overthrow Charles. It was even said that he had poisoned Charles's father, James.[1] These rumours were not simply bandied about by the 'ignorant multitude', but were repeated in ambiguous or attenuated forms in Parliament, and this greatly enhanced their credibility.[2] The Duke's attempts to refute such false rumours seem to have fallen on deaf ears, and Charles for one was convinced that they constituted an orchestrated campaign of disinformation against his favourite.[3] The political importance of these rumours, given the distrust they generated between King and Parliament, is difficult to exaggerate.[4]

As Thomas Cogswell has shown, Buckingham was well aware of the importance of the perceptions of the wider political nation throughout his political career.[5] While the Duke was in Madrid in 1623, as we have seen, his friends in England monitored reports about his conduct that circulated at court and in the city, and attempted to plant favourable information about him. With varying degrees of success, Buckingham sought to attract support for his war policies after his return to England, and he never entirely abandoned hopes of regaining the popularity he had briefly enjoyed when he led the charge to war in 1624.

This final case study will focus on a crisis which revealed the precariousness of Buckingham's position and underlined the practical importance of perceptions to his political standing and the success of his policies. Even at the height of his popularity in the summer of 1624, damaging rumours circulated about Buckingham's loyalty to James, his standing with the King, his health and his mental stability. The first set of rumours, that Buckingham planned to shut the King away in one of his hunting lodges and take the direction of affairs into his own hands, were enthusiastically taken up by various Spanish ambassadors, who wished to create conflict between the favourite and the King in order to derail Buckingham's anti-Spanish foreign policy.

Contemporaries and historians have tended to present rumour as a plebeian mode of discourse, but these reports provide an illuminating case study of the ways in which elites were increasingly willing to seize upon widely circulating mis- and disinformation and exploit it in political battles at court. These manoeuvres prefigured, and perhaps influenced, the accusations against Buckingham on the basis of 'common fame' which formed the basis of the impeachment proceedings against him during the Parliament of 1626. As such, they represent a crucial moment in the political history of the wider Elizabethan and early Stuart period, which saw increasingly radical and destabilising attempts by individuals to appeal to wider opinion as part of their own factional battles, a development which culminated in Parliament's mobilisation of the London crowd in 1641.

Buckingham fell gravely ill as a result of the political pressure that the 'Spanish information' put him under, and this gave rise to a second set of rumours. It was thought that he had been poisoned by the Spanish, had died or had become mentally unstable, and when a guard was put on his door to prevent the access of suitors who were hindering his recovery, it was rumoured that James had imprisoned him. Robert Ruigh presented the 'Spanish information' as a comprehensive own-goal, since it allowed Buckingham to present himself as the victim of a Spanish plot, thus enhancing his popularity with Parliament.[6] Observers at the time were not so sure that the allegations would work in Buckingham's favour. They had the potential to shape perceptions of the Duke, to bring about his downfall and even to change the course of foreign affairs. Although Buckingham survived this turbulent period, it seemed to many as though he was on the brink of falling from power, and that any hope of committing James to a war to reclaim the Palatinate would be dashed. Perceptions helped to shape political reality during this episode.

As we have seen, rumour had a self-fulfilling potential during this period. People preferred conclusive information over ambiguity, tended to believe rumours that they hoped were true and tried to understand current events in terms of common stereotypes and the recent pattern of events. Many of these phenomena are present in the reports that circulated about Buckingham in 1624, but this chapter will expand on this theme by exploring one of the richest elements of rumour – their attribution – in greater detail. Individuals had difficulty believing that rumours about prominent individuals like Buckingham could spring up spontaneously, and tended to believe that they were deliberately spread by his enemies for political purposes, even when that was not the case. Attributing rumours to the deliberate machinations of Catholic slanderers, as I will argue, fulfilled a number of functions. It helped to explain the fact that a rumour was circulating, it falsified unwelcome reports and it externalised fears held by the attributer themselves.

THE 'SPANISH INFORMATION'

The 'Spanish information' against Buckingham created a series of rumours about the favourite's health and political standing. In order to understand these rumours, it is necessary to ask where the original allegations against Buckingham came from, why they were plausible and how both James and Buckingham attempted to exploit them. The first part of this chapter will therefore examine the politics surrounding these allegations.

The context for the 'Spanish information' rumours was Buckingham's return with Charles from Madrid and the 'blessed revolution' in foreign policy that followed.[7] The Prince and the Duke had become convinced during their time in Spain that their hosts were not negotiating in good faith, and that even if they finally concluded the marriage alliance between the Prince and the Infanta, the Spanish would never restore Charles's brother-in-law, Frederick V, to his ancestral lands and titles. The only way for Charles to help Frederick regain the Palatinate was to force Spain to come to terms by waging war. This would require the support or at least acquiescence of James, who still entertained hopes of restoring the Palatinate through a Spanish marriage, but who also realised that a show of belligerence might frighten the Spanish into finally negotiating a solution. War with Spain would also require military alliances with other European powers. In early 1624, George Goring was sent to discreetly sound out the Dutch, while the Earl of Carlisle, Sir Robert Anstruther and Sir Isaac Wake prepared to go to France, Denmark and Venice.

The Spanish ambassadors, Inojosa and Coloma, were alarmed at the direction in which Charles and Buckingham were leading English foreign policy, and in the early months of 1624 they mounted a counter-attack. In mid-January they played the conventional card of offering James fresh proposals for the return of the Lower Palatinate, promising that it would be restored by force of Spanish arms if necessary.[8] When Charles refused to marry the Infanta under any circumstances, however, the ambassadors took the dramatic step in early April of trying to convince James that Buckingham was planning a coup. Buckingham would shut the King away in one of his hunting lodges and take the direction of affairs in to his own hands. These efforts were reinforced in May and June, when in further meetings, James was told that Buckingham intended to displace James altogether and make Charles the King. Both the Privy Council and Charles were said to be aware of, and perhaps complicit in this plot.[9]

The Spanish ambassadors excused the lack of solid evidence against Buckingham on the basis that witnesses were too scared of him to come forward, and although some attempt was made to investigate their claims, they left the country before they could be questioned.[10] Carondelet, the Spanish confessor, was left to explain where the information about the alleged conspiracy against James had come from. Conveniently enough, he claimed that he could not reveal his sources since they had told him of the plot under the seal of confession.[11] Carondelet redoubled his efforts to derail Buckingham's policies by alleging in a further audience with the King that the Duke planned to marry his daughter to Frederick's son. Buckingham, he claimed, had ensured that Charles would be unable to marry the French Princess, and the crown would therefore eventually pass via Frederick's line to the Duke's own descendants.[12] The Spanish ambassadors also sought the support of Buckingham's enemies at court. When they attempted to recruit Lord Keeper Williams, however, he immediately shared the details of their allegations with Buckingham.[13]

By alleging that Parliament would help Buckingham to depose the King if he refused to assent to the Duke's policies, the immediate aim of the Spanish ambassadors was thought to be the dissolution of Parliament, which had not yet approved the subsidy bill.[14] If James could be convinced that Buckingham was involved in a conspiracy against him, the favourite would fall from power and the anti-Spanish party would suffer a major, perhaps fatal, blow. Even if James didn't believe in the plot, however, the allegations could still seriously undermine Buckingham and the policies he championed. Before the allegations were made, the Duke had been relatively free to seek parliamentary support for war. The one-sided account he gave of Spanish perfidy during the match negotiations at a conference of both houses in the early days of the Parliament is an obvious example.[15] Such moves would now play into the hands of those who alleged that the Duke was courting popularity in order to remove the King from power.

The Spanish allegations may seem transparently false, but even those who supported the Duke could understand why they might seem plausible. Indeed, there was a limited sense in which they were true. Even if there was no active conspiracy, the Venetian ambassador did not doubt that many of James's leading councillors would have liked to gradually edge him out of power, leaving the Prince in control.[16] Observers who were disposed to believe in the Duke's treachery had only to look to his apparently incriminating behaviour. Shortly after the allegations were made, it was said that he had burned many of his private papers.[17]

Anti-Spanish observers believed that the attack on Buckingham was being coordinated across Europe as a whole. The Venetian ambassador speculated that the Spanish diplomats had arranged for news of the plot to be printed in a German newsbook so that they could present James with a copy, creating the impression that their allegations had been independently corroborated.[18] Allegations about Buckingham's disloyalty were also repeated in a 'foolish pamphlett written in Fren[ch]'[19] John Chamberlain wrote that the Spanish were orchestrating an even more ambitious campaign of underhand disinformation against Charles, spreading 'scandalous reports both in Rome and all Italie of the Prince to disable him'.[20] Observers tended to exaggerate the Spanish conspiracy against Charles and Buckingham. Diplomats like Inojosa and Coloma may well have believed the charges they made against the favourite, and were not necessarily being deliberately deceitful. What is more, even if Spanish diplomats promoted rumours of Buckingham's plotting, they did not invent them.

Speculation about a conspiracy against James had been circulating widely in England and on the continent for some time. The French ambassador had passed on the rumour of a proposed marriage between Buckingham's daughter and Frederick's son as early as January 1624.[21] An anonymous letter written to James, which claimed to represent the opinions of his ordinary subjects, also reported these rumours.[22] A report circulated in the Spanish Netherlands that James was so angered by Buckingham's behaviour towards the Spanish ambassadors that he had committed him to the Tower of London, and this foreshadowed later reports that James had imprisoned Buckingham for treason.[23] Disgruntled English Catholics did not need outside encouragement to believe that powerful individuals were plotting against James. In February, a priest approached William Trumbull, the English ambassador in the Spanish Netherlands, saying that he had received a letter from a 'man of quality' in England, alleging a conspiracy by Parliament and 'some Great ones in that kingdome, to alter the present gouuernment to the preiudice of his maiesties aucthority'.[24]

These rumours had an important explanatory function. They helped English Catholics as well as continental observers to understand why Buckingham had apparently 'switched sides'. Until his trip to Spain, most had assumed that Buckingham was a supporter of the match. While he had initially made some well publicised noises in favour of Frederick, Buckingham's failure to secure the leadership of the English forces sent to defend the Palatinate in 1620 appeared to alienate him from the Elector's cause.[25] The assumption that his sympathies lay with the Spanish was further cemented later in the year when he wrote a widely circulated letter clearing Gondomar of any attempt to deceive James over the invasion of the Palatinate.[26] In fact, Buckingham's allegiance had never been a straightforward matter, and contemporaries tended to exaggerate his influence over James's foreign policy. Nevertheless, the warm regard many Catholics felt for the Duke began to cool when he quarrelled with Olivares over the terms of the marriage treaty, and was lost altogether when he returned to England and began to oppose the match and support war against Spain.[27] To continental observers who struggled to reconcile Buckingham's recent belligerence with his previous support for the Spanish match, the idea that his real aim was to supplant the King may have provided a simple and satisfying explanation for his apparent change of sides. These rumours also built on intermittent reports circulating on the continent that James's subjects had imprisoned him and replaced him with Frederick.[28]

Rumours about Buckingham's plotting are therefore an example of the interplay between elite and popular rumour that we have already identified. They provided a collective means of explaining the Duke's recent behaviour, and circulated on the continent well before the Spanish ambassadors exploited them. Passing on such rumours to James allowed the ambassadors to cast doubt on Buckingham's loyalty while disowning responsibility for doing so by claiming that they were merely passing on what they had heard.[29] In seizing on these rumours and using them as a political weapon to undermine Buckingham, the Spanish ambassadors further publicised them and gave them a greater air of authority.

James certainly appeared to take the Spanish allegations seriously. John Castle thought the 'mallicious plott' against Buckingham had succeeded in 'putting iealousies in the kings head'.[30] Charles and Buckingham vehemently denied that they were involved in any conspiracy, but the King nevertheless called the Privy Councillors together to swear the Oath of Allegiance, and sent for Sir Francis Nethersole, Elizabeth's secretary, and Sir Dudley Carleton, both of whom were close to Frederick and might be expected to know about any marriage alliance between his son and Buckingham's daughter, to be questioned about the affair.[31] Carleton in particular was thought to be the only person who could 'wype out the last traces' of suspicion.[32] Charles reassured Buckingham that councillors would not risk incurring his wrath by supporting the Spanish accusations.[33] Nevertheless, James's suspicions were slow to fade. A month or so after the allegations, he was still sounding Charles out by asking the Prince if he would like to take charge of affairs.[34]

Some contemporaries thought they could detect a deeper motive behind James's apparent suspicions. The Venetian ambassador thought that James, who had been reluctantly manoeuvred by Charles and Buckingham to the brink of war, was using the Spanish allegations as a way to regain control over foreign policy. The King, who had 'many enemies, few confidents and no party', had put on a public display of suspicion because it provided 'a reason for discredit and a bridle to hold him [Buckingham] back from the good enterprises which the King hates so much'.[35] The 'Spanish information' allowed James to keep the Duke in check and to retain his freedom of action. Although this interpretation is entirely plausible, in a sense it did not matter. Whether James genuinely believed the rumours of Buckingham's plots or not, the rumours still had the potential to derail Buckingham's and Charles's plans for war just as they seemed to be gaining momentum. As Castle noted, Buckingham would now 'not be verie forward to haue the Lord Digby brought vnto question; and the Prince because he hath seene the King so much troubled about the spanish informaccon, doth nowe more & more dispose himself to comply with his humor; being conten[t] to give way to that which he can not safely withstand'.[36] James warned his son about courting popularity with Parliament, and Charles even showed signs of turning against parliamentarians that he had previously attempted to cultivate.[37] Charles was also forced to stay close to the King and arranged to be lodged 'in the kings house hard by his Maiesties chamber' during James's progress.[38] The Prince was said to be against the rise of any new favourite if the Duke was disgraced, but this points to the fact that even Charles doubted Buckingham's standing and would not be able to prevent his fall from power if the King turned decisively against him.[39]

Buckingham and his allies attempted to turn the Spanish allegations to their advantage. The Duke had earlier capitalised on the Spanish ambassador's intemperate suggestion that he should be beheaded for speaking ill of Philip IV.[40] His friends seem to have played a part in revealing and spreading the Spanish allegations, which suggests that he was keen to publicise them.[41] He also directed Sir Robert Cotton to draw up a relation against the Spanish ambassadors, which circulated widely.[42] In this document, Cotton set out the precedents for the punishment of diplomats who had acted against the interests of the state in which they resided. He cleverly suggested that a delegation of MPs should be sent to the ambassadors to demand evidence for Buckingham's supposed plot. If they refused, Parliament could petition James to place the ambassadors under house arrest for their own safety, because the common people were likely to attack them for their malicious plotting.[43] Members of Parliament who were already 'netled at so base a malice' that they were 'mynded to moove his Maiestie to a sharper Course to be taken out of hand' against the Spanish and their English Catholic supporters, would presumably have been eager to comply.[44] Parliament was predisposed to take rumours of Spanish and Catholic plotting seriously, and the actions of the Spanish ambassadors may well have reinforced fears of an imminent popish attack on Parliament in February and March.[45] Placing the ambassadors under house arrest would prevent any further communication with the King.[46] Their actions could even be used as a *casus belli*. Ambassadors acted as proxies for their monarch, and if Philip refused to punish them, their attempt to undermine Buckingham could be interpreted as a declaration of war.[47]

No parliamentary investigation appears to have occurred, however, and this is perhaps because any cooperation between Parliament and the anti-Spanish party at court would only seem to confirm the general thrust of the Spanish allegations. Since Inojosa and Coloma had alleged that Buckingham and

Parliament were conspiring against James, any attempt to use Parliament to attack the ambassadors and exonerate the Duke would merely demonstrate that the relationship between the two was dangerously close. Any assertion of Parliament's right to question foreign ambassadors also had the potential to raise royal fears about parliamentary encroachments on royal power. Even if James did not believe in the conspiracy, a parliamentary backlash could still lead to the sort of confrontation over the balance of power between King and Parliament which had bedevilled previous Parliaments. James was much less eager to pursue the matter than Charles or Buckingham, and observers did not expect him to punish Coloma and Inojosa if their allegations were shown to be false. 'When all is saide and don', wrote Chamberlain, 'I am of opinion we [i.e. James] shalbe nothing sensible of any disgrace or dishonor that may fall upon us from the Spaniard whom we respect and stand in awe of so much either for love or fear'.[48] While Coloma and Inijosa were forced to leave England, they were quickly replaced by Diego de Mendoza, Gondomar's nephew, who raised fresh hopes that a deal with Spain could be negotiated.[49]

BUCKINGHAM'S ILLNESS

Buckingham now became seriously ill. He was 'lett bloud to prevent a feavor' in early April, but soon recovered his strength.[50] In May, however, 'a kinde of yellow Iaundisse', as well as 'many pustules and blaines' broke out on his skin, and it was thought that he might die.[51] He was taken to bed and let blood, and although he recovered slightly, he suffered a serious relapse in June, and did not fully recover until the end of the month.[52] While overwork probably contributed to Buckingham's illness, contemporaries were in no doubt that the Spanish allegations played an important part.[53] John Beaulieu thought that the Duke's health was 'somewhat altered by the greife he conceiued of the Spanish Ambassadors information against him', and described his illness as having come 'rather out of apprehension and griefe of mynde then from any other cause'.[54] How was Buckingham's illness interpreted and explained by observers, and what did it reveal about the potential threat to Buckingham's relationship with James?

Buckingham had a history of psychosomatic illness. In December 1616, when it seemed as though James's passion for Buckingham might be on the wane, Chamberlain reported that 'there is a *sourd bruit* [i.e. muffled rumour] as yf the blasing star at court were toward an eclipse, and that there is some glimpse or sparkling of a lesse comet of the Lord of Mongomeries lighting'.[55] As a result, Buckingham had 'ben crasie ever since he came to Newmarkett'.[56] A further bout of ill health was precipitated by the King's own serious illness in 1619.[57] Buckingham, who had at that point failed to cultivate Charles's affection, would face a bleak future if the King died, and the mental strain this caused manifested itself once again in physical sickness.[58] The Duke's ill-health in 1624 could therefore be read as a symptom of his precarious political situation.

This line of thought may well have encouraged the Duke's friends to marry the physical and the political together in suggesting that their patron was suffering from scrofula, the 'king's evil'. Castle thought that the 'meeting of all symptomes', including the boils and pustules that were breaking out on Buckingham's skin, 'shewed it to be *Morbus Regius*', and therefore 'His Maiesty[s] presence might do much' to cure him.[59] Conveniently enough, proximity to the King was the best cure for Buckingham's political as well as his physical ailments. Access was the most crucial element of any favourite's political power, and attendance on the King was the best way for Buckingham to restore his trust and affection, as well as to prevent the access of any more Spanish ambassadors. This may indeed have been why Buckingham's friends seemed so keen to encourage the Duke to spend time with the King, and to spin his illness as one that James was uniquely capable of curing. Castle reported that the Duke had initially wanted to leave London for Nonesuch Palace, where the better air might aid his recovery, but his friends advised him that it would be better to stay close to the King. 'There was noe pollicie to be so far remooved as Nonesuch from the comforte of that voice which had been so passionate for him a fewe days before', they argued. It would be much better to go to Greenwich, where the King was staying, which had 'far the better ayre while the breathe of a King did blowe vpon it'. To Greenwich Buckingham duly went, 'there to be perfectly recovered by the warme beames of his Maiesties presence'.[60] Worries about Buckingham's health also provided a pretext to prevent any more allegations about him from reaching the King's ears. In early June James refused an audience with Padre Maestro, the Flemish agent, saying 'if I admit Maestro, it will kill the Duke with greefe'.[61]

Given the level of popular hatred towards the Spanish ambassadors, and their apparent willingness to use the most Machiavellian means to effect their ends, it is not surprising that many thought that Buckingham had been deliberately poisoned by 'some Spanishe drugge'.[62] This rumour was given a further burst of life when an Italian charlatan named Carolo Caymo came forward to claim that he had been 'dealt withall by the Spanish ambassador' to poison the Duke, although nothing further seems to have come of this report.[63] Some even believed that the poison had been administered the previous year, while Buckingham was in Spain, but that its effects were delayed.[64] These reports only seemed to confirm earlier fears that the Duke's life was under threat. Buckingham's attendance at a large public wedding raised concerns that he would be assassinated by discontented Catholics.[65]

Poisoning rumours circulated whenever a prominent figure became suddenly ill or when there was anything even faintly suspicious about their death. Lord Keeper Williams, for instance, was rumoured to have been poisoned when he fell ill through overwork, while poison was thought to have contributed to the Marquis of Hamilton's death because his corpse swelled after his death.[66] When reporting the Duke's illness to his superiors, the Venetian ambassador wearily commented that 'the common people, as usual, believe him poisoned'.[67]

Several factors contributed towards the success and longevity of poisoning rumours. Episodes such as the poisoning of Sir Thomas Overbury in 1613 must have given such rumours a much greater air of plausibility to contemporaries than they now possess.[68] They also had the advantage of being impossible to falsify; there was no way to prove that someone had not been poisoned. Such rumours are reminiscent of other 'magical' systems of explanation such as maleficient witchcraft, in that they provided a dramatic and intentional explanation for death when no 'natural' cause could be discovered.[69]

These rumours demonstrate how similar popular tropes could be used of the same individuals in different political circumstances. Rumours that Buckingham had been the victim of poisoning resurfaced in early 1625, when Chamberlain reported the allegation that Lady Purbeck, Buckingham's sister-in-law 'with powders and potions ... did intoxicate her husbands braines, and practised somwhat in that kinde upon the Duke of Buckingham'.[70] These potions were supposedly supplied by John Lambe, the Duke's astrologer, who ironically enough was thought to have practised witchcraft on Buckingham's behalf later in the decade.[71] While Lambe's alleged activities were a sign of the Duke's victimhood in 1624–25, they were a sign of his malign influence in the following years. As Buckingham became more and more unpopular, he was rumoured to have poisoned others himself. Immediately after James's death, rumours circulated that Buckingham had poisoned the King, an allegation given added weight and legitimacy when they were hinted at in Parliament's articles of impeachment in 1626.[72] Buckingham was also thought to have poisoned the Earl of Southampton, the Duke of Lennox and the Marquis of Hamilton.[73] The victim of poisoning in 1624 was transformed in the popular imagination into the prolific poisoner of later years.

Buckingham's political position was not helped by rumours that he had become mentally ill. These rumours may have originated from the fact that the Duke had suffered bouts of delirium during his illness.[74] Chamberlain wrote that 'the world thincks he is more sicke in mind then body', 'a suspicion that grew from frequent blood-letting', a treatment particularly associated with mental illness.[75] Such rumours were given added weight by the fact that Buckingham's brother, the Viscount Purbeck, suffered from periodic bouts of mental illness.[76]

In late May, James forbade visitors from seeing Buckingham, and a guard was put on the Duke's door. Some interpreted this as further evidence that

Buckingham had gone mad, since the King would not wish visitors to see him in such a state.[77] Others saw the guard on the Duke's door as a sign that the King suspected him of disloyalty following the Spanish allegations.[78] Castle was quick to refute the 'false and malicious reportes touching the occasion of setting a guarde at the *duke* of Buck[inghams] doores (as if he had been fallen starke madde; or suspected in his loyaltie)'.[79] In the Spanish Netherlands, Trumbull reported that Buckingham was rumoured to be 'restrayned of his liberty; distracted, irrecouerably sicke, dead, convinced of capitall crymes, and I cannott tell what'.[80] These reports clearly echoed similar rumours earlier in the year that Buckingham had been imprisoned in the Tower.[81]

Anxious onlookers like John Castle and John Wolley eagerly reported any indications that the King was concerned about Buckingham's health. Wolley reported that he could 'giue no credit' to 'common report' that the 'fauor, and credit his *Lordship* possessed in his Ma*ies*tie, should in some kind be deminished' because 'his Ma*ies*tie, hath purposely made twoe Iournyes from Thibolds to visite him as on Saturday, and this afternoon; takeing his house only for a resting place in his passage to Grinwige'.[82] Castle confirmed that the King had visited the Duke two or three times, and sent messengers every few hours to see how well he was.[83] More evidence of the King's compassion came a few days later, when Castle wrote that the King had dramatically told Buckingham 'I pray God either to recouer thee of this sicknesse, or els (the teares breaking downe vp[on] his cheekes while he was speaking) to transfer the same vpon me, as one that would stand in the gapp for the[e]'.[84]

It was widely known that illness could arouse James's sympathy. Almost every disgraced Jacobean courtier seems to have been suspected at one time or another of feigning illness in order to persuade the King to clemency or at least to delay legal action. As Sir Walter Raleigh admitted before his execution in 1618, he had employed the services of a French physician 'to make his face to blister, and to alter the signes of his health, the more to moue the *kings* compassion towards him for the procuring of his libertie'.[85] Sir Thomas Overbury took emetics when he was imprisoned in the Tower in 1613, and a few years later the Countess of Somerset was suspected of following his example by taking 'a dramme' which led her to 'fall that night to casting and scowring', thus delaying her trial.[86] Lady Lake and the Earl of Middlesex were both suspected of similar behaviour when trying to stay out of prison.[87]

The King's feelings towards Buckingham did not always appear to be as tender as his friends might have hoped. 'Notwithstandinge this greate demonstraccon of his Ma*ies*ties tender affection', as Castle wrote, 'some wise men are of opinion that the tincture is not ye[t] out, touchinge the matter informed by the *Spanish* Ambassador; and how[e] deepe that vnhappy brute hath suncke, of a matche proiected betwee[n] the Dukes daughter and the *King of Bohemias* sonne, none can tell'.[88]

To make matters worse, Buckingham's enemies were now circling. The Duke had played a major part in the downfall of the Lord Treasurer, Lionel Cranfield, Earl of Middlesex, who opposed war with Spain on financial grounds and who was rumoured to be involved in the attack on Buckingham.[89] Cranfield had been impeached by Parliament on charges of corruption, but James was reluctant to part with such a capable servant. At the height of the impeachment proceedings, the King spoke in ambiguous terms, but nevertheless sought to exonerate Cranfield from at least some of the accusations against him.[90] Although the Lord Treasurer was found guilty and imprisoned, James released him almost immediately. 'This is the way in England', as Valaresso wrote, 'hardly has the ink dried of a sentence fulminated by Parliament than the king annuls it, and against all reason one sees the resurrection of one who is practically the declared enemy of the prince, and absolutely declared of the favourite Buckingham'.[91] Although Cranfield was not allowed within the verges of the court, James was rumoured to have met him secretly at the Earl of Arundel's house.[92]

Rumours abounded that Cranfield would quickly return to royal favour. It was reported that he had been sworn a gentleman of the King's bedchamber, news which was 'not like to helpe the cure of my Lord of Buckinghams sicknes'.[93] It was even said that the disgraced minister would have a 'kinde of superintendancie' over the treasury, effectively continuing to act as a *de facto* Lord Treasurer from behind the scenes.[94] Letters were said to pass between the King and Cranfield, whose advice would 'still be vsed for matters of the Treasury', and when Pembroke sent for the keys to his court lodgings, the request was denied because the disgraced Treasurer expected to make use of them soon.[95]

The liberation of Cranfield could be interpreted as an act of sabotage by James, since it would inevitably damage the efforts Buckingham and Charles had made to ensure good relations between King and Parliament, a vital precondition to the successful prosecution of any future war. The fact that Cranfield had been freed, and according to rumour, that he would soon have his fine remitted, seemed calculated to enrage Parliament by effectively reversing their decision.[96] This seemed part of a wider turn away from anti-Spanish policies, now that the parliamentary session had ended. It was falsely rumoured that James had allowed the ruler of the Spanish Netherlands, the Archduchess Isabella, to recruit more English troops to use against the Dutch.[97]

During Buckingham's gradual recovery in June, John Castle reported that Cranfield would soon become groom of the stool, although he doubted the rumour because Parliament, which was to assemble again in November, would 'not take it well to see the man so specially countenanced and graced, whome in their sentence they haue banished from Court'.[98] There were also rumours that Arthur Brett, who Middlesex had tried to promote as an alternative favourite during Buckingham's absence, was back in favour with the King, who would soon knight him, make him a gentleman of the bedchamber, and marry him to the dowager Duchess of Richmond.[99] John Digby, Earl of Bristol, who had recently returned from Spain, was also trying to see the King, hoping to clear himself of mishandling the negotiations and blaming Buckingham for the breakdown of the match.[100] To make matters worse, it was rumoured that a new Spanish ambassador was on his way with full power to restore the Palatinate.[101]

The Venetian ambassador anticipated a showdown:

> If Bristol does not fall, and the treasurer does not perish, Buckingham will be ruined, and with him every help of good will be lost. If they go unpunished his favour with the king has already diminished if not utterly gone, and they will have the skill and opportunity to avenge themselves. With Buckingham ruined the prince will lose his right arm and he will never venture anything again, and after that example no one will join him.[102]

Buckingham's situation in early June did not seem to be improving. 'The eyes of this people', Castle wrote:

> could not well be more fixed on a Meteor, then they haue been vpon the moccons of the *Duke* to see whither he diminishe in his light, or holde still the same fulnesse in his Ma*iesties* affection & fauour; And forasmuch as he hath been nowe 5 or 6 dayes at Newehall without beeing visited by the *King* in person; thoughe his Ma*iestie* sent euery day see him, yet these Astrologians (that iudge all by apparances) haue passed their calculaccon on him that the matter of his Light euery day wasting he must needs fall shortly into an extreme diminution. To this purpose, they haue already created a newe fauorite one Clare whome they call the base sonne to the Lo*rd* Walden; & they place him so highe in the *kings* fauour as they allott out digni-ties and honours to him already. Much of which, thoughe it be comment beyond the Text, yet to open my conceipt freely to you I doubt there is some ground for the first supposiccons.[103]

The Duke seemed on the verge of falling from grace, though Castle was obviously reluctant to admit it, perhaps because he was already planning to become Buckingham's client.[104] Buckingham's health and political standing were therefore matters of great personal importance. If the Duke died or fell from grace, Castle would need to find a new patron. Castle was therefore disposed to pour scorn on the hopes of Buckingham's enemies, just as they were inclined to exaggerate the new favourite's chances. In both cases, there was a tendency for courtiers to believe whatever they hoped to be the case.

Buckingham's illness had the potential to damage his political standing in more basic ways. On his return to court in late June, various contempo-raries noted that the Duke's long illness had damaged his previously flawless complexion.[105] This could be taken as evidence of the severity of his illness, but it may have had political implications. Contemporaries understood that the

King had a liking for attractive young men. The Howards had tried to replace Buckingham with a favourite of their own choosing in 1618, 'prancking him up, besides washing his face every day with posset-curd', and Buckingham's physical beauty had played an important part in attracting the King's attention to him in 1614.[106] Any decline in the Duke's appearance might encourage the King to look elsewhere.

DOMESTIC POLITICS AND FOREIGN POLICY

Fears about Buckingham's political position had the potential to become self-fulfilling if his supporters came to believe he was a lost cause. One of the Duke's key allies, Edward Conway, seems to have contemplated giving up his office during his illness. His offer to sell the secretaryship to Carleton had been characterised as 'half-joking', but some thought he was acting in earnest.[107] Castle reported that the secretary, 'doubtinge the stabilitie of the Dukes standinge, vpon which he relyes as on his mayne arche' was trying to give up his office in late May.[108] Even some of those who supported an anti-Spanish foreign policy would have been glad to see Conway go. Wolley followed reports that Conway was trying to give up the secretaryship in July by writing that 'he doth as ill performe [the office] as euer any did I thinck before him'.[109]

If Buckingham was Conway's 'arch', Conway was one of the Duke's pillars, the removal of which could help to bring the favourite down. Conway would have been left in an exposed position if Buckingham had fallen, but the loss of a client in such a sensitive place would have undermined the Duke's own standing at court. Any replacement as secretary might not be as supportive of the anti-Habsburg cause as Conway, and Buckingham would have one less supporter to speak up for him and to carry out his wishes.

The desertion of a great officer of state might also convince others clients that the Duke's power and influence were on the wane, and encourage them to look elsewhere for a patron. This applied as much (or more) to prospective as to established clients. As we have seen, John Castle, who was considering becoming Buckingham's client in 1624, was already worried about the Duke's political standing. Trumbull's and Carleton's own hopes of obtaining offices were also affected by Buckingham's illness. Trumbull's attempt to mobilise the Duke's support for his suit for revocation in 1624 was wasted because he was too ill to present Trumbull's letter to the King.[110] Carleton tried to take advantage of Buckingham's illness to come home and complete negotiations with Calvert for his secretaryship, knowing that no other candidate would be granted the position while the Duke was indisposed.[111] Carleton failed to tell Buckingham about these negotiations, and the Duke was highly displeased to learn about them once he recovered, suspecting Carleton of treachery.[112] It was clear to patrons that the act of leaving a sinking ship might make it sink all the sooner, and this was presumably why Buckingham always insisted that his clients accept him as their sole protector. A client who enjoyed the support of several patrons could easily jump ship if one of them looked to be in trouble. By insisting that clients focus their loyalty on him to the exclusion of all others, Buckingham ensured that such manoeuvres would be much more difficult.

In order to prevent other courtiers from doubting his position, Buckingham put on a show of confidence when he returned to court. Castle told Trumbull that if he saw the way Buckingham was treating suitors, and 'with what elevation he comportes himself with the greatest that haue to doe with him', he would think Buckingham was 'past ieopardie of relapsinge'.[113] The importance of political 'performance' to the Duke's position was clear. 'I will not say', Castle disingenuously added, 'that he personateth a parte, meaning by his stateliness ... to value himself, and recover the other bancke'.[114]

Robert Ruigh argued that by early June, James was 'irrevocably committed to an indirect, covert military confrontation with Spain'.[115] In fact, supporters of the war at home and potential allies abroad had serious doubts about James's commitment. The rumours circulating in the early months of 1624 about Buckingham's health and his standing with the King had the potential to damage the foreign policy the Duke was trying to promote, as well as his domestic position.[116] Buckingham was deeply involved in negotiations with foreign powers designed to create an international anti-Habsburg alliance, and Carlisle, Anstruther and Wake were poised to go on their missions to France, Denmark and Venice. The French extraordinary ambassador, the Marquis d'Effiat, was on his way to negotiate a marriage alliance between the two countries that would form the basis for any joint operations to recover the Palatinate.[117] In the meantime, Count Mansfeld, who had been prevented by the Spanish and papal ambassadors from seeing the French King in April, returned to France in May, carrying with him £20,000 to guarantee English commitment to joint military operations to restore the Palatinate.[118] The machinations of Spanish and dévot forces at the French court forced him to conduct negotiations with Louis XIII through 'secrett Instruments', and these underhand negotiations were still going on as Buckingham lay in his sick-bed.[119] At the same time, the Dutch extraordinaries, Albert Joachimi and Francois van Aerssens, had arrived in England in March in response to offers to renew the alliance between England and the Dutch Republic.[120]

There was already a great deal of mutual distrust between the various parties to this alliance. Relations between James and Louis XIII had never been particularly warm, but in the early 1620s their suspicions verged on paranoia. Louis XIII's military crackdown on the Huguenots in 1621 raised fears of invasion attempts on both sides of the Channel. It was rumoured in September that the French were preparing to land troops in Ireland to forestall any attempt by James to aid his co-religionists in France, and an English fleet was redirected to protect the Irish coast.[121] At the same time, Louis moved his forces to Calais to guard against a rumoured Anglo-Spanish attack.[122] In October, James reportedly warned the French ambassador that if Louis 'took him for a prince incapable of forming any resolution, and who could not obtain money, he deceived himself, as he would find enough and that by God he would chastise him'.[123] If James really made this angry outburst, it shows how bad relations had become, but also demonstrates that James was aware that his reputation for indecisiveness had damaged the credibility of his threats. The poisonous atmosphere that pervaded Anglo-French relations before the return of Charles and Buckingham from Madrid help to explain why James worried that even if the French went through with a marriage alliance, they would immediately leave him 'in the Lurche' to fight Spain alone.[124] It also puts the tortuous course of the later Anglo-French marriage negotiations, as well as the failure of military cooperation under Mansfeld, in a longer context.

The Dutch suspected that James had no intention of breaking with Spain and was merely using the threat of war to extract greater concessions from Philip.[125] They were also negotiating an agreement with Louis XIII, who agreed to give them large annual loans in return for continuing the war against Spain, and were understandably suspicious that James was merely offering an alliance to draw them away from French influence.[126] For his part, James had long suspected that the Dutch merely wanted to embroil him in war with Spain in order to make a separate peace. He had rejected Dutch offers of military cooperation in June 1620 on the grounds that they were merely trying to 'worke theyr own peace' with Spain.[127] Digby was similarly convinced that high-minded Dutch exhortations for James to intervene on Frederick's behalf were entirely self-interested. The Dutch merely wanted to distract the Spanish and prevent them from concentrating their full military and financial might on the Republic.[128] James's suspicions may have been reinforced by rumours of secret negotiations between the Spanish and Dutch, which circulated periodically during the early 1620s.[129] There were particularly strong indications of an imminent new truce just as Charles and Buckingham were trying to construct their anti-Habsburg alliance.[130] Even those like Trumbull who would have welcomed war with Spain worried that the Dutch would banish Frederick from the Republic in exchange for peace, and any such move would increase pressure on James to offer him refuge.[131] James must have feared the prospect of his ally making a separate peace with Spain all the more strongly since this was precisely what he had done in 1604.

James did his best to slow down negotiations, particularly with the Dutch, in the hope of keeping his options open.[132] The King had attempted to appoint the Earls of Arundel and Middlesex, who opposed war with Spain, to the committee organised to oversee the negotiations, although Buckingham and Charles managed to prevent this.[133] He also made requests that he knew the

Dutch would not be willing to grant, demanding new 'cautionary towns' as security for English aid. The Dutch opposed this because they were already getting subsidies from France for free, and by granting James's wish they might either jeopardise these funds or encourage France to demand similar security.[134] James refused to commit to attacking Spain, ruling out the offensive alliance the Dutch had hoped for.[135] These demands, as Castle wrote, made proceedings 'very colde an[d] heavy on both sides', and only increased Dutch fears that James was not acting in good faith.[136] The Dutch ambassadors had not received 'the least incouragement' from James and were thought to be 'much distracted' with English 'irresolutions'.[137] At one point Charles had to intervene to prevent them from breaking off negotiations and returning home.[138] Relations were strained once again by news of the Amboyna massacre, which reached England in May.[139] By the time Buckingham fell ill, a draft defensive treaty had been drawn up but had not been signed by the King.[140]

These negotiations, already in a fragile state, could be delayed, or even derailed, if potential allies came to believe that Buckingham was either dying or had lost all influence with the King, either through mental instability or suspicions about his loyalty. With Buckingham either physically or politically dead, those who were pushing for English intervention in the Thirty Years' War would lose one of the two leaders of their cause. James might well revert to the policy of negotiated settlement he had pursued prior to their return from Madrid. It would be unwise for the French or Dutch to commit themselves to any alliance while Buckingham's standing remained uncertain, because James might simply resume his old friendship with Spain, leaving them to fight on their own.

Buckingham's opponents on the continent were delighted by the prospect of his impending disgrace, and understood that it would have implications for foreign policy. The Infanta's subjects, as Trumbull reported, spoke 'more confidently of the match betwene England, and Spaine, then wee did when his *highness* was at Madrid', because Inijosa's 'false accusaçons' had 'sowen such a seed of Ialous weeds ... as can neuer be rooted out', and had given Buckingham a 'deadly and mortall wounde'.[141] It was even thought that Parliament had been dissolved 'with a disagreement betweene his *maiestie*, and his people; and nothinge ratifyed'. While Trumbull hoped this rumour was false he had to concede that 'some thinges probably in themselues false, doe in the effectes prooue too true'.[142] At the Spanish court, it was said that Buckingham was in custody.[143] Kensington wrote from Paris that since the Spanish allegations had come to light, 'there is not a man in France (myself excepted) that doth not believe but that his Majesty's intentions are changed' about war with Spain.[144]

The Spanish allegations and Buckingham's illness 'greatly hindered' diplomatic and naval preparations.[145] The Venetian ambassador attributed the slowness of the Dutch negotiations to Buckingham's weakened political position, which allowed James to play for time 'and perhaps do nothing eventually'.[46] Supporters of the match at the French court worried that the 'Spanish information' would lead to yet another change in English foreign policy, and their fears were not soothed by the failure to dispatch English diplomats who were tasked with negotiating an anti-Habsburg alliance.[47] Kensington warned that the delay in dispatching Carlisle had plunged the French court into 'new doubts and jealousies ... who do generally beginne to call the sincerity of his Maiesties intention into question'.[48] When he finally left for France in late May, Carlisle excused himself on the basis that 'he had not wished to depart before things were more settled, and before the Spanish imbroglio was out of the way'.[49] Anstruther also delayed his departure until the negotiations with the Dutch ambassadors had been concluded.[50] A parliamentary ally, of Buckingham, Richard Knightley, wrote that MPs were 'almost fallen from that active word hope by your absence', and that the Spanish allegations, as well as delays in Cranfield's impeachment, would 'certainly hinder the subsedies till they be blowne over'.[51] Buckingham's illness also 'greatly damaged' the setting out of a fleet, which as Knightley pointed out, would need to be dispatched soon if it was to achieve anything that year.[52] The sale of provisions intended for the ships led to rumours that Buckingham was 'not soe hote against Spaine as he hes bein of leate', and led some to suspect that James had only bought them to encourage Parliament to pass the subsidy bill.[53] The King, taxpayers, English diplomats and potential foreign allies all waited for someone else to make the first commitment to an anti-Habsburg policy. Little could be achieved without sustained pressure and encouragement from the centre. With Buckingham ill and his political position in doubt, the natural inertia of Jacobean politics reasserted itself. There were many reasons for the delays in funding and dispatching English forces in 1624, but the Spanish information and Buckingham's subsequent illness surely played a major part, and this indicates that Ruigh was wrong to describe the allegations against the Duke as an own goal. Of course, Buckingham did recover, and he was ultimately able to pursue his war policy. Nevertheless, these rumours demonstrated how vulnerable the Duke's position was, and he renewed efforts to remove former supporters of the Spanish match and personal enemies from positions of power. Arundel, Calvert and Williams were dropped from the commission tasked with negotiating the French match in July, and Pembroke was removed in December.[54]

'POPISH RUMOURS'

Those who supported Buckingham's policy of war with Spain were well aware of the potential impact that rumours about him might have on the foreign policy he was trying to promote, and they were anxious to ensure that the truth was reported on the continent. Carleton passed on intercepted letters which supposedly proved that Inijosa's information was a 'plot for the ruin of the Duke of Buckingha*m*', while Conway moved to reassure the French that Buckingham was recovering and that further attempts to poison James's mind against him had been blocked.[155] John Castle also attempted to prevent some of the more damaging rumours about Buckingham from circulating unchallenged on the continent. He repeated the real reason for the Duke's confinement in three separate letters to Trumbull.[156] The guard on Buckingham's door was set there 'at the vehement complaint and peticcon' of Buckingham's doctors, who assured the King that 'vnlesse he would please to remedy the continuall visitts' of clients and suitors, which prevented the Duke from resting, then 'they could not save him with all their arte'.[157] The guard was evidence of the King's concern for the favourite rather than of any suspicions about his loyalty. By passing on the real reason for the guard on Buckingham's door, and by detailing telling episodes which demonstrated the King's continued affection for him, Castle was giving Trumbull the means to 'silence the mouth of vntruth' in Brussels.[158]

News-gatherers like Castle and Chamberlain were quick to identify disgruntled Catholics as the source of the most damaging and scurrilous rumours about Buckingham circulating abroad.[159] 'The papists geve out malicious reports that he [Buckingham] shold be crased in his braine', Chamberlain wrote.[160] The 'Espagniolized spiritts', according to Castle, thought there was a 'digitus dei' in Buckingham's apparent madness. According to Castle, English Catholics thought that God was punishing the Duke for having been the 'cheife perswader of the King to banish the Preists and Iesuites'.[161] John Castle was particularly worried that Catholic priests, whose expulsion Buckingham had encouraged, would carry false rumours with them when they left the country.[162] 'Our vipers in that Courte of yors', he wrote, were trying to 'sewe those absurde and lyinge tales for wonders'.[163]

The association between Catholicism and false rumours was not new.[164] For many Protestants, the existence of 'Church papists', crypto-Catholics who outwardly conformed to Protestant worship to avoid recusancy fines, reinforced the association between Catholicism and dissimulation.[165] Protestants (and indeed many Catholics) attacked the casuistry and mental reservation which allowed some Catholics to reconcile themselves to the Jacobean regime. George Abbot had his own theological explanation for false rumours. 'It hath bene long my observation,' he told Trumbull 'that as Popery itself is made of lies, so it must bee perpetually nourished with vp-springing vntruthes'.[166] Abbot held English Catholic refugees responsible for spreading a rumour that he favoured the Spanish match, and another that the King had taken the responsibility for overseeing the activities of pursuivants out of his hands.[167] The Catholic 'forge' was held responsible for the most unlikely rumours, such as the report that circulated in 1622 that the Earl of Pembroke had driven James out of England with an army of 40,000 men.[168] To Abbot and like-minded contemporaries, false reports were part of the smokescreen of misdirection and superstition with which the Catholic Church deluded Catholics and Protestants alike, a continuation of the Catholic clergy's attempts to exploit the gullibility of super-stitious laymen. The Jesuits had a particular reputation for deception and equivocation. Henry Bilderbeck, one of Trumbull's correspondents, wrote that they would 'deceive God if they could'.[169]

The Spanish Netherlands had a special place in the geography of rumour. 'The place where you live', as Abbot assured Trumbull, 'and the circumiatent Townes of the Archduke, are the very forge of fictions concerning the state of England'.[170] In 1620 Beaulieu wrote that a series of rumours which apparently exaggerated Habsburg military and diplomatic power (some of which later proved only too true) had originated 'from Bruxelles, where I suppose they are forged'.[171] Trumbull sometimes complained that he had little real news to report from the Spanish Netherlands, 'but of forged rumors, and idle gazettas, printed daily in these parts, I could cloye your lordship with a volume'.[172]

Why did individuals so often attribute false reports to Catholics, and what sort of explanatory function did this serve? One reason was that it helped to externalise and discredit their own fears and suspicions about Catholic toler-ation and the broader state of the Protestant cause. A passage from one of Beaulieu's letters to Trumbull, written when the King was considering whether to banish Catholic priests, demonstrates how this attribution functioned:

> I heare the Spanish Ambassadors to breede a jealousie in the myndes both of the Parlement and of the People of the Kings intent therein haue taken vpon them to assure their Clients the Papistes that His Maiestie will neuer be brought to putt anie such thing in execution against them, but that it behoueth him at this present to putt on such a shewe for the necessitie of his affaires.[173]

The rumour, then, was that James was merely making a show of cracking down on Catholics in order to secure subsidies from Parliament, but that he had no real intention of banishing the priests. Given James's track record of chopping and changing between Parliament and Spain, and his habit of threatening or appeasing Catholics depending on the political needs of the day, these reports were entirely plausible. Such suspicions were shared by Protestants who supported war against Spain, as well as Catholics who feared a renewed persecution and hoped that James's gestures against them were empty. By attributing the circulation of these reports to the deliberate foul-play of the Spanish ambassadors, Beaulieu was not simply explaining their origins. He was also implying that they were only believed by a minority of Catho-lics, rather than the larger group of subjects and observers who had reason to doubt James's sincerity. Most importantly, the identification of Spanish ambassadors as the source of these rumours discredited them and helped to reassure Trumbull that they must be false. Mutual distrust between King and

Parliament, this passage suggests, was not a natural state of affairs, but the result of external Catholic plotting.

George Abbot expressed a very similar sentiment when he corrected a false report that he had visited the Jesuit William Baldwin in the Tower of London:

> you are not to marvell that our fugitives do give out false reports, and among them that Baldwyn was visited by my selfe and other LL. In the Tower; for their whole religion consisteth of lies, and the practise of their life by consequence must needs correspond therevnto. In that kinde you must putt their perpetuall talking of liberty or at least connivance in pointe of religion, which I trust in God they shall never trouble themselves withall, albeit so long as this trafficking with Spaine doth hold, it giveth some occasion of suspitious talke to the idler sort of them.[74]

Abbot was 'othering' and externalising well-founded fears that the King favoured toleration as the price for a Spanish alliance by attributing these reports to Catholics. Unwelcome rumours about the completion of the Spanish match or the delay of Charles's return from Madrid were similarly dismissed as 'popish inventions' and 'popish rumour' intended to 'trouble the hearts of religious protestants'.[75]

Catholics were also held responsible for rumours of Protestant military setbacks. Reports that Mansfeld wished to negotiate with the Spanish to disband his army were dismissed as a stratagem 'to make him odious, and bring him into Ialousie, and distrust with his frends'.[76] As with rumours about Catholic toleration or the imminent completion of the Spanish match, these reports had a firmer basis in reality than many supporters of international Protestantism would like to think. Castle dismissed rumours of the shipwreck of one of James's ships, part of the fleet intended to carry Mansfeld's expedition to the continent in 1624, as coming 'from the forge of yor side', the Spanish Netherlands.[77] Unfortunately, this particular report was not as false as Castle might have wished – a week later he was forced to write that the ship had indeed been wrecked, with the loss of £50,000 and 150 lives.[78] The attribution of rumour to the 'other side' was a way of dealing with information that a correspondent was ideologically predisposed to disbelieve, and which they hoped was false. The idea that Spanish ambassadors and English Catholics were engaged in a conspiracy to spread disinformation was frightening, but at least it suggested that there was a means of remedying the situation by rebutting false rumours and silencing those who spread them. It implied that an intentional external force was responsible for doubt and speculation circulating among patriotic Englishmen.

Even false rumours that appeared to favour the Protestant cause could be interpreted as part of a Catholic plot to spread disinformation. One might assume that rumours of a French offer for a match in 1622 would be spread by Protestants who wished to disrupt the Spanish match and see an end to English neutrality in the Thirty Years' War. Trumbull, however, believed they were Spanish 'trickes, to break of the present negotiation ... and to cast vs off, nowe they haue the pray [the Palatinate] in their clutches'.[79] The Spaniards wanted to spread false reports about a possible Anglo-French marriage so they would have a legitimate excuse to end the negotiations now that they had served their devious purpose of preventing James from aiding Frederick. While false (and not so false) reports of Catholic victories could be described as 'bragges and lyes' 'forged' in Brussels, reports of Protestant victories could also be blamed on Spanish plotting.[180] According to Beaulieu, false rumours about a Protestant victory at the Battle of White Mountain were given out by the 'contrarie faction here amongst vs, to asswage the eagerness of the common greife', and to calm popular anger over Frederick's defeat, which might otherwise lead to mob violence against the Spanish ambassador.[181] The Spanish and their English supporters could not win; a few logical contortions could explain almost any rumour as part of a Catholic plot.

Interestingly, Catholic observers appear to have attributed rumours in exactly the same way. In May 1622, an English Catholic in Rome, John Bennett, assured a friend that rumours that James was sending troops to the Palatinate were being spread by the enemies of the Catholic Church designed to serve 'putt doubtes and lettes' in the minds of those who supported a Spanish match.[182]

Mark Knights has drawn attention to the ways in which political battles between Whigs and Tories in the later seventeenth century led to a sceptical crisis in which the interpretation of news was felt to be hopelessly biased by political allegiances.[183] During the early part of the century, there appears to have been a similar division in the assessment of information, but it was religious rather than party political. A good deal of contemporary comment indicates that the readership of news was conditioned by religious allegiances, and that reports were believed or dismissed depending on whether they flattered an individual's religious prejudices. Thomas Lushington complained that people stood 'diverse in Religion, and by their Religion foreknow their News'.[184] Ben Jonson's news factor from *Newes from the New World* even produced different news to suit the religion of his readers. 'I have friends of all rancks, and of all Religions', he says 'for which I keepe an answering Catalogue of dispatch; wherein I have my Puritan newes, my Protestant newes, and my Pontificial newes'.[185] Occasions when individuals dismissed unwelcome information by attributing it to the other side of the confessional divide provides perhaps the strongest and most direct evidence of thisinterpretative division. There is little doubt that Catholics and Protestants interpreted the news differently and believed things that flattered their religious preconceptions, but it is important not to take this division too far. Reports that supposedly originated on one side or the other were in reality common currency. Indeed, the process of dismissing unwelcome information by identifying Catholics as the source may tell us more about the hidden fears and suspicions of Protestants than it does about the reality of discourse among Catholics.

NOTES

1   Roger Lockyer, *Buckingham: the Life and Political Career of George Villiers, First Duke of Buckingham, 1592–1628* (London, 1981), pp. 234, 323, 438–9, 444.

2   *Ibid.*, pp. 323, 329.The thirteenth article of Buckingham's impeachment, for instance, suggested that he had improperly provided medicine for James, but this was clearly a dog-whistle manoeuvre designed to satisfy those who suspected him of poisoning the King while avoiding any direct accusation.

3   *Ibid.*, pp. 429, 441.

4   Thomas Cogswell has recently explored the ways in which the use of Buckingham as a scapegoat for various national woes influenced his assassin, John Felton. See Thomas Cogswell, 'John Felton, popular political culture, and the assassination of the Duke of Buckingham', *The Historical Journal* 49:2 (2006), pp. 357–85.

5   See in particular Thomas Cogswell, 'The people's love: The Duke of Buckingham and popularity' in Thomas Cogswell, Richard Cust and Peter Lake (eds), *Politics, Religion and Popularity in Early Stuart Britain* (Cambridge, 2002), pp. 211–34.

6   Robert Ruigh, *The Parliament of 1624: Politics and Foreign Policy* (Cambridge (MA), 1971), pp. 289–300.

7   See Thomas Cogswell, *The Blessed Revolution: English Politics and the Coming of War, 1621–1624* (Cambridge, 1989); Simon Adams, 'The Protestant Cause: Religious Alliance with the West European Calvinist Communities as a Political Issue in England, 1585–1630' (D.Phil, Oxford, 1973), pp. 333–7.

8   Cogswell, *Blessed Revolution*, pp. 128–30; Ruigh, *Parliament of 1624*, pp. 39–40.

9   John Wolley to William Trumbull, 14 May 1624, Add. 72330, fol. 95r; Wolley to Trumbull, 11 June 1624, Add. 72330, fol. 109v. For the Spanish ambassadors' attempts to discredit Buckingham in the spring of 1624, see Ruigh, *Parliament of 1624*, pp. 264–302; Michael Questier (ed.), *Stuart Dynastic Policy and Religious Politics, 1621–1625* (Camden 5th Series, vol. 34, 2009), pp. 78–9. The Spanish ambassadors, Inojosa and Coloma, as well as Don Francisco de Carondelet, one of the embassy chaplains, were involved at various points in these attempts.

10 'Marquis Inijosa his Leter to King James against the duke of Buckingham and his miscariage in Spaine', Harl. 4761, fol. 85r. It is possible that the Spanish ambassadors genuinely believed some version of their allegations and were hoping to trigger a general attack on Buckingham by encouraging others to make more specific claims to substantiate the general thrust of their accusations.

11 John Castle to William Trumbull, 7 April 1624, Add. 72276, fol. 81r.

12 Lockyer, *Buckingham*, p. 194.

13 'The Heads of that Discourse which fell from Don Francisco, 7 Aprilis, 1624. at 11. of the clock at night', *Cabala, Mysteries of State, in Letters of the Great Ministers of K. James and K. Charles* (1653), p. 90–3.

14 Owen Wynn to John Wynn, 3 May 1624, NLW 9059E/1218; Diary of Walter Yonge, Add. 28032, fol. 57v–58r.

15 Lockyer, *Buckingham*, pp. 180–1.

16 Alvise Valaresso to the Doge and Senate, 24 May 1624, CSPV vol. XVIII, pp. 319–20.

17 Thomas, Earl of Kellie, to John, Earl of Mar, 5 May 1624, in Henry Paton (ed.), *Supplementary Report on the Manuscripts of the Earl of Mar and Kellie*, vol. II, HMC 60 (London, 1930), p. 200.

18 Valaresso to the Doge and Senate, 7 June 1624, CSPV vol. XVIII, pp. 334–5.

19 Castle to Trumbull, 28 May 1624, Add. 72276, fol. 94v.

20 John Chamberlain to Carleton, 17 January 1624, McClure vol. II, pp. 540–1.

21 Questier (ed.), *Stuart Dynastic Policy*, p. 78.

22 Anonymous letter to James, [early 1624], Harl. 1581, fols. 395v, 396v.

23 Trumbull to [Carleton], 16/26 January 1624, SP 77/17, fol. 11r–v. It appears that the reason James was supposed to have imprisoned Buckingham was because the Duke had sent a message to the Spanish ambassador but had presented it as though it were the word of the King. See Questier (ed.), *Stuart Dynastic Policy*, p. 68.

24 Trumbull to Edward Conway, 12/22 February 1624, SP 77/17, fol. 33v. Trumbull thought the priest either intended 'to make me an Instument of defaminge, and accusing others; or els to ensnare my self, and bring me into danger'.

25 Lockyer, *Buckingham*, p. 84.

26 *Ibid.*, p. 85.

27 As Trumbull noted, Buckingham had 'loste a greate parte of our affections' in the Spanish Netherlands since returning from Madrid. Trumbull to [Dudley Carleton], 3/13 December 1623, SP 77/16, fol. 369r.

28 London newsletter, 17 May 1622, Harl. 389, fol. 190v. See also 'Extract of "A moste true Relation", 1621', Harl. 295, fol. 294r.

29 For the usefulness of rumour as a means to avoid full responsibility for one's words, see Tamotsu Shibutani, *Improvised News: a Sociological Study of Rumor* (New York, 1966), pp. 6, 88.

30 Castle to Trumbull, 30 April 1624, Add. 72276, fol. 86r.

31 Beaulieu to Trumbull, 7 May 1624, Add. 72255, fol. 144r; Castle to Trumbull, 28 May 1624, Add. 72276, fol. 94v. According to Ruigh, James merely questioned the Privy Council about Buckingham's conduct in Parliament, not about the 'Spanish information'. See Ruigh, *Parliament of 1624*, pp. 291–2. The Spanish allegations may well have had the effect of making more modest claims – that Buckingham was improperly courting popularity in Parliament – look more plausible.

32 Castle to Trumbull, 18 June 1624, Add. 72276, fol. 101r. Ironically, this service to the Duke may have harmed Carleton and Nethersole's short-term career prospects. When rumours spread that Carleton was likely to be recalled, Nethersole sought Buckingham's support in replacing him, but the Duke, according to Castle, 'dares not vrge to earnestly for him [Nethersole], least the King should suspect it is done by way of recompence for his clearing of the Iealous[y]'. Carleton does not appear to have made a journey to England during this period, however. See Castle to Trumbull, 2 July 1624, Add. 72276, fol. 107v.

33 Charles to Buckingham, 26 April 1624, Harl. 6987, fol. 211r.

34 Valaresso to the Doge and Senate, 17 May 1624, CSPV vol. XVIII, p. 308.

35 Valaresso to the Doge and Senate, 27 May 1624, CSPV vol. XVIII, p. 309.

36 Castle to Trumbull, 28 May 1624, Add. 72276, fol. 94v.

37 Kellie to Mar, 30 May 1624, in Paton (ed.), *Mar and Kellie* vol. II, pp. 203–4.

38 Castle to Trumbull, 18 June 1624, Add. 72276, fol. 101r.

39 *Ibid.* It is possible that Charles's decision to rule without a favourite after the death of Buckingham was made far in advance of the Duke's assassination. See Richard Cust, *Charles I: A Political Life* (Harlow, 2005), pp. 171–80.

40 Thomas Locke to Carleton, 28 February 1624, CSPD 1623–25 (1859), p. 171.

41 The substance of the Spanish allegations found their way into circulation in a number of forms. Carondelet allegedly read Williams a speech he had earlier read to James, and the Lord Keeper communicated its contents from memory to Buckingham. See 'The Heads of that Discourse which fell from Don Francisco, 7 Aprilis, 1624. at 11. of the clock at night', *Cabala*, pp. 90–3. It is possible that Williams exaggerated elements of the allegations in order to damage the ambassadors and present Buckingham in a favourable light. In particular, the claim that the 'Spanish information' amounted to a grand conspiracy against Buckingham, orchestrated by the Pope himself, seems to cast some doubt on the accuracy of Williams's account. See 'Passages between the Lord Keeper and Don Francisco', *Cabala*, p. 77. A separate letter to James, apparently based on Inojosa's original, circulated widely. A draft of it is preserved in the papers of John Coke, one of Buckingham's clients.

42 'A Relation of the proceedings against Ambassadors whoe haue miscarryed themselues', Stowe 159, fols. 112r–118v. I am grateful to Noah Millstone for drawing my attention to this document. News of the document seems to have circulated among people who did not read the relation itself. Owen Wynn reported rumours that the Prince was searching for a precedent to have the ambassadors questioned by Parliament for 'sowing discord between king and people'. See Owen Wynn to John Wynn, 3 May 1624, NLW 9059E/1218.

43 'A Relation of the proceedings against Ambassadors whoe haue miscarryed themselues', Stowe 159, fol. 115v.

44 Castle to Trumbull, 30 April 1624, Add. 72276, fol. 86v.

45 Cogswell, *Blessed Revolution*, pp. 168–9.

46 It was falsely rumoured that the ambassadors had indeed been confined to their embassy. See Valaresso to the Doge and Senate, 24 May 1624, CSPV vol. XVIII, p. 316; Diary of Walter Yonge, Add. 28032, fol. 57r.

47 'A Relation of the proceedings against Ambassadors whoe haue miscarryed themselues', Stowe 159, fols. 112v–118r.

48 Chamberlain to Carleton, 30 April 1624, McClure vol. II, pp. 556–7.

49 Aston did eventually present a remonstrance about the behaviour of Coloma and Inojosa. See SP 94/31, fols. 180r–181v. There is an English translation in Hampshire Record Office, 44M69/G2/502.

50 Castle to Trumbull, 7 April 1624, Add. 72276, fol. 80r; Lockyer, *Buckingham*, p. 194.

51 Castle to Trumbull, 14 May 1624, Add. 72276, fol. 89r; Kellie to Mar, 22 May 1624, in Paton (ed.), *Mar and Kellie* vol. II, p. 203.

52 Francis Nethersole to Carleton, 7 June 1624, CSPD 1623–25 (1859), p. 269; Dudley Carleton Jnr. to Carleton, 14 June 1624, CSPD 1623–25 (1859), p. 275; Lockyer, *Buckingham*, pp. 194–8.

53 Cogswell, *Blessed Revolution*, p. 142.

54 Beaulieu to Trumbull, 7 May 1624, Add. 72255, fol. 144r; Beaulieu to Trumbull, 7 June 1624, Add. 72255, fol. 151r.

55 Chamberlain to Carleton, 7 December 1616, McClure vol. II, p. 41.

56 *Ibid.*

57 Lockyer, *Buckingham*, pp. 55–6.

58 *Ibid.*

59 Castle to Trumbull, 14 May 1624, Add. 72276, fol. 89r.

60 Castle to Trumbull, 28 May 1624, Add. 72276, fol. 94r–v. Castle does not name these friends.

61 Castle to Trumbull, 4 June 1624, Add. 72276, fol. 97r. This was also reported in Wolley to Trumbull, 16 June 1624, Add. 72330, fol. 113v. There is a suggestion that Buckingham's illness was also used as a pretext to delay the trial that Bristol was demanding. See Carleton Jnr. to Carleton, 21 May 1624, CSPD 1623–25 (1859), p. 251.

62 Castle to Trumbull, 14 May 1624, Add. 72276, fol. 89r. This rumour also found its way in to Walter Yonge's news diary. See Diary of Walter Yonge, Add. 28032, fol. 58r.

63 Chamberlain to Carleton, 19 June 1624, McClure vol. II, p. 565; Deliberation of the Privy Council, 20 December 1624, CSPV vol. XVIII, p. 555.

64 Locke to Carleton, 8 May 1624, CSPD 1623–25 (1859), p. 240. These rumours may have derived from the fact that Buckingham had in fact been ill in Madrid. See Charles and Buckingham to James, 20 August 1623, in David M. Bergeron (ed.), *King James and Letters of Homoerotic Desire* (Iowa City, 1999), p. 197.

65 Cogswell, *Blessed Revolution*, p. 99.

66 William Wynn to John Wynn, 9 February 1622, NLW 9058E/1006; Chamberlain to Carleton, 12 March 1625, CSPD 1623–25 (1859), p. 497.

67 Valaresso to the Doge and Senate, 24 May 1624, CSPV vol. XVIII, p. 318.

68 See Alastair Bellany, *The Politics of Court Scandal in Early Modern England: News Culture and the Overbury Affair, 1603–1660* (Cambridge, 2002).

69 Keith Thomas, *Religion and the Decline of Magic* (London, 1971), pp. 638–41.

70 Chamberlain to Carleton, 26 February 1625, McClure vol. II, p. 601; Valaresso to the Doge and Senate, 31 May, 1624, CSPV vol. XVIII, p. 325.

71 Chamberlain to Carleton, 26 February 1625, McClure vol. II, p. 601; Alastair Bellany, 'The murder of John Lambe: Crowd violence, court scandal and popular politics in early seventeenth-century England', *Past & Present* 200 (2008), pp. 59–60.

72 See Lockyer, *Buckingham*, p. 234, 329; Cogswell, 'John Felton', p. 367.

73 *Ibid.*

74 Valaresso to the Doge and Senate, 31 May 1624, CSPV vol. XVIII, p. 325; Wolley to Trumbull, 5 June 1624, Add. 72330, fol. 106v; Trumbull to Conway, 3/13 June 1624, SP 77/17, fols. 190v–1r.

75 Chamberlain to Carleton, 13 May 1624, McClure vol. II, p. 558; Chamberlain to Carleton, 5 June 1624, McClure vol. II, p. 563.

76 Lockyer, *Buckingham*, p. 28.

77 Valaresso to the Doge and Senate, 31 May 1624, CSPV vol. XVIII, p. 325.

78 Castle to Trumbull, 20 May 1624, Add. 72276, fol. 92v.

79 Castle to Trumbull, 28 May 1624, Add. 72276, fol. 94r.

80 Trumbull to Walter Aston, 5/15 June 1624, Add. 36447, fol. 91v. Trumbull included these rumours in his letter to Aston because he was anxious that they should be suppressed, 'presumeinge the lyke fables may haue passed the Perinean Mountaines, and flowen as farre as Madrid'. See also Trumbull to Conway, 3/13 June 1624, SP 77/17, fol. 190v–r.

81 This appears to be another example of the ways in which rumours tended to pick up elements that were fresh in the contemporary imagination, as discussed in Chapter 3.

82 Wolley to Trumbull, 14 May 1624, Add. 72330, fol. 95r.

83 Castle to Trumbull, 20 May 1624, Add. 72276, fol. 92v. For James's apparently affectionate letters to Buckingham during his illness and recovery, see G. P. V. Akrigg (ed.), *Letters of James VI and I* (London, 1984), pp. 436–9.

84 Castle to Trumbull, 28 May 1624, Add. 72276, fol. 94v. See also Wolley to Trumbull, 7/27 June 1624, Add. 72330, fol. 117r.

85 Castle to Trumbull, 24 July 1617, Downshire vol. VI, p. 512; Beaulieu to Trumbull, 30 October 1618, Add. 72252, fol. 149r.

86 David Lindley, *The Trials of Frances Howard: Fact and Fiction at the Court of King James* (London, 1993), p. 146; Chamberlain to Carleton, 18 May 1616, McClure vol. II, p. 1.

87 Chamberlain to Carleton, 20 March 1620, McClure vol. II, p. 296; Castle to Trumbull, 14 May 1624, Add. 72276, fol. 88v; Locke to Carleton, 12 May 1624, CSPD 1623–25 (1859), p. 242.

88 Castle to Trumbull, 28 May 1624, Add. 72276, fol. 94v.

89 For Middlesex's career, see Menna Prestwich, *Cranfield: Politics and Profits under the Early Stuarts: The Career of Lionel Cranfield, Earl of Middlesex* (Oxford, 1966). For rumours of his involvement in the 'Spanish information', see Carleton Jnr. to Carleton, 3 May 1624, CSPD 1623–25 (1859), pp. 232–3. It may be significant that a copy of Inojosa's letter to James, setting out his claims against Buckingham, was in Cranfield's possession. See 'The Marquesse of Inoyoza his lettre to his Maiestie', Kent History and Library Centre, U269/1, O0145.

90 Prestwich, *Cranfield*, pp. 447–8.

91 Valaresso to the Doge and Senate, 14 June 1624, CSPV vol. XVIII, p. 343.

92 *Ibid.*, pp. 343–4. James stayed with Arundel and went hunting with him during Buckingham's illness. See CSPD 1623–25 (1859), p. 267.

93 Beaulieu to Trumbull, 7 June 1624, Add. 72255, fol. 151r. Diary of Walter Yonge, Add. 28032, fol. 59r.

94 Castle to Trumbull, 11 June 1624, Add. 72276, fol. 97v.

95 Castle to Trumbull, 18 June 1624, Add. 72276, fol. 101r; Wolley to Trumbull, 5 June 1624, Add. 72330, fol. 106r.

96 *Ibid.*

97 Diary of Walter Yonge, Add. 28032, fol. 59r.

98 Castle to Trumbull, 18 June 1624, Add. 72276, fol. 101v.

99 Beaulieu to Trumbull, 7 June 1624, Add. 72255, fol. 151r; Wolley to Trumbull, 5 June 1624, Add. 72330, fol. 106v. It is likely that this detailed rumour reflected the aspirations and plans of Brett's backers.

100 Valaresso to the Doge and Senate, 24 May 1624, CSPV vol. XVIII, p. 317. Buckingham had claimed during his address to the Parliament of 1624 that Bristol had misled James about Spain's willingness to conclude the match and restore the Palatinate. Bristol supposedly encourages Charles to outwardly convert to Catholicism when it becomes clear that this is what the Spanish wanted. See 'The effect of the relation to both houses at Whitehall by the Duke of Buckingham', Sloane 826, fol. 19r–v.

101 Beaulieu to Trumbull, 28 May 1624, Add. 72255, fol. 150v.

102 Valaresso to the Doge and Senate, 24 May 1624, CSPV vol. XVIII, p. 318.

103 Castle to Trumbull, 11 June 1624, Add. 72276, fol. 97r.

104 He was hoping to replace Trumbull as Agent in Brussels. See Castle to Trumbull, 4 June 1624, Add. 72276, fol. 96r.

105 Chamberlain to Carleton, 19 June 1624, McClure vol. II, pp. 564–5; Lockyer, *Buckingham*, p. 198. In 1616, when it was suspected that Buckingham had contracted smallpox, Chamberlain wrote that it threatened to ruin his career. See Chamberlain to Carleton, 20 April 1616, McClure vol. I, p. 623.

106 Chamberlain to Carleton, 28 February 1618, McClure vol. II, p. 144; Lockyer, *Buckingham*, pp. 12, 20.

107 Cogswell, *Blessed Revolution*, p. 142.

108 Castle to Trumbull, 28 May 1624, Add. 72276, fol. 95r.

109 Wolley to Trumbull, 23 July 1624, Add. 72330, fol. 130v.

110 Wolley to Trumbull, 5 June 1624, Add. 72330, fol. 105v.

111 Carleton Jnr. to Carleton, 26 June 1624. SP 14/168, fol. 47r. Carleton had been negotiating with Calvert since at least April. The position was on sale for £6,000, another indication that Carleton's credit was healthy. See Carleton Jnr. to Carleton, 6 April 1624, CSPD 1623–25 (1859), p. 209; Carleton Jnr. to Carleton, 3 May 1624, CSPD 1623–25 (1859), p. 231.

112 Carleton Jnr. to Carleton, 15 July 1624, SP 84/118, fol. 190r. Carleton's nephew did his best to reassure Buckingham that his uncle had failed to approach him about the secretaryship simply because he didn't wish to trouble him during his recovery. See Carleton Jnr. to Carleton, 16 July 1624, SP 14/170, fol. 9r.

113 Castle to Trumbull, 30 July 1624, Add. 72276, fol. 112r.

114 *Ibid.*

115 Ruigh, *Parliament of 1624*, p. 300.

116 Much of what follows contradicts Ruigh, who argued that by early June James was

'irrevocably committed to an indirect, covert military confrontation with Spain'. See Ruigh, *Parliament of 1624*, p. 300.

117 Cogswell, *Blessed Revolution*, p. 124.

118 Beaulieu to Trumbull, 16 April 1624, Add. 72255, fol. 139r; Questier, *Stuart Dynastic Policy*, p. 80; Brennan Pursell, *The Winter King: Frederick V of the Palatinate and the Coming of the Thirty Years War* (Aldershot, 2003), p. 222.

119 Castle to Trumbull, 4 June 1624, Add. 72276, fol. 97r; Castle to Trumbull, 18 June 1624, Add. 72276, fol. 101v.

120 John Grayson, 'From Protectorate to Partnership: Anglo-Dutch Relations, 1598–1625' (PhD, University of London, 1978), pp. 290–1; Beaulieu to Trumbull, 20 February 1624, Add. 72255, fol. 120r.

121 Robert Naunton to Buckingham, 28 September 1621, CSPD 1619–23 (1858), p. 293; Lando to the Doge and Senate, 15 October 1621, CSPV vol. XVII, p. 147; Beaulieu to Trumbull, 13 November 1621, Add. 72254, fol. 64r.

122 A. Moote, *Louis XIII, the Just* (London, 1989), p. 134.

123 Lando to the Doge and Senate, 15 October 1621, CSPV vol. XVII, p. 147.

124 Trumbull to Conway, 27 May 1624, SP 77/17, fols. 157v–8r. Edward Herbert, the resident ambassador in France, warned that Louis had little interest in helping James to recover the Palatinate. See S. R. Gardiner, *History of England: from the Accession of James I to the Outbreak of the Civil War, 1603–1642*, vol. v (1886), p. 218.

125 The Prince of Orange had stated this concern in blunt terms when Sir George Goring had attempted to sound him out about negotiations early in 1624. See Lockyer, *Buckingham*, p. 173.

126 The Treaty of Compiègne was signed in June 1624. See J. H. Elliott, *The Count-Duke of Olivares: The Statesman in an Age of Decline* (London, 1986), p. 221.

127 Naunton to Carleton, 26 June 1620, SP 84/95, fol. 301r. His suspicions appear to have been confirmed by a letter written by the Dutch ambassador to France, which Carleton intercepted. See Carleton to Naunton, 2 June 1620, SP 84/95, fol. 179r.

128 Digby to [Carleton], 23 March 1621 (o.s.), SP 77/14, fol. 308r.

129 Diary of Walter Yonge, Add. 28032, fol. 45r; Valaresso to the Doge and Senate, 25 November 1622, CSPV vol. XVII, p. 511.

130 Trumbull to [Carleton], 14/24 April 1624, SP 77/17, fol. 97v.

131 Trumbull to [Carleton], 10/20 December 1622, SP 77/15, fol. 431r.

132 For the Dutch embassy in 1624 see Adams, 'The Protestant Cause', pp. 349–51.

133 Grayson, 'From Protectorate to Partnership', p. 291.

134 Carleton Jnr. to Carleton, 11 April 1624, SP 84/117, fol. 31(a)r.

135 Grayson, 'From Protectorate to Partnership', pp. 291–2.

136 Castle to Trumbull, 16 April 1624, Add. 72276, fol. 82v.

137 Carleton Jnr. to Carleton, 11 April 1624, SP 84/117, fol. 31(a)r; Beaulieu to Trumbull, 16 April 1624, Add. 72255, fol. 139r.

138 Grayson, 'From Protectorate to Partnership', p. 293.

139 Wolley to Trumbull, 5 June 1624, Add. 72330, fol. 106r.

140 Beaulieu to Trumbull, 21 May 1624, Add. 72255, fol. 149v. In fact, James managed to avoid signing the treaty until late June. See Valaresso to the Doge and Senate, 21 June 1624, CSPV vol. XVIII, p. 353.

141 Trumbull to Carleton, 2 July 1624 (n.s.), SP 77/17, fol. 222r.

142 Trumbull to Carleton, 18 June 1624, SP 77/17, fols. 200v–1r.

143 Alvise Corner, Venetian ambassador in Spain, to the Doge and Senate, 18 June 1624, CSPV vol. XVIII, p. 346.

144 Cogswell, *Blessed Revolution*, p. 254.

145 Carleton Jnr. to Carleton, 17 May 1624, CSPD 1623–25 (1859), p. 248.

146 Valaresso to the Doge and Senate, 17 May 1624, CSPV vol. XVIII, p. 310.

147 Kensington to Edward Conway, 16 May 1624, SP 78/72, fol. 205r.

148 Kensington to Conway, 9/19 May 1624, SP 78/72, fol. 188r. The French were particularly worried that Digby, who was on his way home, would bring fresh offers for the restoration of the Palatinate.

149 Valaresso to the Doge and Senate, 31 May 1624, CSPV vol. XVIII, p. 326.

150 *Ibid.*

151 Richard Knightley to Buckingham, [May 1624], in S. R. Gardiner (ed.), *The Fortescue Papers* (Camden 2nd Series, vol. 1, 1871), pp. 196–7.

152 Valaresso to the Doge and Senate, 21 June 1624, CSPV vol. XVIII, p. 354; Richard Knightley to Buckingham, [May 1624], in Gardiner (ed.), *The Fortescue Papers*, pp. 196–7.

153 Kellie to Mar, 30 May 1624, in Paton (ed.), *Mar and Kellie* vol. II, pp. 204–5; Valaresso to the Doge and Senate, 21 June 1624, CSPV vol. XVIII, p. 354.

154 Kevin Sharpe, 'The Earl of Arundel, his circle and the opposition to the Duke of Buckingham, 1618–28' in Kevin Sharpe (ed.), *Faction and Parliament: Essays on Early Stuart History* (Oxford, 1978), p. 226.

155 Carleton to Trumbull, 18/28 July 1624, Add. 72274, fol. 109v; Conway to Carlisle and Kensington, 31 May 1624, SP 78/72, fol. 266r.

156 Castle to Trumbull, Whitson Tuesday 1624, Add. 72276, fol. 103v; Castle to Trumbull, 20 May 1624, Add. 72276, fol. 92v; Castle to Trumbull, 28 May 1624, Add. 72276, fol. 94r.

157 Castle to Trumbull, 20 May 1624, Add. 72276, fol. 92v.

158 Castle to Trumbull, Whitson Tuesday 1624, Add. 72276, fol. 103v.

159 For the relationship between rumour and prejudice, see Gordon Allport and Leo Postman, *The Psychology of Rumor* (New York, 1947), p. 37.

160 Chamberlain to Carleton, 5 June 1624, McClure vol. II, p. 563.

161 Castle to Trumbull, Whitson Tuesday 1624, Add. 72276, fol. 103v; Castle to Trumbull, 20 May 1624, Add. 72276, fol. 92v.

162 For the proclamation banishing priests, see Ruigh, *Parliament of 1624*, pp. 249–52.

163 Castle to Trumbull, 20 May 1624, Add. 72276, fol. 92v.

164 For the oral culture of Catholicism, see Alison Shell, *Oral Culture and Catholicism in Early Modern England* (Cambridge, 2007).

165 For Catholic nicodemism, see Perez Zagorin, *Ways of Lying: Dissimulation, Persecution, and Conformity in Early Modern Europe* (London, 1990), ch. 7. Of course, puritans faced similar accusations of dissimulation when they outwardly conformed. See Zagorin, *Ways of Lying*, ch. 10.

166 George Abbot, Archbishop of Canterbury to Trumbull, 10 July 1616, Add. 72242, fol. 53v. Abbot had attacked the Catholic doctrine of mental reservation in the 1590s. See Zagorin, *Ways of Lying*, p. 198.

167 Abbot to Trumbull, 28 December 1618, Add. 72242, fol. 75r; Abbot to Trumbull, 10 July 1616, Add. 72242, fol. 53v; Abbot to Trumbull, 9 September 1618, Add. 72242, fol. 69r.

168 Beaulieu to Trumbull, 11 October 1622, Add. 72254, fol. 161v.

169 Henry Bilderbeck to Trumbull, 11 January 1612, Downshire vol. III, p. 211.

170 Abbot to Trumbull, 10 July 1616, Add. 72242, fol. 53v.

171 Beaulieu to Trumbull, 6 January 1620, Add. 72253, fol. 85r.

172 Trumbull to Secretary of State, 31 August 1620 (o.s.), SP 77/14, fol. 202v.

173 Beaulieu to Trumbull, 30 April 1624, Add. 72255, fol. 142r.

174 Abbot to Trumbull, 28 December 1618, Add. 72242, fol. 75r.

175 Elisabeth Bourcier (ed.), *The Diary of Sir Simonds D'Ewes* (Paris, 1974), pp. 132–3; London newsletter, 24 September 1623, Harl. 389, fol. 362r.

176 Trumbull to [Carleton], 16/26 January 1624, SP 77/17, fol. 13v; For Mansfeld's negotiations to defect in the summer of 1621, see Arthur White, 'Suspension of Arms: Anglo-Spanish Mediation in the Thirty Years' War, 1621–25' (PhD, Tulane University, 1978), p. 180.

177 Castle to Trumbull, 12 November 1624, Add. 72276, fol. 127v. Mansfeld was rumoured to have drowned. See Trumbull to Conway 10/20 November 1624, SP 77/17, fol. 413r.

178 Castle to Trumbull, 19 November 1624, Add. 72276, fol. 129r.

179 Trumbull to [Carleton], 8/18 March 1622, SP 77/15, fols. 45v–6r.

180 Beaulieu to Trumbull, 6 January 1620, Add. 72253, fol. 85r.

181 Beaulieu to Trumbull, 7 December 1620, Add. 72253, fol. 165r.

182 Questier, *Stuart Dynastic Policy*, p. 7.

183 Mark Knights, *Representation and Misrepresentation in Later Stuart Britain: Partisanship and Political Culture* (Oxford, 2004).

184 Thomas Lushington, *A Sermon preach'd before the University of Oxford, in the year 1624* (London, 1711), p. 2. This comment was also repeated by an acquaintance of John Rous. See Mary Anne Everett Green (ed.), *Diary of John Rous* (Camden 1st Series, vol. 66, 1856), p. 43.

185 Ben Jonson, *Newes from the New World*, II. 40–43, cited in Ian Atherton, '"The itch grown a disease": Manuscript transmission of news in the seventeenth century', in Joad Raymond (ed.), *News, Newspapers and Society in Early Modern Britain* (London, 1999), p. 56.

Conclusion

This study has sought to explore the ways in which information was manipulated, concealed and distorted in Jacobean politics. As we have seen, James's diplomats and Secretaries of State tried to influence the King by providing him with diplomatic news designed to encourage particular courses of action. Sir George Calvert's 'palming' of letters, together with Bristol's stalling over the offer of an Anglo-Spanish partition of the Netherlands and the Scottish Privy Council's refusal to punish those who opposed the five Articles of Perth indicate that during the later years of his reign, James's servants increasingly moderated his instructions or disregarded them according to their own view of his and his subjects' best interests. Ministers and diplomats often suspected that James had no knowledge of instructions issued in his name. The King may ultimately have welcomed or at least benefited from some of this behaviour, since it acted as a safety valve which allowed the King to reconsider rash decisions before they were put in to practice, and also to create different impressions about his intentions among a variety of audiences. In many cases, the latitude he gave his servants was part of the normal running of government. While Charles took responsibility for policies in the hope that knowledge of his personal involvement would ensure obedience and cooperation, James let others enact policies, taking credit if they succeeded and disowning responsibility if they failed. James's sceptical and distrustful attitude set limits on the extent to which his own servants could mislead him, however. Blatant attempts at manipulation would be counter-productive, and anti-Spanish diplomats had to be on their guard against accusations of bias and corruption.

This study has attempted to qualify if not fully reject the view that James retained control over foreign policy until his death. While it remains true that James had the ultimate authority to make decisions, the basis of information on which they were made could be manipulated, and his orders could be significantly distorted or even suppressed by the bureaucratic machinery of diplomacy. The debate over control of Jacobean foreign affairs has tended to focus on James, Charles, Buckingham and Gondomar, but a much larger number of people could influence the process through which policy was created and realised. The pro-war party of Charles and Buckingham did not entirely seize power from James after 1623. Nevertheless, through Conway they were able to use the diplomatic network of information to seek causes of conflict with Spain. The diplomatic news-gathering machinery, if not the actual business of making decisions, passed into the hands of Charles and Buckingham.

James's distrust of many of his own ministers and servants led him to withhold diplomatic news, to conceal his own intentions and to seek advice from small select committees during his later years. This sometimes created the impression that he was not receiving counsel, and this encouraged some of his subjects to fill the apparent gap by writing advisory tracts encouraging the King to change course. James was particularly concerned that opponents of the Spanish match would use information about negotiations in Spain to whip up public discontent, which would damage the progress of the match when reported overseas. During most of the time Charles and Buckingham were in Madrid, James really did restrict knowledge about their negotiations to a remarkable extent, withholding information and excluding virtually all of his councillors from the negotiations. His attempts to maintain secrecy were not always successful, however, and he was unable to prevent high-level leaks by secretaries and bureaucrats to their diplomat friends abroad. The more that access to information was restricted, the more valuable it became, and observers were able to glean rather a lot of information about events in Madrid despite the attempts of both the King and the Prince to maintain a news blackout. The King's policy also had unintended consequences. His unwillingness to share information with some of his diplomats meant that they had less information to share with him. James's secrecy also implied that negotiations with Spain were not going well. As the rumours about the marriage terms circulating during Charles's and Buckingham's stay in Madrid indicate, when James concealed the details of negotiations, observers tended to assume that things were worse than they really were. His secretive behaviour also meant that he was too closely associated with policies which few others knew about, and he risked having no-one else to blame when they went wrong. Secrecy was as important as censorship in James's attempts to regulate discourse that criticised his rule.

James's approach towards secrecy and counsel may have influenced Charles during these years of his political apprenticeship. Charles's attitude towards counsel was not straightforward, and he neither ignored his advisers nor wholeheartedly restored conciliar government as it was supposedly practised before the rise of Buckingham. He regularly attended council meetings, diligently worked through the paperwork they generated, and he has been praised for listening to his Privy Council and tolerating dissent.[1] Nevertheless, he had a tendency to compartmentalise. Committees of the Privy Council, which were convened fitfully under James, became a permanent feature of government under Charles, and members of different committees were largely ignorant about the business of the others. Even if Charles appeared willing to listen to counsel, his meetings with councillors were not always meaningful. Clarendon wrote that Sir Thomas Coventry did not bother to speak in Privy Council meetings because he knew that policies had already been decided before they were discussed there.[2] Like James, Charles preferred to listen to advice about means rather than ends.[3] In this as in other areas, Charles appears to have learnt his kingcraft at his father's elbow during these formative years. While historians no longer simply date all of the causes of conflict in early Stuart England to 1625, as the grand remonstrance did, they have tended to draw a sharp distinction between the abilities of the flexible, wily James and his rigid and untrustworthy son.[4] Mark Kishlansky has warned against 'pulling down the reputation of James' in order to bring him in to balance with Charles.[5] Nevertheless, this study has tended to place greater emphasis on the continuities between the reigns of the two early Stuarts, during a decade in which they faced similar problems and were both under pressure to explain their policies. If Charles deserves even part of his reputation for being secretive and untrustworthy, his behaviour would seem to owe something to his father's style of rule, as well as to his own personality and political circumstances.

One of the consequences of James's habit of concealing information and hiding his intentions was that he was able to present a sometimes misleading impression of what was likely to happen in the future. The King's privileged access to information and his position as the final arbiter in the decision-making process meant that observers scrutinised his every word and gesture in the hope of understanding what was happening and what he intended to do. Uncertainty about James's intentions was partly deliberate and partly accidental. While he saw the value in creating confusion about the likely course of events, decisions about foreign policy and court appointments were often made in a way that struck observers as chaotic and unpredictable.

James's goldfish bowl existence nevertheless created opportunities to shape court and wider public perceptions about the likely course of events. On several occasions, it appears that James tried to whip up a public expectation that he would intervene militarily in the Thirty Years' War in order to put pressure on Spain to come to terms and placate domestic opinion. When negotiations reached their final stages during Charles's and Buckingham's trip to Madrid, he tried to create a false sense of progress and inevitability about the match in order to quell internal dissent and make the successful conclusion of negotiations all the more likely. The huge increase in the circulation of news and the discussion of politics in newsletters, libels and printed material during this period was almost unprecedented. In many ways, James was remarkably quick to adapt to these circumstances, and his ability to manage news, opinion and expectations through his 'outward shewes' was surprisingly sophisticated. James declined to act in court theatricals, but his whole political life can be seen as a series of performances.

These 'outward shows' were a more subtle and ephemeral phenomena than the printed propaganda and proclamations that historians have tended to focus on, and were intended to temporarily influence public expectations about the outcome of specific policies rather than to present a general image of royal virtue. As such, much of James's efforts to influence public politics were examples of spin rather than propaganda. These episodes undermine the traditional distinction between monarchs who were skilled at public display and ceremony, like Elizabeth, and those who were less so, like James and Charles, by indicating that monarchs were on permanent display even in the supposedly private confines of the court.

James's habit of concealing his intentions, and telling different audiences different things created the impression abroad that he could not be trusted, and this severely damaged his diplomacy. The account of James's cunning use of 'outward shows' may seem to further burnish a royal reputation that has been transformed since the 1950s, but it should be remembered that observers both at home and abroad simply did not believe his threats and promises.[6] Very few monarchs, of course, ruled without artifice or deceit in some form, and other European rulers were not exactly paragons of trustworthiness during this period. Nevertheless, James had a particularly bad reputation, and as we have seen, ambiguity, or, if we are less charitable, duplicity, was the hallmark of his style of government. Some continental observers believed that James intended to convert to Catholicism. At the same time, he had to fend off suspicions that he secretly approved of Frederick's actions. James took great pains to deny that he had encouraged Frederick to accept the crown of Bohemia, yet some believed he was privately delighted by his son-in-law's new title.[7] James was also rumoured to have secretly encouraged Frederick's incognito journey to join forces fighting on his behalf in the Palatinate in 1622.[8] James's own diplomats, as we have seen, had severe doubts about how convincing his sabre-rattling against Spain was. While his ambiguous behaviour served him well when playing Spain and her enemies off against each other, it was a severe liability when he came to finally close with one side or the other. James's strategy of tacking between Parliament and Spain risked alienating both in the long run. Buckingham urged him to 'resolue once const[antly] to runne one way. For so long as you wauer [betweene] the spaniard, & your own subiects, to make your aduantage of both, you are sure to doe it with neither'.[9] The Spanish did not trust James to carry out the terms of the marriage treaty in 1623 and insisted on keeping the Infanta in Spain until he had enacted a toleration of Catholics. The Parliament of 1624 would only vote subsidies for James if spending was controlled by parliamentary supervisors. The parties to the anti-Habsburg alliance James reluctantly tried to forge in 1624 so distrusted his promises that he was forced to offer painfully generous terms, and the Spanish accused him of 'levity, and inconstance' in turning against them.[10] The defensive alliance he made with the Dutch pledged most of the money raised by Parliament to maintain English troops in the republic.[11] The marriage treaty with the French involved pledging English ships which were later used against the Huguenots, and Mansfeld's expeditionary force failed to achieve anything in large part due to French distrust.[12] Historians have contrasted James's ambiguity and willingness to compromise with Charles's rigidity and tendency to state matters too starkly and explicitly, usually with the implication that James's style of rule was much better suited to the realities of early seventeenth-century politics. But James's style of rule was not without disadvantages. One observer worried that James was passing on his untrustworthy habits to his son. The Venetian ambassador wrote that 'owing to this facility in his Highness for imbibing his father's ideas one fears that he is being brought up with too much dissimulation and being always pleasant he may find it difficult to throw it off'.[13]

Many of the King's subjects were acutely aware that he tried to manipulate expectations through misleading speeches and gestures, and this helped to foster a sometimes cynical and paranoid political atmosphere. Observers of Jacobean politics who were influenced by the analytical attitudes of Roman historians can be forgiven for suspecting that there was more to James's public pronouncements than met the eye. A sceptical, even cynical attitude towards politics seemed appropriate when the King concealed his intentions and tried to mislead a variety of audiences. While James's management of information and public expectations enriches our understanding of his kingcraft, he was not always as manipulative as many believed. Because James sometimes had secret objectives, and because his every word and gesture was scrutinised for deeper meanings, it was sometimes assumed that the King was dissimulating when he was not. This tendency was partly the result of a preference for complex, intentional explanations for political events. When no dispatches arrived from Madrid in May and June of 1623, for instance, people assumed that James was cleverly hiding the messengers, but in fact no letters had been sent. Observers also believed that James was theatrically trying to whip up rumours of the conclusion of the match by dispatching Rutland's fleet when he was merely acting on the best information available to him at the time. Observers were keen to understand the real reasons that lay behind the public pretexts James gave out, and were highly sensitive – perhaps over-sensitive – to the possibility that they were being misled. Royal 'performances' may often have existed only in the imagination of the observer. Richard Cust has argued that news had a tendency to polarise politics, but it may have been the scrutiny and misplaced cynicism with which contemporaries viewed the news, rather than the news itself, which did most in generating distrust between James and his subjects.[14]

Another consequence of the uncertain news culture that James helped to create was the political rumours that circulated during his later years. Rumours could be created by a process through which errors gradually accumulated, or through the simple drawing of false inference based on the 'outward shows' of political figures. Rumours became exaggerated and increasingly dramatic as they passed from person to person, but they also had a forward momentum, and speculation about things that might happen, such as the death of prominent individuals who had fallen ill, was quickly transformed into apparently conclusive reports that it had happened. Rumours also had momentum in the sense that they tended to conform to the general direction of recent events. Optimistic rumours that the Spanish side had taken several other Dutch towns during the siege of Bergen-op-Zoom demonstrate that if events were unfolding well or badly, it was assumed that they would continue to do so, and rumours that supported these expectations were likely to be believed.

Rumours helped to mitigate the impact of bad news. Reports based on little more than wishful thinking indicating that Frederick's defeat at the Battle of White Mountain was not as severe as was initially thought are an interesting example of this. The attribution of rumours also had a psychological function, helping individuals to deal with unwelcome information. By attributing rumours about Buckingham's political decline to malicious Catholics, for instance, those who supported the Duke could reassure themselves that they must be false. The attribution of rumours helped to 'other' ideas and opinions that the attributors themselves hoped were false but suspected were true, and ascribed blame for their circulation to a small, malign group rather than the wider public who in fact passed them on and shaped their content. Contemporaries simplified this complex reality by assigning responsibility to small groups who were held to have spread them for simple and easily understood reasons. The attribution of rumour was an attempt to understand a complex process, in which responsibility was diffuse, in simple, intentional terms. It mirrored contemporary attempts to explain natural disasters, illness and death in terms of divine or demonic intervention in the natural world.

Spreading and discussing rumours was a form of political discourse that almost everyone could engage in. Rumours were a means for ordinary people to understand and explain politics, but they were also used as political weapons by elites. Rumours flourished in the uncertain atmosphere of the late-Jacobean court, where they were used to boost a candidate's chances of gaining an office or hasten a minister's fall from power. Rumours that circulated outside the court were also used in more important political battles. Reports that were already circulating widely about Imperial or Florentine matches for the Infanta, or about Buckingham's treason, were exploited by foreign ambassadors who hoped to change the course of English foreign policy. Rumour and misinformation were used by the diplomatic and political elite as weapons in a battle for perceptions that was played out across the continent. Individuals could influence the timing of a rumour outbreak or bolster and legitimate reports that were already circulating. While rumours were associated with the many-headed beast of popular revolt, elites were increasingly willing to engage with them and use them, with varying degrees of deliberate deception, as ammunition in political battles. This tactic was not restricted to the court. The use of popular rumours against Buckingham during his impeachment in 1626, and even more so the paranoid rumour-mongering of the Long Parliament demonstrate that vulgar rumours were increasingly exploited and taken seriously by MPs.

Rumours also simplified and explained complicated political events. James's intricate diplomacy was explained by the fact that he had converted to Catholicism, and Buckingham's 'change of sides' in 1623 was explained by the treasonous ambitions revealed by the Spanish ambassadors the following year. Complicated reports of the trial of the Earl and Countess of Somerset for the poisoning of a little-known courtier named Sir Thomas Overbury became reports that James himself had been poisoned. Mere political crisis was misreported as rebellion, and any naval preparations in Spain quickly provoked fears of an invasion fleet. Contemporaries took complex and ambiguous reports about James's health, domestic politics and foreign policy and placed them in boxes bearing simple and familiar labels such as 'James is dead', 'James is a Catholic' or 'there is a rebellion in England'. The famous dictum that journalists should 'first simplify, then exaggerate' was unconsciously followed by those who circulated news long before the advent of periodical news publication.

NOTES

1 Richard Cust, *Charles I: A Political Life* (Harlow, 2007), pp. 173–4; Sharpe, Kevin, *The Personal Rule of Charles I* (New Haven, 1992), pp. 262–3; Kevin Sharpe, 'Crown, parliament and locality: Government and communication in early Stuart England', *The English Historical Review* 101:399 (1986), pp. 343–4; Mark Kishlansky, 'Charles I: a case of mistaken identity', *Past & Present* 189 (2005), p. 51; Conrad Russell, *The Causes of the English Civil War* (Oxford, 1990), p. 189. For an apparently lively council debate in the later 1620s, see Richard Cust, 'Charles I, the Privy Council and the Parliament of 1628', *Transactions of the Royal Historical Society* 2 (1992), pp. 25–50.

2 *Ibid.*, p. 58. See also Caroline Hibbard, *Charles I and the Popish Plot* (Chapel Hill (NC), 1983), p. 9.

3 Richard Cust, 'Debate: Charles I: a case of mistaken Identity', *Past and Present* 205 (2009), p. 210.

4 See for instance Conrad Russell, *The Causes of the English Civil War* (Oxford, 1990), ch. 8. See also the recent debate on Charles's historical reputation, Kishlansky, 'Charles I', pp. 41–80; Richard Cust, Julian Goodare and Clive Holmes, 'Debate: Charles I: a case of mistaken Identity', *Past and Present* 205 (2009), pp. 176–237.

5 Mark Kishlansky, 'Debate: Charles I: a case of mistaken Identity', *Past and Present* 205 (2009), p. 213.

6 Marc L. Schwarz, 'James I and the historians: Towards a reconsideration', *Journal of British Studies* 13:2 (1974), pp. 114–34; Maurice Lee, 'James I and the historians: Not a bad king after all?', *Albion* 16:2 (1984), pp. 151–63; Jenny Wormald, 'James VI and I: Two kings or one?' *History* 68 (1983), pp. 187–209; Ralph Houlbrooke, 'James's reputation, 1625–2005' in Ralph Houlbrooke (ed.), *James VI and I: Ideas, Authority, and Government* (Aldershot, 2006), pp. 183–90. For some more recent work which has emphasised the limits of revision, see Julian Goodare, 'The Scottish Parliament of 1621', *The Historical Journal* 38 (1995), pp. 29–51; Laura Stewart, 'The political repercussions of the Five Articles of Perth: A reassessment of James VI and I's religious policies in Scotland', *Sixteenth Century Journal* 38:4 (2008), pp. 1013–36.

7 Marioni to the Doge and Senate, 22 November 1619, CSPV vol. XVI, p. 53.

8 Thomas, Earl of Kellie, to John, Earl of Mar, July 1622, in Henry Paton (ed.), *Supplementary Report on the Manuscripts of the Earl of Mar and Kellie* vol. II, HMC 60 (London, 1930), p. 127.

9 Buckingham to James, [No date], Harl. 6987, fol. 200r–v.

10 William Trumbull to Edward Conway, 19/29 February 1624, SP 77/17, fol. 39r–v.

11 Thomas Cogswell, *The Blessed Revolution: English Politics and the Coming of War, 1621–1624* (Cambridge, 1989), p. 256. The terms of this treaty were later ameliorated by Buckingham, however. See Roger Lockyer, *Buckingham: The Life and Political Career of George Villiers, First Duke of Buckingham, 1592–1628* (London, 1981), pp. 316–17.

12 *Ibid.*, p. 315.

13 Relation of England of Girolamo Lando, 21 September 1622, CSPV vol. XVII, p. 451.

14 Richard Cust, 'News and politics in early seventeenth century England', *Past and Present* 112 (1986), pp. 60–90.

Bibliography

MANUSCRIPT SOURCES

Bodleian Library

Ms. Clarendon 3 – miscellaneous state papers
Ms. Tanner 73 – miscellaneous state papers

British Library

Additional	4173–5, 4177 – Chamberlain to Carleton (copies)
	28032 – Diary of Walter Yonge
	31112 – Salvetti newsletters
	36444–7 – Trumbull/Carleton to Aston
	48149 – Robert Beale 'Instructions for a Principall Secretarie'
	72242–425 – Trumbull papers
Cotton	Vespasian C/XIII – 'Main points contained in the intercepted dispatch of the count de Onate', July 1620
Egerton	2592–6 – Trumbull/Carleton to Doncaster/Buckingham
Harley	389 – Mead correspondence
	1581 – Trumbull to Buckingham
	7002 – Misc. Castle correspondence
	7010 – Beaulieu to Puckering
Landsdowne	213 – 'Sermon Preach'd at St Maries in Oxford'
Royal	18 A. xxxii – 'O blessed king that heares the poore'
Stowe	167–76 – Trumbull/Carleton to Edmondes

Cheshire Archives

ZCR 63/2/19 – William Davenport's commonplace book

Huntington Library, San Marino, California

Ellesmere	6900 – 'A Collection of the materiall poynts in the intercepted dispatche of the Conde de Onate to the Archduke Alberto, July 1620 deciphred by Phillips'
	7807–7864 – Castle to Bridgewater

Kent History and Library Centre

U269/1 – Cranfield papers

National Library of Wales

466E, 9057–9E – Wynn correspondence

Sheffield Archives

Str P 14 – Wentworth correspondence

Somerset Record Office

DD/PH/227/16 – Robert Phelips, 'A Discourse by way of Dialogue betweene a counsellor of State and Country gentleman who served in the last assembly of the estates in the yeare 1621'

National Archives

State papers, domestic	14/86–185; 16/1–6 – Carleton correspondence
	16/22 – 'Queries against the Duke of Buckingham, grounded on public fame, and delivered into the House of Commons by Dr. Turner', [11 March] 1626
State papers, foreign	77/9–18, 112 – Flanders correspondence
	78/71 – France correspondence
	80/5 – 'Main points from intercepted despatch of Count of Oñate, the Spanish Ambassador, to the King of Spain, 1 August 1622'
	84/72–130 – Holland correspondence
	94/26–7 – Spain correspondence
	105/95 – Abbot to Carleton
Public Records Office	31/3 – Tillières correspondence

Northamptonshire Record Office

FH69 – 'Tom Tell Troth'

PRINTED PRIMARY SOURCES

Agar, Ben, *King James, his apopthegmes, or table-talke* (London, 1643)

Akrigg, G. P. V. (ed.), *Letters of James VI and I* (London, 1984)

Anon, *Cabala, Mysteries of State, in Letters of the Great ministers of K. James and K. Charles* (1653)

Bergeron, David M. (ed.), *King James and Letters of Homoerotic Desire* (Iowa City, 1999)

Bidwell, William B. and Jansson, Maija (eds), *Proceedings in Parliament 1626* vols I–IV (Rochester (NY), 1992–96)

Birch, Thomas (ed.), *Court and Times of James I* vol. II (London, 1849)

Bourcier, Elisabeth (ed.), *The Diary of Sir Simonds D'Ewes, 1622–1624* (Paris, 1974)

Chaucer, *The House of Fame*

Craigie, James (ed.), *The Basilicon Doron of King James VI* vol. I (London, 1944)

Craigie, James (ed.), *The Poems of James VI of Scotland* (2 vols, Edinburgh, 1958)

Ferrini, Roberto (ed.), *Lettere a William Cavendish* (Rome, 1987)

Gardiner, S. R. (ed.), *The Fortescue Papers* (Camden 2nd Series, vol. 1, 1871)

Green, Mary Anne Everett (ed.), *Diary of John Rous* (Camden 1st Series, vol. 66, 1856)

Green, Mary Anne Everett (ed.), *Calendar of State Papers, Domestic Series, of the Reign of James I, 1603–25* (4 vols, 1857–59)

Hacket, John, *Scrinia reserata, a memorial offer'd to the great deservings of John Williams* (1693)

Halliwell, J. O. (ed.), *The Autobiography and Correspondence of Sir Simonds D'Ewes* (2 vols, London, 1845)

Hardwicke, Philip (ed.), *Miscellaneous State Papers from 1501 to 1726* vol. I (London, 1778)

Hinds, Allen B. (ed.), *Calendar of State Papers and Manuscripts Relating to English Affairs Existing in the Archives and Collections of Venice and in other Libraries of Northern Italy* vols. 14–18, 1615–25 (London, 1908–12)

Historical Manuscripts Commission Tenth Report, Appendix, Part IV, HMC 13 (London, 1885)

James I, *His Maiesties declaration, touching the procee[d]ings in the late assemblie and conuention of Parliament* (1621)

Kenyon, J. P., *The Stuart Constitution 1603–1688* (Cambridge, 1986)

Kirk, R. E. G. (ed.), *Report on the Manuscripts of the Duke of Buccleuch and Queensberry,* HMC 45, I (London, 1899)

Larkin, James and Hughes, Paul (eds), *Stuart Royal Proclamations Volume I: Royal Proclamations of King James I 1603–1625* (Oxford, 1973)

Lee, Maurice (ed.), *Dudley Carleton to John Chamberlain 1603–1624: Jacobean Letters* (New Brunswick (NJ), 1972)

Lee, Sidney (ed.), *The Autobiography of Edward, Lord Herbert of Cherbury* (London, 1906)

Lushington, Thomas, *A Sermon preach'd before the University of Oxford, in the year 1624* (London, 1711)

Machiavelli, Nicolo, *Il Principe* (1532)

Maxwell Lyte, H. C. (ed.), *The Manuscripts of the Duke of Rutland,* HMC 24, i (London, 1888)

McClure, N. E. (ed.), *The Letters of John Chamberlain* (2 vols, Philadelphia (PA), 1939)

McGowan, A.P. (ed.), *The Jacobean Commissions of Enquiry 1608 and 1618* (London, 1971)

McIlwain, Charles Howard (ed.), *The Political Works of James I* (New York, 1965)

Notestein, Wallace, Relf, Frances and Simpson, Hartley (eds), *Commons Debates 1621* vol. III (London, 1935)

Paton, Henry (ed.), *The Manuscripts of the Earl of Mar and Kellie* HMC 60 (London, 1904)

Paton, Henry (ed.), *Supplementary Report on the Manuscripts of the Earl of Mar and Kellie* HMC 60 (2 vols, London, 1930)

Powell, W. S., *John Pory 1572–1636: The Life and Letters of a Man of Many Parts* (Chapel Hill (VA), 1977)

Purnell, E. K., Hinds, A. B. and Owen, Gerain Dyfnalt (eds), *Report on the Manuscripts of the Most Honourable the Marquess of Downshire, Formerly Preserved at Easthampstead Park, Berkshire* vols II–VI (London, 1936–95)

Questier, Michael (ed.), *Stuart Dynastic Policy and Religious Politics, 1621–1625* (Camden 5th Series, vol. 34, 2009)

Repplier, Agnes (ed.), *Epistolae Ho-Elianae or the Familiar Letters of James Howell* (New York, 1907)

Roberts, George (ed.), *The Diary of Walter Yonge* (Camden 1st Series, vol. 41, 1848)

Schleiner, Winfried (ed.), *Corona Regia* (Geneva, 2010)

Scott, Harold Spencer (ed.), *The Journal of Sir Roger Wilbraham* (*Camden Miscellany* vol. X, London, 1902)

Scott, Thomas, *Vox Populi* (1620)

Seddon, P. R. (ed.), *Letters of John Holles, 1587–1637* (Thoroton Society Record Series vols 31, 35–6, 1975–86)

Shakespeare, William, *Henry IV Part II*

Shaw, William A. and Owen, G. Dyfnallt (eds), *Report on the Manuscripts of the Viscount De L'Isle*, HMC 77, v (London, 1962)

Spedding, James (ed.), *The Works of Francis Bacon* vol. XII (London, 1857–74)

Tisdale, Robert *Pax Vobis* (London, 1623)

Underdown, David (ed.), *William Whiteway of Dorchester: His Diary 1618 to 1635* (Dorset Record Society, vol. 12, 1991)

Virgil, *Aeneid*

Waszink, Jan (ed.), *Politica: Six Books of Politics or Political Instruction* (Assen, 2004).

SECONDARY SOURCES

Adams, Simon, 'Foreign policy and the parliaments of 1621 and 1624', in Sharpe (ed.), *Faction and Parliament* (1978), pp. 139–72

Adams, Simon, 'Spain or the Netherlands? The dilemmas of early Stuart foreign policy', in Tomlinson (ed.), *Before the English Civil War* (1983), pp. 79–102

Adams, Simon, 'Eliza enthroned? The court and its politics', in Haigh (ed.), *The Reign of Elizabeth I* (1984), pp. 55–77

Adams, Simon, 'Review: *Papers of William Trumbull the Elder, September 1616–December 1618*', *English Historical Review* 112 (1997), pp. 749–50

Alexander, Michael, *Charles I's Lord Treasurer, Sir Richard Weston, Earl of Portland 1577–1635* (Chapel Hill (NC), 1975)

Allport, Gordon and Postman, Leo, *The Psychology of Rumor* (New York, 1947)

Archer, Ian, 'Popular politics in the sixteenth and early seventeenth centuries', in Griffiths and Jenner (eds), *Londinopolis* (2000), pp. 26–46

Atherton, Ian, '"The itch grown a disease": Manuscript transmission of news in the seventeenth century', in Raymond (ed.), *News, Newspapers and Society* (1999), pp. 36–65

Aylmer, G. E., *The King's Servants: The Civil Service of Charles I 1625–1642* (London, 1961)

Beier, A. L., Cannadine, David and Rosenheim, James (eds), *The First Modern Society: Essays in English History in Honour of Lawrence Stone* (Cambridge, 1989)

Bellany, Alastair, 'Rayling rymes and vaunting verse: Libellous politics in early Stuart England, 1603–1628', in Sharpe and Lake (eds), *Culture and Politics* (1994), pp. 285–310

Bellany, Alastair, 'Libels in action: Ritual, subversion and the English literary underground, 1603–42', in Harris (ed.), *The Politics of the Excluded c. 1500–1850* (2001), pp. 99–124

Bellany, Alastair, *The Politics of Court Scandal in Early Modern England: News Culture and the Overbury Affair, 1603–1660* (Cambridge, 2002)

Bellany, Alastair, 'The murder of John Lambe: Crowd violence, court scandal and popular politics in early seventeenth-century England', *Past & Present* 200 (2008), pp. 59–60

Bloch, Mark, *The Historian's Craft* (Manchester, 1992)

Buchanan, Brenda et al., *Gunpowder Plots* (London, 2005)

Burke, Peter, 'Tacitism, scepticism and reason of state', in Burns and Goldie (eds), *The Cambridge History of Political Thought, 1450–1700*, pp. 479–98

Burns J. H. and Goldie, Mark (eds), *The Cambridge History of Political Thought, 1450–1700* (Cambridge, 1991)

Calhoun, Craig (ed.), *Habermas and the Public Sphere* (Cambridge (MA), 1992)

Cano, David Sánchez, 'Entertainments in Madrid for the Prince of Wales: Political functions of festivals', in Samson (ed.), *The Spanish Match* (2006), pp. 51–73

Carter, Charles, 'Gondomar: Ambassador to James I', *The Historical Journal* 7:2 (1964), pp. 189–208

Carter, Charles, *The Secret Diplomacy of the Hapsburgs, 1598–1625* (New York, 1964)

Carter, Charles, 'The ambassadors of early modern Europe: Patterns of diplomatic representation in the early seventeenth century', in Carter (ed.), *From the Renaissance to the Counter-Reformation* (1965), pp. 269–95

Carter, Charles (ed.), *From the Renaissance to the Counter-Reformation: Essays in Honour of Garrett Mattingly* (London, 1965)

Chancey, Karen, 'The Amboyna massacre in English politics, 1624–1632', *Albion* 30 (1998), pp. 583–98

Chudoba, Bohdan, *Spain and the Empire* (Chicago, 1952)

Clarendon, Edward Hyde, Earl of, *History of the Rebellion* vol. I (Oxford, 1888)

Clegg, Cyndia, *Press Censorship in Jacobean England* (Cambridge, 2001)

Clucas, Stephen and Davies, Rosalind, *The Crisis of 1614 and the Addled Parliament* (Aldershot, 2003)

Cogswell, Thomas, 'England and the Spanish match', in Cust and Hughes (eds), *Conflict in Early Stuart England* (1989), pp. 107–33

Cogswell, Thomas, *The Blessed Revolution: English Politics and the Coming of War, 1621–1624* (Cambridge, 1989)

Cogswell, Thomas, 'Phaeton's chariot: The parliament-men and the continental crisis in 1621', in Merritt (ed.), *The Political World of Thomas Wentworth* (1996), pp. 24–46

Cogswell, Thomas, 'The people's love: The Duke of Buckingham and popularity', in Cogswell, Cust and Lake (eds), *Politics, Religion and Popularity* (2002), pp. 211–34

Cogswell, Thomas, Cust, Richard and Lake, Peter (eds), *Politics, Religion and Popularity in Early Stuart Britain* (Cambridge, 2002)

Cogswell, Thomas, '"Published by authoritie": Newsbooks and the Duke of Buckingham's expedition to the Ile de Ré', *Huntington Library Quarterly* 67:1 (2004), pp. 1–25

Colclough, David, *Freedom of Speech in Early Stuart England* (Cambridge, 2005)

Collinson, Patrick, 'The monarchical republic of Queen Elizabeth I', in Collinson (ed.), *Elizabethan Essays* (1994), pp. 31–57

Collinson, Patrick (ed.), *Elizabethan Essays* (London, 1994)

Cressy, David, *Bonfires and Bells: National Memory and the Protestant Calendar in Elizabethan and Stuart England* (London, 1989)

Cressy, David, *Dangerous Talk: Scandalous, Seditious, and Treasonable Speech in Pre-Modern England* (Oxford, 2010)

Croft, Pauline, 'Libels, popular literacy and public opinion in early modern England', *Historical Research* 68 (1995), pp. 266–85

Croft, Pauline, 'Brussels and London: The archdukes, Robert Cecil and James I', in Thomas and Duerloo (eds), *Albert and Isabella 1598–1621* (1998), pp. 79–85

Croft, Pauline, *King James* (Basingstoke, 2003)

Croft, Pauline, 'The Gunpowder Plot fails', in Buchanan et al., *Gunpowder Plots* (2005), pp. 14–19

Cross, Robert, 'Pretense and perception in the Spanish match, or history in a fake beard', *Journal of Interdisciplinary History* 37 (2007), pp. 563–83

Cruickshanks, Eveline (ed.), *The Stuart Courts* (Stroud, 2000)

Cuddy, Neil, 'The revival of the entourage: The bedchamber of James I, 1603–1625', in Starkey (ed.), *The English Court* (1987), pp. 173–225

Cuddy, Neil, 'Reinventing monarchy: The changing structure and political function of the Stuart court, 1603–88', in Cruickshanks, *The Stuart Courts* (2000), pp. 59–85

Cust, Richard, 'News and politics in early seventeenth century England', *Past and Present* 112 (1986), pp. 60–90

Cust, Richard, *The Forced Loan and English Politics, 1626–1628* (Oxford, 1987)

Cust, Richard, 'Politics and the electorate in the 1620s', in Cust and Hughes (eds), *Conflict in Early Stuart England* (1989), pp. 134–67

Cust, Richard and Hughes, Anne (eds), *Conflict in Early Stuart England: Studies in Religion and Politics 1603–1642* (Harlow, 1989)

Cust, Richard, 'Charles I, the Privy Council and the Parliament of 1628', *Transactions of the Royal Historical Society* 2 (1992), pp. 25–50

Cust, Richard, 'Charles I and popularity', in Cogswell, Cust and Lake (eds), *Politics, Religion and Popularity* (2002), pp. 235–58

Cust, Richard, *Charles I: A Political Life* (Harlow, 2005)

Cust, Richard, 'Prince Charles and the second session of the Parliament of 1621', *English Historical Review* 122:496 (2007), pp. 427–41

Cust, Richard, 'Debate: Charles I: A case of mistaken identity', *Past and Present* 205 (2009), pp. 201–12

De Fleur, M. L., 'Mass communication and the study of rumor', *Sociological Inquiry* 32 (1962), pp. 51–70

Dickinson, Janet, *Court Politics and the Earl of Essex, 1589–1601* (London, 2012)

Dooley, Brendan, 'News and doubt in early modern culture or, are we having a public sphere yet?' in Dooley and Baron (eds), *The Politics of Information in Early Modern Europe* (2001), pp. 275–90

Dooley, Brendan and Baron, Sabrina (eds), *The Politics of Information in Early Modern Europe* (London, 2001)

Doran, Susan, *Monarchy and Matrimony* (London, 1996)

Doran, Susan, 'James VI and the English succession', in Houlbrooke (ed.), *James VI and I* (2006), pp. 25–42

Elliott, J. H., *The Count-Duke of Olivares: The Statesman in an Age of Decline* (London, 1986)

Elton, Geoffrey, *Policy and Police* (Cambridge, 1972)

Elton, Geoffrey, 'Tudor government: The points of contact III: The court', *Transactions of the Royal Historical Society*, 5th series, 26 (1976), pp. 211–28

Ettinghausen, Henry, 'The greatest news story since the resurrection? Andres de Almansa y Mendoza's coverage of Prince Charles's Spanish trip', in Samson (ed.), *The Spanish Match* (2006), pp. 75–80.

Evans, F. M., *The Principal Secretary of State: A Survey of the Office from 1558 to 1680* (Manchester, 1923)

Fletcher, Anthony, *The Outbreak of the English Civil War* (London, 1981)

Fletcher, Anthony, 'National and local awareness in the county communities', in Tomlinson (ed.), *Before the English Civil War* (1983), pp. 151–74

Fox, Adam, 'Rumour, news and popular opinion in Elizabethan and early Stuart England', *The Historical Journal* 40:3 (1997), pp. 597–620

Fox, Adam, *Oral and Literate Culture in England, 1500–1700* (Oxford, 2001)

Frearson, Michael, 'The distribution and readership of London corantos in the 1620s', in Myers and Harris (eds), *Serials and their Readers* (1993), pp. 1–25

Freist, Dagmar, *Governed by Opinion: Politics, Religion and the Dynamics of Communication in Stuart London, 1637–1645* (London, 1997)

Gardiner, S. R. (ed.), *Prince Charles and the Spanish Marriage* (2 vols, London, 1869)

Gardiner, S. R., *History of England: From the Accession of James I to the Outbreak of the Civil War, 1603–1642* (10 vols, London, 1883–84)

Gilovich, Thomas, *How We Know What Isn't So* (New York, 1991)

Goodare, Julian, 'The Scottish Parliament of 1621', *The Historical Journal* 38 (1995), pp. 29–51

Griffiths, Paul and Jenner, Mark (eds), *Londinopolis: Essays in the Cultural and Social History of Early Modern London* (Manchester, 2000)

Guthrie, William P., *Battles of the Thirty Years' War: From White Mountain to Nordlingen, 1618–35* (Westport (CT), 2002)

Guy, John, *Tudor England* (Oxford, 1988)

Guy, John, 'The rhetoric of counsel in early modern England' in Hoak (ed.), *Tudor Political Culture* (1995), pp. 292–310

Habermas, Jürgen, *The Structural Transformation of the Public Sphere: An Inquiry into a Category of Bourgeois Society* (Boston, 1989)

Haigh, Christopher (ed.), *The Reign of Elizabeth I* (Basingstoke, 1984)

Haigh, Christopher, *Elizabeth I* (London, 1988)

Hammer, Paul, *Elizabeth's Wars* (Basingstoke, 2003)

Hammer, Paul, 'The smiling crocodile: The earl of Essex and late Elizabethan "popularity"', in Lake and Pincus (eds) *Politics of the Public Sphere* (2007), pp. 95–115

Hardie, Philip, *Rumour and Renown* (Cambridge, 2012)

Harris, Tim (ed.), *The Politics of the Excluded c. 1500–1850* (New York, 2001)

Harris, Tim, '"Venerating the honesty of a tinker": The King's friends and the battle for the allegiance of the common people in Restoration England' in Harris (ed.), *The Politics of the Excluded* (2001), pp. 195–232

Havran, Martin J., *Caroline Courtier: The Life of Lord Cottington* (London, 1973)

Hibbard, Caroline, *Charles I and the Popish Plot* (Chapel Hill (NC), 1983)

Hill, Robert and Lockyer, Roger, '"Carleton and Buckingham: The Quest for Office" Revisited', *History* 88:1 (2003), pp. 17–31

Hoak, Dale (ed.), *Tudor Political Culture* (Cambridge, 1995)

Houlbrooke, Ralph, 'James's reputation, 1625–2005', in Houlbrooke (ed.), *James VI and I* (2006), pp. 183–90.

Houlbrooke, Ralph (ed.), *James VI and I: Ideas, Authority, and Government* (Aldershot, 2006)

Hutton, Ronald, 'The making of the Secret Treaty of Dover, 1668–1670', *The Historical Journal* 29:2 (1986), pp. 297–318

Hutton, Ronald, *Debates in Stuart History* (Basingstoke, 2004)

Jensen, J. Vernon, 'The staff of the Jacobean Privy Council', *Huntington Library Quarterly* 40:1 (1976), p. 32

Kapferer, Jean-Nöel, *Rumors: Uses, Interpretations and Images* (New Brunswick, 1990)

Kettering, Sharon, *Power and Reputation at the Court of Louis XIII: The Career of Charles d'Albert, duc de Luynes (1578–1621)* (Manchester, 2008)

Kishlansky, Mark, 'Charles I: A case of mistaken identity', *Past & Present* 189 (2005), pp. 41–80

Kishlansky, Mark, 'Debate: Charles I: A case of mistaken Identity', *Past and Present* 205 (2009), pp. 213–37

Knights, Mark, *Representation and Misrepresentation in Later Stuart Britain: Partisanship and Political Culture* (Oxford, 2004)

Lake, Peter, 'Constitutional consensus and puritan opposition in the 1620s: Thomas Scott and the Spanish match', *The Historical Journal* 25 (1982), pp. 805–25

Lake, Peter, 'Anti-popery: The structure of a prejudice', in Cust and Hughes (eds), *Conflict in Early Stuart England* (1989), pp. 72–106

Lake, Peter and Questier, Michael, 'Puritans, papists and the "public sphere": The Edmund Campion affair in context', *Journal of Modern History* 72 (2000), pp. 587–627

Lake, Peter, '"The monarchical republic of Queen Elizabeth I" (and the Fall of Archbishop Grindal) revisited', in McDiarmid (ed.), *The Monarchical Republic of Early Modern England* (2007), pp. 129–47

Lake, Peter and Pincus, Steven, 'Rethinking the public sphere in early modern England', in Lake and Pincus (eds), *Politics of the Public Sphere* (2007), pp. 1–30.

Lake, Peter and Pincus, Steven (eds), *The Politics of the Public Sphere in Early Modern England* (Manchester, 2007)

Lambert, Sheila, 'The printers and the government, 1604–1637', in Myers and Harris (eds), *Aspects of Printing from 1600* (1987), pp. 1–29

Lambert, Sheila, 'State control of the press in theory and practice: The role of the Stationers' Company before 1640', in Myers and Harris (eds), *Censorship & the Control of Print in England and France 1600–1910* (1992), pp. 1–29

Larminie, Vivienne, 'The Jacobean diplomatic fraternity and the Protestant cause: Sir Isaac Wake and the view from Savoy', *English Historical Review* 121:494 (2006), pp. 1300–26

Lee, Maurice, 'The Jacobean diplomatic service', *The American Historical Review* 72:4 (1967), pp. 1264–82

Lee, Maurice, *James I and Henri IV: An Essay in English Foreign Policy, 1603–10* (London, 1970)

Lee, Maurice, 'James I and the historians: Not a bad king after all?', *Albion* 16:2 (1984), pp. 151–63

Lee, Maurice, *Great Britain's Solomon: James VI and I and his Three Kingdoms* (Urbana, 1990)

Levy, F. J., 'How information spread amongst the gentry, 1550–1640', *Journal of British Studies* 21:2 (1982), pp. 11–34

Levy, F. J., 'The decorum of news', in Raymond (ed.), *News, Newspapers, and Society* (1999), pp. 12–38

Lindley, David, *The Trials of Frances Howard: Fact and Fiction at the Court of King James* (London, 1993)

Lockyer, Roger, *Buckingham: The Life and Political Career of George Villiers, First Duke of Buckingham, 1592–1628* (London, 1981)

MacDonald, Alan 'Consultation and consent under James VI', *The Historical Journal*, 54:2 (2011), pp. 287–306

Marotti, Arthur (ed.), *Catholicism and Anti-Catholicism in Early Modern English Texts* (Basingstoke, 1999)

Mattingly, Garrett, *Renaissance Diplomacy* (London, 1955)

McDiarmid, John F. (ed.), *The Monarchical Republic of Early Modern England: Essays in Response to Patrick Collinson* (Aldershot, 2007)

McElligott, Jason, '"A couple of hundred squabbling small tradesmen"? Censorship, the stationers' company, and the state in early modern England', in Raymond (ed.), *News Networks in Seventeenth Century Britain and Europe* (2006), pp. 85–102

Merritt, Julia, 'Power and communication: Thomas Wentworth and government at a distance during the personal rule, 1629–1635', in Merritt (ed.), *The Political World of Thomas Wentworth* (1996), pp. 109–32

Merritt, Julia (ed.), *The Political World of Thomas Wentworth, Earl of Strafford, 1621–1641* (Cambridge, 1996)

Milton, Anthony, *Catholic and Reformed: The Roman and Protestant Churches in English Protestant Thought: 1600–1640* (Cambridge, 1995)

Milton, Anthony, 'Licensing, censorship, and religious orthodoxy in early Stuart England', *The Historical Journal* 41:3 (1998), pp. 625–51

Milton, Anthony, 'A qualified intolerance: The limits and ambiguities of early Stuart anti-Catholicism', in Marotti (ed.), *Catholicism and Anti-Catholicism in Early Modern English Texts* (1999), pp. 85–115

Moote, A., *Louis XIII, the Just* (London, 1989)

Morrill, John, *The Revolt of the Provinces: Conservatives and Radicals in the English Civil War, 1630–1650* (London, 1976)

Morrissey, Mary, 'Presenting James VI and I to the public: Preaching on political anniversaries at Paul's Cross', in Houlbrooke (ed.), *James VI and I* (2006), pp. 107–21

Myers, Robin and Harris, Michael (eds), *Aspects of Printing from 1600* (Oxford, 1987)

Myers, Robin and Harris, Michael (eds), *Censorship & the Control of Print in England and France 1600–1910* (Winchester, 1992)

Myers, Robin and Harris, Michael (eds), *Serials and their Readers: 1620–1914* (Winchester, 1993)

Neale, John (ed.) *Essays in Elizabethan History* (London, 1958)

Neale, John, 'The Elizabethan political scene', in Neale (ed.) *Essays in Elizabethan History* (1958), pp. 59–84.

Parker, Geoffrey, *The Dutch Revolt* (New York, 1977)

Parker, Geoffrey, *The Thirty Years' War* (London, 1984)

Patterson, W. B., *King James VI and I and the Reunion of Christendom* (Cambridge, 1997)

Peacey, Jason, 'Print and public politics in seventeenth-century England', *History Compass* 5:1 (2007), pp. 85–111

Peck, Linda Levy, *Northampton: Patronage and Policy at the Court of James I* (London, 1982)

Peck, Linda Levy, *Court Patronage and Corruption in Early Stuart England* (Boston (MA), 1990)

Peck, Linda Levy (ed.), *The Mental World of the Jacobean Court* (Cambridge, 1991)

Prestwich, Menna, *Cranfield: Politics and Profits under the Early Stuarts: The Career of Lionel Cranfield, Earl of Middlesex* (Oxford, 1966)

Pursell, Brennan, 'The end of the Spanish match', *The Historical Journal* 45:4 (2002), pp. 699–726

Pursell, Brennan, *The Winter King: Frederick V of the Palatinate and the Coming of the Thirty Years War* (Aldershot, 2003)

Quintrell, Brian, 'The Church triumphant? The emergence of a spiritual lord treasurer, 1635–1636', in Merritt (ed.), *The Political World of Thomas Wentworth* (1996), pp. 81–108

Raab, Felix, *The English Face of Machiavelli: A Changing Interpretation* (London, 1965)

Randall, David, *Credibility in Elizabethan and Early Stuart Military News* (London, 2008)

Raymond, Joad, *The Invention of the Newspaper: English Newsbooks 1641–1649* (Oxford, 1996)

Raymond, Joad (ed.), *News, Newspapers and Society in Early Modern Britain* (London, 1999)

Raymond, Joad (ed.) *News Networks in Seventeenth Century Britain and Europe* (Abingdon, 2006)

Redworth, Glyn, 'Of pimps and princes: Three unpublished letters from James I and the Prince of Wales relating to the Spanish match', *The Historical Journal* 37:2 (1994), pp. 401–9

Redworth, Glyn, *The Prince and the Infanta: The Cultural Politics of the Spanish Match* (New Haven, 2003)

Ruigh, Robert, *The Parliament of 1624: Politics and Foreign Policy* (Cambridge (MA), 1971)

Russell, Conrad, 'The foreign policy debates in the House of Commons in 1621', *The Historical Journal* 20 (1977), pp. 289–309

Russell, Conrad, *Parliaments and English Politics 1621–1629* (Oxford, 1979)

Russell, Conrad, *The Causes of the English Civil War* (Oxford, 1990)

Salmon, J. H. M., 'Seneca and Tacitus in Jacobean England', in Peck (ed.), *The Mental World of the Jacobean Court* (1991), pp. 169–88

Samson, Alexander (ed.), *The Spanish Match: Prince Charles's Journey to Madrid, 1623* (Aldershot, 2006)

Schneider, Gary, *The Culture of Epistolarity: Vernacular Letters and Letter Writing in Early Modern England 1500–1700* (Newark (NJ), 2005)

Schreiber, Roy E., *The First Carlisle: Sir James Hay, First Earl of Carlisle as Courtier, Diplomat and Entrepreneur, 1580–1636* (Philadelphia (PA), 1984)

Schwarz, Marc L., 'James I and the historians: Towards a reconsideration', *Journal of British Studies* 13:2 (1974), pp. 114–34

Shagan, Ethan, 'Rumours and popular politics in the reign of Henry VIII', in Harris (ed.), *The Politics of the Excluded* (2001), pp. 30–66

Sharpe, Kevin (ed.), *Faction and Parliament: Essays on Early Stuart History* (Oxford, 1978)

Sharpe, Kevin, 'Parliamentary history 1603–1629: In or out of Perspective?' in Sharpe (ed.), *Faction and Parliament* (1978), pp. 1–42

Sharpe, Kevin, 'The Earl of Arundel, his circle and the opposition to the Duke of Buckingham, 1618–28', in Sharpe (ed.), *Faction and Parliament* (1978), pp. 209–44

Sharpe, Kevin, 'Crown, parliament and locality: Government and communication in early Stuart England', *The English Historical Review* 101:399 (1986), pp. 321–50.

Sharpe, Kevin, 'The image of virtue: the court and household of Charles I, 1625–42', in Starkey (ed.), *The English Court* (1987), pp. 226–60

Sharpe, Kevin, *The Personal Rule of Charles I* (New Haven, 1992)

Sharpe, Kevin and Lake, Peter (eds), *Culture and Politics in Early Stuart England* (London, 1994)

Sharpe, Kevin, *Image Wars: Promoting Kings and Commonwealths in England, 1603–1660* (London, 2010)

Shell, Alison, *Oral Culture and Catholicism in Early Modern England* (Cambridge, 2007)

Shibutani, Tamotsu, *Improvised News: A Sociological Study of Rumor* (New York, 1966)

Siebert, Frederick, *Freedom of the Press in England 1476–1776: The Rise and Decline of Government Controls* (Urbana (IL), 1952)

Smuts, Malcolm, 'Public ceremony and royal charisma: The English royal entry in London, 1485–1642', in Beier, Cannadine and Rosenheim (eds), *The First Modern Society* (1989), pp.65–93

Smuts, Malcolm, 'Court-centred politics and the uses of Roman historians, c. 1590–1630' in Sharpe and Lake (eds), *Culture and Politics in Early Stuart England* (1994), pp. 21–43

Sommerville, J. P., *Politics and Ideology in England 1603–1640* (Harlow, 1986)

Starkey, David (ed.), *The English Court: From the Wars of the Roses to the Civil War* (Harlow, 1987)

Stewart, Alan and Wolfe, Heather (eds), *Letterwriting in Renaissance England* (London, 2004)

Stewart, Laura, 'The political repercussions of the Five Articles of Perth: A reassessment of James VI and I's religious policies in Scotland', *Sixteenth Century Journal* 38:4 (2008), pp. 1013–36

Stone, Lawrence, *An Elizabethan: Sir Horatio Palavicino* (Oxford, 1956)

Thomas, Keith, *Religion and the Decline of Magic* (London, 1971)

Thomas, Werner and Duerloo, Luc (eds), *Albert & Isabella 1598–1621: Essays* (Turnhout, 1998)

Thrush, Andrew, 'The personal rule of James I, 1611–1620', in Cogswell, Cust and Lake (eds), *Politics, Religion and Popularity* (2002), pp. 84–132.

Tomlinson, Howard (ed.), *Before the English Civil War: Essays on Early Stuart Politics and Government* (London, 1983)

Weldon, Anthony, *The Court and Character of King James* (London, 1650)

Wilson, D. H., *James VI and I* (London, 1956)

Wilson, Peter H., *Europe's Tragedy: A History of the Thirty Years' War* (London, 2009)

Wormald, Jenny, 'James VI and I: Two kings or one?' *History* 68 (1983), pp. 187–209

Zagorin, Perez, *The Court and the Country* (New York, 1970)

Zagorin, Perez, *Ways of Lying: Dissimulation, Persecution, and Conformity in Early Modern Europe* (London, 1990)

Zaller, Robert, *The Parliament of 1621* (London, 1971)

Zaller, Robert, '"Interest of State": James I and the Palatinate', *Albion* 6:2 (1974), pp. 144–75

THESES

Adams, Simon, 'The Protestant Cause: Religious Alliance with the West European Calvinist Communities as a Political Issue in England, 1585–1630' (D.Phil, Oxford, 1973)

Cockburn, D. A. J., 'A Critical Edition of the Letters of the Reverend Joseph Mead, 1626–7' (PhD, University of Cambridge, 1994)

Courtney, A., 'Court Politics and the Kingship of James VI and I, c. 1615–c. 1621' (PhD, University of Cambridge, 2008)

Grayson, John, 'From Protectorate to Partnership: Anglo-Dutch Relations, 1598–1625' (PhD, University of London, 1978)

Henneke, Christian, 'The Art of Diplomacy under the Early Stuarts, 1603–42' (PhD, University of Virginia, 1999)

Marshall, Albert, 'Sir Dudley Carleton and English Diplomacy in the United Provinces, 1616–1628' (PhD, Rutgers University, 1978)

Mears, Natalie, 'The "Personal Rule" of Elizabeth I: Marriage, Succession and Catholic Conspiracy, c. 1578–1582' (PhD thesis, St Andrews, 1999)

Uddin, Imran, 'William Trumbull: A Jacobean Diplomat at the Court of the Archdukes in Brussels, 1605/9–1625' (PhD, University of Leuven, 2006)

White, Arthur, 'Suspension of Arms: Anglo-Spanish Mediation in the Thirty Years' War, 1621–25' (PhD, Tulane University, 1978)

INTERNET SOURCES

Alastair Bellany and Andrew McRae (eds), 'Early Stuart Libels: an edition of poetry from manuscript sources', Early Modern Literary Studies Text Series I (2005) (http://purl.oclc.org/emls/texts/libels)

Oxford English Dictionary Online (www.oed.com)

Oxford Dictionary of National Biography, Oxford University Press; online edn (www.oxforddnb.com).

Index

Abbot, George, Archbishop of Canterbury 15, 34, 37–8, 124, 133, 157–8, 198–200
Aberdeen 22
Aerssens, Francois van, Lord of Sommelsdijk 194
Albert, Archduke 28, 31, 63, 65, 105
Allport, Gordon 83, 85, 98
Amboyna massacre 36
Anstruther, Sir Robert 182, 194
Arundel, Thomas Howard, Earl of 60, 191, 195, 197
assassination plots 29–30, 98, 104
Aston, Sir Walter 21, 55, 145, 151, 153
Austria 32

Bacon, Francis *see* St. Alban
Baldwin, William 200
Balmerino, James Elphinstone, Lord 25
Bavaria 15
Bayly, Lewis, Bishop of Bangor 86
Beale, Robert 12, 124
Beaulieu, John 1, 35, 53–4, 63–4, 71, 82, 86, 89, 90, 93–4, 101, 143, 148, 150, 159–60, 199, 201
Bellany, Alastair 2, 105
Bennet, Sir John 125
Bennett, John 201
Berghen-op-Zoom 18, 90, 92, 94–7, 216
Bilderbeck, Henry 93, 199
Bohemia 15–16, 32, 63–4, 66, 70, 89, 93
Book of Sports 86
Bouillon, Henri de la Tour d'Auvergne, Duke of 37
Breda 18, 33
Breslau 86
Brett, Arthur 123, 191
Bristol, John Digby, Earl of 15–17, 37, 51, 59, 101, 104, 127, 145–7, 151, 153, 157, 160, 162, 168, 186, 192, 195, 211
Brno 86
Brunswick, Christian, Duke of 93, 95
Brussels 17, 29, 31, 52, 65, 95–6
Buckingham, George Villiers, Duke of 25, 65–6, 72, 118, 127, 131–2, 146
and 'blessed revolution' 13, 18–21, 24, 26, 29, 60, 181–2
and 'popularity' 180, 183
bypasses Privy Council 49, 58, 60, 167
illness of 7–8, 180–202, 216
impeachment 106, 180–1
rumours about
imprisonment 184, 190, 196, 198
loss of favour 53–4, 180, 182, 190–4, 216
mental illness 181, 189–90, 198
poisoned 181, 188–9
poisoning of James I 99, 106, 180, 189
speaks for Protestant cause 56
trip to Madrid 7, 18, 22, 35, 66, 73, 82, 89, 101, 123, 139–68, 212–13
conceals news of negotiations 140, 144–55
monitors opinion in England 161–2, 164, 180
Burghley, William Cecil, Baron 117
Buwinkhausen, Benjamin 93

Cadiz 106, 162
Calvert, Sir George 22–5, 37–8, 51–2, 58, 67, 131–2, 148, 193, 197, 211
Carey, Robert 151
Carey, Sir Henry 133
Carleton, Sir Dudley 1, 20, 22–4, 26–7, 30–1, 33–6, 54–5, 64, 70, 90, 92–3, 95–7, 99, 102, 105, 116,

and formation of policy 4, 12–14,
  19–39, 211
as news gatherers 33, 52
exchange news with colleagues 54–5,
  72
ignored by James I 51–3
informal contacts in England 53–5, 116
loyalty of 33–8
dissimulation 5
Dohna, Christopher 16, 64
Dort, Synod of 53
Dover, Treaty of 149
Dunkirk 22–3
Dutch Republic 14–16, 18, 20, 22–3, 25,
  29–32, 34, 36–7, 58, 64, 66–7,
  88, 92–7, 102–3, 141, 146–7,
  154–6, 182, 194–6, 215

Edmondes, Sir Thomas 30, 37, 118, 131
Effiat, Antoine de Ruze, Marquis d' 194
Elizabeth, Electress Palatine 15, 23, 30,
  34–5, 92, 97–8, 141–2, 144, 185
Elizabeth I 4, 13, 28
  and Anjou match 59, 149
  and royal display 5, 49–50, 214
  decision-making 68
  relationship with councillors 4, 12–13,
    24, 38, 59, 117–18
Ellesmere, Thomas Egerton, Baron 87,
  125–6
Exchange, Royal 1

Ferdinand II, Holy Roman Emperor 15–
  17, 30–2, 37, 51, 93, 100–2, 141
Ferdinand III, Holy Roman Emperor
  100–2, 104
Ferdinando II, Duke of Florence 100
Finch, Heneage 85
Finet, Sir John 130
five articles of Perth 25, 71
Fleurus, Battle of 18, 95
Fox, Adam 48, 84, 104
France 15, 18–19, 21, 25, 27, 34, 88, 101–2,
  142–4, 146, 152–3, 194–6, 197
Frankenthal 21, 87, 90
Frederick Henry, Prince of Orange 91

Frederick V, Elector Palatine 15–17, 20, 23,
  29–30, 32, 34–7, 50–1, 53, 55, 57,
  63–6, 93–5, 141–2, 144, 182–5,
  190, 195, 201, 214, 216
free speech 17
French match 18–19, 21, 59, 72–3, 149,
  166–7, 195, 197, 200–1, 215

Gabor, Bethlen, Prince of Transylvania 15,
  86, 88, 93, 99
Gage, George 160
Gondomar, Diego Sarmiento de Acuña,
  Count of 19, 21, 30, 38, 64–5,
  70, 102–4, 184, 187, 211
Goring, Sir George 1, 125, 182
Grandison, Oliver St. John, Viscount 120
Gresley, Walsingham 150, 153
Gruffith, Owen 85
Guiana 15

Habermas, Jürgen 3
Hague, The 1, 22
Hamilton, James, Marquis of 23, 71, 149,
  165, 189
Hatton, Sir Christopher 117
Hay, James *see* Carlisle
Heidelberg 18, 31
Henrietta Maria 18, 126
Henri IV of France 15, 29, 144
Henry VIII 84
Herbert of Cherbury, Edward, Baron 27,
  101, 146, 152–3
Hipsley, Sir John 162
Hochst, Battle of 17
Holland, Henry Rich, Earl of 197
Holles, John *see* Clare
Huguenots 18, 142, 194

Ile de Ré 104, 162
Infanta *see* Maria Anna
Inojosa, Juan Hurtado de Mendoza,
  Marquis of 72, 146–7, 159,
  182–4, 186–7, 196
intercepted letters 30–3, 197–8
invasion scares 29, 37, 64–5, 85, 99,
  102–4, 194, 217

Index

Isabella, Archduchess 17, 21, 32, 34, 52,
63, 65, 105, 191

James I
and ministers
appointment of 117–19, 132
fosters divisions among councillors 13
ignores Privy Council 55–61,
141–55, 157, 167, 212
permits 'excuseable disobedience'
4, 12–13, 24–5, 38
refuses to protect 118
and news
concealment of 4, 7, 139–40,
144–55
source of 1, 115
and parliament 16–18, 50, 56
and the spoken word 62–3
appears indecisive 68, 118
assassination plots 29–30, 98, 104
Basilikon Doron 61, 63
death 19, 99
distrust of 214–15
foreign policy
Anglo-Spanish attack on Dutch
Republic 142, 146–7, 211
avoids committing to war with
Spain 194–7
control of 4, 12–13, 19, 27, 38–9, 50,
185, 211
gives diplomats independence 14,
27
peaceful diplomacy 13–19, 35, 48,
53
threatens war over Palatinate
16–17, 21, 50–1, 63–6, 70, 213–14
threatens war with Dutch 22–3
presents self as transparent 61
public display 49–50
rumoured conversion to Catholicism
25, 67, 89, 103, 122, 214
scepticism about public announce-
ments of 67–72, 141, 160–7, 215
visits Scotland 71, 86
Joachimi, Albert 194

John George, Elector of Saxony 32
Jonson, Ben 201

Kellie, Thomas Erskine, Earl of 1, 69,
142, 148, 150–1, 153–4, 160–1, 167
Killigrew, Peter 150
Kirk, Scottish 25, 71
Kishlansky, Mark 49, 213
Knightley, Richard 197
Knights, Mark 201
Kronberg, John Schweikart von, Elector
of Mainz 32

Lake, Peter 3, 50
Lake, Sir Thomas 117–18, 121–2, 131
Lambe, John 189
Lambert, Sheila 48
Lando, Girolamo 29, 32, 56–7, 65, 67–9,
100, 145, 147–8
Lee, Sir Thomas 85
Leith 22
Lennox, Ludovic Stuart, Duke of 71, 165,
189
Levy, F.J. 2
Lewkenor, Sir Lewis 130
Ley, Sir James 85
libels 2, 48
Lionello, Giovanni 29
Lipsius, Justus 5, 122, 127
Locke, Thomas 54, 165
Lockyer, Roger 66
London, Treaty of 14
Lord Keeper 19–20, 25
Lords, House of 66
Lorkin, Thomas 102
Louis XIII of France 15, 18, 53, 85, 88,
102, 142–4, 146, 194–5
Louis XIV of France 118
Lushington, Thomas 201

Machiavelli, Niccolò 5
Madrid 15, 29, 55, 101
Male, Jean Baptiste Van 28, 31, 63
Manchester, Henry Montagu, Earl of
123–5, 130
Mansell, Sir Robert 16, 64, 102–3